Electronic Enterprise: Strategy and Architecture

Andrew S. Targowski
Western Michigan University, USA

IRM Press
Publisher of innovative scholarly and professional information technology titles in the cyberage

Hershey • London • Melbourne • Singapore • Beijing

Acquisitions Editor:	Mehdi Khosrow-Pour
Senior Managing Editor:	Jan Travers
Managing Editor:	Amanda Appicello
Development Editor:	Michele Rossi
Copy Editor:	Ingrid Widitz
Typesetter:	Amanda Appicello
Cover Design:	Michelle Waters
Printed at:	Integrated Book Technology

Published in the United States of America by
IRM Press (an imprint of Idea Group Inc.)
701 E. Chocolate Avenue, Suite 200
Hershey PA 17033-1117
Tel: 717-533-8845
Fax: 717-533-8661
E-mail: cust@idea-group.com
Web site: http://www.irm-press.com

and in the United Kingdom by
IRM Press (an imprint of Idea Group Inc.)
3 Henrietta Street
Covent Garden
London WC2E 8LU
Tel: 44 20 7240 0856
Fax: 44 20 7379 3313
Web site: http://www.eurospan.co.uk

Library of Congress Cataloging-in-Publication Data

Targowski, Andrzej.
Electronic enterprise : strategy and architecture / Andrew Targowski.
p. cm.
Also available in electronic form.
Includes bibliographical references and index.
ISBN 1-931777-77-2 (soft cover) -- ISBN 1-931777-78-0 (ebook)
1. Information technology. 2. Industrial management. I. Title.
HD30.2.T3685 2003
658'.05--dc21

2002156241

British Cataloguing in Publication Data
A Cataloguing in Publication record for this book is available from the British Library.

New Releases from IRM Press

- **Multimedia and Interactive Digital TV: Managing the Opportunities Created by Digital Convergence**/Margherita Pagani
ISBN: 1-931777-38-1; eISBN: 1-931777-54-3 / US$59.95 / © 2003
- **Virtual Education: Cases in Learning & Teaching Technologies**/ Fawzi Albalooshi (Ed.), ISBN: 1-931777-39-X; eISBN: 1-931777-55-1 / US$59.95 / © 2003
- **Managing IT in Government, Business & Communities**/Gerry Gingrich (Ed.)
ISBN: 1-931777-40-3; eISBN: 1-931777-56-X / US$59.95 / © 2003
- **Information Management: Support Systems & Multimedia Technology**/ George Ditsa (Ed.), ISBN: 1-931777-41-1; eISBN: 1-931777-57-8 / US$59.95 / © 2003
- **Managing Globally with Information Technology**/Sherif Kamel (Ed.)
ISBN: 42-X; eISBN: 1-931777-58-6 / US$59.95 / © 2003
- **Current Security Management & Ethical Issues of Information Technology**/Rasool Azari (Ed.), ISBN: 1-931777-43-8; eISBN: 1-931777-59-4 / US$59.95 / © 2003
- **UML and the Unified Process**/Liliana Favre (Ed.)
ISBN: 1-931777-44-6; eISBN: 1-931777-60-8 / US$59.95 / © 2003
- **Business Strategies for Information Technology Management**/Kalle Kangas (Ed.)
ISBN: 1-931777-45-4; eISBN: 1-931777-61-6 / US$59.95 / © 2003
- **Managing E-Commerce and Mobile Computing Technologies**/Julie Mariga (Ed.)
ISBN: 1-931777-46-2; eISBN: 1-931777-62-4 / US$59.95 / © 2003
- **Effective Databases for Text & Document Management**/Shirley A. Becker (Ed.)
ISBN: 1-931777-47-0; eISBN: 1-931777-63-2 / US$59.95 / © 2003
- **Technologies & Methodologies for Evaluating Information Technology in Business**/ Charles K. Davis (Ed.), ISBN: 1-931777-48-9; eISBN: 1-931777-64-0 / US$59.95 / © 2003
- **ERP & Data Warehousing in Organizations: Issues and Challenges**/Gerald Grant (Ed.), ISBN: 1-931777-49-7; eISBN: 1-931777-65-9 / US$59.95 / © 2003
- **Practicing Software Engineering in the 21st Century**/Joan Peckham (Ed.)
ISBN: 1-931777-50-0; eISBN: 1-931777-66-7 / US$59.95 / © 2003
- **Knowledge Management: Current Issues and Challenges**/Elayne Coakes (Ed.)
ISBN: 1-931777-51-9; eISBN: 1-931777-67-5 / US$59.95 / © 2003
- **Computing Information Technology: The Human Side**/Steven Gordon (Ed.)
ISBN: 1-931777-52-7; eISBN: 1-931777-68-3 / US$59.95 / © 2003
- **Current Issues in IT Education**/Tanya McGill (Ed.)
ISBN: 1-931777-53-5; eISBN: 1-931777-69-1 / US$59.95 / © 2003

Excellent additions to your institution's library!
Recommend these titles to your Librarian!

To receive a copy of the IRM Press catalog, please contact (toll free) 1/800-345-4332, fax 1/717-533-8661, or visit the IRM Press Online Bookstore at: [http://www.irm-press.com]!

Note: All IRM Press books are also available as ebooks on netlibrary.com as well as other ebook sources. Contact Ms. Carrie Skovrinskie at [cskovrinskie@idea-group.com] to receive a complete list of sources where you can obtain ebook information or IRM Press titles.

To Stan

Electronic Enterprise: Strategy and Architecture

Table of Contents

Part II: Enterprise Information Infrastructure

Part III: The Internet Ecosystem

Part IV: IT Development and Management

Preface

The purpose of this book is to provide big-picture strategies and system architectures which evolve an enterprise. The synthesis of about 300 IT technologies is presented in a consistant manner under the form of graphic modeling. To analyze each of these technologies one must read about 300 books, which is a tough task. However, if we look at the library shelves, such an amount of different books on IT applications in an enterprise exists, if not more.

Therefore the book is recommended for those readers who are interested mainly in general solutions of IT in the enterprise. Among such readers one can include:

- Business exccutives
- Information executives
- IS/CIS/MIS major students of the cup-stone curriculum courses
- MBA students who take a course on IT management
- IT technicians who would like to understand how their specific solutions fit into a bigger-picture solution

The book concept is presented in the following model.

Chapter 1 analyzes paradigm shifts in enterprise management caused by the applications of information technologies (IT). As a result of it, a new set of business rules is defined.

Chapter 2 defines eight evolutionary enterprise configurations triggered by the implementation of advanced applications of IT. This is a very important approach in understanding how to manage the development of IT applications to achieve the right end-solution at a given time.

Chapter 3 portrays five layers of the Enterprise Information Infrastructure (EII), which evolves from islands of automation. To manage a modern enterprise it is necessary to understand how to develop and manage EII, which is composed of hundreds information technologies.

Chapter 4 defines architectures of major application systems within the framework of the enterprise-wide solutions. These architectures identify endless number of components and their relationships, which control the flow of information ("content") in decision-making processes of an enterprise.

Chapter 5 describes major solutions that determine so called enterprise electronization and integration. Several emerging standards which support these processes are presented. Also their relationships are provided under the form of a web's services.

Chapter 6 defines the Internet Ecosystem in terms of its layers and major applications in business. The "dot.com" issue is analyzed and its impact upon the future of the Internet.

Chapter 7 present the major trends in developing IT solutions, among them such ones as design strategies and methodologies and 10 specific developmental approaches. Some future trends of IT developments are sketched.

Chapter 8 depicts issues and solutions on how to manage an IT-driven enterprise. The fundamental rule is to integrate business and system strategies and choose the right strategic applications. A set of management key indicators, based upon a balance scorecard, how to manage such enterprise is provided.

The author is very grateful to anonymous reviewers who provided very important suggestions on how to improve this book.

Andrew S. Targowski

The Book Architecture

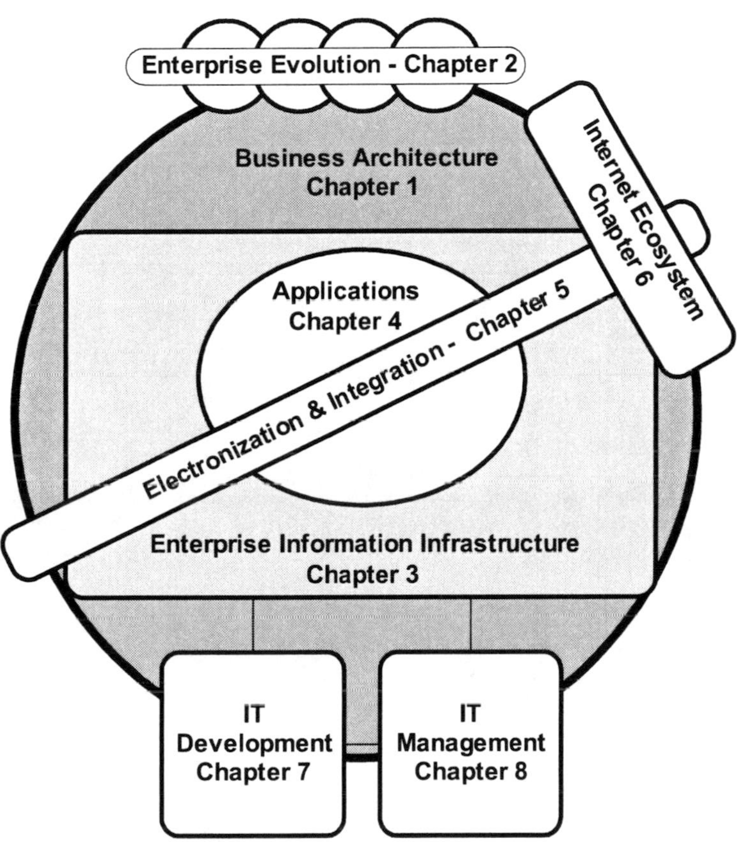

Part I

Enterprise Evolution

Chapter I

The New Informated Business Architecture[1]

Andrew Targowski
Western Michigan University, USA

Thomas Carey
Western Michigan University, USA

INTRODUCTION

The fall of the Berlin Wall, the collapse of the Warsaw Pact, and the disintegration of the Soviet Union are certainly monumental events in the history of the human race as the 20th century nears its close. Monumental changes are taking place in business organizations and in the managers who run them. The business community is shifting its paradigms and the manner in which it does business.

To avoid "*Future Shock,*" one must look beyond the trends of the past and discover the rules that will govern business in the Twenty-First Century, the Information Age. By knowing the nature of such changes and how to anticipate them, the strategist can elicit extraordinary leverage in shaping the future. Drucker (1980) in *Managing Turbulent Times*, writes that one of the most important skills during times of turbulence is anticipation.

This chapter explores the effects of the information age (Figure 1) upon the global business enterprise which is shifting from an old paradigm to a new one, in the way Kuhn (1970) described paradigm shifts in science in *The Structure of Scientific Revolutions*. We will also suggest that since all major business dimensions have shifted paradigms, a new era in business requires a new set of rules.

This chapter offers an integrative strategic model for a new informated business architecture which operates in the new Electronic Global Village (Targowski, 1991, 1996). In this village, planet Earth, computers, communications, and cognition (3C) will globally connect islands of business, customers, and citizens between diminishing national boundaries. These new tools develop computer and human networking within a new informated, more abstract, or icon driven environment (Tapscott and Caston, 1993).

SHIFT OF POWER

The most easily recognized paradigm shift is that of power: political, economic, and social.

The Political Perspective

At the end of World War II, the United States was preeminent in all areas of commerce and industry with 52% of the world's GNP. This singular leadership by *Pax Americana* was seriously eroded during the decade of the 1980's and has evaporated altogether with the collapse of the Soviet Union and the reemergence of Japan and Germany as economic superpowers. Perhaps the most dramatic shifts of the second half of the 20th century have occurred in the areas of political, economic, and social power. The polar competition between capitalism and communism has ended without an unboastful victor while the former communists are busily transforming themselves into fledgling democracies (Huntington, 1996).

The Economic Perspective

The year 1991 marked the end of the old military industrial arms race and the beginning of economic warfare conducted by stateless corporations (Korten, 1995). Since 1991, large corporations have moved away from local or national boundaries toward cosmopolitan and global ones without borders. For example, IBM had 62% of its sales in countries other than the U.S. Similarly, Colgate had 64% of its sales outside of the U.S. while Coca-Cola did 54% of its business abroad (1991, annual Reports). In these instances, companies thought to be American are in fact global competitors, serving global markets, with global products. But to whom are they responsible? They wield the power and financial resources which rival that of many nations. This shift from local to global has eroded the previous power of a single nation. For centuries many corporations served their own nation, while today many nations serve as markets for the multi-national corporations.

This change of a global environment has led to changes in regulation—the creation of G-7; changes in production and marketing—from mass consumption to highly differentiated global markets; changes in employment—from full employment to structured unemployment; changes in organization design—from hierarchical core units to joint ventures, peripheral units, and expanded partnerships or Keiretsu; and changes in the state, from a military—welfare society to an industrially competitive—self-supporting society (Elliott, 1996).

In 1992 the trade barriers fell among twelve countries—Belgium, Denmark, France, Germany, Greece, Ireland, Italy, Luxemburg, the Netherlands, Portugal, Spain, and the United Kingdom, which had formed one integrated economic market – European Union (E.U.). In 2004 another ten countries from Central and Eastern Europe will join E.U. Rather than being pawns in a rapidly escalating trade war between the U.S. and Japan, the nations of EU have opted to form a single entity that will become the third economic superpower, with a population of 520 million and gross national product of over 10 trillion dollars in 2010 (Targowski and Korth, 2000).

It has been said that "economics controls politics." The successful integration of the rapidly-growing American (including Latin America) market and simultaneous slow growth of the European market may lead towards the further integration of the two components of Western Civilization. As a result, the Americas may integrate with Europe into the *FTA* of *the North Atlantic* (FTAAT), with at least 50 Western-Civilization countries forming the world's largest market.

Several factors will propel Europeans in that direction. Both areas already trade much more with each other than with Asia. Furthermore, Great Britain trades twice as much with NAFTA as it does with its E.U. partner, and would prefer to have its own currency and political identity as a member of FTAAT rather than as a member of a political union (Black, 1999). Also, Italy and Central Europe have strong ethnic ties with the United States as a result of massive migration from Europe to the U.S. These are only some of the influences that may lead to the emergence of FTAAT. FTAAT could have half of the world's market and 1.5 billion consumers — more than in China.

The rest of the world will grow faster than in the first decade of the new century. Due to the expansions of NAFTA and the E.U., as many as 40-50 countries will join either FTAA or the E.U. The remaining 140-150 countries will be strongly stimulated by the four larger markets. There will also be benefits as more and more of these countries open their economies to world markets and capitalism. Therefore, economic growth of close to 4% per year is reasonable. And there are some potentially very strong countries in that group: in addition to the "tigers and dragons," India, South Africa, Australia, and the oil producers. All have favorable potential. India might very well compete with China as the most dynamic of all of the major developing countries. Also, the possible success of other integrated regional markets, such as ASEAN, or any group involving India, should be considered.

The coming generation will be a period of great change – political as well as economic. The evolution toward multi-country economic integration will continue – especially in the Atlantic and ASEAN regions. Today's economic powers will continue to dominate in the coming years. China may well become the world's largest individual economy. However, the United States, which is very likely to integrate with larger groups of countries into a massive free-trade area, will continue to be a dominant world economic force.

The proliferation of Internet access will open intriguing scenarios. On one hand, windows of opportunity will be offered for developing markets (e.g., India and Brazil already have booming software-development industries). Also, ready access to the communication and information opportunities provided by the Internet may help stimulate education, improve health, and encourage entrepreneurs – thereby improving living standards and stimulating the economies. On the other hand, the dissemination of information, together with the ready access to free worldwide communication, can abet terrorist groups such as has been seen with al Qaeda. Also, as widespread cyber attacks have shown, the Internet is open to abuse – from anywhere in the world.

The Social Perspective

For most of mankind's history the individual worked either on the farm or as a craftsman and was solely responsible to himself or the guild, with a resulting per capita income of approximately $300 per year. Then at the end of the 18th century, the industrial revolution was started in England by entrepreneurs and their families, an event that radically transformed productivity and personal income. In America, men such as John Rockefeller, Henry Ford, and Andrew Carnegie created, financed, and managed their own businesses. These early entrepreneurs were the first capitalists and their offspring today control at least 25% of the stock in over one third of the present day Fortune 500. During the first half of the 20th century, the role of the capitalist was assumed by individual stockholders, while entrepreneurs provided the knowledge and the vision, but not necessarily the capital to start a business. By 1950 "managerial capitalism had gained ascendancy over family and financial capitalism." In the 2000's the managerial class caused some serious crisis trying to rob stakeholders, as is best exemplified by the Enron and WorldCom cases. This shift in economic power has had a great impact upon the blue collar work force. Prior to the 1980's the manufacturing cost of direct labor was approximately 25% of sales and almost a third of the workforce was employed in manufacturing. Today the U.S.'s average cost for direct labor in manufacturing is less than 5% of sales, while fewer than 16% of the workforce is employed in manufacturing. The collective voice of labor has also been muted. Union membership among manufacturing workers had a post-war high of 25% in the 1950's, while today barely 10% of all U.S. manufacturing workers are unionized (Krugman,

Figure 1-1: From Hierarchy to Networking

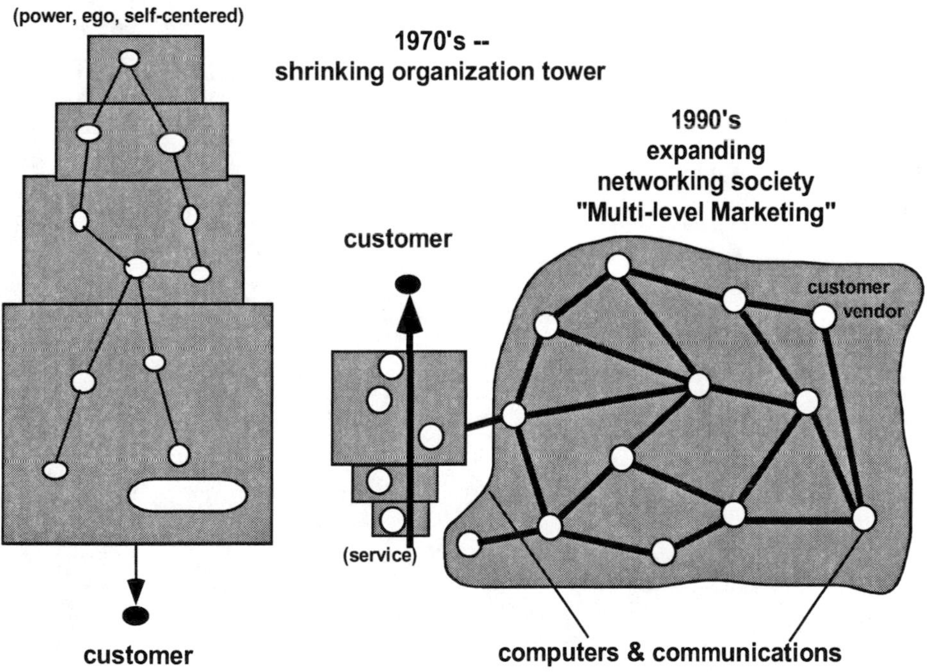

Forbes, and Lawrence, 1996). The evolution of economic, and thus social power is shown as a model in Figure 1-1.

SHIFT IN STRATEGIC RESOURCES

The raw materials paradigm will actually shift along two dimensions: from more resources to fewer resources, and from quantity and quality to the

Figure 1-2: A Shift of Strategic Resources

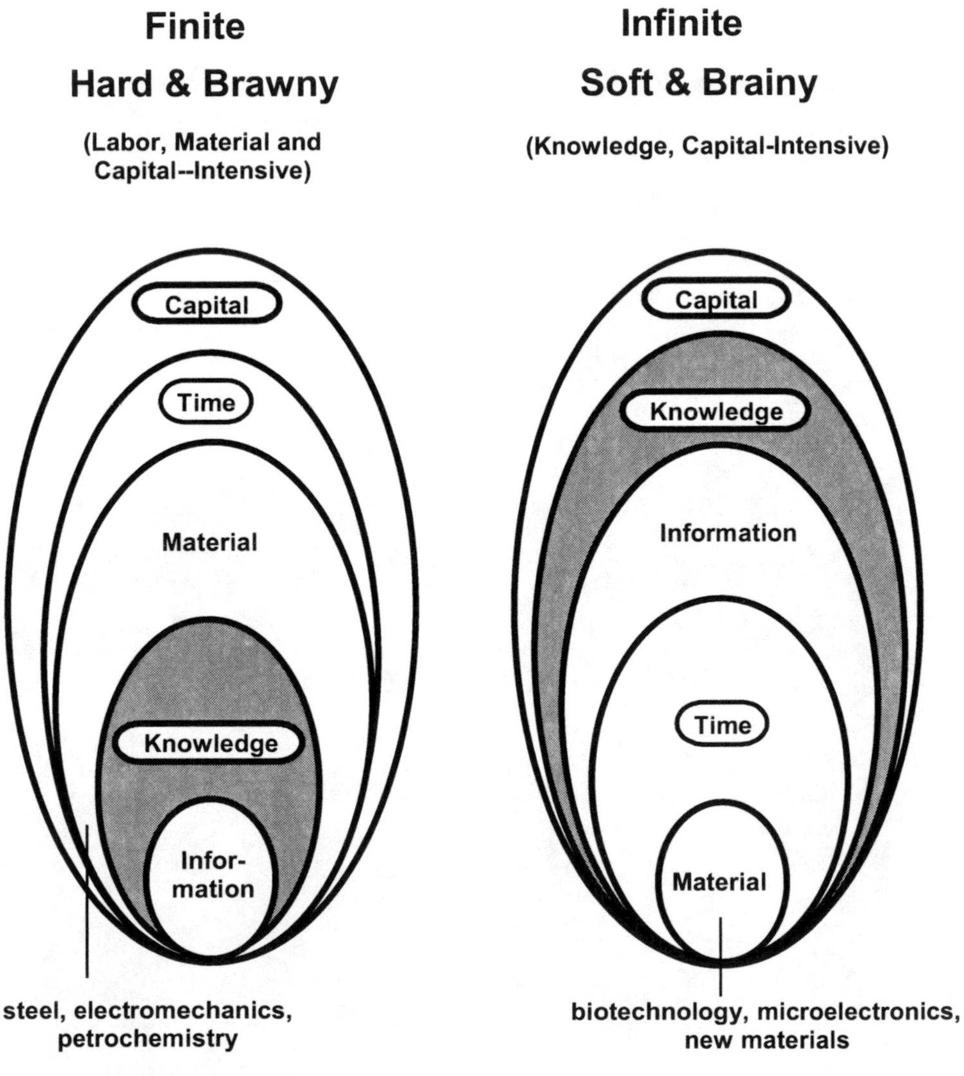

timeliness of resources. Plastics and synthetic materials actually replace heavier, more labor intensive and scarcer materials. For example, the vacuum tube was replaced by the smaller, more knowledge intensive, but less labor intensive transistor, which in turn was replaced by silicon chips and now by molecule sized chips etched by single electrons. Even automobiles have fewer parts, fewer cylinders, with less direct labor and a tremendous increase in quality. Fewer parts, less labor, and diminished resources have actually resulted in a better automobile. New electric motors have fewer parts, require less direct labor to produce, less energy to run, and are virtually maintenance free. Total product redesign adds product value by employing fewer resources.

The other paradigm shift (Figure 1-2) involves product development. Companies no longer have the luxury of waiting decades to see new products or technologies brought to market. Computer producers would love to have the luxury of more time between development cycles, but neither the competition nor the customer will allow it. Likewise, service companies live with new time constraints. One such example is the United Services Automobile Association, which recently settled three hail damage claims to one of the author's cars in less than 43 hours, with an apology that the claims were not settled in 24 hours — their corporate goal.

SHIFT OF THE ENTERPRISE STRUCTURE

A modern business organization represents one of the most complex forms of social organization. By the end of the 19th century and the beginning of the 20th century, most firms grew through vertical integration: by moving back in the productive process, by the owning of raw materials and minerals, or by forward moving in the distributive process toward direct sales. This was typical of U.S. Steel, Standard Oil, American Tobacco, Ford Motor Co., and almost all large manufacturers. During the 1920's and 1930's companies grew by horizontal integration, a movement toward expansion of similar activities throughout a wide geographical area. This type of integration was typified by the chain-store movement, like Sears & Roebuck. During the post-World War II period, the pattern of growth for most enterprises has been through heterogeneous growth with concentric and conglomerate diversification into new and varied fields, exemplified by General Motors, General Electric, United Technologies, General Dynamics, LTV, and ITT. This approach has greatly increased the complexity and size of the business organization.

The corporate structure that emerged from WW II was designed for the era of *Pax Americana*. The structure was organically simple: an isolated enterprise which competed as a complete manufacturer in both the domestic market and international trade (Elliott, 1996). As late as 1950, 24 out of 25 cars sold in the U.S. were made in the U.S.

Playing suppliers off against each other keeps each short of capital to modernize and unable to compete in the global economy. That is one reason why American factories have more outmoded equipment than the plants of other industrialized countries. The average age of the U.S. plant and equipment is approximately 14 years, which experts believe is double the figure for Japan and Europe.

In the 1980's *Pax Nipponica* tried to replace[2] *Pax Americana* as Japan became a major manufacturer of industrial goods and a country which enjoys a large trade surplus. The Japanese corporate structure is organized around a concept of *vertical—horizontal keiretsu*. Together the Summitomo, Sanwa, Mitsui, Mitsubishi, Fuyo, and Dai Ichi Kanguyo groups account for roughly one-fourth of Japan's total business assets and revenues. The vertical dimension of keiretsu is a pyramid of companies that serve a single master. Every large manufacturer, regardless of its affiliation with a horizontal group, dictates virtually everything, including the prices it will pay to hundreds of suppliers that are often prohibited from going outside the keiretsu. At the pyramid's base is a swarm of job shops and family ventures with primitive working conditions and subsistence-level pay and profits (Ferguson, 1990).

Horizontal groups provide security and stability to promote risk-taking and long-term investment. Keiretsu members, collaborating on research and production, deliver new products ahead of independent rivals. U.S. companies are now forming some organizations that could be even better than the Japanese keiretsu. American industry is shifting from the isolated enterprise to a network-cooperative, virtual enterprise with the goal of strengthening its own position in the global marketplace by improving the quality of products and by quickly getting them to the market. What is emerging is the virtual enterprise model that borrows from Japan's keiretsu, with a reliance upon cooperation and alliances among manufacturers, researchers, suppliers, and financiers, where commitment is a virtue and free choice is desirable (Dyer, 1996). The virtual enterprise is shifting its orientation from a monopoly to a niche corporation which balances scale and scope while focusing on customer-oriented products. A monopoly could manufacture 100 products at high volume as a follower (IBM as a PC producer), while a niche corporation (a contract manufacturing) makes 1,000 products at low volume, but as an inventor.

The virtual enterprise structure (Handy, 1995) (Figure 1-3) works in the following manner:

- Corporate Partnership operates on a project-by-project basis, with ideas coming from people throughout both organizations. The main criterion for

Figure 1-3: The Architecture of a Virtual Enterprise

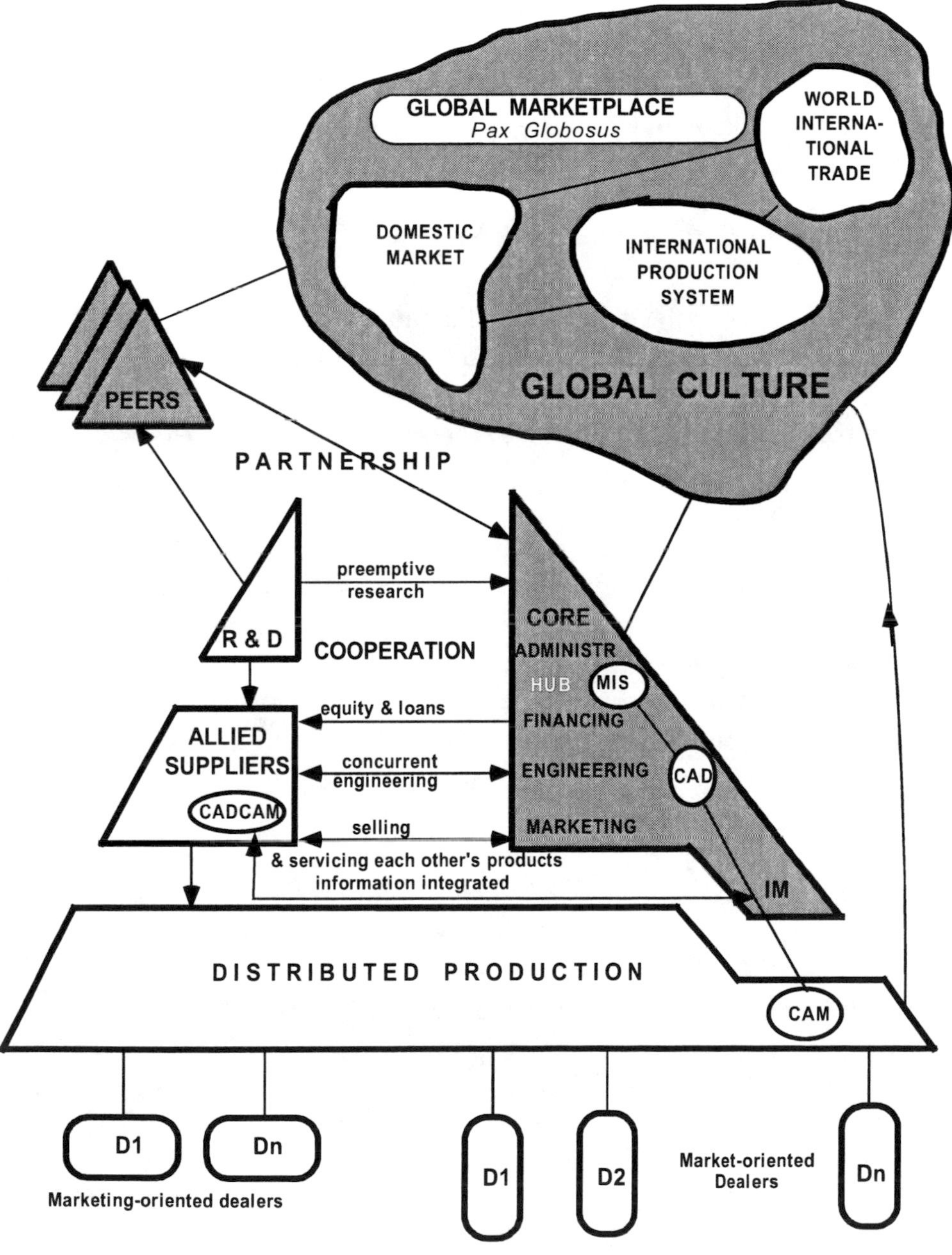

Figure 1-3 The Architecture of a Virtual Enterprise

approving an idea is that it must benefit both companies. The secret of the successful partnership between Ford and Mazda is such that neither side wants to be a part of the other (Moore, 1996).

- Research and Development are concentrated in a consortium funded by peer companies to provide preemptive (precompetitive) research and technology for distinctive products. Since 1982, when Microelectronics & Computer Technology Corp. was initiated by 22 shareholders and 51 associate members, more than 250 new R&D consortiums have been operating. Thus, American companies have begun forming direct research links with competitors. For example, with the help of $120 million from the federal government, the Big Three car manufacturers have jointly developed a new battery technology for electric cars (Brandenburger and Nalebuff, 1996).

- Financing allows the strategic suppliers and startups working on promising technology to receive equity or loans from hub companies. Other cash-rich investors, such as IBM, Ford Motor Co., or Intel sometimes invest up front, instead of on delivery, for research or product-development (Tufano, 1996).

- Engineering is provided concurrently by trusted and organized alliance suppliers and major manufacturers in new-product designs. This process helps avoid time-wasting traps that occur in the final stages of product development. The best suppliers are totally responsible for designing components and subprocesses or subsystems. Harley-Davidson buys 50% of the production value of motorcycles from suppliers, who have been reduced in number from 320 to 120. The buyers are still the boss, but are constrained by their augmented dependence upon the suppliers to be an ally or partner. IBM has invited Motorola Inc. to send engineers to IBM's advanced Semiconductor Technology Center in East Fishkill, N.Y., to help develop a new chipmaking technique (Adler et al., 1996).

- Production is distributed overseas to Pacific Rim Countries or Mexico through single-source contracts or strategic partners. IBM is teaming up with Germany's Siemens, a competitor, to launch joint production in an IBM plant for the next generation of memory chips with 32-megabit dynamic random-access memories (DRAM's). These contracts set strict product quality, cost, and delivery schedules for components that are to be delivered just-in-time and assembled into the final product. Manufacturers and suppliers are becoming partners in production. At Deere & Co., workers now solve problems with their counterparts at suppliers such as McLaughlin Body Co.

- Marketing is performed by manufacturers and suppliers each selling and servicing the other's products. For example, Wang sells IBM products.

- Information Management processes for suppliers and manufacturers are integrated through Computer Aided Design (CAD), Computer Aided Manufacturing (CAM), and Management Information Systems (MIS), all composing Computer Integrated Manufacturing (CIM), sometimes sharing electronic mail, via local, wide, and global area networks (LAN, WAN, GAN). A supplier has to follow the assembly master plan of a manufacturer who retrieves and updates the suppliers' production schedule in order to compete in time and cost through the just-in-time approach. When GM announced that it would not deal with any supplier that had to send it paper documents instead of electronic ones, the company adopted the manufacturing automation protocol (MAP) (Keen, 1988; Targowski, 1990).

Table 1-1 provides a summary of the shifting enterprise structure.

Table 1-1: The Shifting Paradigm of Enterprise Structure

Element	From	To	Permanency
World Power	Cold War *Pax Americana*	Single superpower and terrorists *Pax Globosus*	Dynamic
Enterprise Type	Isolated	Virtual	Temporary
Products Program	Economy of Scale	Economy of Scope	Long-term
Relationship with Suppliers	Disposal	Alliance	Long-term
Market	Domestic	Global/Regional	Long-term
Culture	National	National/Global	Long-term

SHIFT OF MANAGEMENT CONTROL

From the Hierarchical to the Networking Model

Anthony's (1965) model of planning and control consists of three categories: strategic planning, management control, and operational control. This model has dominated the theory and practice of business for the last 25 years. Anthony's model reflects a closed system concept of the isolated enterprise in a formated (machines and materials) national economy. This economy was based on the division of a specialized and massive labor force similar to the military in World Wars I and II with a rigid command structure. The 1980's were the last decade when this model could be successfuly applied in business without major modifications.

The 1990's are a decade of an emerging global and informated (computers and communications) economy in a post-industrial era, where "borderless-stateless," multi-national companies, and national companies compete with foreign products and services through innovation, price, and time. The competition, cooperation, and partnership among company peers, research centers, and suppliers through enterprise-wide computer information systems has shifted the management structure. It has been transformed from a tall to a flattened hierarchy of four or fewer layers with network communications subordinated to results-oriented performers within and among temporary (ad hoc) project teams. This new structure reminds one of university governance. In essence, this new multidomestic enterprise has two rules: "each person is his/her own boss" and "think globally, act locally."

The steep hierarchy in the post-industrial, Global Information Age era is no longer an adequate base of power. Today's managers get work done by building a lateral network of information-sharing relationships, and by developing commitment rather than compliance to a shared vision. They also find new sources of ideas and opportunities and broker deals across internal and external corporate boundaries. Effective managers are integrators, conductors, facilitators, and "fertilizers," not watchdogs or supervisors.

A network is a recognized group of managers (seldom more than 100, often fewer than 25) assembled by senior management. Network membership solution criterion is simple, yet subtle: what select group of managers, by virtue of their business skill, personal motivation, drive, and control of resources are uniquely positioned to shape and deliver a winning strategy? Networks, the new social architecture, are important for the change of organizational behavior: the frequency, intensity, and honesty of the dialogue among managers determines the outcome of priority tasks. The network operates at its best when it guarantees the visibility and free exchange of information to all participating members (Halal, 1996).

In companies such as Conrail, Dun & Bradstreet Europe, MasterCard International, General Electric (some business units), Du Pont, and Royal Bank of Canada, networking plays to the participants' best interests by achieving commitment for specific tasks. Over time, the network induces emotional energy, builds commitment, and enjoys the work.

Twenty years from now, the typical large business will have half the levels of management and one-third the management personnel of the present firm. Work will be done by specialists brought together in project teams that will perform across traditional functional departments. Coordination and control will largely depend upon the employees' willingness to discipline themselves (Drucker, 1988). Behind these changes lie communications and computers. Networked computers process and communicate information faster and better than multiple layers of middle management. Traditional departments won't be where the work gets done. According to Drucker (1988), the best organizations won't have middle management at all. This outcome, however, may be too unrealistic for business as a socio-technical system, evolving constantly, with changes and shifts that must be skillfully managed. The tasks for mid-level management are shrinking, but probably won't disappear entirely.

To survive, business will have to shift from armies of clerical soldiers into organizations of knowledgeable associates (demonstrating intellectual curiosity and a global mind-set) who are flexible, and well-informed specialists or generalists unified by a shared vision, and organized into ad-hoc, interactive teams. This type of merito-cracy is called a "webarchy" (Evans and Wurster, 1997). There will also be less structured career development, with fewer assured routes for promotion, but more opportunities for recognition, innovation and entrepreneurial success. Managers will become facilitators and conductors of culture change enhanced through cross-cultural communication in a business informated environment.

Business Innovation

The strategy of trimming companies in the 1980's through massive layoffs, often executed with the finesse of a Prussian drill instructor ("my way or the highway"), has left the atmosphere at many firms alive with alienation. There is tremendous frustration and tension between employers and their employees. Mutual cynicism and mistrust seem to be at an all-time high. Into this human resources ruin comes a new breed of management expert and executive, who preach a gospel of full worker participation in managing the company. Such a philosophy has already won reformers at Ford Motor Co., Goodyear, and General Electric. Management must stress collaboration, ingenuity and creativity, rather than internal conflict.

Management must develop new solutions and recognize a new language. They have to replace the stale culture with a new one with its own new rules and postulates. A permanent learning process must be implemented so as to prod the worker's mind to accept more innovation, competition and cooperation in a turbulent information-rich environment. Leadership must then provide atypical solutions.

The Campus Model

Figure 1-4 depicts a synthesis of existing practices and postulates solutions for a new campus structure of management in the network-cooperative enterprise. Since knowledge becomes a strategic resource, knowledge-based firms will evolve into university-like organizations (Davis and Botkin, 1994). As such they will turn to a campus-like organizational structure with a dual process, a formal administrative one and an informal one for the faculty. The campus administration provides procedures, funds and services to the faculty and students, while the typical president is more a facilitator than a powerful czar.

The faculty produce knowledge, solve problems, discover new theories, and teach students. In the campus structure for business organizations the old, steep hierarchical structure is inverted and flattened. The new structure is divided along three time dimensions: long, medium, and short range. It is also electronically integrated by an enterprise-wide communications and computer information processing system. Outside the halls of academia this model has been fully embraced by Microsoft.

In the campus model, business administration must provide the vision, motivation, corporate culture, agenda, goals and strategy, communication, profitability, discipline, and equilibrium. Business administration is a long-term management function carried-out by a CEO and managers who ensure a spirit of competition and cooperation. They must also provide new opportunities and customers. The skills required are intellectual, with a global strategic conceptualization of the business.

The new campus organization revolutionizes the *modus operandi* for business, the economy, and government, as well as the workers and executives who during the 1990's and beyond must learn to apply new knowledge and

Figure 1-4: The Architecture of a Campus Management Apparatus

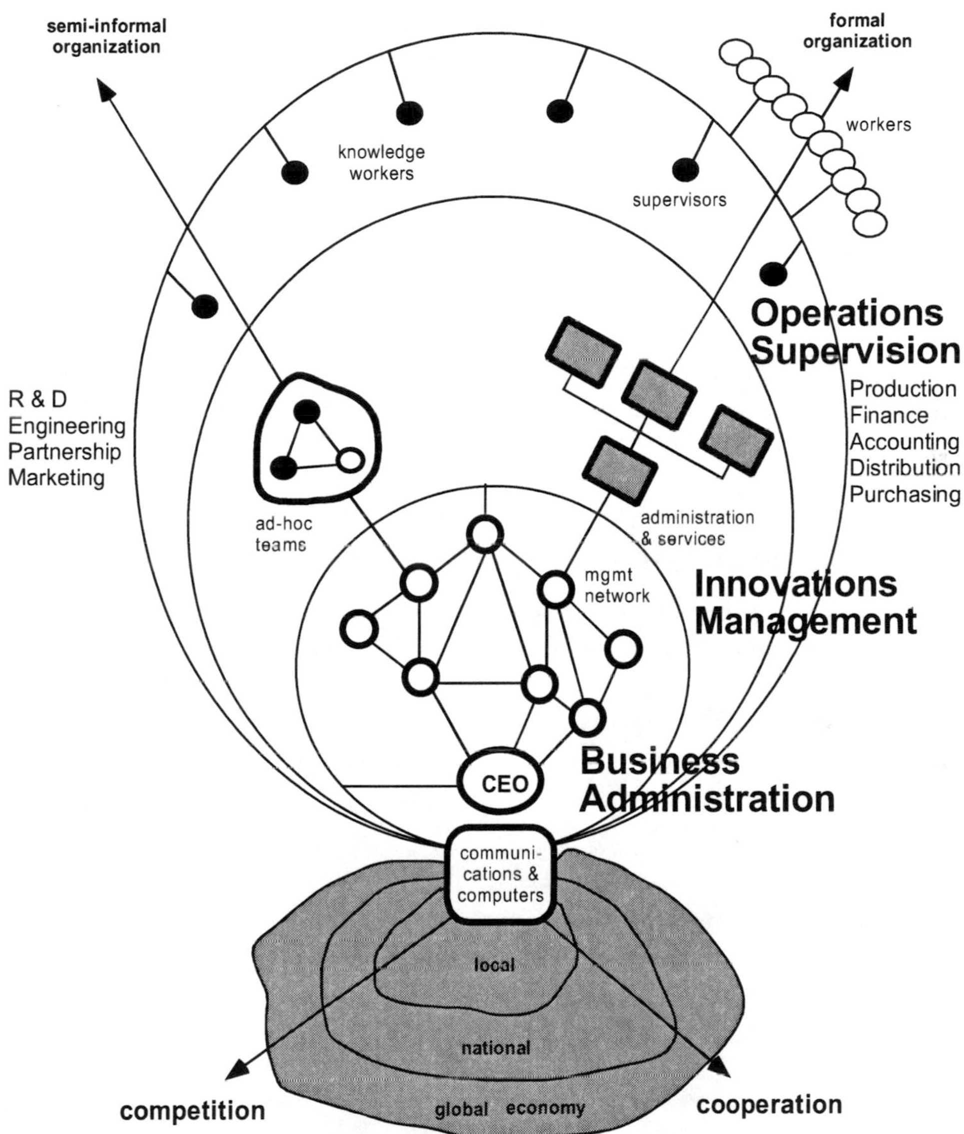

techniques. These new techniques mean that the administrative level of management is one of service and facilitation for other managerial levels. In other words, business administration is now like the roots of a tree feeding a dynamic, innovative, and productive enterprise whose leaves are green throughout the seasons. The ancient Chinese emperors who were in service to their citizens fully understood leadership as a service occupation. The critical layer of global business, to the surprise of many, is the highly knowledgeable middle manager, who creates and implements the innovations that ultimately decide business survival and success. Of course, the middle manager who is only involved in information collecting and processing has no guarantee of survival since this position itself is being computerized.

This new managerial role requires open-minded CEO's, CFO's, COO's, and CIO's who can build networks for motivated "associates" who collaborate to achieve innovation, productivity, customer satisfaction, and profitability. The network starts locally, becomes national, and more frequently emerges globally. A new type of executive is necessary, not one who can only use a computer, but one who can learn to communicate easily with collaboration-oriented performers and who is not intimidated by the expertise of others. These executives are not necessarily the youngest or the oldest, but simply the best.

From Tasks to Culture Control

Management has shifted from Goals-Objectives-Tasks to Vision-Culture-Results Management. Once a worker becomes his or her own boss and the manager becomes a facilitator, managerial control shifts from quantitative to qualitative aims. To support this new orientation and work ethic, executives must learn how to become leaders to provide a vision, to negotiate from the bottom-up with top-down goals, and to create a culture supportive of excellent performance.

A corporate vision must be provided by business leadership which integrates long-term value and architecture (a multi-dimensional, harmonic configuration of the company and its customers) with a defined philosophy, goals, and culture. This vision should also be generated by all the "associates" from within the firm. Such a generation of vision requires better horizontal communication which will energize the employees' spirit and joy for work.

SHIFTS OF INFRASTRUCTURE

From Formative to Informative Products and Economy

A shift from formative to informative products and economy, and a shift from hardware to brainware, is driven by a shift from traditional materials and energy to new composite materials and knowledge-based products and services. New products are lighter and more functional, new houses consume fewer materials and energy, new American airplanes consume 30% fewer materials than a decade ago. The new Boeing 767 couldn't be built without computer aided design (CAD) and computer aided manufacturing (CAM). This new wave continues to expand: six billion microprocessors are embodied in all types of smart products, more than the population of the Earth.

The relationship between capital, labor, energy, and knowledge is shifting toward knowledge as a source of wealth. Big business relies upon mass markets funded by large capital requirements. But the small and innovative companies which can quickly produce new knowledge, products, processes, and services are the most profitable and have the fastest rate of growth. They may eventually become a large corporation, like Microsoft. Such as machine-tools are extensions of human muscles, microcomputers are extensions of the mind and will be gradually incorporated into many smart products and processes. New products and processes will self-control, self-repair, and self-reproduce. Robot factories will even produce other robots.

Previously, the informative economy required continual expansion, or so-called "growth." Now, a key of the informative economy is "downsizing," or "rightsizing," which leads to more niche-oriented products and services while it eliminates unnecessary operations and materials. Firms are producing more with less direct labor, but with better methods and automation, with empowered workers who do not separate thinking from doing. The empowered worker is often a white collar worker since direct labor is often below 5% of a manufactured product's selling price (Targowski, 1996).

From Automation Islands to Federated Systems Architecture

The business of information is big business, and is rapidly growing larger. American companies spend 2% to 4% of total corporate sales on information services each year (2000 CPM Media, Inc.). Technology has made information an economic good that can be produced, bought and sold like many other goods in the marketplace. But information must be managed wisely and as productively as any other company resource. Most computer application systems were developed on an ad hoc basis. Each application was considered a separate entity with little or no connection to other computerized applications existing within the business organization (McKenney et al., 1982). Without an enterprise-wide flexible supersystem, there is no clear mechanism, from a holistic business perspective, for the transformation of data into information and knowledge which will impact the business decision making.

Integrated, architecturally-designed, organizational computer-information programs can best be conceptualized through hierarchies of interconnected systems and subsystems which one can label "federated information systems." The following federated C&C (Computers & Communications) blocks include: Federated Information Systems, Data/Information/Knowledge Base, Company Software, Computer Systems, and Communications Networks. These enterprise-wide, federated systems create a business-driven "blue-print" for systems planning and the integration of information which allows the company to better compete in time, cost, product functionality, manufacturing quality, and customer service within the global economy (Targowski and Rienzzo, 1991).

A good example of such systems is a concept of ERP (Enterprise Resource Planning) provided by SAP, Baan, JD Edwards, Oracle, and others[3].

From National and Traditional to Cross-Culture and Electronic Communications

Numerous service companies and retailers have learned to transcend national boundaries and to conduct business globally. For example, the Limited, headquartered in Columbus, Ohio, uses electronic links with Asian based manufacturers to make and ship by air the latest fashions in a matter of weeks. Suppliers, shippers, and retail outlets are all linked by telecommunications, resulting in a competitive advantage for the Limited. Similarly, U.S. airlines are linked via computers and telephones with reservation clerks based in Ireland where wages are low and the level of education is high. Even the Fortune 500 has developed transcultural operations that yield in excess of one-third of the Fortune 500's total profits.

Ken Ohmai's "Borderless World" is a reality. Large technology firms are large only because of extensive foreign operations, as exemplified by the computer giants. In 1991 Apple Computer had foreign sales of 44.8% of revenues, while Compaq had 58%, IBM had 50%, and Hewlett Packard realized 56% of revenues from foreign operations (1991 annual Reports). Coca-Cola had soft drink sales of 2.6 billion in the United States, but had 7.2 billion in sales from international operations [4]. But a cold Coke tastes good anywhere in the world. The world leader in international operations as a percentage of sales is the ubiquitous Nestle, which had 95% of sales and 97% of profits from outside its native Switzerland. Even small U.S. companies such as those producing computer modems have belatedly realized that high growth almost solely relies upon international sales.

From the Known to Unknown and the Dot.Com Crisis[4]

The management of a turbulent environment is very challenging. We can learn about the factors that influence dynamic global corporations, but only indirectly, and often long after their impact has been made. A simplistic predictive model of corporate excellence is fun to believe in, but unfortunately, unrealistic.

For example, in the late 1990's the emergence of e-commerce known as a "dot.com" business created the economic boom, which later transformed into the speculative bubble. The boom stage of the Internet bubble lasted from October 1998 to April 2000. During that period, more than 300 Internet firms did IPO's (Initial Public Offerings of stocks). On March 10, 2000, the NASDAQ closed above 5,000. On April 14, 2000, the NASDAQ had dropped 1,727.33 points, or 32%. The Dow Jones Composite Internet Index was down 53.6% from its March 9 high. In just one week, $2 trillion of stock market wealth had been eviscerated, Micosoft alone had lost $240 billion in market capitalization since its peak, Amazon.com had lost 29.9%, and Yahoo! had lost 34.8%. The collapse of the NASDAQ was caused by unscrupulous alliances of entrepreneurs, venture capitalists, stock analysts, investment bankers, and too optimistic journalists who helped to expand and prolong the bubble. This failure can be named "*from dot.com towards dot.con.*" John Cassidy (2002) states that–"the collapse of the NASDAQ was a turning point in American history." Because, "for the past five years, the stock market, particularly the NASDAQ, had been a symbol of American technological leadership and economic power. Most of all, it had been a symbol of American self-confidence." The myth of the American technological might had been exposed. Unexpectedly, instead of the premise that the future is illimitable, the U.S. faced a future of economic, political, and cultural limits.

September 11, 2001

The terrorist attacks hit the post-bubble economy, particularly punched in the minds of consumers. When the stock market opened on Monday, September 17, it suffered a fall of 1,300 points, or 14.8%, to 8,235.81. The sell-off represented investors' uncertainty about the future, and the attacks had largely emphasized existing limitations in the economy. The slow-down of the economy slowed investments in information technology too. However, the Internet remains a technological wonder and despite of the fact that many dot.com ("dot.con") companies are long forgotten, we should look back on the 1990's as the time during which the information society became a reality. For example, the online edition of The Wall Street Journal has about 500,000 subscribers, most of whom also buy the print edition. Merrill Lynch offers online trades for $29.95, but the greater part of clients also employ the firm's brokers, who charge much more for their services.

NEW RULES OF POST-MODERN BUSINESS

We suggest a new revolution — not the end of history, but the dawn of a new era, as informated global business with new rules:

Rules of The Informated Global Business:

1. From one stakeholder and system to many.
   There used to be a stockholder and one system that now are extended to more agents/systems influencing a firm's performance, such as employees, managers, communities, governments, NGO, and their systems.

2. Act locally, think and profit globally.
   Almost every local producer and service provider is affected by foreign competitors, hence the formers must organize themselves having in mind the global competition.

3. Customers, not executives, drive a business.
   The introduction of agile production supports mass customization which puts emphasis on how to please a customer, who chooses more suitable solutions and decides about a firm's success.

4. Knowledge is as important a strategic resource as capital.
   Knowledge embedded in products makes them more sophisticated and better at satisfying customers.

5. Cooperation precedes and is integrated into the competitive process.
   One firm is unable to spend enough resources on R&D and marketing,

hence must look for alliances to compete with stronger companies/alliances.

6. Lead time, innovation, quality, and utility satisfy a customer.
A nowadays customer is more demanding from producers and service providers who must compete at the level of cost, quality, and lead time, which add value.

7. Do not separate thinking from doing.
Advanced technological systems require that their operators are problem solvers.

8. The integration of the islands of automation into an enterprise information infrastructure leads to the gateway of the Electronic Global Village.
The system's integration leads to less redundant components and communication which take place locally, nationally, and globally through telecommunication networks and the Internet.

CONCLUSION

Perhaps in no time of history has the human race faced a brighter, but less defined and less tangible future. The historical paradigms of business simply no longer apply. We are at the beginning of a new era, and as exemplified by the Russian proverb, we must "break the glass." We must break our old paradigm and create a new one based upon an informated business architecture. Knowledge will allow us to accomplish more, with less, but this accomplishment will require new paradigms and much change.

On the other hand, we cannot exaggerate the role of information technology in the economy. Despite the rapid growth of the Internet and information technologies in general, firms still spend more money of industrial and agricultural capital equipment than they do on computers and networks. Many big industries that employ millions of workers, such as health care, catering, and construction are largely unaffected by the Internet. In the concluding analysis, manufacturing still has more to do with assembling parts of wood and metal than with processing information. The Information Wave just optimizes the Agricultural and Industrial Waves but does not replace them. Without these two Waves, the Information Wave could not have the reason to exist.

BIBLIOGRAPHY

Adler, P. S., Mandelbaum, A., Nguyen, V. & Schwerer, E. (1996). Getting the most out of your product development process.. *Harvard Business Review*, March-April, pp. 134-153.

Anthony, R. N. (1965). *Planning and Control Systems: A Framework for Analysis*. Boston: Harvard University Press.

Applegate, L. M. et al. (1999). *Information Technology for Managers, Business Fundamentals Series*. Cambridge, MA: HBS Press.

Cassidy, J. (2002). *dot.con, The Greatest Story Ever Sold.* New York: HarperCollins Publishers.

Davis, S., & Botkin, J. (1994). The coming of knowledge-based business. *Harvard Business Review*, September-October, pp. 165-189.

Drucker, P. (1980). *Managing in Turbulent Times*. New York: Harper & Row.

Drucker, P. (1988). The coming of the new organization. *Harvard Business Review*, January-February, pp. 45-53.

Dyer, J. H. (1996). How Chrysler created an American Keiretsu. *Harvard Business Review*, July-August, pp. 42-60.

Elliott, M. (1996). *The Day Before Yesterday: Reconsidering America's Past, Rediscovering the Present.* New York: Simon & Schuster.

Estes, R. (1996). *Tyranny of the Bottom Line.* San Francisco: Berrett-Koehler Publishers.

Evans, P. & Wuster, T. S. (1997). Strategy and the new economics of information. *Harvard Business Review*, September-October.

Ferguson, C. K. (1990). Computers and the coming of the U.S. Keiretsu. *Harvard Business Review*, July-August, pp.55-70.

Halal, W. E. (1996). *The New Management*. San Francisco: Berett-Koehler Publishers.

Hamel, G. (2000). *Leading the Revolution*. Cambridge, MA: HBS Press.

Handy, C. H. (1995). Trust and the virtual organization. *Harvard Business Review*, May-June, pp.40-54.

Huntington, P. S. (1996). *The Clash of Civilizations and the Remaking of World Order*. New York: Simon & Schuster.

Keen, P. W. (1988). *Competing in Time*. Cambridge, Massachusetts: Ballinger Publishing Co.

Korten, D. C. (1995). *When Corporations Rule the World.* West Hartford, CT: Kumarian Press.

Krugman, P., Forbes, S., & Lawrence, R. (1996). Workers and economists. *Foreign Affairs*, 75(4), pp. 164-181.

Kuhn, T. (1970). *The Structure of Scientific Revolutions*. Chicago: The University of Chicago Press.

Means, G. (ed.) (2000). *MetaCapitalism: The e-Business Revolution and the Design of 21st Century and Markets*. New York: John Wiley & Sons.

Moore, J. F. (1996). *The Death of Competition*, New York: Harper Business.

Robertson, B. & Scribar, V. (2002). *The Adaptive Enterprise: IT Infrastructure Strategies to Manage and Enable Growth*. Boston, MA: Addison-Wesley Professional.

Tapscott, D. (1997). *Digital Economy*. New York: McGraw-Hill Trade.

Tapscott, D. & Caston, A. (1993). *Paradigm Shift: The New Promise of Information Technology*. New York: McGraw-Hill Inc.

Tapscott, D. et al. (2000). *Digital Capital: Harnessing the Power of Business Webs*. Cambridge, MA: HBS Press.

Targowski, A. (1990). *The Architecture and Planning of Enterprise-Wide Information Management Systems*. Harrisburg, PA: Idea Group Publishing.

Targowski, A. (1991). Emergence of the international production system. *Proceedings of Facing East/Facing West: North America and the Asia/Pacific Region in the 1990s.* WMU-Fetzer Business Development Center, Kalamazoo, MI, September 13-15, pp. 199-207.

Targowski, A. (1991). Strategies and architecture of the electronic global village.. *The Information Society*, 7, pp. 187-202.

Targowski, A. (1996). *Global Information Infrastructure*. Harrisburg, PA: Idea Group Publishing.

Targowski, A. & Korth, C. (2000). China or NAFTA: Which will control the world's largest market in the 21st century, *The Proceedings of The Third Facing East/Facing West Conference*, Fetzer Business Development Center, Western Michigan University, Kalamazoo, Michigan, June 2-3.

Tufano, P. (1996). How financial engineering can advance corporate strategy, *Harvard Business Review*, January-February, pp. 136-147.

Weil, P. & Broadband, M. (1998). *Leveraging the New Infrastructure: How Market Leaders Capitalize on Information Technology*. Cambridge, MA: HBS Press.

Wheelwright, S. C. (1994). Regaining the lead in manufacturing. *Harvard Business Review*, September-October, pp.108-143.

ENDNOTES

1 An informated enterprise is such one where its information resource can generate a value added knowledge about its business/organizational processes for the purpose of optimizing decision making.

2 However, Japan is in a long recession (1994-2002) and its *Pax Nipponica* did not succeed.

3 More information on ERP systems is provided in Chapter 4.

4 More on this topic is in Chapter 6.

Chapter II

Enterprise Configurations

INTRODUCTION

The new economy requires a new enterprise organization. It obligates most companies to redefine their mission, goals, and strategy. The emerging 21st century enterprise is a more complex organization than the 20th century industrial enterprise. Since the enterprise consists of small teams running their affairs from a single office, the lean organization is also a subject of the emerging trend of outsourcing and creating partnerships. Managing those relationships will be the key strategy of the IT support.

Enterprises that once handled everything internally now find they must concentrate on their core competencies, so they outsource much more than they once did. Moreover, many of the new relationships are international and global. In 1995, the Institute for the Future in Menlo Park, California, found that the number of international joint ventures has grown 25% a year since 1990.

Time to reach market is critical when products have a competitive life span of one year, one month, one week, or one afternoon, as in the case of some products in financial services. Innovation, rather than access to resources, plant, and capital, is what counts most.

ENTERPRISE CLASSIFICATION

The enterprise organization can be classified by many criteria. For the purpose of this book we will apply two criteria: the geographic criterion and the IT criterion.

According to the geographic criterion, one can distinguish the following types of enterprise:

- A local enterprise, whose area of sales is limited to a given city or region (e.g., a state, like Spartan Stores),
- A national enterprise, whose area of sales is within national borders (like Kroger Food),
- An international enterprise, which has an international division, which manages its operations in selected countries (like Steelcase),
- A multidomestic enterprise (multinational enterprise – MNE, or multinational corporation – MNC) allows each of its foreign country operations to act with some autonomy, by designing and producing in Italy for the Italian market and in South Korea for the South Korean market,
- A global enterprise (multinational enterprise – MNE, or multinational corporation – MNC) integrates its operations that are located in different countries. In this enterprise, the development of capabilities and the decisions to disperse them globally are essentially made in the enterprise's home country (e.g., Royal Dutch/Shell Group, General Electric, Toyota Motor, Ford Motor, Nestle, Unilever, and so forth)[1].

According to the IT criterion, one can distinguish the following types of enterprise:

- Off-line enterprise, in which data processing operates in a batch mode, not on-line and not in real-time,
- On-line enterprise, which processes information on-line through computer networks,
- Integrated enterprise, which applies a common, enterprise database for the majority of applications,

- Agile enterprise,
- Informated enterprise, which applies knowledge management systems in decision-making,
- A communicated enterprise,
- Mobile enterprise,
- Electronic enterprise,
- Virtual enterprise, which applies communication technology in connecting different worker locations, when the workers very often operate from their own home, a hotel, a car, or a customer's location[2].

The above sequence of the enterprise evolution is a simplified model, as each model is. In practice, some components of these enterprises can appear in just one enterprise and very often in a sequence different than the evolutionary model. However, very often such enterprise having a piece of each configuration can be considered as an unfinished solution with questionable benefits of information technology. The purpose of the enterprise evolution is to know its requirements for each configuration's architecture, budget, developmental skills, and the timeline.

The combination of solutions in different enterprises is provided in Table 2-1.

Table 2-1: The Combination of Solutions in Enterprises

	Local	*National*	*International*	*Multi-domestic*	*Global*
Off-line	Yes				
On-line	Yes	Yes	Yes	Yes	
Integrated	Yes	Yes	Yes		Yes
Agile	Yes	Yes	Yes		
Informated	Yes	Yes	Yes	Yes	Yes
Communi-cated	Yes	Yes	Yes	Yes	Yes
Mobile	Yes	Yes	Yes	Yes	Yes
Electronic	Yes	Yes	Yes	Yes	Yes
Virtual	Yes	Yes	Yes	Yes	Yes

OFF-LINE ENTERPRISE

The off-line enterprise is a typical solution for the industrial enterprise, which operated in the 1950's and 1960's. Several applications such as payroll, stock control, production control, and customer orders had been processed independently and their data were provided in batches. Rooted in the 1980's and 1990's, such data processing modes can be found in small enterprises, such as small retail stores or small repair shops. A model of such an enterprise is shown in Figure 2-1.

Figure 2-1: A Model of Off-line Enterprise

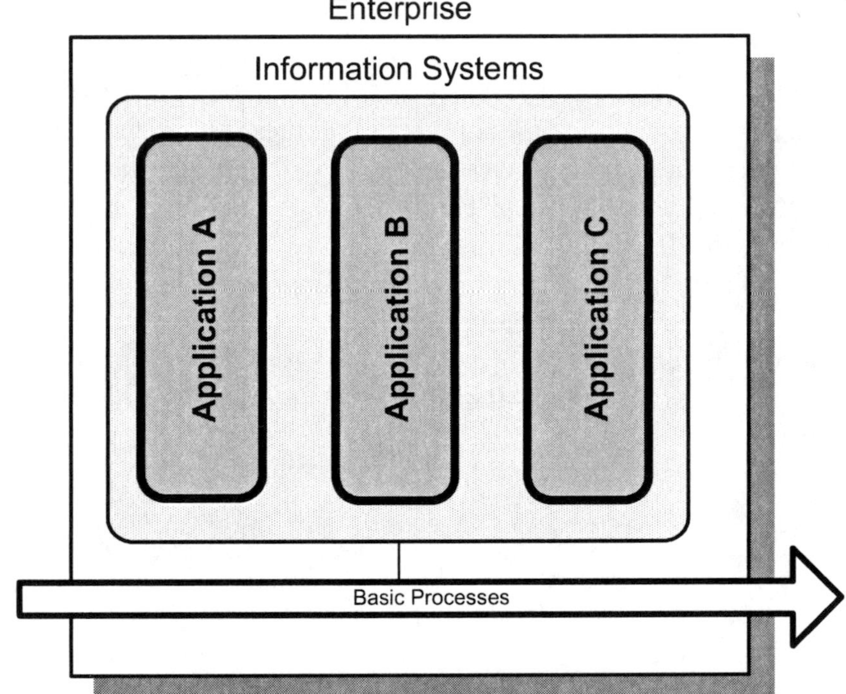

ON-LINE ENTERPRISE[3]

The organization of an on-line (networked) enterprise is based upon computer networks such as Local Area Network (LAN), Metropolitan Area

Network (MAN), Wide Area Network (WAN), Value-added Network (VAN), and Global Area Network (GAN), and the Internet. A network enterprise can have the following types of organization:

- Internal enterprise network among its own organizational units,
- Single partner collaboration,
- Multiple external collaboration (extended enterprise),
- Internet-based enterprise,
- Combination of the above.

Computer networks enable the transformation of a hierarchical organization into a "network" organization, which is characterized by the following attributes (Alstyne, 1997):

- Its purpose is to advance co-operation,
- Horizontal integration is stronger than a vertical one,
- Decentralized, internetworking teams,
- Trust is moderate and even high,
- Conflict resolution is based on negotiations and reciprocity,
- Tasks are carried out through the internal management of the project,
- Decision-making is based upon persuasion and consensus, and
- Strong support of computer networking.

These attributes create an on-line (networked) enterprise, which at the same time can be:

- The horizontal enterprise,

- The extended enterprise,
- The Internet-driven enterprise.

The *horizontal enterprise* reflects the philosophy of work organization, which largely eliminates both management hierarchy and functional and departmental boundaries. In its purest state, the horizontal enterprise may be composed of a skeleton group of senior executives at the top in such traditional support functions as finance and human resources. But everyone else in the enterprise works together in multidisciplinary teams that perform core processes, such as product development or sales generation. As a result, the enterprise might have only three or four layers of management between the chairman and the staff in a given process.

Simple downsizing in the 1980's and 1990's did not produce the dramatic rises in productivity many companies had hoped for. Gaining quantum leaps in performance requires rethinking the way work gets done. To do that, some companies are adapting a new organization model. Here is how it might work (Byrne, 1993):

- Organize around process, not a task. Instead of creating a structure around functions or departments, build the company around its three to five "core processes" with specific goals. Assign an "owner" to each process.
- Flatten hierarchy. To reduce supervision, combine fragmented tasks, eliminate work that fails to add value, and cut the activities within each process to a minimum. Use as few teams as possible to perform an entire process.
- Use teams to manage everything. Make teams the main building blocks of the organization. Limit supervisory roles by making the team manage itself. Give the team a common purpose. Hold it accountable for measurable performance goals.
- Let customers drive performance. Make customer satisfaction – not stock appreciation or profitability – the primary driver and measure of performance. The profits will come and the stock will rise if the customers are satisfied.

- Reward team performance. Change the appraisal and pay systems to reward team results, not just individual performance. Encourage the staff to develop multiple skills rather than specialized know-how. Reward them for it.

- Maximize supplier and customer contact. Bring employees into direct, regular contact with supplier or customer. Add supplier or customer representatives as full working members of in-house teams when they can be of service.

- Inform and train all employees. Do not just spoon-feed sanitized information on a "need to know" basis. Trust the staff with raw data, but train them how to use it to perform their own analyses and make their own decisions.

Companies moving toward this new organization model:

AT&T Network Systems Div. reorganized its entire business around processes; now sets budgets by process and awards bonuses to employees based on customer evaluation.

Eastman Kodak. Kodak unit has over 1,000 teams, ditched senior v-ps of administration, manufacturing, and R&D in favor of self-directed teams.

General Electric. Lighting business scrapped vertical structure, adapting horizontal design with more than 100 processes and programs.

Lexmark International. Former IBM division axed 60% of managers in favor of cross-functional teams worldwide.

MOTOROLA. Government Electronics group redesigned its supply management organization as a process with external customers at the end; team members are now evaluating peers.

XEROX. Develops new products through multi-disciplinary teams that work in a single process, instead of vertical functions or departments.

The horizontal enterprise is a solution that is gaining currency and one that will increasingly demand people who think more broadly and thrive on change, who manage process instead of people, and who cherish teamwork as never before.

The *extended enterprise* is emerging from computer networks which link suppliers with producers and customers. This form of integration of partners creates so-called supply-chain management (advanced logistics). A supply-chain coordinates customer requirements with a producer's internal planning and scheduling and suppliers' delivery of materials and components.

> Wal-Mart has transformed business and has become a successful retailer through inter-enterprise networking with its most important suppliers. It allows Wal-Mart to reduce inventory and improve product availability on the shelves. Today when someone buys a skirt at Wal-Mart, a stream of computer applications is processing information across the computer networks, all the way to the factory that makes the skirt. The new skirt, however, did not first go into a central warehouse. It was sent directly to the store from the manufacturers, as 97% of all Wal-Mart's goods never pass through a warehouse.

Figure 2-2: A Model of an On-line (Networked) Enterprise as the Extended Enterprise

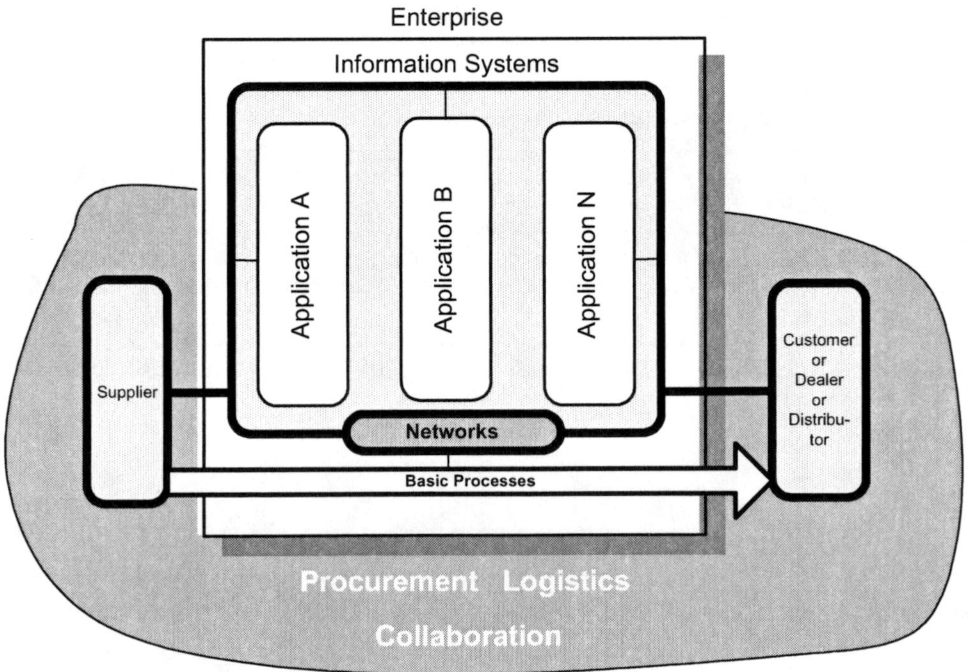

> Chrysler has won kudos from suppliers and shareholders alike for its highly regarded SCORE program – the acronym stands for Supplier Cost Reduction Effort – in which cost savings stemming from suppliers' suggestions are shared with suppliers. Since 1989 the Auburn Hills, Michigan-based automaker has received some 25,000 supplier proposals that have yielded $3.7 billion in cumulative cost savings. Every week suppliers submit more than 100 ideas or proposals that offer practical ways for Chrysler to reduce costs (Industry Week, 2.02.1998).

The networked enterprise model is shown in Figure 2-2.

INTEGRATED ENTERPRISE

Once an enterprise is equipped in computer networks, the next step in its evolution is the integration of application around a common enterprise database. This integration leads to so-called enterprise-wide computing and the development of enterprise-wide information systems and services. Companies are stockpiling ever-larger amounts of data on products, customers, and transactions in an effort to understand and control what sells, reach new customers, and make better business decisions.

Companies that implement enterprise-wide systems usually acquire software packages. Those companies no longer want packages that merely automate existing processes. Instead, they want packaged applications that support integration between functional modules, can be quickly changed or enhanced, and that present a common graphical look-and-feel, thereby helping to drive down training and operating costs.

Furthermore, companies require suites of applications that support their desires to operate worldwide. The cost of maintaining custom applications has been growing, and the packaged suite of applications (called ERP - Enterprise Resource Planning) has emerged as a solution.

The enterprise-wide software is provided by several vendors and is customized and implemented by several "integrators." Among leading software packages one can mention the following:

- **SAP (*Systeme Anwendung Produkte*)**, a German company which has about 30% of the market. The company sells the R/3 software package which supports a high degree of integration and multi-site, multi-currency operations. The R/3 package integrates Financial Accounting, Treasury Management, Sales And Distribution, Human Resources, Product Data Management, Computer-Integrated Manufacturing, and Enterprise-Wide Reporting. The R/3 package is supported in the local languages of 35 countries.

- **OCA (Oracle Cooperative Applications)** are integrated around Oracle relational database system, which is supported on multiple platforms. OCA is composed of six enterprise-wide applications; Supply Chain Management, Manufacturing, Financial Management, Project Accounting, Market Management, and Human Resources Management. Oracle has also introduced a family of applications for the Web, such as Oracle Web Employees, Oracle Web Customers, and Oracle Web Suppliers.

- **PeopleSoft** sells an integrated package which contains the following integrated applications: Human Resources Management System, PeopleSoft Inventory, PeopleSoft Order Management, PeopleSoft Purchasing, PeopleSoft Manufacturing, PeopleSoft Distribution, and PeopleSoft Financials. PeopleSoft applications run on several top databases, including DB2, Oracle, Informix, Sybase, and MS SQL Back Office.

- **Baan Co.**, from the Netherlands, sells a software package which supports such applications as: Supply Chain Management, Project Control/Planning, Suppliers scheduling, Self-Billing, Financials, Logistics, Process Control, Shop-Floor Monitoring, EDI, a product Configurator, Distribution, and Simulation.

- **Software 2000** offers a package containing the following applications: Financial Management, Human Resource Management, Material Management, and Manufacturing. In addition, the vendor provides a user interface for access to management and business analysis information. Software 2000 provides Web access to information for customers.

The ERP software systems are very complex; for example, SAP R/3 has about 500 million lines of code, 80,000 tables, and 10,000 icons. Its implementation is a very complex and costly undertaking, which can take several years and millions of dollars. To make a successful implementation of

ERP it is necessary first to adapt business processes (about several hundreds) to new software requirements. Failure to do so is one of the main reasons for many difficulties, even business malfunction. For example, Kellogg had to replace Oracle's ERP by SAP R/3 at the cost of $400 million.

The implementation of ERP systems is provided by so-called system integrators. System integration and outsourcing is a $300 billion business. Selecting an IT integration service provider is the most important decision an information executive ever makes. The average company spends one-fifth of its budget each year on these experts, relying on them to fill huge skills gaps, cope with technological complexity, and ultimately, to help drive a new business.

Among the 10 top integrators one can include the following:

- Andersen Consulting,
- EDS,
- Pricewatershouse-Coopers,
- Ernst & Young,
- KPMG Peat Marwick,
- Deloitte Consulting,
- IBM Global Services,
- Computer Science Corp.,
- Compaq/Digital,
- Hewlett-Packard.

Among the most popular integration and outsourcing services one can mention are the following:

- Application development,
- PC support and procurement,

- Network integration and management,
- Data centers management,
- Internet hosting (e-commerce),
- Help desk,
- ERP integration,
- Extranets.

Along the long-term dangers IT organizations face in using integrators and outsourcers to augment internal staff is the risk that their very best employees will be eliminated, or that they may not develop essential skills and know-how to manage and maintain new systems.

A model of an integrated enterprise is shown in Figure 2-3.

Figure 2-3: A Model of an Integrated Enterprise

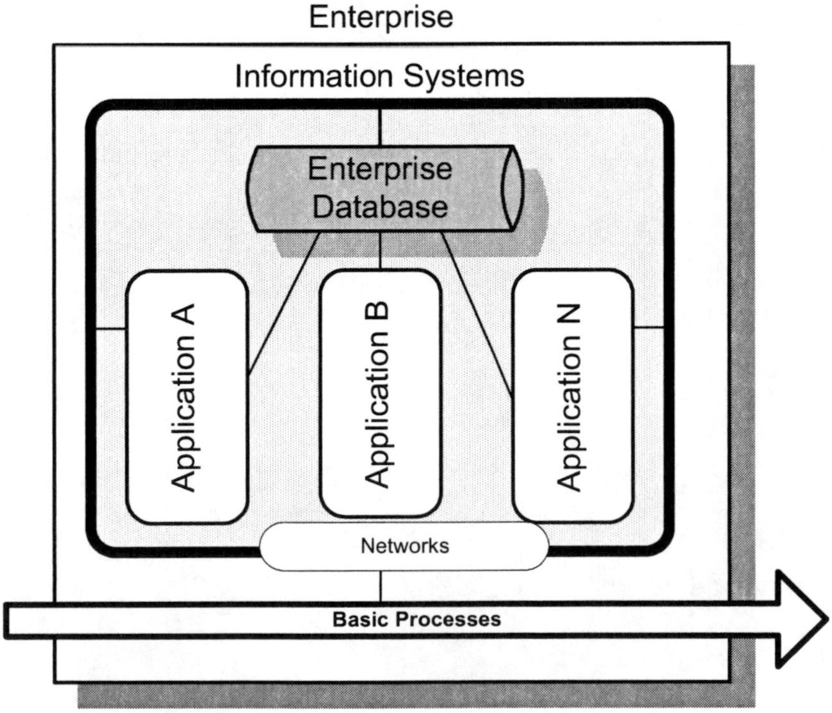

Examples

IBM installed SAP R/3 software for its own internal information processing. This decision saved millions of dollars, not only through faster flows of consistent information, but also as a result of the elimination of hundreds of other software programs. IBM had 47 different order-entry systems and about 6,000 applications; today that figure is down to 300. IBM expects to have 26,000 employees using SAP.

The R/3 Supply Chain application was able to reduce IBM's demand/supply calendar – the time it takes the company to rebalance supply with changes in product demand globally – from 60 to 20 days. The process improvements obtained from the shift to SAP's applications package are impressive. Prior to installing the enterprise system, the entire process of handling a purchasing request took two days; today it requires just two and half hours. The time needed to give a customer a committed date for shipping a PC – previously a day – now can be done over the phone immediately. Orders can be scheduled or rescheduled in real-time, compared with the former overnight wait.

IBM formerly offered about 3,000 different PC system units; today the company offers 150 systems. The time to bring new hardware to market was reduced from 54 to 16 - 18 months. As a result, sales advanced from 1.9 to 2.2 million units, and from 8.2% (1995) to 8.7% of the market (in 1998). In the disk-drive unit, the integration of IBM's enterprise systems via SAP enabled the unit to cut its manual workload from three-fourths of all orders and shipment to zero. The 15 to 20 minutes it took someone to respond to a customer's question about a bill was reduced to an immediate response. The job of shipping a customer a repaired or replacement part, which used to take three to 44 days, now takes two days. IBM has slashed information systems expenses dramatically, from $4.3 billion in 1992 to about $2.3 billion in 1996. Much of the savings came from consolidating the firm's 155 data centers around the world into only 28, eight of which are manned; the remaining 20 are fully automated.

As a result of these improvements, IBM's stock has risen from $40.62 in 1993 to $179 in late May of 1998 (Industry Week, 07/07/1998). However, in the 2000's IBM's stock went down, but mostly due to the decline of almost all technology stocks.

With more than 10,000 employees and annual sales approaching $5 billion, one large global chemical company chose to differentiate itself by being first in its industry to use the ERP system. The company's aggressive corporate goals called for accelerating revenue growth, identifying and quickly developing new income streams from emerging market segments, and establishing itself as an industry leader. The first phase established the EMC Enterprise Storage Network™ (ESN) at the company's headquarters to support corporate SAP R/3 operations. The second phase brought the Microsoft Exchange environment, currently supporting 9,000 users and rapidly becoming a lifeline for business communications, under the same high availability of the IT environment as SAP R/3. In the third phase the company broadened the ESN to tie into their information infrastructure the rapidly growing number of applications such as ERP (SAP), customer relationship management (CRM), supply chain management (SCM), and data warehousing (DW). These applications in turn support the company's business processes that are carefully mapped to corporate goals and strategies. By placing information at the center of this environment, the company is well positioned to make sound business decisions based on timely information, adjust rapidly to changing business conditions, maintain tight control over manufacturing, order processing, and distribution functions, and maximize customer satisfaction. The following results have been achieved: significant improvement in company's performance, $510,000 annual savings in people costs, $1.4 million annual savings for disaster recovery contract, and others.

AGILE ENTERPRISE

The mass production of standardized goods was the source of America's economic strength for generations. But in today's turbulent business environment, mass production no longer works; in fact, it has become a major cause of the nation's declining competitiveness. The most innovative companies are rapidly embracing a new paradigm of management – mass customization – which allows them the freedom to create greater variety and individuality in their products and services at desirable prices.

New ways of managing, together with new technology, now enable savvy businesses to provide each customer with the attractive "tailor-made" benefits of the pre-industrial craft system at the low cost of modern mass production. Companies that have discovered and successfully implemented mass customization are swiftly outpacing their competitors in gaining new customers and achieving higher margins.

Among the firms that are leading their industries to this new frontier are McGraw-Hill, which can deliver custom-made classroom textbooks in quan-

Table 2-2: Evolution of the Factory

Factory Focus	Mass Production	Flexible Production	Mass Customization
Period	1900 - 1970	1971 - 2000	2001 - 2020
Typical Number of Machine-tools	150	50 – 30	25 – 20
Products Made	10 to 15	100 to 1000	Unlimited
Products Reworked Due to Poor Quality	25% or More	0.02% or Less	Under 0.0005%

Source: Business Week: Special 1994 Bonus Issue, p.158.

tities under 100 copies; Motorola, which can manufacture any one of 29 million variations of pagers within twenty minutes after receipt of the order.

The evolution of the factory is shown in Table 2-2.

Flexible production is characterized by the integration of Computer Aided Design (CAD) and Computer Aided Manufacturing (CAM) under the supervision of Management Information Systems (MIS) and within an environment of Office Automation (with e-mail). This type of integration is called Computer Integrated Manufacturing (CIM), and in a broader sense - Computer Integrated Operations. This programmable technology may deliver 100 to 1000 different products, or, still standardized ones for a given group of customers. The next step in the development of the factory is the creation of variety and customization through flexibility and quick responsiveness to individual customer needs.

Mass customization is emerging, and is caused by the following factors (Pine II, 1993):

- Demand for individual products has been unstable. What used to be a large demand for standard mass-market products has fragmented into demand for different "flavors" of similar products.

- Because demand has fragmented, the large, homogeneous markets have become increasingly heterogeneous. The niches are becoming the market, shifting power to buyers who demand higher-quality goods that more closely match their individual desires.

- Along with a shorter development cycle comes a shorter product life cycle. Driven by the need to more closely fulfill customer desires, products and technologies are constantly improved upon and replaced.

Advances in the speed, capacity, efficiency, effectiveness, and suitability of IT constantly lower the cost of increased mass and customization in service as well as in production. One can recognize the following ways of managing mass customization:

- The integration of CAD, CAM, MIS, and Office Automation systems into one Computer Integrated Operation, which is reprogrammable and reduces setup and changeover times, and lowers run size and the cost of customization.

- Just-in-time delivery and processing of materials and components that eliminate process flaws and reduce inventory carrying costs.

- Compressing cycle times throughout all processes in the value chain, which eliminates waste, decreases costs, and increases flexibility and responsiveness.

- Producing upon receipt of an order instead of a forecast, which lowers inventory costs, eliminates fire sales and write-offs, and provides the information necessary for individual customization.

The new competition on total process efficiency results in joint management/worker involvement in defining and improving the process: the integration of *thinking and doing*. This attitude leads to the elimination of waste in the process.

One example is the perception that work-in-progress (WIP) is no longer a buffer and hedge against uncertainties of the process and the market, but rather it is waste that adds costs and inefficiency. One measure of this is WIP turnover: the ratio of total sales to the value of the WIP inventory. In the late 1970's, when American automobile manufacturers were operating about 10 WIP turns a year, Japanese caretakers were between 50 and 200; by 1982 Toyota was turning over its WIP inventory more than 300 times due to the just-in-time system (Abegglen and Stalk, 1985). Abeggten and Stalk estimate an increase of 35% to 40% with every doubling of WIP turnover through the just-in time-system. This is certainly a positive factor.

> It is 2010, and you need a new suit – fast – for overseas business trip. No problem. You head to the department store at the mall. You step into a kiosk-like contraption, and an optical scanner automatically

measures your body. Seconds after you record your choice of style and fabric, the information is relayed to a plant, where lasers cut the cloth precisely to your size. A few days later, the suit is ready (*Business Week*, Special 1994 Bonus Issue, p. 158).

Not only clothes, but a huge variety of goods, from autos to computers, are manufactured to match each customer's taste, specifications, and budget. Mass customization marks the synthesis of the agile enterprise. Some of the production work that went offshore in the 1980's has been returning in the 1990's. One reason is that companies have discovered that moving products through an international pipeline eats up more time than the labor savings are worth. Items that have come back to agile factories range from some of Caterpillar Inc.'s huge earthmoving equipment, for a while made in Korea, to

Figure 2-4: A Model of Agile Enterprise

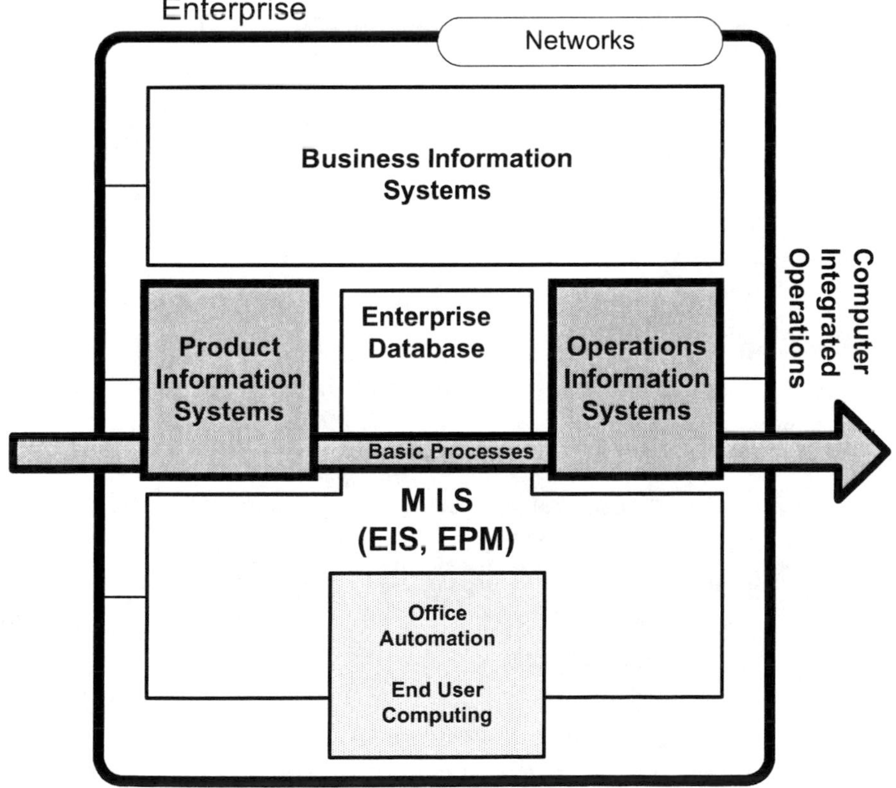

computer modems from U.S. Robotics Inc., which used to outsource the production of components to Mexico.

The agile enterprise might do more for U.S. employment than the post-industrial work that was supposed to supplant manufacturing. Nobody expects blue-collar jobs will grow. Agile factories will be smaller, with fewer but smarter machine tools that need only token human care – yet they will turn out a far richer variety of goods. So, shop-floor employment is heading the way of farm labor. However, agile technology is also spawning new white-collar jobs in support industries, just as modern agriculture has created a myriad of jobs in packaging design, food engineering, marketing, and other services (Port, 1994). A model of an agile enterprise is shown in Figure 2-4.

The number of U.S. workers employed in manufacturing in 1998 has fallen by 3.2 million since the peak of 21 million in 1979. Yet the manufacturing output has remained stable as a percentage of the gross national product. As these factory jobs vanish, a new manufacturing-driven economic sector is emerging – industries such as computer software, robot making, and countless services that add jobs to supply leaner manufacturing operations. These support industries, with their high component of knowledge skills, constitute nothing less than a second tier of the manufacturing industries. A smaller percentage of the workforce will be in production, but a much larger percentage will be supporting that. Systems analysts, computer programmers, and software engineers will increasingly be selling their wares around the globe.

INFORMATED ENTERPRISE

Once the installation of computer networks and the integration of enterprise systems has been completed, companies look for the added value that information systems can bring to management and business. So far the computerization of information processing has been based on automating information routines and integrating them into a cycle of "planning – control." This approach is called OLTP – On-line Transactions Processing, while the next step in computerization leads to OLAP – On-line Analytical Processing, containing such systems as EIS-Executive Information System, EPM-Enterprise Performance System and others.

As IT has automated blue and white-collar jobs, achieving unprecedented speed and consistency, it has also robbed workers of whatever skill and gratification they might retain, and has increased the impersonality and remoteness of management. The same technology, however, may "informate," empowering ordinary working people with overall knowledge of the production/service process, making them capable of critical and collaborative judgment about production/service and distribution/sales. As these new opportunities unfold, the function of management and the conventions of work organization are being transfigured. Ironically, Zuboff (1988) argues, if those in command choose to automate rather than "informate," many commercial advantages of the computerization will be lost.

An informated enterprise is such one where its information resource can generate a value added knowledge about its business/organizational processes for the purpose of optimizing decision making.

We know that the source of wealth is knowledge, a uniquely human attribute. If we apply knowledge to tasks we already know how to do, we call it *productivity*. If we apply knowledge to tasks that are new and different, we call it *innovation*. Only knowledge allows us to achieve these two goals. The next step in the enterprise evolution is the development of computer-driven knowledge management.

Knowledge is composed of scientific data, rules, laws, and behavioral patterns that are used to interpret a given concept (*increasing awareness of a decision-maker*) and choose (*applying his/her wisdom*) among actions to achieve established goals/objectives. Knowledge may be recorded in an individual's brain or stored in the enterprise's processes, products, systems, and documents. Such intellectual capital requires investments and recognition.

Knowledge management, the process of capturing a company's collective expertise, is big business; about $5 billion is paid annually to consulting firms. Knowledge management is appealing to companies ranging from Big Six consulting firms to Big Three automakers.

A variety of information systems can make up knowledge management systems (KMS):

- Decision Support Systems (DSS),
- Expert Systems (EXS),
- Data Warehouse, Data Mart, and Data Mining,
- Neural Networks,
- Artificial Intelligence,

- Groupware, and
- Other.

The architecture of an Informated Enterprise is shown in Figure 2-5.

The backbone of KMS is a data warehouse and data mining. A *data warehouse* is an extract of the most important data from a production database. The latter is usually closed for end-users, which could harm it either on purpose or unintentionally, due to a lack of skills. *Data mining* is a process which uses mathematical algorithms to find patterns in data, for example, about customers' behavior. Perhaps the first solution of KMS was the emergence of enterprise information portals in 1999, also called corporate portals, enterprise knowledge portals, and collaborative portals[4].

Figure 2-5: A Model of Informated Enterprise

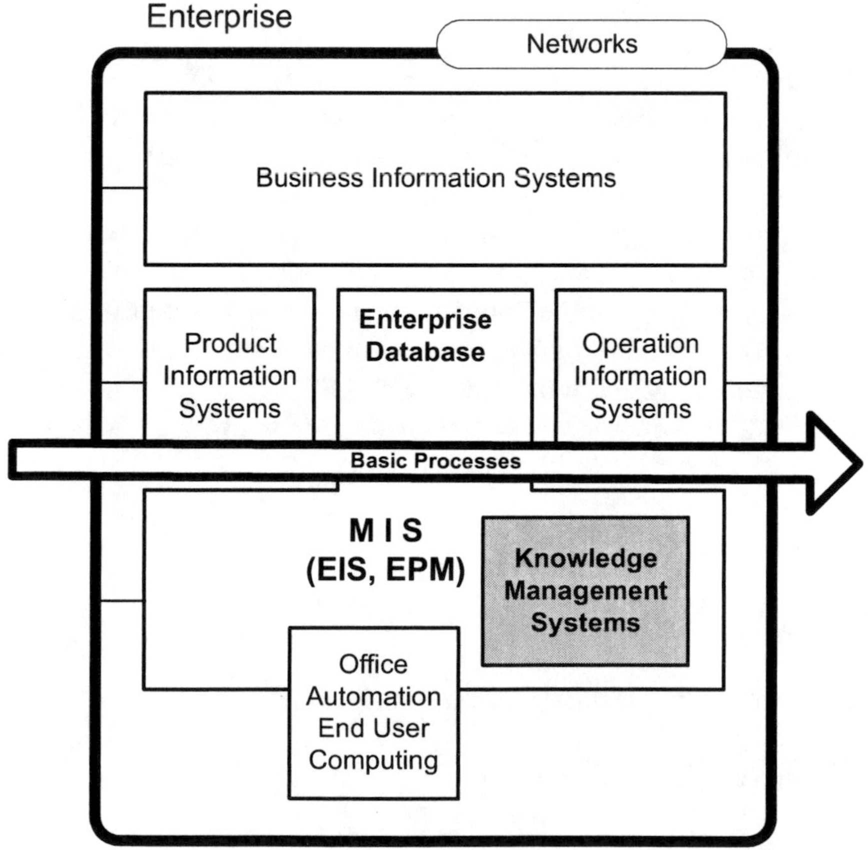

Knowledge management is the broad process of locating, organizing, categorizing, storing, retrieving, accessing, transferring, interpreting, and using expertise within an enterprise. Knowledge contains everything from creating a filtered newsfeed containing competitors' press releases, to assessing patent portfolios to identify licensing opportunities, to providing initial and continuing employee education.

Networked computing environments facilitate users' easy access to unstructured information in a narrative text form from different internal and external sources. Very often it contributes to information overload, the antithesis of knowledge management. The task of good knowledge management is to structure information under the form of scientific data, rules, laws and their systems as well as behavioral patterns of stakeholders.

> Consider the following scenario: Tim is the manager of a retail chain that specializes in upscale travel gear. When he reviews the monthly reports he sees that sales and profits for most of the franchises are down, for the third month in a row. Bad news, he thinks, we really have to do something. The question is, what? Reduce overhead, change the product line, increase the marketing and advertising effort, change the management team, or close some of the stores?
>
> This dilemma provides a simple illustration of the most common information problem, and the facts are not enough. Instead, the facts have to be seen within a context to give them meaning. In this case, the context includes information about other retailers in this market, information about individual products in the product line, details about the relative performance of the franchises to one another, changes in the productivity of the employees, and news that might affect business in general. Only within such a context do performance statistics become truly valuable as the basis for making an informed decision.
>
> By generating a variety of other performance reports, Tim can get answers to his questions about how various stores and products performed relative to one another. He notes that the stores in the Southwest are doing particularly poorly, but that the corporate ad campaign and promotional sales increased sales at all locations, including the underperforming stores. By displaying and sorting several news items to which he subscribes, he finds that the largest

> employer in that area recently announced major layoffs, which would help explain the substandard performance of those stores. By querying his company's database on competitive information, he finds that the competitors' nationwide results are even worse. And by checking his travel statistics, he sees that pleasure travel is at its lowest point in years. Given that context, the bad news suddenly starts to look good.
>
> However, he also sees that product Y, a new product in the product line, is not selling as well as projected by several market surveys. He sends an e-mail to his key sales people to ask them about their experiences with the product. The result surprises him, as most sales associates do not know how to properly position or sell the product. A search of available training courses shows that none of them cover how to get the most benefits from this type of product. He calls his training manager, Sandra, and they decide to address the problem with a one-hour course, filmed with a live trainer and delivered via Internet technology to the sales associates of each store. Sandra proceeds to search the company's Human Resources database for a course developer with experience in both the product area and in developing courses for distance learning.
>
> Tim's discussion with Sandra raises another issue: a large number of new employees are having problems with the end-of-day reconciliation procedures. After observing several employees at this task and talking with them about their difficulties with the procedure, Sandra decides that a job aid would solve the problem. This time she searches the Human Resources database for a technical writer, who reports that an existing procedure in the system documentation could be easily modified to show simple instructions right beside the actual work area on the screen (mySAP.com White Paper).

Here we concentrate our attention on IT's application in knowledge management (mySAP.com White Paper):

> Just as the Web as a way to communicate between businesses and their customers has grown explosively, the corporate Intranet has become the primary way to communicate with employees. In just a few years, over 90% of organizations now have some sort of

Intranet. These sites generally combine corporate information for all with specialized access for certain groups, and the ability to meet personal information needs. At SAP, for example, employees can see daily corporate news, video clips of speeches by executives, and corporate policies and benefits. They can order material via linked B2B transactions, search for people, apply for vacations, register for courses at the corporate university, find and contribute to project documents, or find someone who has a rare Beatles album.

The SAP Knowledge Warehouse provides a repository to manage site and navigation structures of internal or external websites, as well as the tools for creating and editing content and links. It is simple to use for knowledge consumers and occasional authors and provides complex possibilities for modeling and managing content for administrators. Its abilities to grant (or not to grant) role-based access to whole structures or single documents and to manage multiple versions and languages make the Knowledge Warehouse a powerful solution for managing international information of different degrees of sensitivity.

Every company needs to create and distribute information about itself. One audience of such information are an organization's employees, who need to stay informed on corporate strategy and who need to access corporate policies, instructions on how to do their work, and so on. Another audience are potential customers, who need to find out whether a product will meet their needs. Because this information needs to grab attention and convince, many companies go beyond printed materials to provide Web animations on their sites or multimedia presentations at trade shows or on CD-ROM.

The following uses for knowledge management provide an overview of the breadth of knowledge needs within an organization. Depending on your company's needs, one or all of these scenarios may be of interest:

- Creating a Web presence and an Intranet,
- Creating information products,

- Supporting collaboration,
- Creating corporate universities,
- Developing certification programs,
- Supporting SAP implementations and continued improvement,
- Supporting SAP end-user training and performance.

The idea that knowledge should be shared is obviously not new. The pursuit of any significant human activity, including business management, typically leads to the knowledge acquisition by those with better know-how skills. When the knowledge process can be captured, and communicated and shared with others, it can enable subsequent practitioners – or even generations – to build on earlier experience and obviate the need of costly rework or of learning by making the same repetitive mistakes. We do not need to continually re-invent the wheel.

Today, a range of technologies from computers to teleconferencing for distance learning offers unprecedented opportunities to disseminate know-how (knowledge) and insights rapidly and cheaply to a world-wide audience.

COMMUNICATED ENTERPRISE

The importance of communication in business is central to management success. In fact, the network of communication channels, methods, and skills are paramount, regardless of one's business major or type or size of business enterprise. Communication is critical to any business. It takes place among the enterprise's stakeholders (owners, customers, executives, managers, workers, and society).

The purpose of communication in a business enterprise is to establish a common experiential base, a system of significant, indexed concepts and relationships that enables mutual understanding which is required to accomplish business aims by stakeholders. Communication is an interactive process in which communicants exchange a message (content) that must be understandable in order to support meaningful performance.

A communicated enterprise applies a developed matrix of mediated channels, such as:

- Telephone,
- Fax,
- E-mail,
- Workgroup,
- Internet,
- Intranet,
- Extranet,
- E-commerce,
- E-meeting,
- Teleconferencing,
- Telecommuting,
- Other.

These channels (technologies) will be analyzed in more detail in Part II of this book. These channels' matrix facilitates the following communication methods:

- *Interpersonal Communication* – takes place among individuals who transfer personalized and psychological information to emphasize reciprocal feelings and bonds that determine a relationship.
- *Business Communication* – takes place under the form of business speaking, written business reports, letters, memos, and visual techniques.
- *Organizational Communication* – takes place in formal and informal structures in the context of communication networks, climate, culture, and targets: power, politics, and influence.

- *Professional Communication* – takes place among professionals from the same kind of profession; it applies a given profession's symbolic contents, context, culture, and channels.

- *Managerial Communication* – takes place among managers (peer communication techniques), between managers and subordinated workers (superior/subordinate techniques) in modes of command/control, negotiation/motivation, conflict management, information exchange, and issue management. It emphasizes feedback, motivation, and performance.

- *Cross-culture Communication* – takes place among communicants from different cultures that have different values, virtues, communication styles, and tradition. Usually this takes place at the international level, but is not limited to it.

It is necessary to notice that an informated enterprise uses some sort of basic communication technologies, however in a limited manner, while a communicated enterprise is based upon an intensive use of all sorts of communication media. When an enterprise is informated it is time to communicate its content-based messages around stakeholders. A vice-versa process may increase "empty" communication that very often takes place in practice.

The media-communicated enterprise is equipped in computer networks, integrated, and informated. Because the enterprise is also "communicating," it is relatively easier to communicate "knowledge" among enterprise stakeholders. So far knowledge has been generated in the informated enterprise, which has limited media to communicate. At the stage of the media-communicated enterprise (MCE) it is much easier to share knowledge among stakeholders. The development of MCE is necessary if knowledge generation and dissemination is a target.

The architecture of the communicated enterprise is shown in Figure 2-6. The inter-organizational communications trigger the development of inter-organizational IS such as Supply Chain Management (SCM), Customer Relations Management (CRM), and e-commerce.

The communicated enterprise is based on the *Internet* and its derivatives such as *the Intranet* and *Extranet*. Customers, as well as producers, escape the limits of geography. Until recently, if you needed a mortgage, you would stop at the local bank. Now, you can electronically travel to Bancrate.com and shop for the best mortgage rates from financial institutions across the country.

Figure 2-6: A Model of Media-Communicated Enterprise

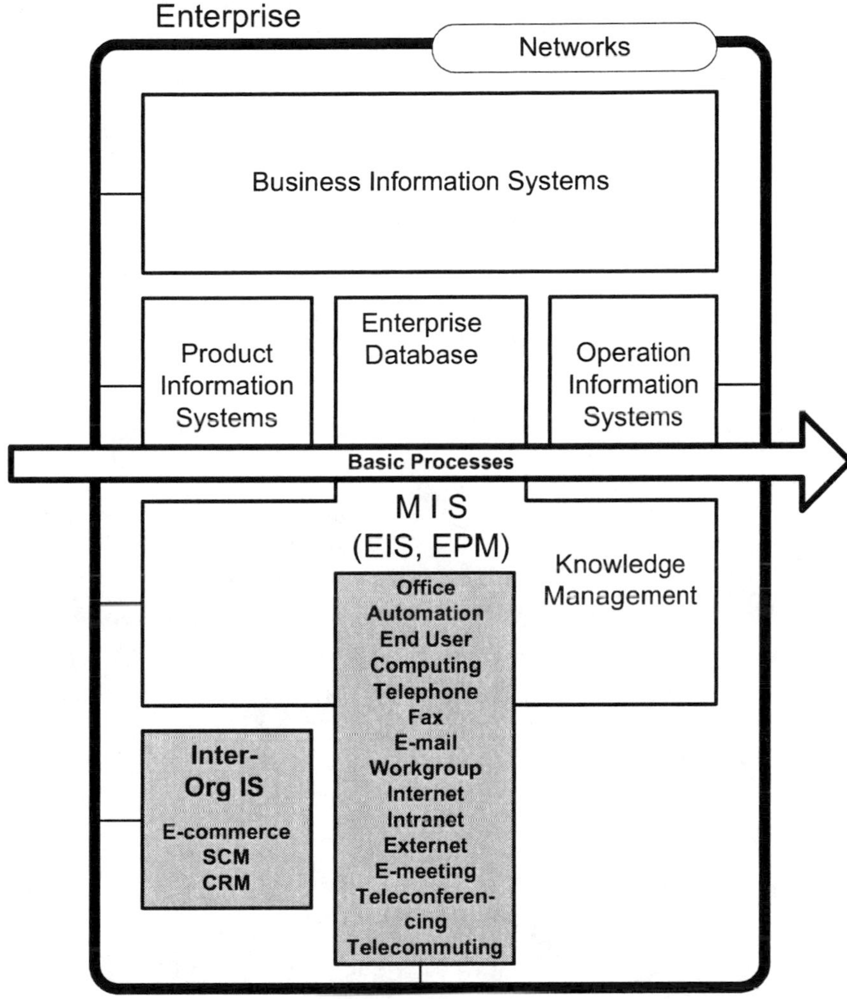

E-commerce breaks every business free of its geographic moorings. Amazon.com bookstore spans the globe, selling 20% of its books to foreign destinations. A physical bookstore serves an area of a few square miles, while e-Amazon sells in France and Nigeria and is a click away.

The death of a distance makes it difficult for producers to set different prices around the world. This is already a reality for software that is paid for and downloaded over the Internet. No longer is a customer willing to pay $200 in Warsaw for a piece of software that costs $100 in Detroit. On-line commerce is destroying these discrepencies. No company will be able to charge a premium when consumers know precisely what goods cost elsewhere.

New types of e-business communities (EBC: customers, producers, suppliers, distributors, and commerce providers) are evolving in the new economy (Tapscott, 1998, and the author):

- **Value Chain EBC**. One of them is Cisco Systems, which makes networking products, such as routers, that shuffle data from one computer to another over the Internet or corporate computer networks. About 64% of its $8.5 billion in annual sales are made on-line. Yet it does not actually manufacture anything. It sits at the top of the "food chain," marketing and managing customer relationships. All other functions are outsourced. Cisco is successful because it carefully and efficiently manages the flow of information from customer input (customers order directly through the Web site) to product development. In the process, it manages to achieve $585,000 in revenue per employee, about double that of more traditional competitors. And Cisco is always working with the best possible team of players. A network of distributors, manufacturers, and suppliers constantly compete with one another, which drives innovation. Information is shared among competitors, leading to a healthy combination of competition and collaboration. This level of coordination would be unthinkable without the Net.

- **Open Market EBC**. Priceline.com is a Web site that lets consumers bid for their plane tickets, and more recently cars and hotel rooms. Buyers submit a "guaranteed bid" for desired flights – the lowest price they think they can get away with. Priceline forwards the bid to participating sellers. The first airline to accept gets the sale. Priceline completes the transaction. As an open market EBC, Priceline creates a market on the Web for buyers and sellers. Not all of Priceline's partners have joined the system with enthusiasm, and some airlines have refused to participate. As a liquidation channel, Priceline threatens the industry's ability to offer seats at different prices for the same flight because it lowers the perceived value of full-fare tickets.

- **Aggregation EBC**. HomeAdvisor, Microsoft's answer to home buying, does not just offer hundreds of listings on its Web. It also has developed a variety of partnerships to provide real-time mortgage calculators, crime and school statistics, maps covering every U.S. metro area, live e-mail updates, and loan qualification service. What HomeAdvisor offers is a total home-buying solution – from searching to financing. This is called an aggregation EBC master, where one company positions itself as an intermediary between producers and consumers. Unlike the Priceline model where bids are directed to several sellers, an aggregator sells a branded set of products and services at stable prices. For now HomeAdvisor only brokers loans, but like Priceline, it has strategically positioned itself between buyers and sellers. In consumers' minds, it will not make sense to shop for a house through one group of people, and then shift industries to finance the purchase if they can do it all through the same channel. Priceline "mind share" is a major achievement. And home buyers might one day even negotiate their mortgages directly with the "Microsoft Bank."

- **Alliance EBC**. The most evaluated type of EBC is illustrated in the 3Com PalmPilot case. It is an example of an Alliance EBC – the most "virtual" and free-flowing type of EBC. PalmPilot is unique because most of its product development happens outside the company. But unlike Cisco, there is no one in charge. The EBC instead works more like a giant on-line jam session. Rather than guarding its programming secrets, 3Com makes its "code" available to one and all. The result? A huge community of users (most of them hackers) and partners are developing support software, parts, and accessories. PalmPilot benefits from an increase in the number of functions it performs, not to mention a growing community of users. Another example is Boeing, which becomes a design, networking, project management and marketing company, working with suppliers and customers in EBC to design aircraft in cyberspace.

- **Business-to-Consumers (B2C)**. An example is the electronic bookstore Amazon.com, which sells 3 million books and whose market value is greater than Barnes & Noble's bookstores.

- **Business-to-Business (B2B)**. An example is General Electric's practice of marketing and selling its industrial products through the Web to the EBC for its products.

- **Creators-to-Consumers (C2C)**. The singer known as Prince sold 100,000 CD's directly to fans on-line, by-passing all distribution channels.

Constant change has become a part of doing business. Today as geography has receded in significance, relationships have replaced products and services. The most important trait for winning in business will not be having the best products or services but having the best relationships (based on communications).

MOBILE ENTERPRISE

A mobile enterprise emerges along with the applications of mobile handheld devices such as personal digital assistants (PDA), handheld personal computers (HPC), computer panels, Web-enabled mobile phone handsets, and in-home consumer Internet access appliances. These devices take advantage of the General Packet Radio Service and Wireless Application Protocol (WAP). At the first glance, a mobile enterprise looks like a communicated enterprise. It is true, however, that the former requires a different *modus operandi* than the latter, as its operations require more complex business processes and management.

Wireless networks and satellite technology have developed to the extent that, in most places, one can connect to a LAN, WAN, and GAN. These networks are evolving to achieve the higher speeds, greater reliability, and easier access.

The applications of mobile devices differ among countries. In Japan and in most of the Asian countries mobile computers are used as desktop computers because of limited desk space. In Asia the young generation for years has been used to cellular phones, so it is natural for it to extend functionality of wireless phones in accessing enterprise systems or end-user computing.

In Europe and the U.S the populations have been familiar with using smart card in buying and paying almost for everything, so it is natural for them to expand capabilities of those cards under the form of expanded (digital) phones. In Finland, Nokia's country, there are more wireless phones than wired phones.

Those types of users are natural candidates for the users of a mobile enterprise. The power and features of mobile phones and handheld computers will overlap. Hybrid devices that add PDA functions to mobile telephones will be more successful than PDA's that add voice capability.

Among the most popular mobile applications are:

- E-mail,
- Personal Information Management,

Figure 2-7: A Model of a Mobile Enterprise

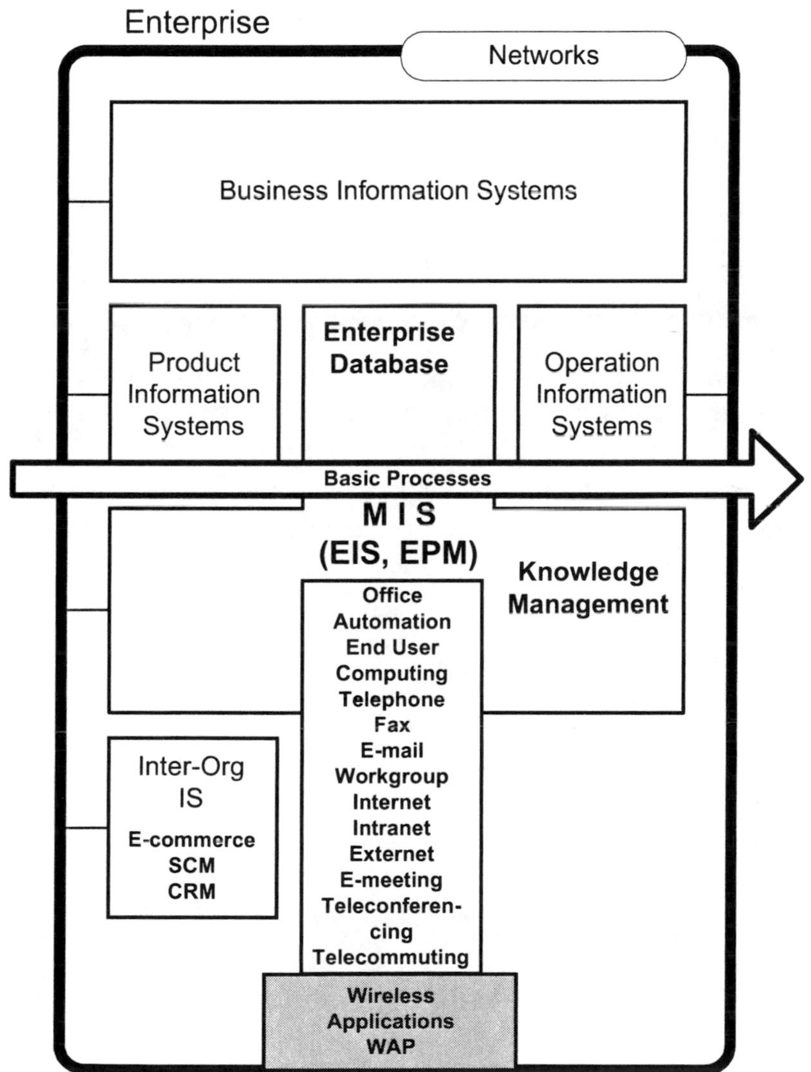

- Access to Workflow Systems,
- Accessing an Enterprise Information Portal,
- Accessing ERP and CRM systems for status and fulfillment,
- Field-based updating of enterprise systems, such as a stock control system, maintenance information system, sales information system, and others,
- Field-based communications with the enterprise dispatching system,
- Other.

A model of a mobile enterprise is presented in Figure 2-7.

ELECTRONIC ENTERPRISE

The combination of technology and work organization creates an e-enterprise. In its full implementation it can include the previous enterprise configurations: off-line, on-line (networked), integrated, agile, informated, communicated, and virtual. Of course such an enterprise is very difficult to develop and manage. For many enterprise stakeholders such a multi-dimensional enterprise can trigger culture shock. Many companies develop their work and technology unaware of the high degree of complexity they precipitate.

A model of an electronic enterprise is shown in Figure 2-8, where the mission-critical systems are driven by the following solutions:

- Strong application of Web technologies to integrate all enterprise systems, for example by using the XML standard for data compatibleness,
- Enterprise Information Portal (EIP) for external and internal stakeholders,
- Electronic Document Management System (e-DMS),
- Workflow System,

Figure 2-8: A Model of an Electronic Enterprise

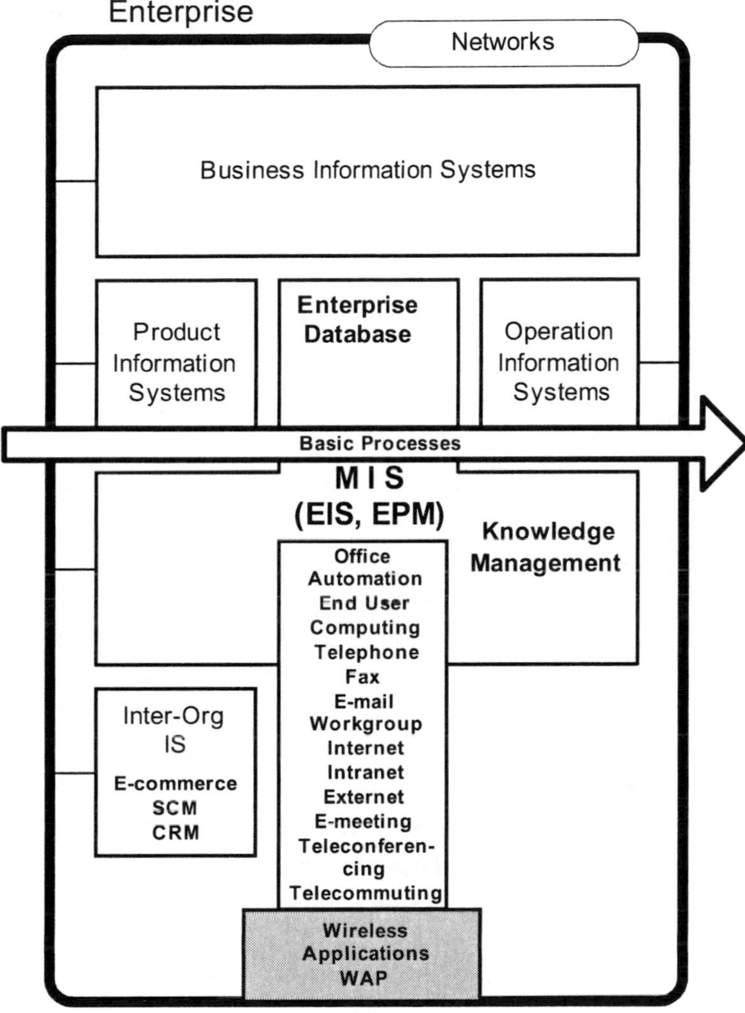

- E-Business (converting business information systems into Web-driven solutions).

The goal of the electronic enterprise is to implement all major applications to build the extended enterprise that functions as a paperless organization, whose units and workers process information and communicate via all layers of the Enterprise Information Infrastructure.

VIRTUAL ENTERPRISE

As mass customization becomes more popular, organizations are finding it increasingly difficult to perfect and maintain all of the competencies needed to provide customer specific product/services. In light of this trend, it is becoming progressively more practical to form strategic alliances with other business entities which offer competencies complementary to the enterprise's own. Due to shorter product/service life cycles, the duration of such strategic alliances, which tend to be product/service specific, are often ephemeral. These short-term strategic alliances are often referred to as virtual enterprises (Goldman, Nagel, and Preiss, 1995).

A virtual enterprise is formed dynamically, in response to customer demand, and is dissolved as soon as it becomes economically unviable. In order to appear seamless to the customer, the virtual enterprise depends to a great extent on information-communication technology (IT) (Goldman et al., 1995). In ideal cases, the virtual enterprise is fully connected through IT, and there is total sharing of information among all constituent organizations. It is possible, however, to achieve most of the advantages associated with the virtual enterprise without maintaining the total integration of systems.

Virtual enterprises are different from joint ventures and strategic alliances in their dynamism, since the former are more dynamic. They also differ in the fact that there is no obligation for the virtual enterprise to continue functioning as an entity after the current project is completed (Rampal, 1998).

The virtual enterprise does not refer to a single unit (company, firm, plant, and department) but to a network of independent business agents, whose business activities co-operate to achieve a common objective/task: research, development, production, marketing, sales, customer service. The virtual enterprise operates as a single entity towards the final customer/consumer who often is not aware of the complexity behind the product/service he/she is buying (Bielli, 1998). The architecture of a virtual enterprise is shown in Figure 2-9. The advantages of this enterprise system are:

- competitive position,
- reliance on non-transferable knowledge,
- innovations generation,
- expertise sharing,

Figure 2-9: A Model of a Virtual Enterprise (MIS–Management Information System, CSS–Communication Systems and Services)

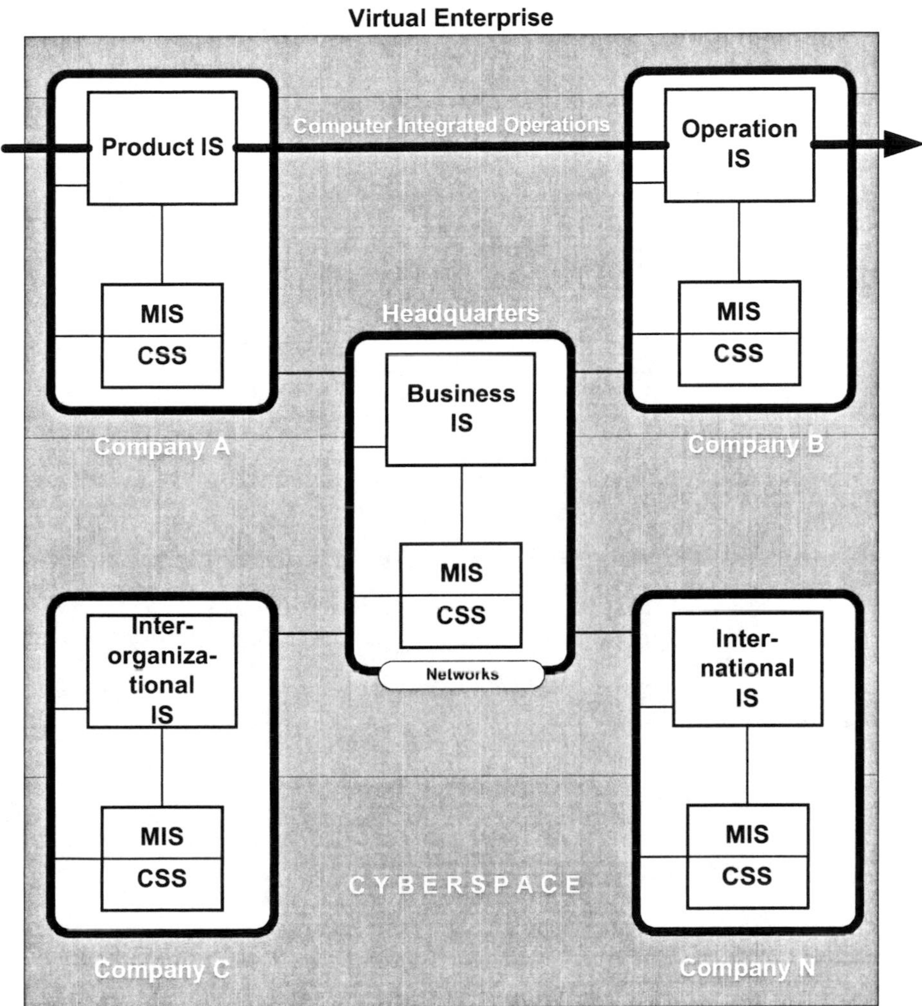

- operations flexibility,
- short timeliness,
- transaction cost reduction,

- financial gains from synergetic effects,
- other.

The overall characteristics of a virtual enterprise have the following attributes:

1. Confrontation of a very competitive market,
2. Business network membership of several independent business units (companies, firms, plants, departments),
3. Common objective/task of the members,
4. Strong trust among the members,
5. Each unit-member contributes its own specialization and expertise,
6. Co-operation based on inter-organizational processes,
7. Common life as long as it is necessary to achieve a common objective,
8. Ad-hoc of specialists and business people (virtual teams),
9. Single enterprise image from the customer view point,
10. Support of and collaboration based on IT.

The virtual enterprise is considered as an ideal model which is being applied within the emerging new economy in developed countries. The virtual enterprise breaks down the linear sequence of a value chain and substitutes almost a parallel one for it. It means a shorter delivery time of products and services. There are many ways to implement a virtual enterprise, as it is practice in The United States, Japan, and Western Europe. One example of a virtual enterprise is presented here.

> Diesel is an Italian company of the sportswear industry, producing jeans and garments (with several collections every year) with a strong image and high quality/price ratio. Explicit results demon-

strate Diesel's success: from 1.5 to 400 million dollar in 22 years, yearly growth rate (turnover) of about 15%, 12 subsidiaries around the world.

Peculiar is the production process at Diesel: only a few activities are kept within the company, those with the highest added-value for the final customer (R&D, communication, quality control, order collection). Everything else is subcontracted to small producers who are strongly specialized. This picture is common to the majority of fashion and garment producers in Italy, which count on powerful textile districts. However, two issues need clarification, as they differentiate Diesel and compare to a virtual enterprise: flexibility in selecting the subcontractors and the use of IT.

Even if Diesel has been operating in the same location since its foundation, it does not rely on stable relations with a single group of sub-contractors. Depending on the tendencies in their seasonal collections (in terms of fabric, sewing technologies, and accessories), Diesel involves a certain group of subcontractors and leaves others free, depending on the task at a given time.

The relationships among units are not purely of a subcontracting nature, as Diesel cooperates with them in order to find the best solution (from technical and economical points of view) for producing a specific article or for obtaining a specific effect (e.g., in dyeing or ironing fabrics). Flexibility for Diesel implies the ability of responding to market needs (fades and trends in fashion) with the most suitable collection, without being linked to existing expertise and materials. If a fabric is available in the Far-East, they want to be able to purchase it there without any geographical constraints. The second peculiarity at Diesel is the use of IT: while operating in an industry mainly based on human creativity and taste, Diesel applies IT whenever is possible and appropriate. The following IT systems are applied:

- CAD systems for engineering of collection,
- Databases of models and accessories are available for all designers,

- Groupware applications to communicate among participants,
- Common information systems operate in all units,
- Electronic layouts are transferred to all shops.

The ability to balance IT and trust-based relations is one of the most important goals of Diesel (Bielli, 1998).

In a virtual enterprise in which processes are partially internal and partially outsourced, subcontractors are treated as partners who are involved in a common process of accomplishing the task. Since new products/services require high levels of innovation, the search for that type of expertise is stretched from the local to global partners. The global reach of a virtual enterprise depends on the elaboration of trust and IT application among partners.

FUTURE TRENDS - *THE 21ST CENTURY CORPORATION*

At the beginning of the 21st century, the Industrial Economy is giving way to the New Economy and corporations are at another crossroads. Attributes that made them ideal for the 20th century could cripple them in the 21st century. The Darwinian struggle of daily business will be won by the people and the organizations that adapt to the new world that is unfolding.

The Real Assets: Ideas. The turn of the millennium is a turn from hamburgers to software. Software is an idea; hamburger is a cow. There will be hamburger makers in the 21st century, of course, but the power, prestige, and money will flow to the companies with indispensable intellectual property. You can see it already. At the end of the year 1999, Microsoft Corp., with just 31,000 employees, had a market capitalization of $600 billion. McDonald's Corp., with 10 times as many employees, had one tenth of the market cap.

Or take Yahoo! Inc. – a virtual place in a virtual medium, the Internet. Although far below its peak price, Yahoo in 2000 trades at more than 40 times book value. If USX Corp.'s U.S. Steel Group traded at the same multiple to book as Yahoo, its market capitalization would be nearly $90 billion, instead of less than $2 billion.

In an economy based on ideas rather than on physical capital, the potential for breakaway success like Yahoo is far greater. That is because ideas, like germs, are infectious. They spread to a huge population seemingly overnight. And once the idea – say, a computer program – has been developed, the cost of making copies is close to zero and the potential profits enormous.

With the possibility of gargantuan returns, it's no wonder that idea-based corporations have easy access to capital. In 1999 U.S. companies received nearly $50 billion in venture capital, which is 25 times as much as in 1990. The amount of money raised in U.S. initial public offerings in 1999, nearly $70 billion, was 15 times the amount in 1990.

In the New Economy, based on the creation of ideas, the most important intellectual property isn't software or music or movies. It's the stuff inside employees' heads. When assets were physical things like coal mines, shareholders truly owned them. But when the vital assets are p e o p l e there can be no true ownership. The best that corporations can do is to create an environment that makes the best people want to stay.

There will be the Industrial Economy jobs in the 21st century, but high-tech employment will grow much faster as it is reflected in Table 2-3.

The most valuable companies today have fewer employees than those of a decade ago. And they are less capital-intensive. In the same way that the economy is losing weight – software instead of steel – corporations are getting lighter, too.

Management by We. The Net gives everyone in the organization, from the lowest clerk to the chairman of the board, the ability to access a mind-boggling array of information – instantaneously, from anywhere. Instead of seeping out over months or years, ideas can be zapped around the globe in the blink of the eye. That rapid flow of information will permeate the organization. Orders will be fulfilled electronically without a single phone call or piece of paper. The "virtual financial close" will put real-time sales and profit figures at every

Table 2-3: Jobs of The Future 1999-2008

TOP FIVE IN TOTAL JOBS ADDED			TOP FIVE IN PERCENTAGE GROWTH		
	JOBS ADDED	PERCENTAGE GROWTH		JOBS ADDED	PERCENTAGE GROWTH
System analyst	577,000	94%	Computer engineer	323,000	108%
Retail salesperson	563,000	14	Computer support specialist	439,000	102
Cashier	551,000	17	System analyst	577,000	94
General manager	551,000	16	Database administrator	67,000	77
Overall	20,300,000	14	Overall	20,300,000	14

Source: Business Week, August 28, 2000, p. 80.

manager's fingertips via the click of a wireless phone or a spoken command to a computer. The organizational chart of a large-scale enterprise had long been defined as a pyramid of ever-shrinking layers leading to an omnipotent CEO at its apex. The 21st corporation, in contrast, is far more likely to look like a web: a flat, intricately woven form that links partners, employees, external contractors, suppliers, and customers in various collaborations. The players will grow more and more interdependent. Fewer companies will try to master all the disciplines necessary to produce and market their goods but will instead outsource skills – from research and development to manufacturing – to outsiders who can perform those with greater efficiency. Cisco Systems has taken the concept to an extreme. It owns only two of the 34 plants that produce its products. Roughly 90% of the orders come into the company without ever being touched by human hands, and 52% of them are fulfilled without a Cisco employee being involved.

Managing the intricate network of partners, spin-off enterprises, contractors, and freelancers will be as important as managing internal operations. Indeed, it will be hard to tell the difference. All these constituents will be directly linked in ways that will make it nearly impossible for outsiders to know where an individual firm begins and where it ends.

It's Mass Customization. The previous 100 years were marked by mass production and mass consumption. Companies sought economies of scale to build large factories that produced cookie-cutter products, which they sold to the largest numbers of people in as many markets as possible. The company of the future will tailor its products to each individual by turning customers into partners and giving them the technology to design and demand exactly what they want. Mass customization will result in waves of individualized products and services, as well as huge savings for companies, which will no longer have to guess what and how customers want.

It's global. In the beginning, the global company was defined as one that simply sold goods in overseas markets. Later, global companies put manufacturing facilities in numerous countries with cheap labor. The company of the future will call on talent and resources – especially intellectual capital – wherever they can be found around the globe. Indeed, the very notion of a headquarters country may no longer apply as companies migrate to places of greatest advantage. The new global corporation might be based in the U.S. but do its software in Sri Lanka, its engineering in Germany, and its manufacturing in China. Every outpost will be seamlessly connected by the Net so that employees and freelancers can work together in real time.

It's about speed. The computer-driven speed of action, the speed of deliberations, and the speed of information flows is faster and faster. That means that old, function-oriented corporations must radically revamp. With everything from product cycles to employee turnover on fast-forward, there is simply not enough time for contemplation and bureaucracy.

It's the end of job. In the later half of the 20th century, power flowed to corporations, where bodies were as replaceable as light bulbs. Today, with the transition to a knowledge-based economy and global connectivity, the power is shifting to those with skills. To cater to the shift of an expanding and contracting labor force, workers will be auctioning their services, becoming the just-in-time employees. Bucking the trend are companies that offer careers – but as a series of projects, not as a static job. But increasingly, companies will keep their most prized employees on site and outsource everything else. Experts predict that workers will have as many as 20 different positions in their lifetimes. Think of yourself as a volleyball player in a floating boat. Among them, those who will handle ambiguity will be leaders.

The corporate ecosystem of the 21st century will be characterized by a blurring of once distinct boundaries: between public and private, foreign and domestic, insider and outsider, friend and foe. The effect will be liberating in many ways. Corporations will be freer to pursue opportunities wherever in the world they find it, and exploit it according to the requirements of circumstance, not blind dictates of tradition. Outsourcing will become ever more prevalent, transforming many corporations into super-efficient, virtual facsimiles of their old selves.

The growing fluidity of vital business relationships will require constant vigilance and improvisation by all concerned. Like it or not, corporations also will assume a larger role in education and other public-sector preserves, taking over tasks that government either is unwilling or unable to do it itself.

Toward the Global Rules

The Internet and the rise of globalization are creating new pressure to develop a commercial code that is recognized from Hong Kong to Chicago. Think for a moment about a world that now faces New Economy giants such as America Online Inc., Amazon.dot, and Yahoo! Inc. As they sell products and services to an increasingly global marketplace, these companies face a patchwork of conflicting local regulations. Europe's privacy rules are much tougher than those in the U.S. A digital signature that seals a deal in Albany may be invalid in Kuala Lumpur. Thousands of different sales taxes are levied around the world.

Regulating the global economy will require international cooperation. Here is how commercial law will evolve in key areas:

- *Taxes*. Internationally, tariffs will largely disappear. Multinational agreements will assure that companies pay the tax they owe, but protect them from being double-taxed.

- *Finance*. Worldwide accounting standards will increasingly develop. Efforts are already underway to create global capital rules for banks.

- *Privacy*. Business and government will form partnerships to create minimum privacy standards for commercial transactions.

- *Antitrust*. Governments will sign multilateral agreements spelling out acceptable business practices. The new global standard will be aimed at increasing competition.

How long will this take? Many decades – if history is any guide. But make no mistake: as business seeks simplification and predictability, the rules of the 21st century will be developed faster, because the *speed* is a paradigm of a New Economy.

CONCLUSION

The IT-driven enterprise evolution leads towards more complex organizations that require sophisticated operational and management knowledge and skills. Employees of such enterprises must know IT quite well; otherwise they will not be able to work in them.

The virtual enterprise is perhaps not the last phase in the enterprise evolution, although even nowadays it is not the optimal solution for many firms. In general, the IT-driven enterprise rationalizes the scope of employment at the times when the population growth is global. This contradiction is the challenge for the politicians and business executives who must solve "unsolvable" problems.

BIBLIOGRAPHY

Abegglen, J.C. & Stalk, G. (1985). *Kaisha, the Japanese Corporation*, New York: Basic Books, pp. 112-115.

Alstyn, M. van. (1997). The state of network organization: A survey in three frameworks. *Journal of Organizational Computing and Electronic Commerce*, 7(2/3), pp. 83-151.

Bielli, P. (1998). Virtual enterprises and information technology: An ambiguous relationship, *Proceedings of 1998 Information Recourse Management Association.* Boston, May 17-20.

Bradley, S.P. & Nolan, R.L. (1998). *Sense & Respond: Capturing Value in the Network Era.*, Cambridge, MA: HBS Press.

Byrne, J.A. (1993). The horizontal corporation. *Business Week*, December 20, pp. 76-81.

Chorofas, D.N. (2001). *Enterprise Architecture and New Generation Information Systems.* Boca Raton, FL: Saint Lucie Press.

Cook, M. A. (1996). *Building Enterprise Information Architecture: Reengineering Information Systems*. Upper Saddle River, NJ: Prentice Hall.

Cummis, F.A. (2002). *Enterprise Integration.* New York: John Wiley & Sons.

Goodyear, M. (ed). (1999). *Enterprise System Architectures: Building Client Server and Web Based Systems.* Boca Raton, FL: CRC Press.

Haeckel, S. & Slyvotzky, A.J. (1999). *Adaptive Enterprise: Creating and Leading Sense-And-Respond Organizations*. Cambridge, MA: HBS Press.

Pickard, J. (1998). Fountain of knowledge, *People Management*, 4(2), p. 37.

Pine, J.B., II. (1993). *Mass Customization, The New Frontier in Business Competition.* Boston: Harvard Business School Press.

Rampal, R. (1998). Communication Technologies in Virtual Enterprise: A Case Study. *Proceedings of 1998 Information Recourse Management Association*, Boston, May 17-20.

Roberts, B. & Scribar, V. (2002). *The Adaptive Enterprise: IT Infrastructure Strategies to Manage Change and Enable Growth.* Boston: Addison-Wesley Professional.

Ruh, W.A. et al. (2000). *Enterprise Application Integration*: A Wiley Tech Brief. New York: John Wiley & Sons.

Spewak, S.H. & Hill, S.C. (1993). *Enterprise Architecture Planning: Developing a Blueprint for Data, Applications and Technology*. New York: John Wiley & Sons.

Twenty-first (21st) Century Manufacturing Enterprise Strategy. (1991). Bethlehem, PA: Leigh University Press.

Zuboff, S. (1998). *In The Age of The Smart Machine.* New York: Basic Books.

ENDNOTES

1 Synonyms for a global corporation are transnational corporation (TNC) and a stateless corporation.

2 A virtual enterprise emerged historically before an electronic enterprise, however, the former performs better if it is electronic.

3 In the early stage of the On-Line Enterprise development (the 1960's and 1970's) "on-line" meant just having remote terminals connected on-line to a mainframe; later, with the advent of LAN's and WAN's (1980's and 1990's) the "on-line" solution evolved into one that is described in this section.

4 The KMS will be described in depth in Chapter 4.

Part II

Enterprise Information Infrastructure

Chapter III

Enterprise Information Infrastructure (EII)

STRATEGY AND RATIONALE

The American business in the Information Wave in the 21st century increasingly relies on computer and information networks for the conduct of vital operations. The computerized telecommunications networks, customer interfaces, services, applications, and related technologies create the Enterprise Information Infrastructure (EII). The industry which supports the development of EII and other information infrastructures (NII – National Information Infrastructure, GII – Global Information Infrastructure, and Local Information Infrastructure) is valued domestically at about $1 trillion in 2000. Not surprisingly, with this kind of money at stake, the emerging technologies that will define information infrastructures in the future have become the subject of much discussion and many grand schemes.

But suppliers are not the only ones anticipating benefits from the new information infrastructure. Business users also hope to increase their productivity and quality of life through the application of technologies and services in a wide variety of contexts. But despite all the great expectations of industry insiders and technology users, the general business practitioners remain largely unaware of exactly what is taking place because the majority of these services are invisible to the naked eye.

The EII includes more than just the physical facilities used to transmit, store, process, and display voice, data, images, and video. It encompasses:

- A wide and ever-expanding range of equipment including cameras, scanners, keyboards, telephones, fax machines, computers, telecom switches, compact disks, video and audio tape, cable wire, satellites, optical transmission lines, microwave nets, switches, televisions, monitors, printers, and much more,

- The information itself, which may be in the form of print-outs, scientific or business databases, images, sound recordings, library archives, video programming, and other media,

- Applications and software that allow users to access, manipulate, organize, process, and digest the proliferating mass of information that EII's facilities will put at the users' fingertips,

- The network standards and transmission codes that facilitate interconnection and inter-operation between networks, and ensure the privacy of persons and the security of the information carried, as well as the security and reliability of the networks,

- The people—largely business professionals—who create the information, develop applications and services, construct the facilities, and train others to tap its potential.

Hence, the EII is an array of computerized networks, online devices, intelligent appliances, applications, standards, and services that people use to interact with digital information. One feature that distinguishes the EII from the previous computing environment is an unprecedented degree of distributed user empowerment. Never before in the history of communication has anyone possessing relatively an inexpensive, networked personal computer had such access to and control over information.

The goal of EII is to support the urban, agricultural, industrial infrastructures in order:

1. To empower an enterprise in better positioning itself in the marketplace through the optimization of using resources from other infrastructures (urban, agricultural, industrial, etc.),

2. To empower an enterprise's workers and executives in broadening their cognition about operated/managed processes and resources.

The strategy of EII should lead towards the gradual development of a comprehensive, compatible, reliable, secure, and safe complex of digital resource processes and services according to the master plan. Such EII should fit into an array of other EII's (e.g., in a Supply Chain Management System), NII, GII, and LII's.

This chapter covers the main concepts and components of the Enterprise Information Infrastructure (EII) whose mission is to exchange a message in a service manner. It is very difficult to separate the communication process from the information process in computer and software environments, computer-telecommunication networks, and the Internet. Hence, one can call these processes info-communication processes and systems.

EII GENERAL ARCHITECTURE

In the 2000's, funds spent on information management are at the level of 15% of the Gross Domestic Product, which means that these funds exceed $1 trillion. The cost of information management in the United States is comparable to the cost of health care, which is the number one industry in this country. Such an amount of funds requires tremendous developmental and operational stages and phases at the strategic, tactical, and operation levels. Similar to civil engineering projects, information management projects require planning of general solutions and designing of detail outcomes.

The difference between the architectural approach and the engineering approach is in the level of abstraction. The architectural solutions are more conceptual whereas engineering outcomes are more technical. The architectural approach is the response to the complexity of expected outcomes. Prior to spending a few million dollars for a new information system, one must provide its information architecture and the business and social implications associated with it.

The enterprise information architecture should be at the level of synthesis as a result of empirical experience and theoretical knowledge. An architect is more an artist than an engineer; he/she must know more principles governing the planning process and have strong intuitive instinct about what principles (rules) should be chosen for a given architectural project.

The system architect begins his/her work when the user's business strategy and preliminary budget have been determined. Thus, system architecture planning begins with the task of harmonizing business/corporate strategies with information technology (IT) potential and user needs. Good system architecture should be driven by the following principles which determine what is possible and what is effective in a given information architecture:

1. Cybernetization - good system architecture should be "viable" and open-ended

2. Systematization - good system architecture should have a goal, structure, and measurable outcomes

3. No redundancy - good system architecture should avoid component redundancy

4. Categorization - good system architecture should recognize self-contained components at the same levels of abstraction

5. Primitiveness - good system architecture should be based on generic components and relationships.

6. Completeness - good system architecture should recognize all major components and their relationships

7. Value engineering - good system architecture should not contain unnecessary components

The information management discipline is very young; it is at most 50 years old. However, its professional development has been very strong, especially in the last two decades of the 20th century. Since the beginning, IS have been developed as islands of automation that have been a consequence of an autonomous and eclectic (non-architectural) approach. In the 1980's personal computers triggered the creeping, quiet revolution known as the Computer Age. In the 1990's, the Internet launched the Communication Age and the phenomena of telecommunication networking and video services. We no longer deal with IS only; we now have to include into an information architecture other forms of information-communication systems and services.

These new systems and services require a new approach towards IT applications in the enterprise. A set of these systems and services is what I call the Enterprise Information Infrastructure (EII). This is the second civilization infrastructure, which follows the already developed urban infrastructure.

Figure 3-1 depicts the architecture of EII. The EII is composed of the following levels:

1. Telecommunications Layer – physical information transmission over public telecommunications lines and facilities,

2. Computer Networks Layer – managed online information transmission among associated computers,

3. Internet Layer – public cyberspace for information exchange,

4. Computing Layer – physical processing of information,

5. Communication Layer – facilities and systems of providing online information,

6. Application Layer – final result of info-communication handlings and processings applied by the end-users.

The EII architecture should lead towards the definition of:

- System strategy and its integration with a business strategy,
- Prioritized systems and services application projects,
- Data modeling,
- Software needs,
- Computer needs,
- Network needs,
- Staff needs,
- Budget,
- Implementation schedule,

Figure 3-1: The EII Generic Model (U2A–User-To-Application, A2A–Application-To-Application, B2B–Business-To-Business, B2C–Business-To-Consumer, C2C–Consumer-To-Consumer)

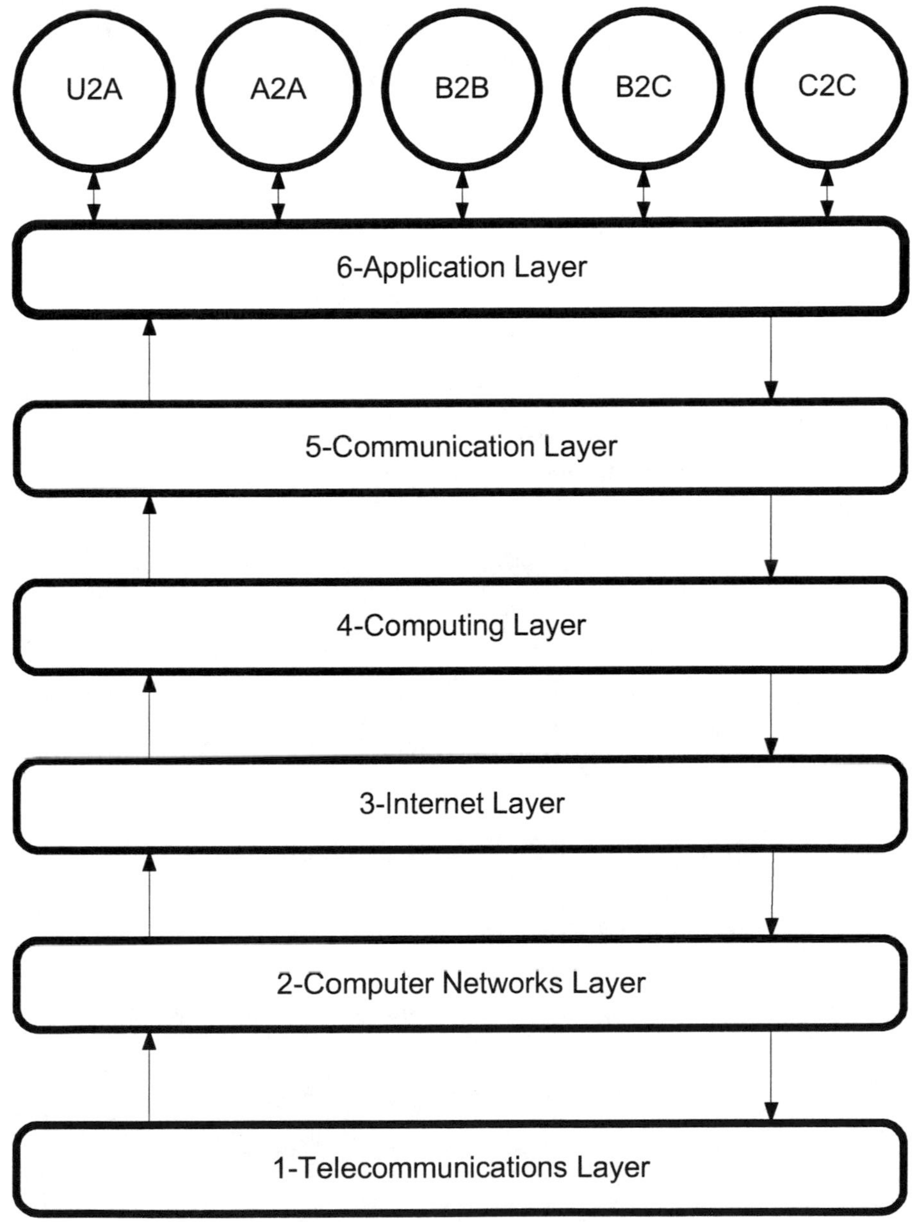

- Training plan,
- Other.

The EII layers will be described in the following sections and chapters (Application Layer). The set of these layers creates an interconnected matrix or even a labyrinth of technology, where it is very difficult to separate one technology from another.

TELECOMMUNICATIONS LAYER

The Telecommunications Layer emerged from the telegraph (1837), and evolved to the telephone (1876), satellite (1945), wireless (1958), cable (1960), and "the information super-highway" (1990's) which transmits voice, data, graphics, and video in one packet.

The universal access to telecommunications services and its integration with computer services and network services transforms these technologies into the information utility technology, which can be characterized by the following attributes:

1. Central online real-time facility,
2. Many subscribers at remote locations,
3. Information storage, retrieval, processing provided,
4. Services provided at the subscriber's own location,
5. Service is fast, immediate, easy to understand, and reliable,
6. Service is relatively inexpensive, based on the unit costs,
7. Other.

Telecommunications provides the means to transmit messages over distances through the following levels:

1. Access and transmission technologies, such as:
   - Telephony (intra-LATA-local services, IXC-interexchange carriers-long distance, and specialized common carriers (SCC), such as Telenet and Tymnet,
   - Cable television,
   - Nonwireline media – microwave radio, digital radio, satellite communications, cellular communications.

2. Switching technologies which are provided in two categories:
   - Circuit switching, when the customer pays per used time of transmission,
   - Packet switching, when the customer pays per volume of sent messages. These messages are organized into "packets" or "cell relays" or "frame relays." The second technology leads to so-called broad band transmission (B-ISDN) and the third technology supports narrow band transmission (N-ISDN).

3. Telco switching networks that make connections among 170 million subscribers in the U.S. via:
   - Integrated Digital Networks – they integrate voice, data, graphics, and voice into one binary stream transmitted through a digital path connecting switching equipment and transmission lines. AT&T provides such a service, called ISDN (Information Services Digital networks), which is controlled by a programmable software.
   - Intelligent Networks – consist of integrated hardware and software, distributed throughout the telecommunications service provider's network. Vendors can easily develop telecommunications services that deliver certain communications service under the form of software-oriented "building blocks," e.g., a "900" number which charges those who call them.
   - Advanced Intelligent Networks – are the intelligent networks whose services can be designed by CAD-Computer Aided Design software. This ability dramatically reduces the time between conception of a service and its implementation.

It is important to notice that these telecom networks are invisible networks for user computer networks such as LAN, MAN, WAN, and GAN that are described in the next section. The latter networks are built upon the telecom networks. However, LAN is the only network which is out of the telecom facilities since it is developed inside a company's building. Although there are some examples of outsource LAN's, they have to operate through the telecom facilities.

COMPUTER NETWORKS LAYER

This layer interconnects computers and applies the Telecommunications Layer for information's physical transmission. If telecommunications services are invisible for end-users, this layer is visible for them.

LAN

Local Area Networks (LAN) allow a great number and variety of user computers and devices such as printers to exchange large amounts of information at high speed over limited distances. LAN interconnects users within an area of 16 miles. LAN is a private network. Design elements for LAN fall into three main categories (Digital, 1982):

- Topology
- Access and control methods

A network topology is created by the geometric arrangements of the link and nodes that make up a network. A link (also called a line, channel or circuit) is the communications paths between two nodes. A node can be defined as an end point to any branch of a network. The hardware and software chosen for each node is determined by the functions of that node in the network.

Most LAN's are based on simple structure topologies, like the bus, star or ring. These topologies are shown in Figure 3-2.

Bus topology is organized as an open ring. Messages placed on the bus are broadcast out to all nodes. Nodes must be able to recognize their own address in order to receive transmissions. However, unlike nodes in a ring, they do not have to repeat and forward messages intended for other nodes. As a result, there is neither the delay nor the overhead associated with retransmitting messages at each intervening node, and nodes are relieved of network control responsibility at this level. The bus topology is now the most popular solution. Its commercial name is Ethernet, which has a branching-bus topology, with a

Figure 3-2: LAN Topologies

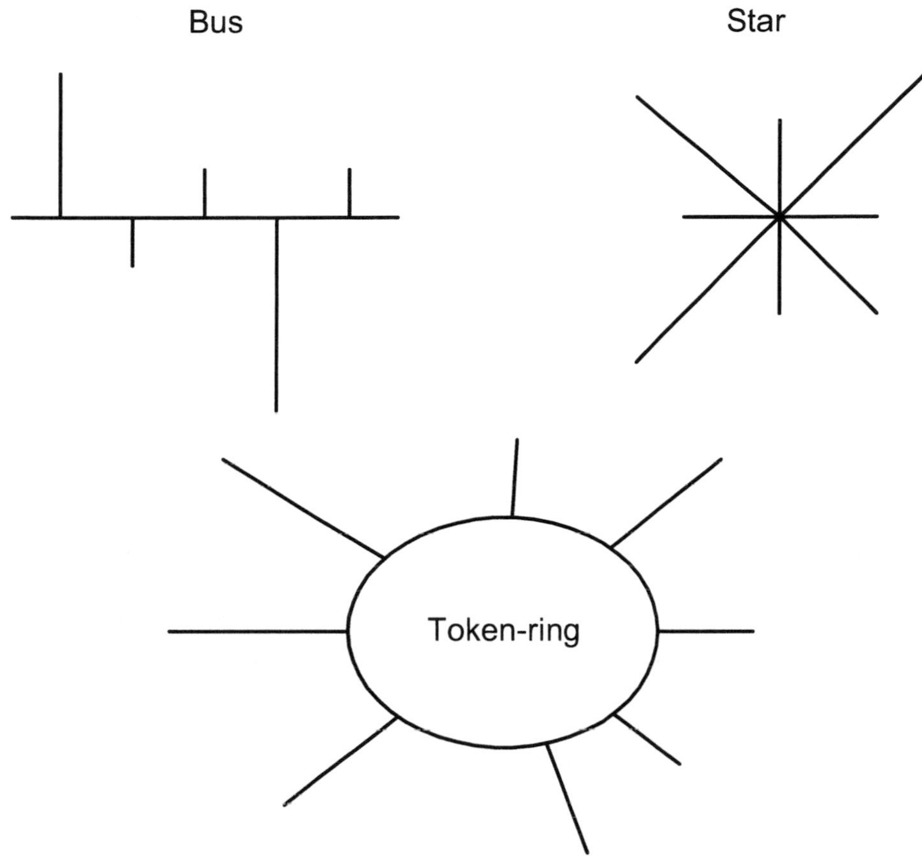

maximum distance of 1.6 miles between the two furthest nodes. Up to 1,024 nodes can be tapped onto the Ethernet coaxial cable, allowing a connection of thousands of devices.

Star topology is frequently used for networks in which control of the network is located in the central node or switch. When this is the case, all routing of network messages traffic – from the central node to outlying nodes, between outlining nodes and from nodes to remote points – is performed by the central node. This has the effect of relieving outlining nodes of the control function. In all star networks the central control is a single point of network failure. If it goes down, so does the entire network. The star topology is often seen in academic timesharing systems, with the central node serving as the timesharing host. It is also quite common in PBX telephone networks, adapted as LAN.

Ring topology has nodes connected in an unbroken circular manner. Transmitted messages travel from node-to-node around the ring. Each node must be able to recognize its own address in order to accept a message. In addition, each node serves as an active repeater, retransmitting messages addressed to other nodes. To transmit a message, a node has to receive a token from the network server. Then, the node with a token gains exclusive access to the channel.

Figure 3-3: LAN Components

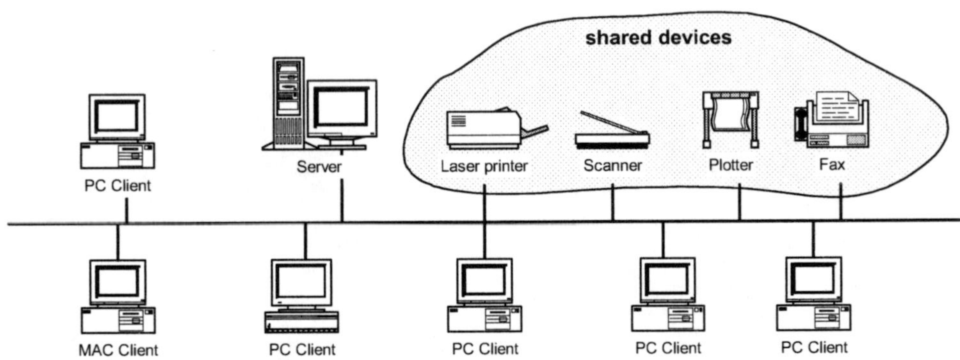

LAN is a popular solution of the client/server computer configuration, where the following devices are interconnected: servers, clients, and share printers, OCR readers, scanners, and high-resolution monitors (Figure 3-3). It is also an infrastructure for the Intranet.

MAN

A Metropolitan Area Network (MAN) is usually a public network which interconnects LAN's, hosts, and clients of many organizations located in the same metropolitan area within a radius of 60 miles. Some of the applications of MAN's include:

- Remote online transactions processing,
- Host-to-host (channel-to-channel) connections,
- CAD to CAM interconnection,
- Teleconferencing,
- Gateway to Wide and Global Area Networks,
- Other.

MAN is implemented in a dual ring architecture which in case of a node breakdown will send a message by the second unbroken bus. MAN's are built of fiber-optic cable which allows for the speed of 100+ MB/s. Control of MAN is provided by the central node equipped in the Switched Multi-Megabit Data Service (SMMDS).

WAN and VAN

Wide Area Network (WAN) can be a private or public telecommunications network over a large geographic area such as a state or country. Mainframes, minicomputers, microcomputers, workstations, and terminals can be linked together using inter-exchange carrier circuits (AT&T, MCI, US Sprint), satellites, or microwave relay links. WAN's transport information without significant enhancement or change of character in information (Figure 3-4).

A national WAN interconnects a company's different LAN's and MAN's into one national Enterprise Information Infrastructure. Here are some examples of WAN applications:

- Internal e-mail,
- Internal teleconferencing,
- Internal workgroup collaboration,
- Remote and online transactions processing,

- On-line enterprise database retrieval,
- CAD-CAM connection,
- Computer power leveling,
- EDI,
- EFT,
- Internet,
- Intranet,
- Other.

The architecture of WAN's has been evolving in two directions:

1. Circuit switching networks, mostly proprietary IBM, Compaq (Digital), HP, and Unisys networks based on leased circuits from long-distance telecommunications companies. Regardless of transmitted information volume, the circuit's provider charges the user on per time base.

Figure 3-4: Wide Area Network in a Ring Topology

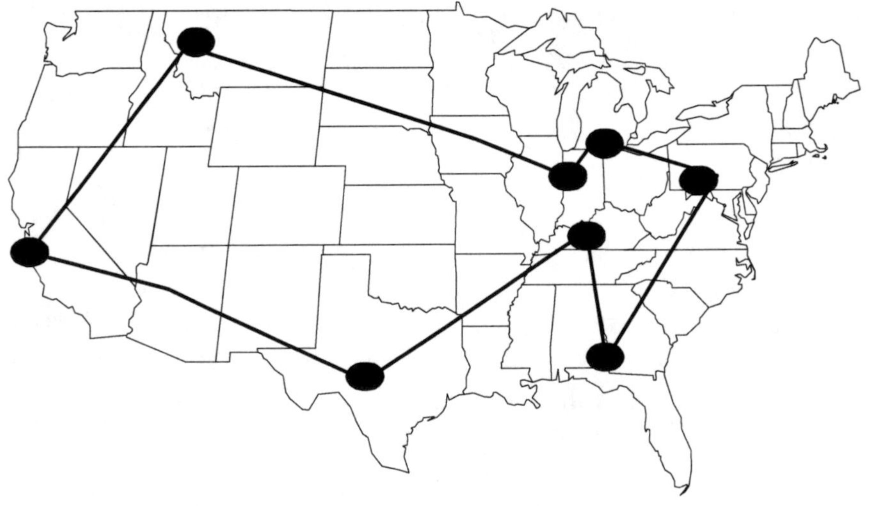

2. Public switching networks (PSN) transmit information in packets and charge the user per information sent volume. These networks are more effective for users.

The public packet switching networks are called Value Added Networks (VAN) since they provide additional services for the users, such as problem shooting, private network management, storage renting, and software renting, as well as training and turn-key installation of networks. Among the largest VAN's one can recognize:

- Telenet, the world's largest network, owned by U.S. Sprint with nodes in all major American and world cities
- Tymnet, owned by Boeing (after the merger with McDonnell Douglas), provides local access for users of America on Line, Prodigy and other similar services
- Accunet, owned by AT&T, covers all major American cities
- National networks in a majority of developed and developing countries

GAN and VAN

To support the development of a global economy and its global corporations, called consortia, Global Area networks (GAN) are implemented at the international level. GAN's interconnect LAN's, MAN's, and WAN's from different countries. Among the most popular applications transmitted through GAN's are the following ones:

- Global purchasing,
- Global inventory control,
- Global distribution,
- Global trading of commodities and stocks,
- Global fund transfer,

- EDI,
- E-commerce,
- Teleconferencing,
- Global service or production scheduling,
- Global human resources management,
- Other.

GAN's can be private or public. The latter is a typical VAN, which can support all users' needs, from the network installation to trouble shooting and

Figure 3-5: Global Area Network in a Ring Topology

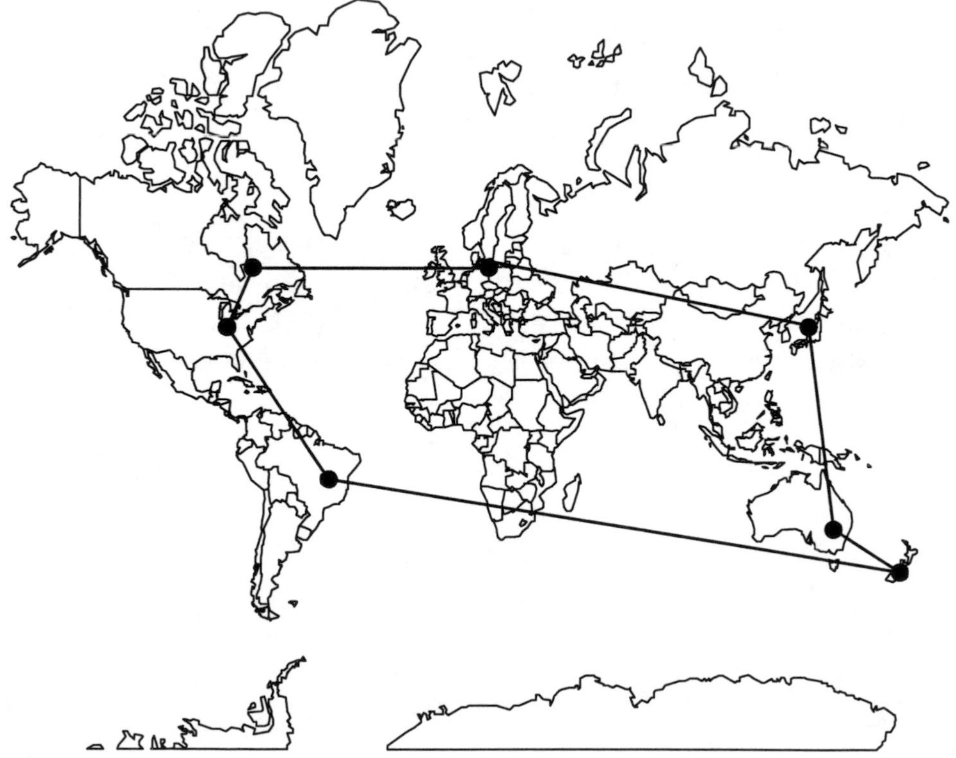

private network management. The architecture of a GAN is illustrated in Figure 3-5.

INTERNET LAYER

Internet

The Internet is a public, global network of web-driven computers (servers) that provide free access to the majority of info-communication services for individual and organizational users. The Internet is an international computer network of networks that connect government, academic, and business institutions as well as individual users. In the 1960's the Department of Defense developed the Internet. Its first Wide Area Network was called the ARPANET after the name of the Advance Research Project Agency. Then in 1983 ARPA opened the ARPANET for public applications, and since then this network has been called the Internet. It is an open system since the technical specification needed to build Transmission Control Protocol and Internet Protocol (TCP/IP) is open for everyone who wants to develop network tools and applications. By the year 2000, the Internet was used by several million servers and over 100 million individuals. The Internet as a whole reaches around the globe, connects computers from personal computers to supercomputers, and is not administered by a single authority.

The Internet architecture is shown in Figure 3-6, which is composed of the following components:

- Backbone Network Services at the speed of 3 TB (Tera Bits per second = 1000 GB per second) between the Internet main nodes composed by the computer super centers;
- Internet Registrars are responsible for registering Internet domain names, such as *www.cnn.com*, to people and organizations. They are overseen by boards made up of representatives from private and public institutions;
- Internet Registry tracks the connections between Internet addresses such as 125.34.24.21 and domain such as *www.zdnet.com*;
- Internet Society steers the direction of the Internet and its development in the scope of its technological and architectural issues, e.g., how TCP/IP and other Internet protocols should work.

Figure 3-6: How the Internet Runs

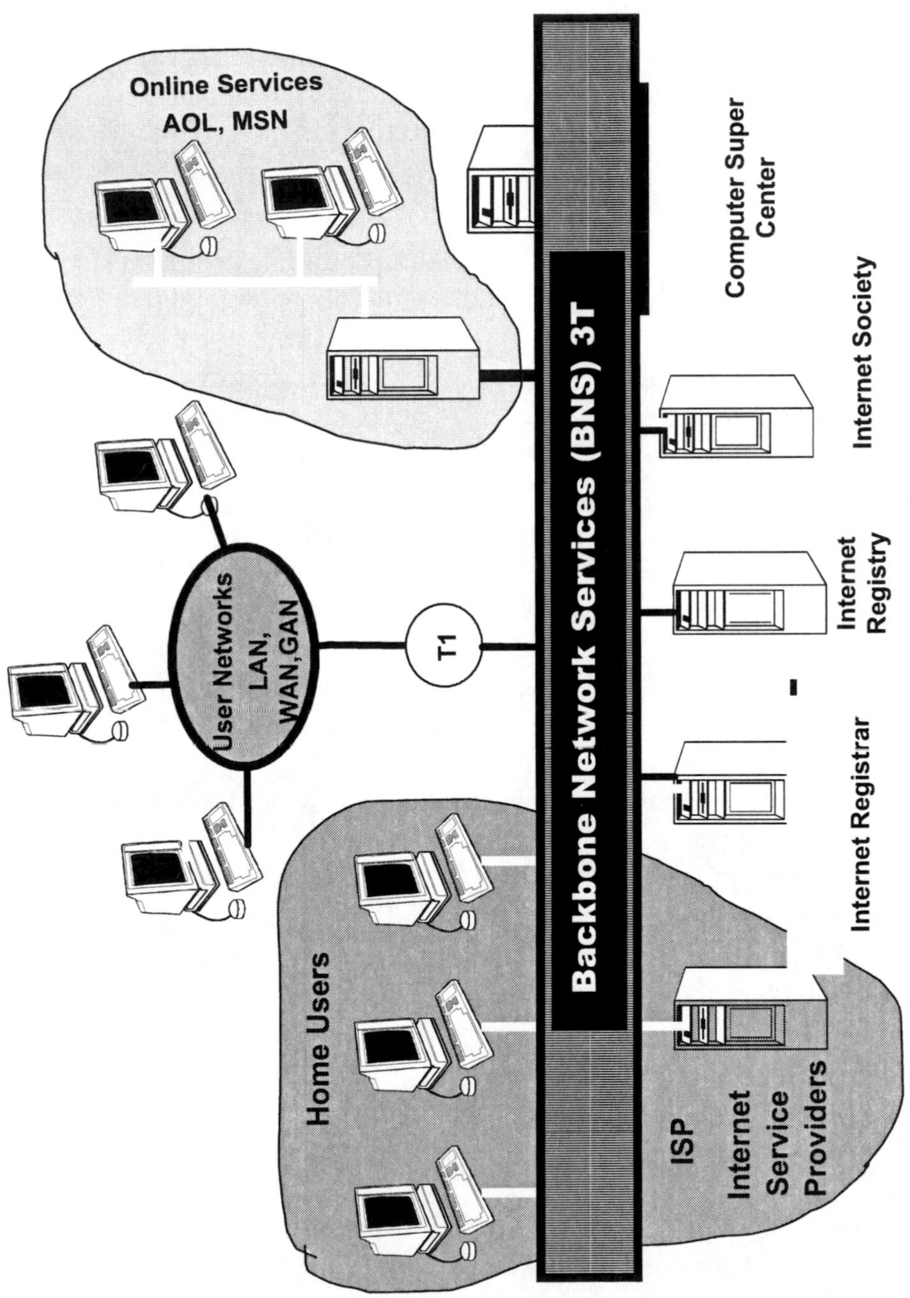

- Internet Service Providers (ISP) provide a paid access to the Internet for home users and small organizations;
- Corporate Networks – provide an access for their users;
- Online Services such as America Online or MSN provide a paid access to extended information services and the Internet.

Names and Addresses. Each server connected to the Internet has its own net IP-address, and an organization's domain name, which contains data about the type of the organization (Table 3-1) as well as a country code (Table 3-2), with the exception of the U.S. Since users from the United States are the largest users' group of the Internet, they do not have to write the country code in domains and e-mail addresses.

Table 3-1: Domain Types on the Internet

Code of Domain Type	Type of Organization	Example	Organization
edu	educational organization	tiger.wmich.edu	"tiger" server of Western Michigan University
gov	government organization	whitehouse.gov	White House
mil	military organization	airforce.mil	Air Force
net	network organization	archie.sura.net	net indexing tool applied at the University of Maryland
org	Other organizations	telecity.org	Kalamazoo teleCITY
com	commercial organization	americaonline.com	America on Line

Table 3-2: Country Codes Used on the Internet

Code	Country	Code	Country	Code	Country
AQ	Antarctica	FR	France	NZ	New Zealand
AR	Argentina	GR	Greece	PR	Puerto Rico
AT	Austria	HK	Hong Kong	PT	Portugal
AU	Australia	HU	Hungary	PL	Poland
BE	Belgium	IE	Ireland	SE	Sweden
BR	Brazil	IL	Israel	SG	Singapore
CA	Canada	IN	India	TW	Taiwan
CH	Switzerland	IT	Italy	UK	United Kingdom
CL	Chile	JP	Japan	US	United States
DE	Germany	KR	Korea	VE	Venezuela
DK	Denmark	MX	Mexico	ZA	South Africa
ES	Spain	NL	The Netherlands		
FI	Finland	NO	Norway		

Each domain is unique and provided to an organization after consulting the Domain Name System (DNS), which is a worldwide distributed database of names and addresses. An organization can register for a domain name, selecting a unique name and using the above provided codes: for example, the Digital Kalamazoo County in the U.S. selected a name *telecity.org*. The DNS database will assign the IP address of this organization server. The IP address is a set of four groups of numbers separated by periods, such as 123.567.55.2, which is the IP address for a connection of a given organization.

In the e-mail systems, user ID is composed of a first and last name, @ character, and organization domain, for example: *ian.smith@wmich.edu*. In addition to the user ID, a password is required in e-mail systems.

Most Internet service providers (ISP's) and many large organizations maintain DNS servers that serve as the source of information about DNS entries for a specific set of domains. The servers also cache used domain names and their IP addresses in a local lookup table. When a request to resolve a domain name arrives, the resolver parses the components of the domain name right to left, starting with the top-level domain (such as .com or .edu) and queries the DNS server for that domain, which redirects it to a DNS server for the second-level domain (such as telecityglobal.com); this process proceeds until the address is resolved or an error is encountered. In practice, recently used DNS entries are cached by the local resolver for possible reuse. If a website is hosted on servers belonging to an ISP, the IP address belongs to the ISP, even though the domain belongs to the customer. If the Web server operator changes ISP's, then the IP address will change as well, but the domain name will not.

The Internet Services and Systems. The classification of the Internet services is provided in Figure 3-7. They are grouped in the following manner:

- Net Tools, which allow the user either to navigate the Internet or to build its applications,
- End-User Communications, which allow communicating among people,
- E-commerce, systems that allow the pay-per-exchange transactions (Chapter 5),
- Education resources that allow students and instructors to seek help and support for their studies,

- Entertainment resources that allow the user to look for games, chat rooms,
- Information Services, such as news and magazines,
- Electronic White and Yellow Pages,
- Other.

Figure 3-7: The Classification of the Internet Services

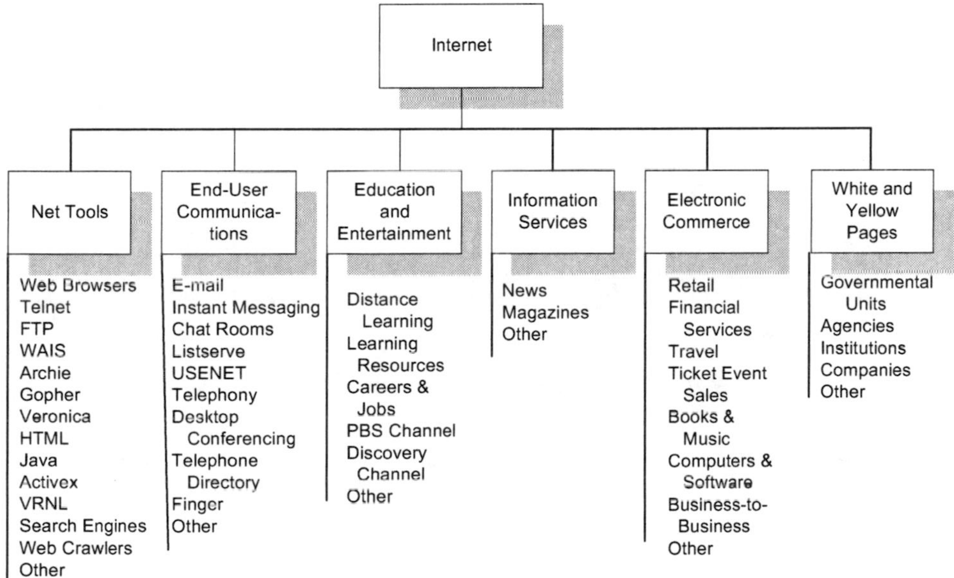

Net Tools. Among net tools one can distinguish the following:

- *World Wide Web (WWW)* browsers for the navigation of the Internet home pages and databases. Among the most popular navigators are *Netscape* and *Internet Explorer*. The location of each Web page within WWW is given by its URL, or Uniform Resource Locator; for example, the URL for the Kalamazoo teleCITY posting home page is *http://www.telecity.org*. HTTP stands for Hyper Text Transfer Protocol, which is a communication language used by Web servers and clients.

- *Telnet* – a tool enabling you to log on to remote computer sites. You can log on to the Library of Congress in the following manner: *$telent>open locis.loc.gov* (where $ is a prompt character on your server).

- *FTP – File Transfer Protocol* is a tool allowing the transfer of files from another site to your computer. For example, you may transfer a file (software) from the anonymous site, accessible to all users in the following manner: *$ftp wuarchie.wustl.edu*, login as *anonymous*, and use your *e-mail address* as a password. You will obtain software from The Washington University Public Domain Archives.

- *Archie* is a tool allowing the search for a file on an archie server. To do this you telenet to a distance location:

  $telenet archie.rutgers.edu
  login: archie
  archie> "type a file name"
  make a note of the file location
  archie>quit
  buy
  apply *FTP* to transfer the found file to your computer

- *WAIS – Wide Area Information Servers* for searching databases' contents.

- *GOPHER*[1] is a retrieval tool applying a system of menus. Log on as *gopher* and retrieve menus from an educational institution in Australia *info.anu.edu.au.*

- *Veronica*[2] - a search tool which searches gopherspace only; however, you do not have to quit it and use FTP as in Archie, so it is possible to retrieve the file instantly. Type *gopher* and select other *Information Sources and Gopher Servers* menu, select *Veronica* and type your search criteria *Apollo 1*. Navigate the selected menus and find your word: *Apollo 1*.

- *Search engines*: are computers with programs that retrieve a list of websites that match some user-selected criteria such as "light cotton and tuxedo." The user navigates to the search engine's sites and their URL addresses:

• Yahoo	*www.yahoo.com*
• Infoseek	*www.infoseek.com*
• Excite	*www.excite.com*
• Alta Vista	*www.altavista.com*
• Lycos	*www.lycos.com*
• Inktomi	*www.inktomi.com*
• Open Text	*www.opentext.com*
• WebCrawler	*www.webcrawler.com*
• WWW Worm	*www.webcrawler.com*
• Other	

- *Web crawlers* – are also called spiders, ants, robots, bots, and agents because they traverse the Web automatically to collect index data about home pages' contents.

End-User Communications include the following systems and services:

- E-mail.

- Instant Messaging – a service of America Online and MSN which delivers e-mail messages to a desktop screen's dialog box for "instant" communication.

- Chat Rooms – participants communicate in real-time.

- *Listserv* – gets its name from "list server" and is an automatic discussion list service. It is a program that handles all the list administrative functions such as subscribing and unsubscribing users to and from interest groups. It is an e-mail-based discussion forum. All new contents of listserv are sent to the user's e-mail address and are shown in his/her "new mail." Responses sent by subscribers are sent to all other subscribers.

- *USENET* – is a service to support discussions, interest groups, and conferences. These communications are transmitted on the USENET network, which can be transmitted across the Internet. About 3 million people participate in the USENET idea exchange. USENET is a conferencing service and is not considered an e-mail system. It is an open

and uncensored environment, where people from different facets of life spend time together "reading," "responding," and "posting news." USENET is divided into about 10,000 different newsgroups devoted to a special topic. Each newsgroup is made up of articles, which are similar to e-mail messages. Major news categories include: com-computer, misc-topics that do not fit anywhere else, news-groups dealing with USENET administration, recreational subjects, sci-topics on established sciences, soc-socializing and world culture topics, talk-debates, and biz-business topics. Some examples of newsgroups (entered through the browser):
    - *sci.military*
    - *rec.humor.funny*
    - *soc.women*

- *Telephony* – Internet telephones let users talk across the Internet to any PC/Mac computer around the world, for the fee of the Internet connection. Of course the two communicating computers must have installed the Internet telephone software. The user can download the phone packages for free from the following websites:
    - Netscape's CoolTalk *www.netspeak.com*
    - Intel's Internet Phone *www.intel.com*
    - IBM's Internet Connection Phone (IC Phone) *www.ibm.com*

- *Desktop conferencing* – is a real-time Internet-based telephone connection with video of conferencing parties. The user needs to install a desktop camera and the supporting software of *www.compaq.com*.

- *Telephone directory* – there is a free service in which users can look up the names, phone numbers, and addresses of friends, colleagues, and businesses:
    - *www.switchboard.com*
    - *www.bigbook.com* with 3-D pictures of business sites

- *Finger* – is a service of finding people when we know on which computer (server) they operate. One can usually use any part of the person's name and Finger will return essential data on all the users with that name on that computer. You need to type *$finger@remote-host-name*. Not every server provides the Finger service for security reasons.

Education resources include mostly websites that provide tools and information for teachers, professors, pupils, students, and administrators about curricula, syllabi, textbooks, laboratories, online classes, projects, issues, and equipment. Look for:

- The University of Phoenix Online Campus *www.uophx.edu/online*
- The Louisiana College *www.lacollege.edu/lconline.html*

Entertainment resources – there are plenty of resources that provide entertainment; look for:

- Discovery Channel Online *www.discovery.com*
- PBS Online *www.pbs.org*

Electronic White and Yellow Pages – are directories that contain listings of many people/organizations.

Without a doubt, the Internet is ushering in an era of sweeping change that will leave no business or industry untouched. In just the five years from 1995 to 2000, the Internet has gone from a playground for nerds into a vast communications and training center where some 300 million people swap information or deals around the world. Remember: it took radio more than 30 years and television 30 years to reach 60 million people! Never has technology caught fire so fast.

Intranet

Many companies have built internal networks using the same software standards as the Internet. Companies use intranets to distribute information and speed data exchange among offices. Intranet activities usually take place behind secure "firewalls" so that only authorized users have access. An intranet can span multiple business locations via the Internet. Recently the intranets are being implemented under the form of enterprise information portals (EIP)[3].

Extranet

When a company throws open its internal network – or intranet – to selected business partners, the intranet becomes an "extranet." Suppliers, distributors, and other authorized users can now connect to the company's network over the Internet or through virtual private networks. Once inside, they can view data the company makes available.

Companies ranging from Mobil Corp. to NationsBank Corp. are embracing intranets to key business partners over the Internet. Extranets use open software standards to shave networking costs and open the door to innovative applications. Prudential Health care figured that out. The managed-care plan has an extranet linking its internal systems to the corporate networks of large subscribers. That permitted the benefits managers at companies to enroll new employees themselves – rather than sending paperwork or dialing Prudential's call center. It also allows people to check their eligibility and claim status, or change doctors at any hour of the day. The payoff is sweet for Prudential too: the self-service extranet cuts hundreds of calls a day to the company's 800 number.

Extranets are about more than just saving money, though. They also can be a way to forge more intimate business links among partners, allowing them to share business data, even collaborate on product design and development.

Hewlett-Packard Co. and Procter & Gamble Co., for instance, have extranet links to their advertising agencies to swap marketing plans and speed the review of ad comparing. A winemaker, Robert Mondavi Corp., which buys satellite images from NASA to spot problems in its vineyards, aims to push those images out over an extranet to its independent growers. That would improve the grapes within the Mondavi business and also improve relationships with its subcontractors.

Adaptec Inc., a leading supplier of computer-storage products invested $1 million for an extranet. Adaptec does not make the chips it uses in its products. Adaptec saves money that way. But the company cannot move as quickly, in some sense, as rivals that build their own chips. In this business you are either fast or forgotten. To speed up communications with Adaptec's Taiwanese chip suppliers, Adaptec developed the extranet to tie all the companies in a kind of virtual *keiretsu*. Now, messages from Adapytec flow in seconds from its headquarters to partners in Asia. More important, the two-way communiqués include not just parts orders but also engineering drawings and detailed manufacturing instructions. Adaptec has reaped great benefits, reducing the time between the order and delivery of its chips from as long as 112 days to 55 days – the same cycle enjoyed by companies that make their own chips. The time for processing purchasing orders fell from six days to minutes, and suppliers stopped having to manually re-enter faxed orders – eliminating the potential for disastrous errors. Adaptec also saved $9 million on its work-in-process pipeline.

The complexity of networking based upon the Internet, Intranet, and Extranet is shown on Figure 3-8, where a mythical merchant Cool Sportz (designed by Business Week) uses the Internet for e-business.

> Cool Sportz has a private company intranet to communicate with branch stores and employees in remote offices.

Figure 3-8: The Internet-based Cool Sportz Company

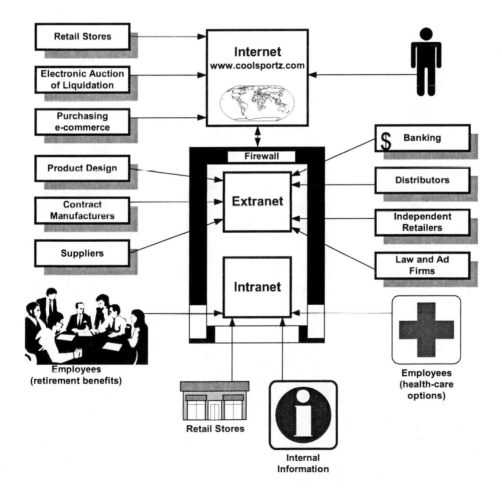

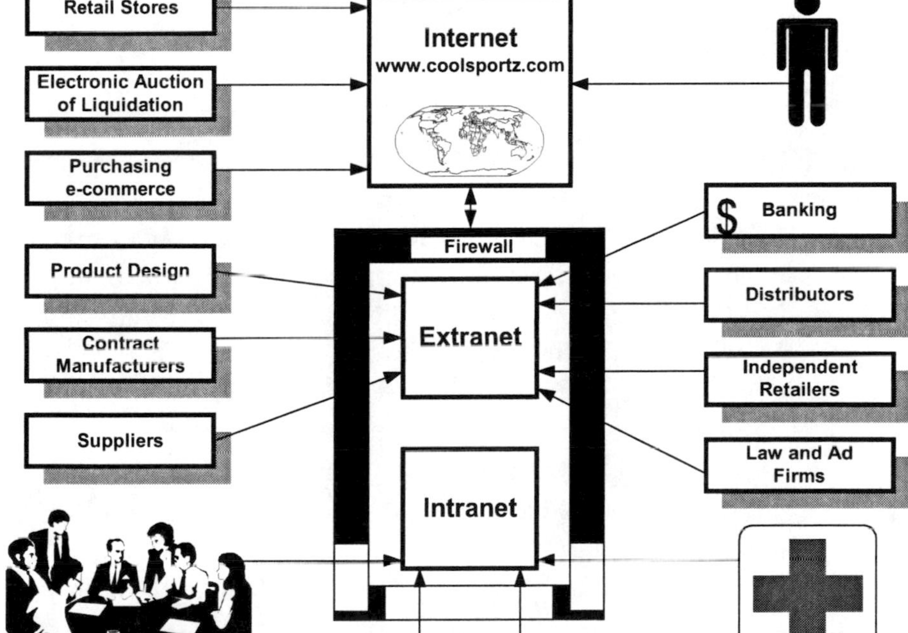

The Internet.

Consumers. Cool Sportz's website is promoted in TV ads, and gets thousands of hits a day. From a survey of its site, Cool Sportz collects demographic data,and it advises registered surfers on sales and new products.

Electronic auction. When products do not sell, Cool Sportz auctions them through an online brokerage. The company posts information about the goods at minimum price. Potential buyers enter bids, and Cool Sportz ships the goods to the winning bidder.

The Extranet.

Product design. Cool Sportz enlists freelance designers to create CoolWear products. The designers exchange drawings with Cool Sportz over the extranet. Then Cool Sportz staff and designers can mark them up while talking together live over the extranet.

Manufacturing. For years, Cool Sportz has placed orders with contract manufacturers using Electronic Data Exchange (EDI), an old software standard that is neither cheap nor flexible. Now, Cool Sportz saves money by moving some of these orders over the extranet.

Suppliers. Cool Sportz used to order shoes, ski gear, and camping goods by phone and fax. Now, the company saves time and money by sending orders electronically over the extranet. Some suppliers let Cool Sportz enter their private networks to place orders.

Distributors. Cool Sportz sells its CoolWear products through 2,500 independent sporting-goods stores around the country. Distributors who supply these shops use Cool Sportz's extranet to check on their commissions and read up on new merchandise-marketing programs.

Law and ad firms. To help efficiency, Cool Sportz requires its law firm, accounting firm, and ad agency to belong to the corporate extranet. This ensures privacy and security for e-mail and electronic files. Cool's marketers brainstorm over the extranet with the ad agency.

Banking. While awaiting standards for the Net-based electronic banking, Cool Sportz sends invoices by secure e-mail, which reduces paperwork and speeds up payment. The CFO likes collecting bills faster, but is less eager to see accounts payable go electronic.

The Intranet.

Retail stores. The company collects data from its 1,200 retail stores around the country and fills hundreds of product reorders electronically. All stores are on the Cool Sportz intranet, a secure link that traverses the Internet. Cool Sportz also "pushes" information on promotions and discounts to its stores.

Employees. Instead of phoning the Human Resources department, Cool Sportz staff refer to an electronic version of the employee book on the company intranet. They use a Java-based application to change their investment and health-care options and calculate their retirement benefits. Expense reports filled via the intranet are paid within 48 hours.

COMPUTING LAYER

A computer environment supports information processing in EII through the following building blocks:

1. Computer sets, divided into the following classes:
   - Supercomputers (ex. Cray T90),
   - Mainframe (e.g.: IBM ES/9000),
   - Midrange (e.g.: IBM AS/400),
   - Server (e.g.: IBM RS/6000),
   - Desktop PC,
   - Mobile PC,
   - Network Computer, NC (IBM Network Station),
   - Internet browsers (e.g.: WebTV),
   - Hand-held computers,
   - Other.

2. Operating systems (a layer software that resides between hardware and application, which manages the execution of programs and the data flow among devices), such as:
   - Server/host operating systems (IBM MVS, VSE, VM, OS/400, DEC VMS),
   - Server operating systems (Novell NetWare, MS Window NT server, Unix),

- Desktop operating systems (DOS, Windows, MS Window NT Workstation, MacOS, Unix, Linux),
- Mobil operating systems (MS Windows CE, GEOS, Magic Cap, Apple Newton).

3. Programming languages:
   - 3 GL - generation languages (e.g.: COBOL),
   - 4 GL - generation languages (e.g.: Information Builders FOCUS),
   - Object languages (ex. C++),
   - Visual languages (ex.: Visual Basic),
   - Other.

4. Data Management:
   - Database Management Systems (Oracle, Access, SQL),
   - Data Warehouses (IBM Visual Warehouse, OmniWarehouse),
   - Data Mining (KnowledgeSeeker, IBM Intelligent Mining Tool).

5. Developmental tools:
   - Computer Aides Software Engineering (CASE) for system design and analysis, source code generation, documentation creation, and so forth (Oracle Designer, 2000),
   - Object-oriented Development Environments (IBM Visual Age, DEC Visual Smalltalk),
   - Component Base Development (CBD) such as enterprise objects ("customer," "employee," "product,"),
   - GUI (Graphic User Interface) toolkits (HyperCard, CenterLine, HP C+++),
   - Web tools for the presentation of information, design of transaction systems and information retrieval (ex.: Front Page, Sapphire/Web, WebObject, NetCraft),
   - Other.

Computer platforms are organized into the following computer configurations:

- Independent computer configuration – one computer used by in-house users,

- Computer interconnection configuration – at least two or more computers are organized into clusters in order to increase the reliability of real-time applications, such as at banks, air-traffic control, or military command and control,

- Computer distributed configuration – where according to the 20/80 rule 20% of information processing takes place at the headquarters level and 80% of information is processed at the departmental level. A network of departmental computers is connected to the headquarters' computer,

- Computer multi-system configuration – where several computers are geographically dispersed among a company's units and interconnected through a network,

- Client-Server configuration – is organized around a Local Area Network (LAN) where servers store files and application software which are accessible by client computers with a limited scale of their own resources,

- Network computers (NC) configuration – inexpensive, "thin" computers are connected to Local Area Networks (LAN) or to Value Added Networks (VAN) which on the fly mode provide necessary software and files to client NC's.

COMMUNICATIONS LAYER

PBX

Private branch exchange (PBX) is one of the oldest communication services. It connects external telephone callers with internal extension numbers. PBX is also applied to data transmission at a speed from 19.2 KB/s to 196 KB/s within ISDN service. The latter is AT&T Integrated Services Digital Network (ISDN), which provides multimedia transmission through a twisted pair of telephone lines. Instead of building an autonomous LAN, PBX may be applied as a LAN.

Voice Mail

In voice mail the sender can record a verbal message (voicegram) and send it later either to one or to many receivers (broadcasting). The most frequent procedure is to store a voicegram on the receiver's answering machine. A voicegram can also be forwarded to more receivers by any one of the receivers. Voice mail is the most popular telephone-based system of communications. This system can avoid the following negative factors:

- wasted time on unsuccessful attempts ("telephone tag") to reach a party,
- many calls to individuals by broadcasting messages that are in nature one-way communication,
- costs associated with chatting by sending a voicegram during off peak time, when rates are lower.

E-mail

A typical electronic mail (e-mail) system provides the following functions:

- new mail message composition, including spelling checker,
- address book handling,
- message management which includes such functions as:
    - scanning the incoming messages,
    - filtering incoming messages for unwanted contents,
    - replying to received messages,
    - forwarding received messages,
    - redirecting received messages,
    - broadcasting new messages,
    - organizing folders; message filing and retrieval,
    - automating signature,
    - managing written attachments,
    - managing video and audio attachments,
    - managing attached Web pages,
    - notifying message, received and/or read by the receiver,
    - saving and/or printing messages,
    - other.

- security management,
- other.

With the advent of the Internet, an e-mail client had a simple mission: to transfer e-mail across the Internet or across a proprietary, in-house system. But as the number of e-mail users has increased dramatically and their addresses have become a target of marketers, e-mail systems have become more complex now. Their mission is to manage all messages that land in the user mailbox. These messages include news digests, notices about software updates, and messages from mailing lists, including junk mail that has become an occupational hazard for eager e-mail users. Many users have more than one account and new systems take care of managing all the user's accounts.

From simple communication programs, e-mail clients are evolving into true productivity applications that help the user work smarter and faster. Among such e-mail software are Eudora, Lotus Mail, Netscape Communicator, Microsoft Outlook, Pegasus, and others.

E-meeting

A typical electronic meeting (e-meeting) takes place in a room with interconnected client computers. Each participant of a meeting has one client computer and takes part in the live meeting through interactive written messages. A moderator organizes discussion by sorting and ranking participants' messages and concentrating discussion on those issues that interest all or the majority of participants.

An e-meeting has an advantage over a traditional meeting when brainstorming and consensus are required. Such meetings are suitable for developmental issues such as a conceptualization of a new business, new product, new strategy, and other solutions of this type.

The e-meeting is supported by a Local Area Network and application software which manages the meeting and supports the moderator's task.

Computer Conferencing

Computer conferencing is created by forming a network of participants who communicate through their remote, client computers. This is a system that supports communications in a mode of many-to-many. Participants send typed messages and comments to a central host computer, where a moderator organizes these messages by subject and stores them for eventual further retrieval by other conferees.

In such a manner, conference members may participate at any time and from anywhere; home or office or from a laptop in a car or on an airplane. In computer conferencing, participants contribute their ideas, positions, with one idea/position building on another until after a few hours or days or weeks or months, there may be a dozen or hundreds of comments, all stored and read in that conference waiting to reach either conclusion or further reference. Such a conference is sometimes called a Group Decision Support System (GDSS).

For example, Harvard University has organized a computer conference among 215,000 living alumni worldwide and senior professors. This conference enables the faculty to be current with business practice issues and the alumni also to be in touch with this famous campus.

Most computer conferencing systems organize messages into conferences according to subject matter. Other terms for these organized topics are Special Interest Groups (SIG), mailing lists, or news group (USENET). Very often such a computer conference creates a social group or an existing social group organizes itself as a computer conference - a virtual community such as the WELL in San Francisco.

Many systems keep lists of conferences that can be used to discover what conferences exist. For example, for the Internet one can look for USENET newsgroups.

Bulletin Board Systems (BBS)[4]

A BBS is an electronic bulletin board for posting information and comments. A list of categories and topics is displayed by the moderator (administrator). A user may post messages per category and per topic. A BBS is a rudimentary single machine, a non-interactive conferencing system with a small number of topics available, without a sophisticated user interface. A user posts a message without any idea who will read it or reply to it.

A BBS is organized in:

- Conferences (non-interactive),
- Message exchanges,
- Item posting,

- Notes recording,
- Files handling,
- Administration services.

In business, among other applications, BBS's are applied within customer service to post customers' comments about products/services. In such a manner the vendor's staff can trace customers' opinions and improve their own products/services.

Groupware

Groupware is software that allows selected groups to share (collaborate) documents electronically and perform tasks such as writing, editing, and electronic note-taking. It encourages collaboration among teams in the formation of original documents (written, graphic, spreadsheet). It also helps to establish online and off-line discussion subjects that act as ad hoc collaborative teams and it documents a meeting's results and helps in organizing a project's history.

Groupware permits common access to the same:

- word processing documents,
- spreadsheet documents,
- database documents,
- file-distribution subsystem,
- automated calendaring-scheduling application,
- threaded-computer conferencing,
- whiteboards,
- e-discussion administration, and
- development and migration tools.

Implementing a groupware package in a large company is expensive and requires more administrative and technical support than a comparable e-mail system. Among the most popular systems are Lotus Notes and Microsoft Exchange. Groupware systems will play a critical role in implementing virtual offices and enterprises in the future.

Work Flow Systems (WFS)

A Work Flow System (WFS)[5] is the automation of business/organization information movement as it flows through the steps from start to finish that make up the work procedure by maintaining a record of changes in status and the state of the document or transaction. Key to WFS is the tracking of process-related (e.g., a car loan's path in a bank's procedures) information and the status of each process' operation as it moves through a firm/organization.

The WFS fell into two categories:

- Collaborative WFS – a project team located in different locations uses a WFS to facilitate communication and development of documents (can apply a groupware software),

- Production WFS – is applied in mission-critical processes or transaction processes, usually within one department. It includes document image storage and retrieval capabilities, intelligent forms, database access, and ad hoc capabilities. This system is usually applied in claims processing by insurance companies or in loans processing by banks.

Teleconferencing

Any live, point-to-point, electronically aided conversation is a teleconference. Technically, two people talking over an intercom are engaged in a teleconference. Such a conference is called an audiographic conference. Finally, if you beam a live, full-motion television picture from location A to location B or to many locations and add two-way telephone communications, you have a videoconference.

Meeting tables at Pharmacia-Upjohn can now stretch across oceans. A room with video conferencing equipment went into service in 1990 in Kalamazoo-Portage, Michigan. Similarly equipped rooms have been put into operation at Upjohn sites in Brussels, Belgium and Crawley, United Kingdom.

Videoconferencing involves the use of television equipment to conduct meetings between people at different locations. Television signals are transmitted from location to location using fiber-optic cable and/or satellite transmission systems. Applications include: reviews of advertising pieces, discussions of marketing plans, and exchanges of competitive information.

Primary objectives of Pharmacia-Upjohn's Global Videoconferencing System are:

- To improve home office - field communication,
- To deliver worldwide live information,
- To reduce travel time and expense,
- To speed up decision-making,
- To enhance training and education efforts,
- To allow reception of other programming,
- Other.

Almost every Fortune 500 company applies a video-conferencing system, and those companies that do not have such a system can rent facilities from about 10,000 public videoconferencing rooms.

Telecommuting

Telecommuting is a work-at-home or telework center through office automation that interconnects a workplace with an organization place. Telecommuting means teleworking from the house or teleworkplace (a shared, informated office in a residential area).

If telecommuting catches on, it will not be the first time telecommunications has reshaped the urban landscape. The telephone helped to separate office from factory, allowing knowledge workers to be concentrated in urban skyscrapers, and creating our modern pattern of moving suburban workers to the urban center.

We are now attempting the reverse: moving jobs to workers. Corporate headquarters are being relocated to suburban office parks. This merrily brings urban gridlock closer to home, forcing even the urban escapees to consider telecommuting options like suburban satellite offices linked to their headquarters. Telecommuting from home will also increase. In the 1990's about 10% of the labor force was telecommuting.

Fax

A facsimile (fax) system is, after a telephone, the simplest business telecommunication technology. Its function is to send a paper-based document over a telephone line. Its commercial use took place in the 1980's and today almost every organization and many homes are equipped with a fax station.

Fax machines work by the telecommunication transmission of scanned image data. At the sending machine, a document is illuminated to recognize white or dark places that are subsequently converted into a sound and sent over the telephone lines. At the receiving station a printing process takes place.

A fax machine is an info-communication system which contains several useful functions such as: broadcasting, delayed dialing, storing, and storing-and-forwarding. In the former case, the sender transmits the facsimile message to an intermediary distributor who sends the message when the circuitry to the receiver is open, usually during morning hours. The fact that a fax connection can handle a paper message through several functions determines that the faxing process belongs to a system nature.

A PC is more frequently applied as a fax machine too.

EDI

Electronic Data Interexchange (EDI) is a system of transmitting standard, business, digital documents among two or more computers. By its nature EDI is of an inter-organizational nature. For example, an assembly plant may apply EDI to transmit an assembling schedule to component subcontractors' computers in order to modify their manufacturing schedules. Instead of faxing paper-based schedules, involved companies exchange electronically computer-to-computer digital documents that are incorporated into their own enterprise information systems, in this case in a production planning subsystem.

EDI is application software which uses telecommunications lines and it integrates applications of different organizational units, either of its own company or with another company or companies.

EDI speeds up the process by which companies conduct their business. A purchase decision is made and communicated to the supplier at once, instead of waiting for a purchase order to make its way through the typing pool and then the postal system.

EDI takes on strategic importance by enhancing relationships between companies and their suppliers on one side and their customers on the other side. EDI helps companies to reduce their inventories and associated carrying costs. In a number of industries, such as the grocery industry, where margins are slim, the cost/benefit that EDI yields can significantly increase productivity.

EDI has a great future as a time-driven, integrative component of the organizational electronic infrastructure. New applications are continually being designed for such industries as aerospace and the ready-to-wear apparel industry, where electronic graphics are important in the purchasing process because blueprints or drawings are required to support the purchase decision.

EFTS

In order to take full advantage of the banking and stock exchange systems, the Electronic Fund Transfer System (EFTS) was invented. It replaces paper money with electronic money processed by computers and their networks. EFTS is a tool to communicate, transport, integrate, and share information among financial institutions and their customers.

On October 28, 1974, the Congress of the United States provided for the creation of a National Commission on Electronic Fund Transfers. It is a new information infrastructure for the facilitation of payment mechanisms. But not only is it an electronic tool for payments, it is also a tool for the generation of new financial and information services.

Once EFTS is in operation, online exchanges can take place. Not only users from financial institutions, but also consumers and private investors can fix deals electronically via Automated Teller Machines (ATM), Point-of-Sales (POS) machines, credit and debit cards, smart cards (with a chip), and information kiosks located in such public places as malls, libraries, hospitals, airports, bus and railroad stations, and other.

FURTHER TRENDS

Future trends in the EII development are:

- Broadband capacity should radically increase the speed and carrying capacity of telecommunications and computer networks,

- Data compression should squeeze more information into a smaller space and therefore should accelerate the speed of digital services,
- Network intelligence and flexibility should improve the ability of service suppliers and end users alike to customize the management of online information resources,
- Interactive capabilities will allow for loading and retrieving the most complex information such as a video anytime, anywhere,
- Multimedia applications and services should allow for teleconferencing anytime, anywhere,
- Intelligent information appliances, such as pocket-size telephones (PCS) and multimedia personal digital assistants (PDA's) should improve the mobility of the enterprise's workers and their ability to access and retrieve information anytime, anywhere,
- Navigational tools should allow for the application of intelligent agents to navigate that information which is right for a given user,
- Reliability, security, and safety improvements in order to make EII more robust,
- Wireless communication should improve the delivery of the applications to/by the mobile workforce and consumers, increasing the velocity of transactions and decision-making.

CONCLUSION

A business enterprise is not any more supported by a single (e.g., MIS) or system set (e.g., ERP) of applications. The latter evolves into an Enterprise Information Infrastructure (EII), a system of six layers handling thousands of IT components that support business/organization processes.

The same process of emerging information infrastructures takes place at the level of:

- Local, supported by the Local Information Infrastructure,
- Nation, supported by the National Information Infrastructure,
- Global, supported by the Global Information Infrastructure.

These four information infrastructures are being interconnected, creating a new civilization information infrastructure, following and interacting with the 10,000+ years old agricultural infrastructure, 6,000 years old urban infrastructure, and the 200+ years old industrial infrastructure. The purpose of the EII/LII/NII/GII is not to replace the other two civilization infrastructures but to optimize their development and operations.

BIBLIOGRAPHY

Anderson, R.H. (1999). *Securing the U.S. Defense Information Infrastructure, A Proposed Approach.* Santa Monica, CA: RAND.

Bradley, J.C. (1995). *A Quick Guide to the Internet.* New York: An International Thomson Publishing Company.

Comer, D.E. (1995). *The INTERNET Book.* Englewood Cliffs, NJ.: Prentice Hall.

Drake, W. J. (1995). *The New Information Infrastructure, Strategies for U.S. Policy.* New York: The Twentieth Century Fund Press.

LaQuey, T. (1993). *INTERNET Companion.* Reading, MA: Addison-Wesley Publishing Company.

Muller, N.J. & Davidson, R.P. (1990). *LANs to WANs, Network Management in the 1990s.* Boston, MA: Artech House.

Pitter, K., Amato, S., Callahan, J., Kerr, N., & Tilton, E. (1995). *Every Student's Guide to the Internet.* San Francisco, CA: McGraw-Hill.

PriceWaterhouse. (1997). *Technology Forecast.* Menlo Park, CA.

Reinhard, A. (1998). Extranets, Log on, Link up, Save big, *Business Week,* June 22, pp. 132-138.

Targowski, A. (1996). *Global Information Infrastructure.* Harrisburg, PA: Idea Group Publishing.

Targowski, A. (2001). *Enterprise Information Infrastructure.* Boston, MA: Pearson.

Ware, H. W. (1998). *The Cyber-Posture of the National Information Infrastructure.* Santa Monica, CA: RAND.

ENDNOTES

[1] This service was used at the beginning of the Internet Era, nowadays has been replaced by www.

[2] This service was used at the beginning of the Internet Era, nowadays has been replaced by www.

[3] More on EIP's in Chapter 4.

[4] This system is less frequently used now; however we speak about it to complete a list of potential Internet systems and services.

[5] WFS is described in depth in Chapter 4.

Chapter IV

Application Layer[1]

STRATEGY AND RATIONALE

The goals of the Application Layer of the Enterprise Information Infrastructure are:

1. To empower the organization (via enterprise computing-EC) in optimizing the use of resources, such as manpower, money, material, machines, management, and the marketplace in business,

2. To empower individuals (via end-user computing-EUC and enterprise computing (EC) - Figure 4-22) in gaining cognition about managed resources and processes in the business environment.

The strategy of implementing these goals is based on the growing expansion of the applications' integration across all business functions in the networked and Web-driven environment.

The integration of business applications in an enterprise is the natural process that follows the pattern of reproduction processes in nature. The first stage in these processes is the growth by division of functional organs; and the next stage is the consolidation of these organs into a non-redundant wholeness. In such a way the evolution of nature takes place with feedback from the environment.

The applications' integration follows the premises of the General System Theory, defined (in the 1930's and 1940's) by a German-American biologist, Ludwig von Bertalanffy (1968), who argued that artificial systems, to be fully effective, should copy the construction of biological systems, the most perfect in our world. The contribution to that theory was provided by Norbert Wiener (1948) who defined cybernetics as knowledge about communicating in animals and machines through feedback. For almost the second half of the 20th century these theories were applied only as "the approach" and in a limited manner, since the tools of their applications were just in a conceptual or developmental stage.

The rapid development of computer networks, the Internet, and the Web technology have made it possible to apply in practice these theories in the integration of business application in such a way that the enterprise becomes more coherent, more "organic," less redundant in subsystems, more communicative, and responsive to business challenges.

At the same time, the "feedback" from this type of development raises awareness and skills among business executives and professionals who pursue with rapid decisions the transformation of information islands into an information continent. Those who lead this transformation in the 21st century will become the richest people in the world, as took place with the initial leaders of the Industrial Wave at the end of 19th century. One can say after 100+ years that history has repeated itself and now the new Information Wave is absorbing the best minds of developers and entrepreneurs, just as was the case in the Industrial Wave.

SEMANTIC LADDER – ARITHMETICS OF INFORMATION PROCESSING

To understand computer applications in organizations one must understand the concept of information, which determines the scope and limits of those applications.

It is evident that the dynamics of the universe are determined by the cognitive relationships that govern the purposeful development of the natural and artificial systems. These relationships convey units of cognition whose substance is "mental" and create a "mind event." In man's environment, his state of mind (cognition) steers the environment. In an animal's environment, the state of mind (instincts and natural laws) controls its environment. In the world of the inanimate object, particularly in the scope of machines, their internal logic is steered by scientific ideas applied by the designers.

Cognitive relationships operate through the pragmatic process of communication, which conveys meaning via transactions, data, information, concepts, knowledge, and wisdom.

A *transaction* is an activity that reflects the nature of the organization. An example: manufacturing companies are based on activities that transform labor, materials, and money into finished goods; accordingly, transactions in these companies describe sales, receipts, expenditures, changes in personnel, and changes in inventory levels.

A *datum* is a measuring unit of cognition that describes transactions between natural, artificial, or semantic systems. In the business system, data measures the performance of production, distribution, transportation, or service. For example, *Time* magazine sold one million copies in 1985. Thermometer readings describe the temperature of the air. In September of 1986, there were 255 male and 187 female registered members of the Dynamic Health Club in Portage, Michigan. The rate of return on short-term bond funds in the 401 K plan has risen 6.8% for the last quarter.

Information is a comparative unit of cognition that defines a change between the previous and the present state of the natural, artificial, or semiotic systems. The business system, for example, can provide a consensus that a given business is in a normal state, a conflict state, or a crisis state. Through the comparison of actual data from two different periods of business operations, the difference between which is compared to standards for analyzed performance areas, one can draw a conclusion about the change in business. Continuing with the previous examples, *Time* magazine was the best selling magazine in 1985. The difference between two thermometer readings taken at different times indicates changes in air temperature. In September of 1987, membership of males dropped by 15% at the Dynamic Health Club in Portage, Michigan, while female membership increased by 30%. The rate of return on short-term bond funds in the 401 K plan rose 1.5% since the last quarter.

A *concept* is a perceptive unit of cognition, which generates thoughts or ideas that create our intuition and intention, a sense of direction. Applying this to the previous examples, more *Time* magazines should be printed and made available in Europe. The phrase "it is too hot" indicates the perception that the air is not comfortable. Women are becoming increasingly more health and weight-conscious while men are losing interest in health and fitness. As a participant in the 401 K plan, I should increase my contribution in short-term bond funds.

Knowledge is a reasoning unit of cognition that creates awareness based on facts, rules, coherent inferences, and well-defined methods. This knowledge provides a point of reference; a standard for our way of analyzing data, information, and concepts. The following types of knowledge are recognized: personal knowledge (kp), domain knowledge (kd), societal knowledge (ks), and moral knowledge (km). Once again elaborating on the previous situations, an increasing demand for a product necessitates an increase in the supply of the product; therefore, a wider distribution of *Time* magazine is needed. "Hot weather can be dangerous" is a conclusion based on past experience. Surveys on fitness show that men are more interested in body building and that women tend to enjoy aerobics and cardiovascular exercise. The rate of return on short-term bond funds will continue to be high if interest rates remain high.

Wisdom is a pragmatic unit of cognition which generates volition, a chosen way of acting and communicating. It is a process of choosing ordered routines which provide success and eliminate obstacles in performance. Concluding with our examples, *Time* could be printed in Mexico, where there are lower labor costs. To increase the number of men joining and staying with Dynamic, the club will invest in more body building equipment such as weight lifting apparatus and Nautilus machines. "Do not allow the patients to exert themselves in this heat." Economists predict that interest rates will begin to fall in the near future; therefore, I will decrease my contribution to short-term bond funds and channel the majority of my contributions into another option in the 401 K plan that is less susceptible to change in interest rates.

A hierarchy of cognitive units creates the semantic ladder, which identifies the process of cognition from the simplest to the most complex units. The semantic ladder is shown in Figure 4-1.

At the silent level, happenings within the environment, objects, and processes are described as data (D) and inserted into the linkage of the human communication system. This data is subsequently processed into information (I) and concepts (C). At the verbal level, we find the men (M) who create information, which contains the user's intentions (communication reaction). Once data has been processed and human information has been provided, they create the intentional level of cognition where the user assigns significance to the silent and verbal levels of happenings. As a result, other alternatives of information and new concepts are created. From the information and concepts emerge the semantic structures under the form of the previously discussed types of knowledge (K). At this level of cognition, reasoning takes place. Wisdom (W) is applied at the value level, where reasoning is utilized with the aim of deciding between the various available courses of action. Cognitive wisdom is

Figure 4-1: Semantic Ladder (Targowski Model)

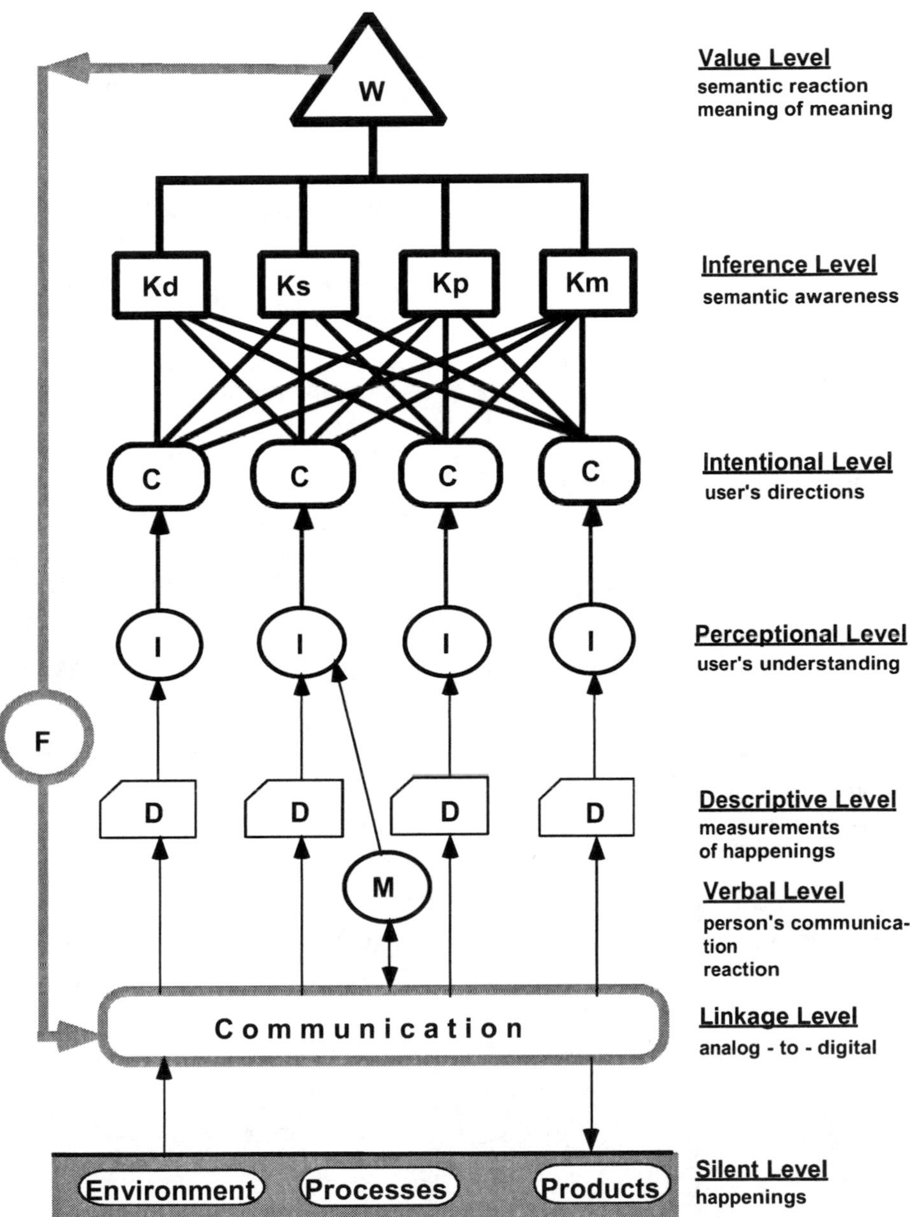

a pragmatic apparatus which formulates a communication frame (F) composed of a message and reflecting information (intentions). That frame enters the cognitive communication system and interacts at the verbal and silent levels with the natural and artificial systems. The frame closes the loop of the cognition process, causing two events. The first is a semantic and communication reaction of the man to the data coming in from the external realm. The second is the increase of semantic correlation between knowledge and wisdom as a part of the learning process.

A pass from one semantic level to another takes place under the form of semantics processing. Semantics processing is composed of the following operations: transmitting, editing, calculating, controlling (selections and loops), storing, retrieving, and maintaining. The organized semantics operations create either the regular-manual information system (RIS) or the computer-based information system (CIS). Semantics processing and its paradigms are shown in Figure 4-2.

Data processing organizes a description of transactions into data (data collection, data preparation, data entry, data storing, updating, retrieving, and report generation). The paradigm of data processing is measurement of transactions via so-called Transaction Processing Systems (TPS).

Information processing converts data into information through comparisons of different data sets in order to define a change at the verbal and silent levels. At this level, concepts (ideas) are created which determine a sense of direction. The paradigms of information processing are the assessment of change and direction. In this category fall a majority of the applications, such as Executive Information Systems (EIS), Enterprise Performance Management (EPM), Enterprise Resource Planning (ERP), Supply Chain Management (SCM), and Customer Relation Management (CRM) systems.

Concept processing converts situations into certain levels of affairs (normal, conflict, success, crisis, and failure) that are rules-driven. These systems are Expert Systems (EXS).

Knowledge processing converts data, information, and concepts into rules and a way of reasoning. The paradigm of knowledge is awareness. Through awareness we can verify incoming data, information, and concepts. Do they fit into our frame of reference? Can we use them as a basis for decision-making? Among this category of systems one can mention Knowledge Management Systems (KMS) and Expert Systems.

Wisdom processing converts knowledge into the choice of an action course. The communication frame is created and volition of communication and

Figure 4-2: Semantics Processing by Information Systems

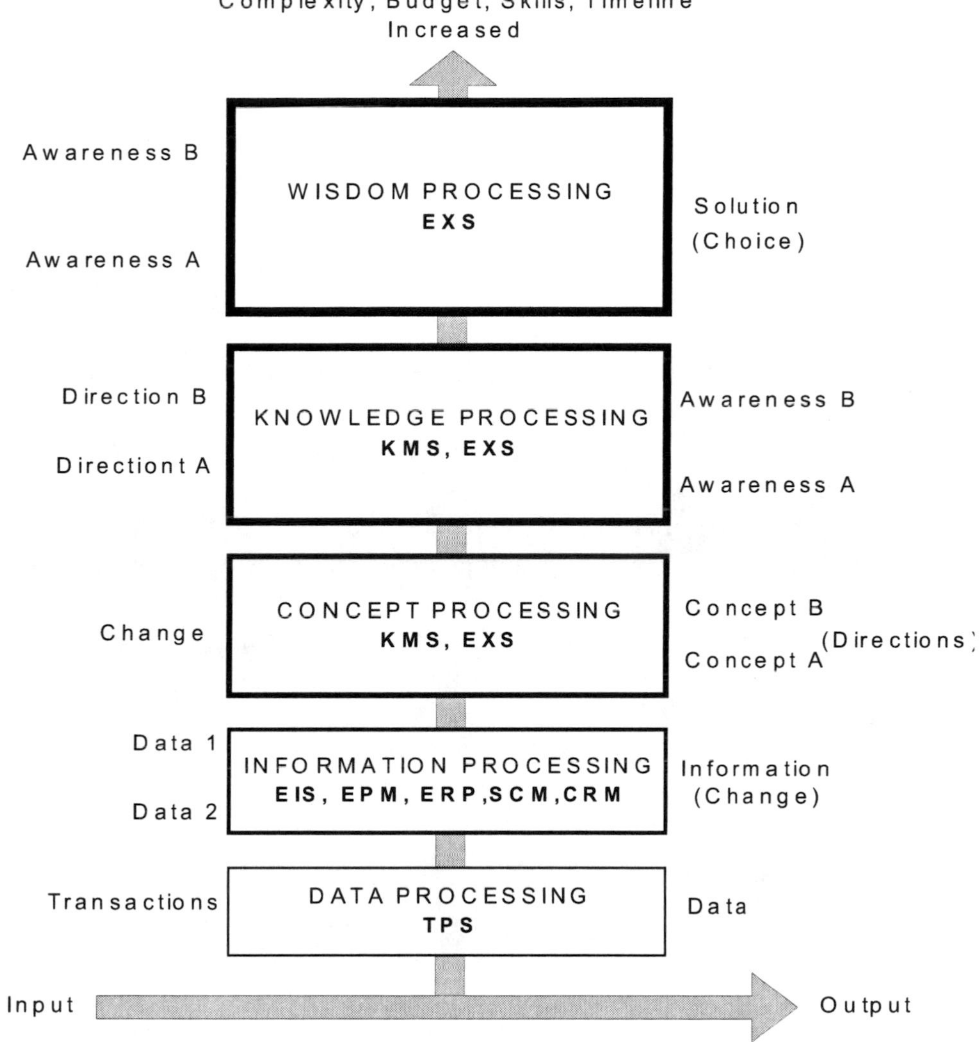

action is expressed. The paradigm of wisdom processing is choice, which can be implemented through Expert Systems.

The knowledge of semantics processing paradigms allowed for the design of correct information systems. We should be "aware" of the requirements from the data processing system. Its purpose is to process transactions and to measure them, nothing more. However, information processing should lead to more advanced systems, such as the Enterprise Performance Management System which can identify the state of the organization (normal, conflict, crisis, success, failure) through the analysis of change ("planned" vs. "actual"). From this analysis, the EPM will create some sort of direction for future courses of action. The output from information processing may pass through the phase of knowledge processing to filter solutions that are correct. Such devices as Data Mining from KMS or Expert Systems (EXS) can be used to create or improve awareness of the decision-maker. At the next level, one can use an Expert System that possesses preprogrammed volition when making a decision. This system provides a way for the choice to be made by the expert in a given field of authority.

It is necessary to notice that the next level of semantic processing requires more complex system architecture, bigger budget, higher skills of developers, and longer time for the system development.

The main purpose of such information systems is to minimize effects of asymmetric information in decision-making. The next section provides the examples of such situations.

ASYMMETRIC INFORMATION

Three Americans won the Nobel Prize for economics in 2001 for research into how the control of information influences everything from used car sales to the boom in its very own motion sensitive-alerts you when high-tech stocks during the 1900's. George A. Akerlof of the University of California at Berkley, A. Michael Spence of Stanford University, and Joseph E. Stiglitz of Columbia University shared the award.

The laureates laid the foundation in the 1970's for a general theory about how players with differing amounts of information affect a wide range of markets. Research into "asymmetric information" gave economists a way to measure the risk, for example, faced by a lender who lacks information about a borrower's creditworthiness.

This sphere of economics deals with situations where agents on one side of the market know something that agents on the other side do not: for example, a seller of a second-hand car may have knowledge of its qualities unknown to a potential buyer. Such situations are very different from those dealt with in the more conventional analysis which assumes that the buyers and sellers have the same information about goods being sold.

It also explored how people with inside knowledge of a high-technology company's financial prospects gain an edge over other investors, while people who don't fully understand a company's finances may invest unwisely. The theory helps economists explain why the recent bubble (1998-2000) in high-technology stocks burst.

Situations of asymmetric information seem to be widely prevalent in the real world, so that moving beyond the conventional analysis yields fascinating and handsome awards.

A good introduction to the idea of asymmetric information is provided by the well-known story of Solomon's wisdom (Hillier, 1997). In this story, King Solomon, in a dream, has his wish for "an understanding heart to judge the people, that I may discern between good and bad" granted by God. Solomon's wisdom is illustrated by a story concerning two women who appear before him seeking judgment.

Two women have a young baby with them and each claims to be its mother. Each woman claims that although the other woman also gave birth to a baby it died in the night, and that the other woman is the mother of the dead child and not of the living one. Solomon responds to the women's contradictory claims by instructing a servant to bring a sword and divide the child in half.

On hearing Solomon's command, the true mother of the child responds by saying she is not the mother of the child and that it should be given to the other woman. The other woman says that the child indeed should be divided in two. Solomon is then able to tell who is the real mother and instructs that the child should be not killed but given to the true mother, who was prepared to give it away rather than see it die.

This story illustrates a number of points which explain the idea of asymmetric information. First, there is a clear asymmetry of information: the women knew whose baby if the child is, but Solomon does not. Second, there is a conflict of objectives; Solomon would like to have the information that is available to the women in order to better achieve his goals. Third, the true mother would like to transmit the information but cannot easily do so because of the actions of the other woman, who also lays claim to the child. Finally,

Solomon devises a contract to offer the women, which causes them to reveal him.

This case illustrates the points that are characteristic of many market situations. For example, an insurance company offering accident insurance to car drivers, some of whom are naturally more cautious and less accident-prone than others. The insurance company is like Solomon because it cannot tell who a safe driver is and who is a risky one, but it would like to be able to do so in order to charge higher premiums to riskier drivers. The drivers are like the women, since both safe and risky drivers will claim to be safe to try to obtain cheaper insurance. Thus the insurance company, like Solomon, has to try to devise a contract to offer the drivers which will cause them to reveal themselves truthfully. Unlike Solomon, the insurance company is unlikely to be able to solve its problem perfectly. In practice, the presence of the risky drivers prevents the safer ones from getting as good an insurance deal as they would otherwise be offered.

The application of information role in macroeconomics begins at the level of the theory of games and its application to the calculations of the price equilibrium by John Nash, who, however, applied symmetric information to all bidders' demand schedules. In a Nash equilibrium all players take the strategies of all the other players as given and learn in the process from the moves of other players. Nash's grounding in economics had taught him that people normally operate so they reach a position of mutual benefits, and he developed systems for understanding these non-zero-sum situations. He also pointed to the differences that exist between situations where competitors sit together and cooperate to produce an outcome and those where there is no cooperation. To sort it out he introduced the concept of an equilibrium point – a collection of the various players' strategies where no individual player can improve his or her outcome by changing strategy. Nash relied on the standard asset pricing theory that all market participants possess the same information. Although, the equilibrium that results under asymmetric information is quite different from one that would prevail under full information.

However, in reality different traders hold different information. Some traders might know more than others about the same event or they might hold information related to different events. Even if all traders hear the same news in the form of a public announcement they still might interpret it differently. Therefore, financial markets cannot be well understood unless one also examines the asymmetries in the information dispersion and assimilation process (Brunnermeiere, 2001). Exploration of the consequences of imperfect information in economic decision-making is now a standard consideration of economic theorists.

Taking down macroeconomic decisional situations to the microeconomic level (e.g., at the level of traders) of asymmetric information requires two significant departures from conventional analysis. One departure involves recognizing and modeling the various types of asymmetry, and the second involves seeing how the asymmetry affects the nature of the contract entered into by the participants in the market (Hillier, 1997).

At the microeconomic level the analysis of information impact on decision-making took place in the last 30 years in management science under the form of a value of perfect information under certainty and uncertainty. In business communication there is an approach to evaluate media-communicated information richness, which can be interpreted as a value of additional information in perfect decision-making. Both approaches provided the foundation for the development of all sorts of management information systems, including decision-support systems and recently, data mining systems penetrating data warehouses.

The impact of the Information Wave on the examination of economic theories is not unique. One can observe the similar impact upon the theory of physics as well. Since 100 years ago when Albert Einstein developed its famous theory, the role of information was neglected, not felt at all. Even in the further developments in the theory of the atom we do not see any informational considerations. Meanwhile, the whole universe is dynamic and driven by info-communication processes, either observational or hidden.

Summing up, when asymmetric information is taken into account, the economic/business situation becomes an important determinant in decision-making. Gathering information to minimize the effects of asymmetric information is usually costly and can be more effective along with the development of more sophisticated information systems.

The understanding of the role of asymmetric information may lead to further research on how psychological, anthropological, and sociological factors may impact economic/business decision-making. A tool which may help in these undertakings is information technology and its numerous applications.

APPLICATION LAYER MODEL

The Application Layer (AL) is the key component of the whole Enterprise Information Infrastructure (EII). Its architecture evolves from routines (1960's) to applications (1970's), to information systems (1980's), to enterprise-wide system packages such as ERP, SCM, and CRM (1990's). In general, one can recognize three major components of AL:

- Enterprise Computing (EC):
  - Business Information Systems (BIS),
  - Product/Service Information Systems (PIS),
  - Operation Information Systems (OIS),
  - Management Information Systems (MIS),
  - Inter-Organizational Systems (IOS),
  - E-Business applications,

- End-User Computing (EUC).

- Inter-organizational Computing (IOC) as an exit to B2B, B2C and EII to NII, GII, LII links through computer networks.

These systems are supported by info-communication systems from the Communication Layer:

- Info-Communication Systems:
  - E-mail,
  - Internet, Intranet, Extranet,
  - Groupware,
  - Work Flow System,
  - E-Conferencing,
  - Enterprise Information Portal,
  - Information Services.

The AL interacts with other EII layers such as the Communication Layer and the Computing Layer. This last layer makes AL more dynamic by the interaction with the Computer Networks Layer. All the systems and interacting layers are depicted in Figure 4-3.

From the formal point of view one can classify a set of Business Information Systems (BIS) as follows:

Figure 4-3: The Generic System Architecture of Application Layer (CAA–Computer-Aided Advertising, CAP–Computer-Aided Publishing, DBMS–Data Base Management System, DMS–Document Management System, RMS–Records Management System, WFS–Work Flow System) (The Targowski Model)

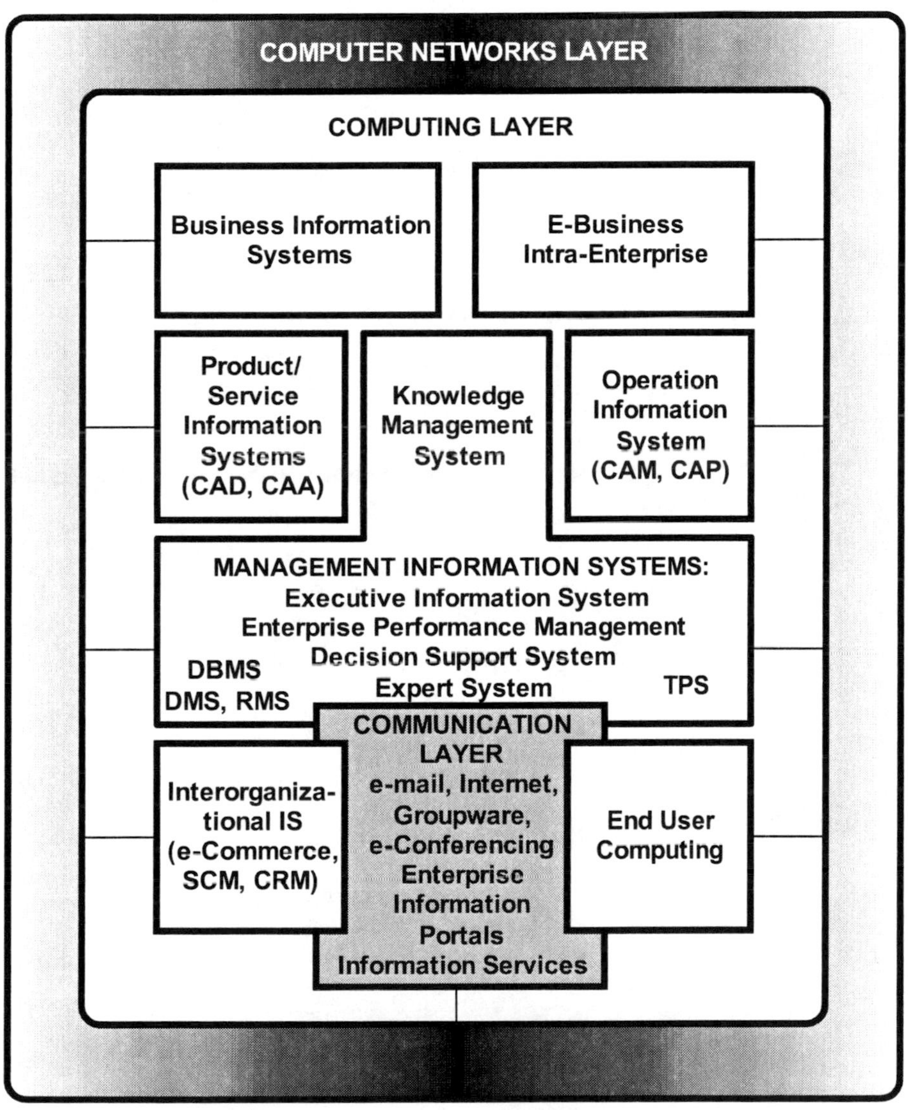

- Marketing Information System,
- Financial Information System,
- Accounting Financial System,
- Human Resources Information System,
- Legal Information System,
- Administration Information System,
- Other.

It is interesting to notice that the Marketing Information System evolves into CRM-Customer Relationship Management system, and Financial IS and Accounting IS evolves into one integrated IS as it takes place in PeopleSoft's implementation.

A set of Product/Services Information Systems (PIS) can be classified into the following categories:

- Computer Aided Engineering (CAE),
- Computer Aided Editing (CAED),
- Computer Aided Drafting (CAD),
- Computer Aided Advertising (CAA),
- Computer Aided Drafting and Design (CADD),
- Computer Aided Planning (CAPP),
- Computer Aided Software Engineering (CASE),
- Geographic Information System (GIS)
- Other.

These systems are implemented as stand-alone workstations with customized software for a given engineering job. Also, CADD systems are very often integrated with Computer Aided Manufacturing Systems (CAM) as CADCAM systems in a so-called Computer Integrated Manufacturing system (described later).

Operation Information Systems (OIS) can be recognized as a set of the following categories:

- Process Control System,
- Computer Aided Manufacturing (CAM),
- Computer Aided Publishing, and other,
- Data Collection System,
- Quality Control System,
- Automated Material Handling System,
- Automated Storage and Retrieval System,
- Production/Service Operations Planning System,
- MRP I (Material Planning Requirements) System,
- MRP II (Manufacturing Resources Planning) System,
- Inventory Control System,
- Shop-Floor Control System,
- Service Management,
- Plant/Organization Maintenance System,
- Project Management System,
- Other.

Management Information Systems (MIS) are described in this chapter later. Inter-organizational Systems (IOS) evolve into e-commerce and the so-called B2B (Business-To-Business), B2C (Business-To-Consumer), and C2C (Consumer-To-Consumer systems) described in Chapter 6. E-Business applications are of a different substance, and very often are limited to e-commerce applications. In a broader sense, they are singular business routines implemented in Web technology and they are described in Chapter 6.

A combination of BIS, PIS, OIS, MIS, IOS, and e-Business applications evolves into a set of integrated applications called ERP (Enterprise Resource Planning); associated with them are more independent combinations of BIS and OIS such as SCM (Supply Chain Management) and CRM (Customer Relations Management). Each of these combinations (varied from vendor to vendor) is modeled in the following sections.

Data Management Systems evolved from file management systems into Database Management Systems (DBMS) that in the 1980's became relational databases, composed of multiple, related tables (RDBMS). A typical DBMS is composed of three subsystems:

- Data Description Language (DDL) for defining and loading data,
- Data Manipulation Language (DML) for querying data, recently known as SQL (Sequential Query Language), which became the standard,
- Data Dictionary (DD), which describes properties of data elements.

Whatever the database technology, there are certain business-critical requirements that apply to applications, irrespective of the complexity of their information structures:

- An acceptable total cost of ownership, with simple administration,
- 24x7 availability of service,
- A consistent view of current data to all users, wherever they are and whatever their mode of access is,
- Reliable access for all current users,
- Strong security.

Among the most popular RDBMS are IBM DB2, Oracle, MS SQL, and Informix.

Transaction Processing Systems (TPS) are the simplest of all applications; however, they are also the most important since they feed data to all other applications, mostly through DBMS.

ERP SYSTEMS – *BACK-OFFICE AUTOMATION*

The ERP system emerged from the gradual integration of several enterprise-wide applications. At the first stage of integration in the 1970-80's the MRP I (Material Requirements Planning) system was formed from such applications as BOMP (Bill of Material Processor), Net Requirements Planning, and Gross Requirements Planning. At the next stage of integration in the 1980's the MRP II (Manufacturing Resources Planning) system was created as a result of integrating such applications as Capacity Requirements Planning (CRP), Production Planning, Subcontracting Planning, and others.

In the 1990's all of the above systems were integrated into the ERP system, which also incorporated other applications of the back-office, such as Financials, Human Resources, Project Management, Plant Maintenance, and others. Typically, an ERP system is a software package composed of several applications supporting such business functions as sales, productions, finance, human resources, and others, providing for the horizontal integration of data across an organization's business processes that can be customized with specific design-programming tools of the 4th generation (Computer Aided Software Engineering).

Core ERP Applications include:

- Financials – accounting, financial processes, budgeting, assets management,
- Human Resources – payroll, benefits, compensation, performance assessment and enterprise total employee information, assuming compliance with requirements of multiple jurisdictions and tax authorities in the Global Economy,

- Manufacturing (or Operations[2]) – production/operations planning and execution, including a Bill Of material processor (BOMP), shop floor management, and quality control,

- Project Management – planning of project schedules, costs, contracts, and resources according to a budget.

Extended ERP Applications include:

- Product Life-cycle Management (PLM) – supports product planning and design and product information sharing with suppliers to optimize development of products,

- E-Procurement – helps buyers to acquire goods via online catalogues, auctions, and requests for quotes (RFQ),

- E-Logistics – supervises the transportation and storage of goods within the SCM,

- Customer Relations Management (CRM),

- Supply Chain Management (SCM),

- Business Intelligence – collects information from external and internal sources to analyze them for managers in their decision-making,

- Other.

ERP is the concept of developing applications that are fully integrated and can be used to automate many of the business routines of running a company. The advantage of ERP is the ability to integrate the data across a company. ERP systems, for example, allow manufacturing companies to adjust production and inventory automatically to meet fluctuating sales.

The ERP system reflects a generic solution based on a series of best practices in a given industry. It is contrary to the proprietary systems developed according to the specific requirements of a given organization. This approach imposes its own strategy and logic of applications, which forces changes in the way of doing business by a given company. If this is not the case, very often the ERP system's implementation can be a failure. For example, FoxMeyer

Drugs, a $5 billion pharmaceutical wholesaler, filed for bankruptcy protection due to an incorrect implementation of the ERP system. Also, FoxMeyer filed a lawsuit against SAP's U.S. subsidiary and its implementation partner, Accenture Consulting, for $500 million each for allegedly providing misleading assurances about the software's potential. On the other hand, the ERP vendor insists that the user did not introduce changes in business practices that are required by the SAP R/3 software.

Among top ERP vendors are SAP, PeopleSoft, Baan, Oracle, J.D. Edwards, and others.

ERP - SAP R/3 Application Software Model

The most popular ERP software package is one developed by the German firm SAP (*Systeme Anwendungen und Programme in Der Datenverarbeitung*) as a SAP R/3 version (1992), which in fact is the enhanced version of IBM COPICS (Communication-Oriented Production Information Control System). This system was developed from a business point of view and became the important factor in reengineering legacy information systems in the 1990's. Figure 4-4 illustrates a concept of SAP R/3.

The R/3 software is a large-scale system which has about 500 million lines of code, 80,000 database tables, and 10,000 icons. It is a result of 30 years developmental effort by 1,000+ specialists, and it standardized 800 main business processes and converted them into an enterprise integrated information system.

The R/3 software system is composed of five main components:

1. SAP business standard applications, developed by the SAP corporation and configured for a given enterprise-user,

2. SAP business applications developed for a given, specific user, either by the SAP consultants or by third party integrators, or by the user itself,

3. mySAP.com Workplace is an enterprise portal which provides a single point of access via Web browser to all internal and external information via the Internet to accomplish your daily tasks, thereby delivering a complete e-business environment,

4. SAP Basis provides kernel functions that are used by application modules, and which plays a role of a middleware software. It has the role of

Figure 4-4: The General Architecture of R/3 Software System (The Targowski Model)

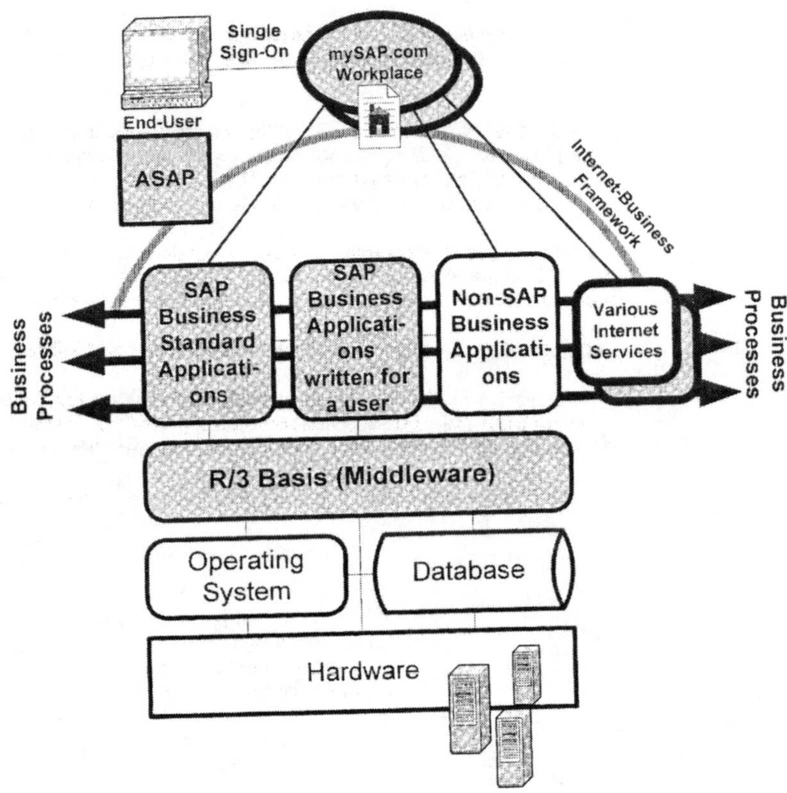

an abstraction layer and thus hides the application modules from all details of underlying operating system, database, and window system,

5. ASAP-AcceleratedSAP, which is a rapid implementation solution designed to streamline and standardize the implementation process to achieve mission critical business functionality as soon as possible (ASAP). ASAP's methodology is called the Roadmap, which supports the R/3 software system's implementation through five phases of:
   - **Phase 1: Project Preparation** (objectives, senior level management support, strategy for change, qualified team),
   - **Phase 2: Business Blueprint** (analysis of required business processes and associated information to include into standard and customized SAP applications),

- **Phase 3: Realization** (standard applications configuration, testing, and tuning)
- **Phase 4: Final Preparation** (final system testing and end-user training)
- **Phase 5: Go Live and Continuous Change**

mySAP.com Workplace allows you access to both SAP and third-party applications and Internet services. Its Cockpit provides MiniApps (intuitive, easy-to-use Web applications or Web documents), which include key reports from the SAP Business Information Warehouse, e-mail, and document alerts, as well as the following services:

- Small previews of full transactions (for example, system monitoring tools, lists of documents that are currently on hold, or lists of customers with overdue accounts),
- Commonly used functions that require a small amount of input where the user does not need to launch an entire application,
- Shared folders,
- Ad hoc queries,
- Wizards and navigation accelerators,
- Interfaces to third-party applications.

In the same way, the following mySAP.com components are integrated in the Workplace:

- Employee Self-Service (ESS) enables employees to be actively involved in human resources business processes. Employees can display, create and maintain certain types of data, anytime, anywhere, with an easy-to-use Web browser,
- Business-to-Business Procurement (BBP), e-commerce business process that enables employees to purchase goods and services directly from the provider,

- Advanced Planner & Optimizer (APO), a software solution for dynamic supply chain management; that is, active processing of the entire logistic chain (supply chain) from the vendor to the customer,

- Customer Relationship Management (CRM), umbrella term covering all aspects of business relationships with customers with the aim of fostering long-term customer loyalty,

- Strategic Enterprise Management (SEM), a group of tools and processes enabling managers to introduce company-wide value-oriented management procedures. It helps managers to translate their vision into real world actions. SEM links a strategy with operative activities and value drivers and thus turns the strategy into everyday business for every employee,

- Knowledge Warehouse (KW), integrated environment for creating, translating, presenting, distributing, and administering multimedia content through the application of a comprehensive range of tools and functions,

- Business Information Warehouse (BW), enables the evaluation of data from both SAP and non-SAP applications, often called data mining.

The R/3 Basis, as a software middleware, is composed of the following components:

- GUI – Graphic User Interfaces provided for each application,

- ABAP/4 Development Workbench to change standard applications or develop new applications that have the same properties as SAP's standard business applications,

- Database interface, where a database can be one of the commercial databases, such as Oracle, IBM DB 2, Microsoft SQL, Informix, and so forth,

- Workflow system, a support tool that can be used to optimize the execution of activities. Work steps carried out consecutively can be automated to coordinate a flow of information. Workflows bring the *right* work in the *right* order at the *right* time to the *right* people working in different departments/divisions,

- Mail system among all users and administrators,

Figure 4-5: The Architecture of ERP SAP R/3 Systems Complex (The Targowski Model)

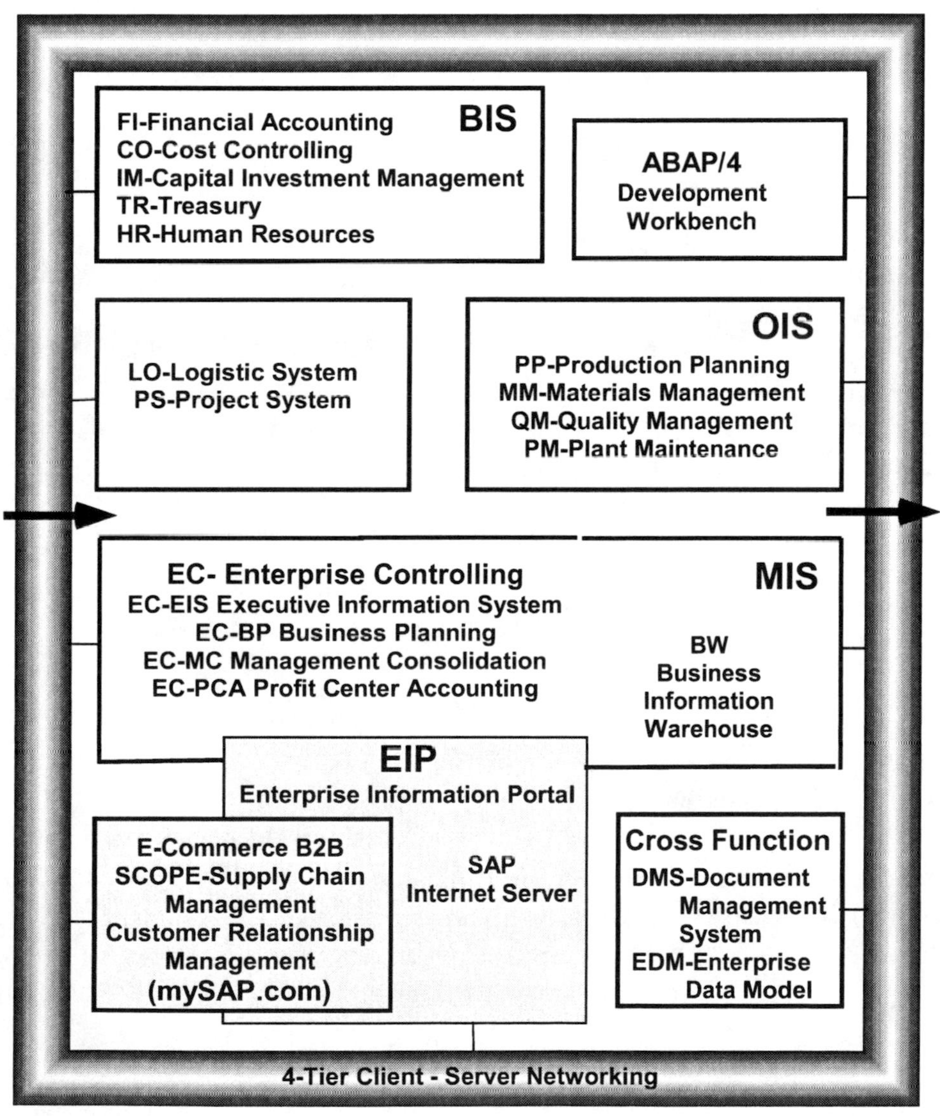

- Desktop's user presentation integration with appropriate business applications and system administration,
- Background processing to support concurrent processing of several tasks of the R/3 software system,
- Spool system to speed up a flow of data, procedures, and command among involved software components,
- System administration tools,
- Communication interfaces to external systems,
- Other.

The R/3 software system can work under main commercial operating systems such as UNIX (Sun Microsystems only), Windows NT+, IBM AS/400, and others.

The SAP R/3 system package is composed of about 25 modules (depending on how they are grouped) which are illustrated in Figure 4-5. When customized changes are introduced to one module of the package, other related data elements and modules are automatically updated.

MIS-MANAGEMENT INFORMATION SYSTEMS

In the past, Management Information Systems reflected all static systems developed for business information processing, characterized by their high-volume of transactions and lengthy reports, programmed in COBOL (user unfriendly language). These types of "systems" nowadays are called legacy systems. However, according to our AL generic model in Figure 4-3, MIS reflect systems that manage the whole enterprise, as is illustrated in Figure 4-6.

The system components of the MIS federation have the following purposes:

- GUI – Graphic User Interface – an on-screen menu which is easy to navigate through the enter key and arrow keys.

Figure 4-6: The Generic Architecture of Management Information Systems (The Targowski Model)

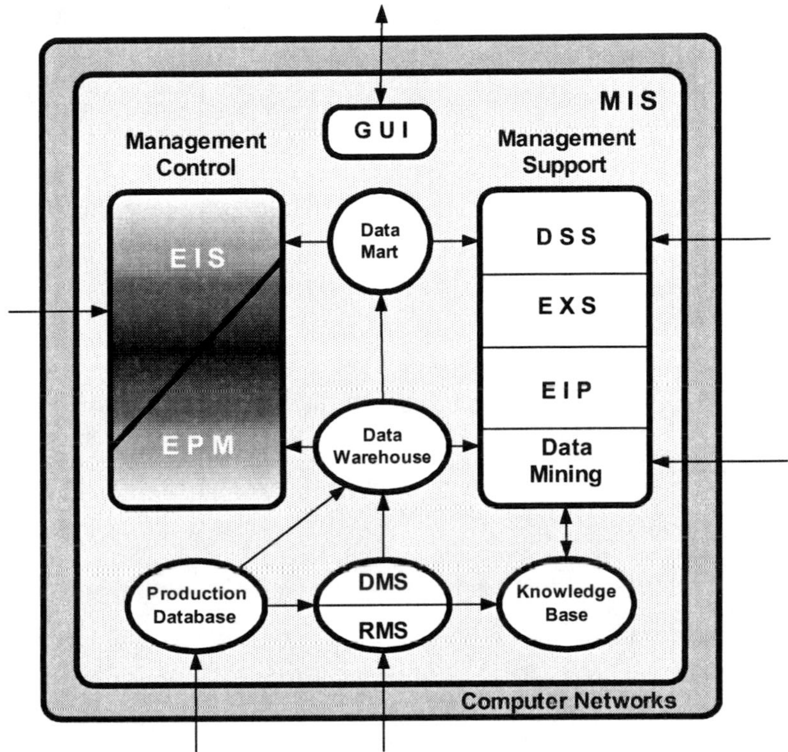

- EIS – Executive Information System – a system which is easy to use, containing a summary of information (mostly in a graphic manner) about the performance of the enterprise or its departments' key indicators.

- EPM – Enterprise Performance Management System – a system which contains information about the performance of the enterprise or its departments' key indicators in a scope of plan-actual.

- DSS – Decision Support System – a system which is based on mathematical models such as spreadsheets, linear programming, etc., is applied, for example, to recalculate a budget or optimize a production or transportation plan.

- EXS – Expert System – a system which is based on artificial intelligence is applied in the decision-making automation when decisions are well structured, ill-structured, or unstructured.

- EIP – Enterprise Information Portal, later described in this chapter.

- Data Mining – software which analyzes the content of Data Warehouse in order to find behavioral patterns of customers (and other stakeholders) and units.

- Production Database – a database software which stores the enterprise's unredundant data elements created from transactions or other actions. This database is applied in processing the majority of the enterprise applications, such as payroll, accounting, sales, production planning, stock control, and so forth.

- Data Warehouse – a database which is a copy of the most applied data elements in cross-functional systems, such as EIS, EPM, DSS, EXS, and so forth.

- Knowledge Base – a database which stores business rules and behavioral patterns (knowledge management) defined by the data mining software.

- Data Mart – a database which stores data, information, and knowledge for a given user or a function/activity to discover patterns and trends for specific issues.

- DMS – Data Management System manages the document life cycle by supporting:
  - Document creation, applying templates and style sheets,
  - Document modification and tracking its versions,
  - Document security through access restrictions,
  - Document approval by different officers via WFS,
  - Document distribution/publishing via e-mail, on a Website or on a paper,
  - Document archiving on optical disks,

- RMS – Records Management System manages multi-media-based images (e.g., images of Kellogg's cereal boxes, movies) and directories[3].

Data Warehouse, Data Marts, Knowledge Base, and Data Mining are components of a Knowledge Management System which is described in this chapter later.

EIS-Executive Information System

The objective of this system is to gather, analyze, and integrate internal (corporate) and external (public) data into dynamic profiles of key corporate indicators for senior managers. Depending on the nature of the organization's business, such indicators may relate to the status of high-priority programs, health of the economy, inventory and cash levels, performance of financial markets, relevant efforts of competitors, utilization of manpower, legislative events, and so forth. The indicators are displayed as text, tables, graphics, or time series, and optional access is provided to more detailed data/information. The data/information comes not only from the organization's internal sources but from external sources too. By simply pointing and clicking on various "Who, What, When, and Why" buttons, the user can select and investigate such critical areas as workers' utilization, revenue analysis, census comparisons, cash flows, current bookings levels, vendor performance, inventory valuation, past due work orders, accounts receivable and accounts payable aging, and much more.

In military organizations, the approximate equivalent of EIS is the Command-Control System (CCS). EIS makes use of computational aids for data classification, modeling, optimization, and simulation. These capabilities are characteristic of Decision Support Systems (DSS) and Expert Systems (EXS). The latter are applied for ill-structured and unstructured decisions, supported by artificial intelligence (including neural computers and networks) to enhance EIS with adaptive and self-organizing abilities by means of learning from the executives' changing information needs and patterns of decision-making in practice.

In the 2000's the SAP software was expanded by Strategic Enterprise Management (SEM) system[4], which is according to the enterprise model a classic EIS.

The SAP SEP is a mySAP.com application component that supports completely strategic enterprise management processes in an organization on various levels. It is comprised of the five following components:

- Business Information Collection (BIC) automates the sourcing of unstructured business information from the Web,
- Business Planning and Simulation (BPS) links strategic planning and simulation with cross-functional enterprise planning, for example applying scorecards,

Figure 4-7: Strategic Enterprise Management (SAP SEP)

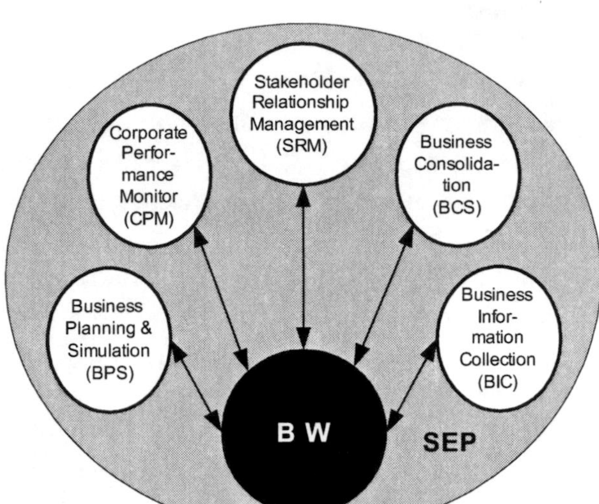

- Business Consolidation (BCS) consolidates financial and management components,
- Corporate Performance Monitor (CPM) communicates and monitors performance and strategy through Balanced Scorecard, Management Cockpit, and Value Driven Trees,
- Stakeholders Relationship Management (SRM) integrates the most important stakeholders into your enterprise management process.

SEM applications operate on a common OLAP database composed of Business Warehouse (BW) and InfoCubes, as it is illustrated in Figure 4-7.

EPM-Enterprise Performance Management System

The system evolves as an internal system which applies such techniques as Balanced Scorecard, Value-based Management, Critical Success Factors, and Key Performance Indicators. But measurement alone is not enough.

Cross-organization research (www.lotus.com) indicates that:

- 60% of companies are not able to articulate and communicate their strategy effectively throughout their organization,
- Only 10% are able to deliver on their strategy,
- 90% believe that a clear, action-oriented understanding of their strategy will significantly influence their success.

The research shows that organizations need a way to formalize, accumulate, and leverage their knowledge about performance and how to manage performance. In today's fast-changing, networked enterprises, a configurable intranet or groupware solution such as EPM system is essential.

The ADBS – EPM system, designed by Arthur Andersen, applies the Show Business Toolset available from Show Business and Lotus Development. The ADBS' content is organized in four perspectives: Customer, Financial, Internal Business Process, and Learning and Growth, according to thc Balanced Scorecard concept (Kaplan and Norton, 1996) to provide a strategic and balanced view for decision-making. This is a tool to mobilize the workforce to fulfill the company's mission and strategy. Through these four dimensions executives and workers can align individual, organizational, and cross-departmental initiatives and identify entirely new processes for meeting customer and shareholders' objectives.

The ADBS-EPM system includes:

- A customized set of indicators to the user's needs,
- Tracking of corrcctivc actions to complction,
- Quick overview of measures, with traffic-lighting to show trouble spots,
- Easy-to-use report catalog, containing all relevant reports in cross-sections of the past, present, and future,
- Easy to navigate paths through the report databases, using the Notes or intranet infrastructure,

- Workflow for knowledge requests,
- Clear action reports, which are updated immediately.

The example of the EPM system based on the Balanced Scorecard is illustrated in Figure 4-8.

The architecture of the EPM system is open, scaleable, and ultimately an ideal platform on which it is possible to build business intelligence systems. For example, PeopleSoft Enterprise Warehouse draws from the vendor's applications as well as from other ERP applications and legacy systems to stage, store, and make information available for decision-making and analysis.

To evaluate an enterprise's performance one must compare key indicators with targets to discover at what state of affairs there is a managed enterprise or its unit. The present solutions of EPM systems compare a target with its actual value and draw conclusions about the change, either negative or positive. However, the computer can do more if we recognize the following states of affairs:

- The normal state – measure coming from *data processing,*
- The conflict state – change coming from *information processing,*
- The crisis state – judgment coming from *concept processing,*
- The success state – judgment coming from *concept processing,*
- The failure state – judgment coming from *concept processing.*

Compare the outcomes with the Semantic Ladder from the beginning of this chapter.

The standard value for each state is arbitrarily set by the user-decision maker, in reference to the enterprise's plans, performance practice, and the perception of market conditions.

Let's apply this concept for company XYZ which produces cereal and whose packaging unit's performance is evaluated. The manager of this unit suggested that computers have the most impact in the packaging area, at least in the aspect of control, because standards are more easily set and measured. He claimed that the actual production of the cereal is more an art than a science, thereby making it difficult to implement computer control. However, he

Figure 4-8: The Example of Enterprise Performance Management System as a Balanced Scorecard

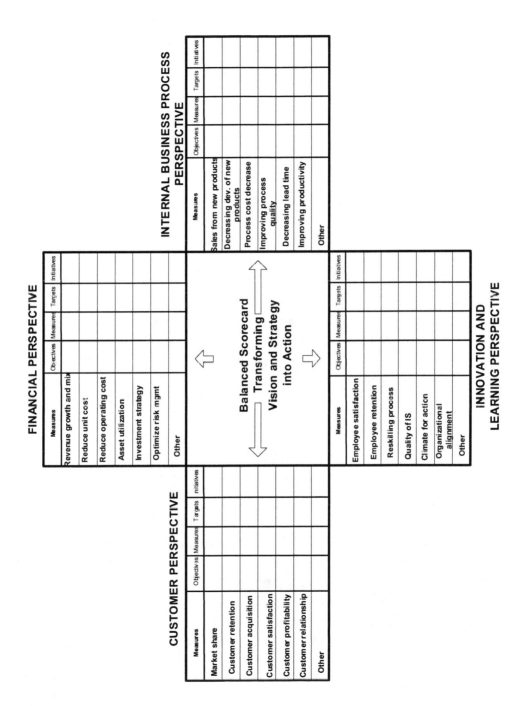

FINANCIAL PERSPECTIVE

Measures	Objectives	Measures	Targets	Initiatives
Revenue growth and mix				
Reduce unit cost				
Reduce operating cost				
Asset utilization				
Investment strategy				
Optimize risk mgmt				
Other				

INTERNAL BUSINESS PROCESS PERSPECTIVE

Measures	Objectives	Measures	Targets	Initiatives
Sales from new products				
Decreasing dev. of new products				
Process cost decrease				
Improving process quality				
Decreasing lead time				
Improving productivity				
Other				

Balanced Scorecard Transforming Vision and Strategy into Action

CUSTOMER PERSPECTIVE

Measures	Objectives	Measures	Targets	Initiatives
Market share				
Customer retention				
Customer acquisition				
Customer satisfaction				
Customer profitability				
Customer relationship				
Other				

INNOVATION AND LEARNING PERSPECTIVE

Measures	Objectives	Measures	Targets	Initiatives
Employee satisfaction				
Employee retention				
Reskilling process				
Quality of IS				
Climate for action				
Organizational alignment				
Other				

emphasized that packaging was a very important part of the production process because governmental regulations and customer satisfaction are both important as the company tries to make a profit.

Several key indicators are used in cereal plant performance monitoring and control. Three key indicators have been chosen that relate to the quality control of packaging and also to the quantity packaged. The indicators for a given product are as follow:

	Weight	Fullness	#Produced
a. Normal state	12 oz.	3 in.	2.5 K
	Lowest/ Highest	Lowest/ Highest	Lowest/ Highest
b. Conflict state	10/14	2.7/3.3	2.3/2.8
c. Crisis state	8/16	2.4/3.6	1.9/3.2
d. Failure state	6/8	2/4	1.25/3.85
e. Success state	11.85	2.9	2.48

The EPM system can display/print results in different colors, and furthermore, if each state of affairs is preprogrammed with ways of action, then a manager not only has a concept of the state of affairs but also knows what to do in the case of negative outcomes.

KMS-KNOWLEDGE MANAGEMENT SYSTEM

General Architecture

The desire to preserve knowledge is as old as our civilization. The practice of keeping records in archives was used in 4,000 B.C. in Syria, and later in 4th century B.C. a large library (*Bibliotheca Alexandrina*) was created in Alexandria in Egypt, which lasted almost 1000 years, and at its peak storaged about 700,000 handwritten works. Copies of these documents were distributed by this library throughout the world. The development of papyrus allowed us to record academic and administrative documents and it took almost 1400 years (between 5th century B.C. and 9th century A.D.) to develop a reliable technology. At the same time the alphabet was transformed from mnemonic into phonetic and it allowed for reading and writing as common skills around the 12th century A.D. The discovery of print in the middle of the 15th century pushed the development and dissemination of knowledge very fast. As a consequence, modern sciences were defined and the social analysis in the Age of Enlightenment (18th century) led to the American and French Revolutions that created democracy and modern capitalism, which triggered the Industrial Wave and eventually led to the Information Wave. The latter developed digital media (computers, their networks, and databases) for knowledge recording and dissemination.

From this short review of how knowledge supported the development of civilization one can find that knowledge has the same potential for the development of business if it is properly created and disseminated within the organization. Hence, knowledge potential is better understood by many business leaders who develop Knowledge Management Systems in their own organizations to achieve a competitive advantage in the marketplace.

A Knowledge Management System creates, captures, and shares knowledge from internal and external sources through an interactive computer application. By *knowledge* in the enterprise ecosystem we understand an intangible business resource that helps people to be better aware of problems and their solutions. Using the models developed by Saint-Onge (1995), Nonaka and Hirotaka (1995), Pollard (2000), and others, one can assume the following structure of knowledge in the enterprise ecosystem:

1. Tacit Knowledge (Human Capital) – skills, competencies, know-how, and contextual knowledge in people's heads;

2. Explicit Knowledge (Structural Capital) – the knowledge that is captured or codified in the company's knowledge-bases, tools, catalogues, directories, models, processes, and systems;

3. Customer Knowledge (Customer Capital) – the collective knowledge about and of the company's customers, their people, their needs and buying habits;

4. Innovated Knowledge (Innovation Capital) – the collective knowledge about as-yet undeveloped or unexplored markets, technologies, products, and operating procedures.

Knowledge creation is largely a result of converting Human Capital to Structural Capital, and afterwards knowledge is applied by Customer Capital and Innovation Capital which impact Financial Capital and Physical Capital, which later provide a feed-back to Human Capital. This cycle is illustrated in Figure 4-9.

Examples of where and how to invest in enterprise knowledge are provided by each type of knowledge:

- Human Capital – salaries for new expert hires, training programs, mentoring and retention programs, and profit sharing programs;

- Structural Capital – call center with customer history database, e-commerce systems, competitive analysis database, and accelerated solutions center;

- Customer Capital – customer satisfaction survey with follow-up visit blitz, multimedia marketing & branding program;

- Innovative Capital – New Product and Knowledge-embedded Product Incubator, Product & Service Life-Cycle value-add program, Value Exchange program, Pathfinder, and thought leadership program.

Figure 4-9: The Enterprise Capital's Cycle Management

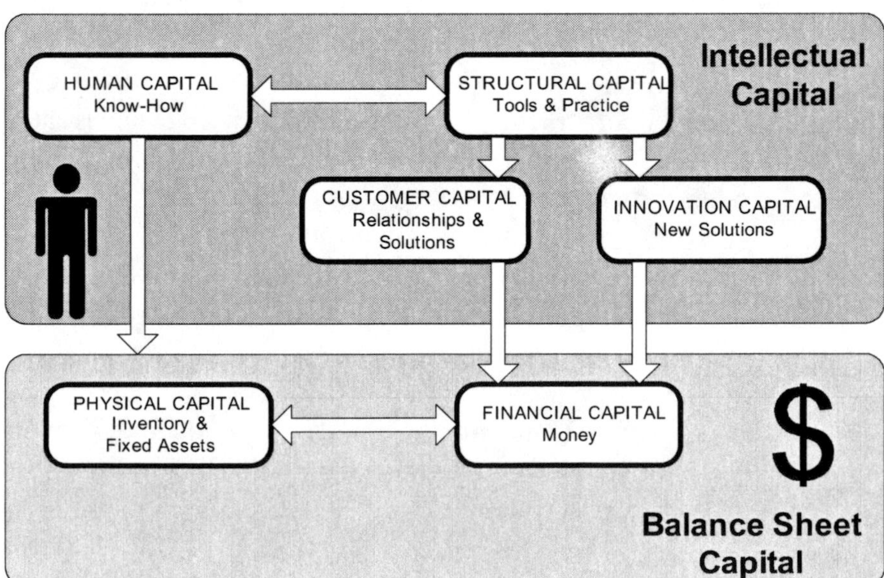

A Knowledge Management System, such as the one which is provided by Ernst & Young, is composed of a mix of:

- Catalogues and Directories – that allow users to browse sequentially through relevant knowledge (analogous to reading a book's Table of Contents);
- Search Engines – that allow users to find a list of knowledge objects that contain certain keywords or meet other specified search criteria (analogous to reading a book's index);
- Portals – that point users to a small, organized subset of knowledge from a much larger knowledge warehouse which can be browsed;
- Road Maps – that provide users with dynamic step-by-step instructions to learn or find pertinent knowledge about a particular subject;
- Profiling or Subscribing – using the Net to continuously catch knowledge that meets specific criteria.

The process by which the user navigates through knowledge warehouses often involves both "push" (into e-mail) and "pull" (via browsers) mechanisms. The results of the application of KMS are as follows:

- New behavioral patterns of stakeholders,
- New business rules,
- New success and failure practices,
- Other.

For example, Wal-Mart has discovered a certain customer behavioral pattern that after weekends men buy pampers and beer, apparently replenishing a home's inventory which was used during that time. Hence, the store puts both products on the same shelf to facilitate the sale.

Data Warehouse

A data warehouse (DWH) is an organized database for the purpose of supporting business and management Online Analytical Processing (OLAP). The architecture of data warehousing processes is illustrated in Figure 4-10. It identifies the data sources, management processes, analytical tools, and their applications. An average DWH package usually contains the following features:

- Data extraction from different sources and transformation (data integration for a given model and summarization) tools,
- Data loading from different sources in real-time,
- Design/developmental tools such as a visual data modeller,
- Database Management System,
- OLAP tools (data mining, statistical, optimization, spreadsheets, reports, vertical applications, etc.),
- Extensive use of wizards for configuring activities,
- Excellent Graphic User Interface,
- English query facility to retrieve query,
- Easy to use system management tools of maintaining DWH in a right status,
- Scalability – to Very Large Database (several terabytes) and Very Large Memory,
- Other.

Data warehousing in the business modern environment is an ongoing affair. Without proper administration the warehouse will soon fail or become redundant for all practical purposes. The overriding requirement in data warehouse management is the ability to maintain central control over metadata from

Figure 4-10: Data Warehousing Process

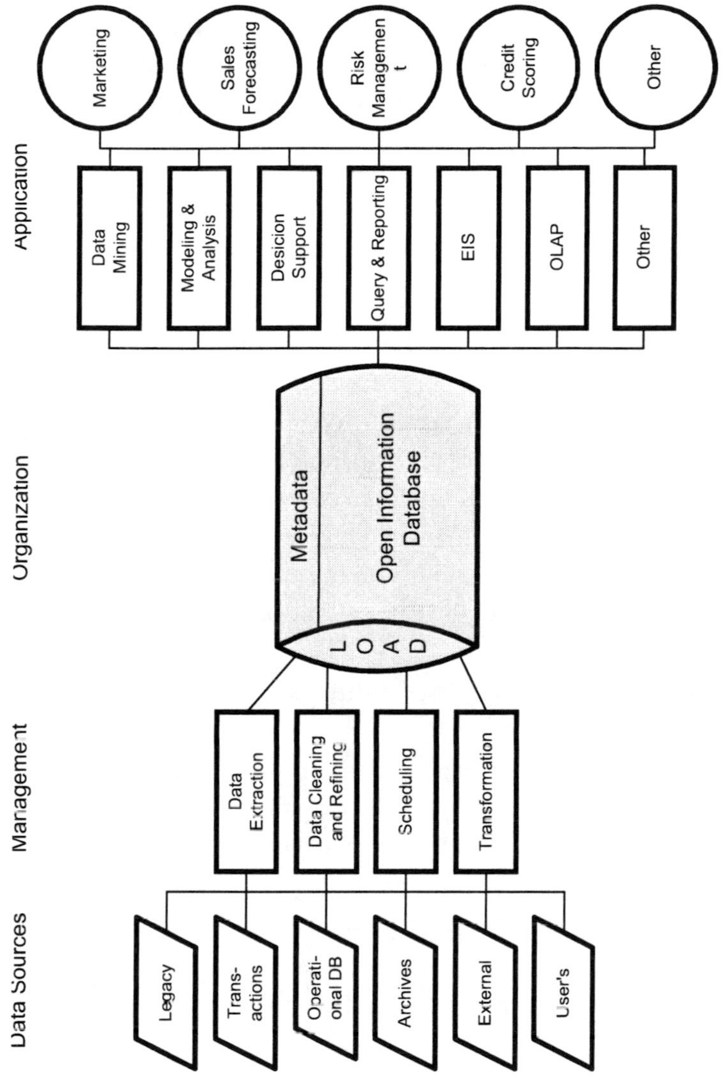

different sources. Data warehouses are non-dynamic when compared to the databases they exist in and are an important part of a dynamic environment.

Data Mart

A data mart is a subset of data for a specific enterprise function or activity; for example, measuring the impact of marketing promotion, or measuring and forecasting sales performance, or measuring the impact of new product introductions on company profits, or measuring and forecasting the performance of a new company division.

Data marts may store substantial data, even hundreds of gigabytes, but they contain less data than an enterprise's data warehouse. Because data marts are less expensive to implement than data warehouses, they therefore become a popular alternative to data warehouses.

Data Mining

Data mining is a computerized process of discovering patterns and trends of an enterprise's activities based on a large volume of stored data in data warehouses to solve a business problem. For example, data mining tries to determine the most significant factors involved in the question "Why do low sales take place in the Midwest, while high sales occur on the West Coast?" In traditional database querying we can find out the basic fact, for example, "What is the difference in sales in both mentioned regions?," but we won't find out "why" this difference happens. The data mining tool does not require special assumptions in computing, it just discovers hidden patterns and trends based on a large volume of stored (archived) data.

The typical business problem solving may focus on:

- Which of my customers are most profitable?
- Who is most likely to purchase this type of product?
- Which customers are most likely to leave?
- What other products is this customer likely to buy?
- What is the best channel to reach my customer base?
- Which customers may not pay their bills?
- How can I tell if a transaction is fraudulent?
- What will the demand be for a particular product?

According to Groth (1998) and others, data mining processing is composed of the following stages:

- Business understanding – defining a problem or a task to be solved,
- Data preparation – data cleaning (from synonyms such as "Pepsi," "Pepsi Cola," and "Cola"), correcting missing values, creating derivations (e.g., differences in sales in different periods), merging data from different sources into two-dimensional tables, etc.,
- Defining a study – defining a goal, .e.g., "To understand customers who are loyal versus those who are lost to competitors,"
- Building a model – gathering all indicators, (e.g., frequencies, weight, conjunctions, differentiations, etc.) for a given study that will be criteria for screening data sets,
- Understanding the model – analyzing correlations among indicators, developing a data distribution and a summary,
- Prediction – choosing the best possible outcomes based on historical data, e.g., "a customer was overdrawn," and understanding why a prediction was made in a discovered manner,
- Decision-making – based on discovered knowledge, the right decision should be made.

Data mining models are very extensive, since they can apply a lot of mathematical techniques which have been defined through the whole last century but could not be implemented since there was not enough data and warehousing technology. Among the most popular techniques one can mention: decision trees, genetic algorithms, neural networks, intelligent agent networks, statistics, and hybrid models.

Data mining can be illustrated in the following example. The Big Bank had a target of acquiring 200,000 new accounts, a number that would require mailing offers to 10 million prospects using a 2% return rate, an expected rate for direct mail. Instead, The Big Bank used the data mining technique to mail to a "refined" subset of all prospects yielding a response rate of 12%. Instead of mailing to the 10 million prospects, discovered patterns of customers' behavior allowed the bank to send mail only to 2 million, which generated required new accounts at a five times smaller cost. In addition to reducing cost, the average profitability of an acquired customer was 3 times higher than usual because data mining had targeted the customers whose needs best matched The Big Bank's services.

Some examples of data mining applications in business are as follows (Dan Pratte – www.techrepublic.com):

- Revenues and profitability:
  - Identify the products, services, and channels driving a company's revenue and profit,
  - Rank customers and customer locations by profitability,
  - Automatically alert when critical costs, such as non-billable overtime rates, fall out of control,
  - Know when a company's sales reps/managers are on target and when it is necessary to intervene in time to make a difference.

- Customer relationship management:
  - Identify low-value customers and try to improve their value or take them out of a company's business,
  - Spot customer relationship problems early by monitoring leading satisfaction indicators, such as product or service quality.

- Marketing and sales:
  - Target high-volume customers in order to lower my marketing risk,
  - Rank the success of product promotions to know what is effective by product and market segment,
  - Know what is in a company's pipeline.

Data mining provides a way of unlocking the value hidden within collected data. This technique is an example of "How to informate?" rather than "How to automate information processing?" and achieve an added value from data assets.

A role of data mining in the data warehouse evolution can be perceived in the following stages:

1. Reporting – WHAT happened at the strategic level? Answered through integrated different sources of information within one data warehouse and with pre-defined queries;

2. Analyzing – WHY did it happen at the strategic level? Answered with increased ad hoc queries (questions are unknown in advance) and through human discovery (query, OLAP tools, SQL);

3. Predicting – WHAT will happen at the strategic level? Solved with analytical modeling through machine-assisted discovery (statistics a la SAS, machine learning, data visualization and processing of hundreds of complex metrics for hundreds of thousands (or more) of observations);

4. Operationalizing – What IS happening at the tactical level? Solved with continuous updating and time sensitive queries. It typically means providing access to information for immediate decision-making in a field. For example: inventory management with just-in-time replenishment or scheduling and routing for package delivery. To make useful decisions, information must be extremely fresh and up-to-date and query response time must be very fast.

5. Active warehousing – What do I WANT to happen? Solved with event-based triggering of patterns and rules. For example, the updating of prices on shelf labels with traditional Mylar labels may be replaced by digital labels controlled by the computer from a remote location without any manual labor. A data warehouse may serve as sophisticated price management to control mark-down strategies in a labor free environment; otherwise it is prohibited by high costs (Brobst and Rarey, 2001).

Analytical solutions of typical business problems are provided in Table 4-1.

Table 4-1: Typical Data Mining Business Problems and Analytical Solutions

Business Problem	Data Mining Analytical Model
Segmentation	Clustering, Factor Analysis, Ranking
Propensity to Buy	Induction Trees, Logistic Regression, Neural Nets
Attrition	Induction Trees, Logistic Regression, Neural Nets
Life Time Value	Net Present Value, Structural Equation Modeling
Purchase Sequence	Association and Sequence Analysis, Affinity, Time Series
Prospecting and Lead Generation	Induction Trees, Logistic Regression, Neural Nets
Profitability Analysis	Activity-based Costing, Process-based Costing
Campaign Effectiveness Assessment	Induction Trees, Logistic Regression, Neural Nets, Discriminant Analysis

The application of data mining in the Customer Relations Management is illustrated in Figure 4-11.

Figure 4-11: Data Mining Makes CRM Smarter (NCR Teradata)

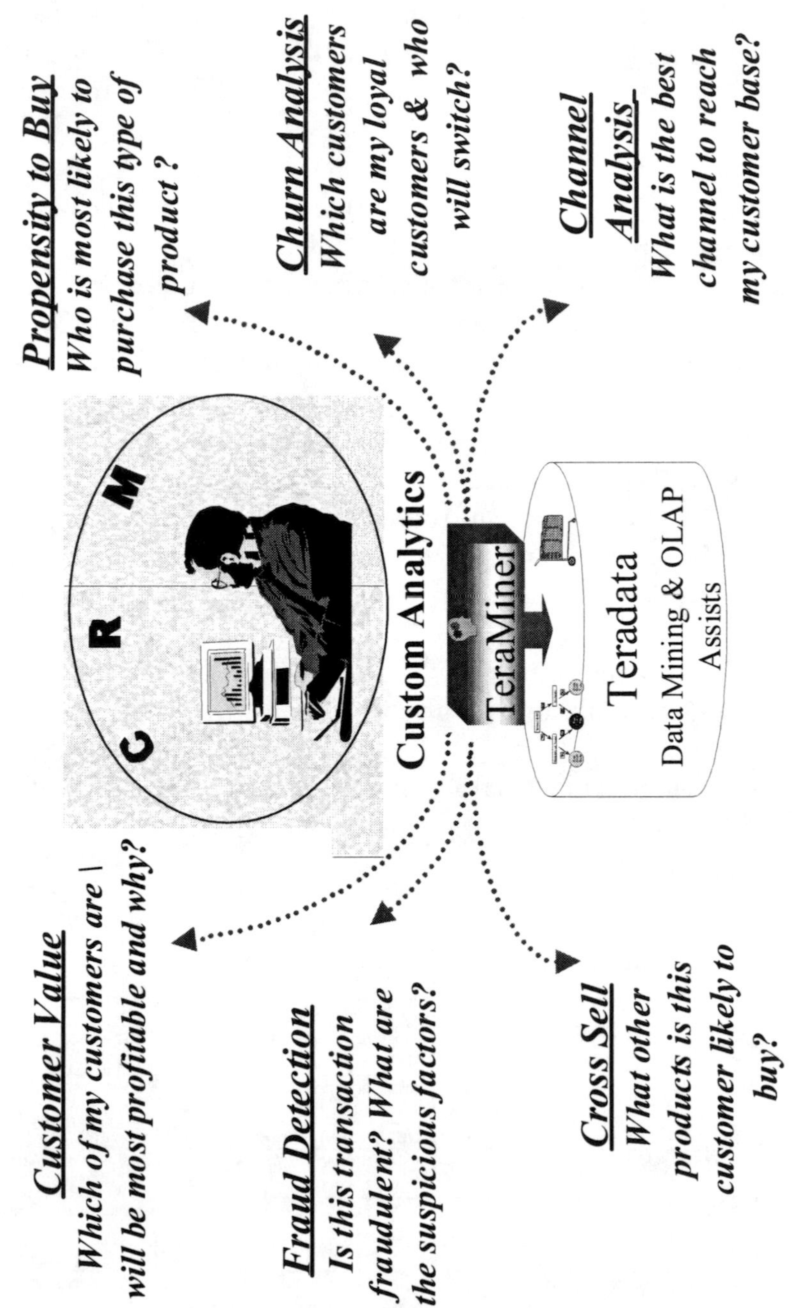

KMS Generic Architecture

The generic architecture of a KMS is shown in Figure 4-12.

A model in Figure 4-12 illustrates a relationship between a Data Warehouse, Data Miner, Data Mart, and Knowledge Base within a KMS. A Data Warehouse provides a source of data repository which provides inputs to a Data Miner engine, which categorizes data and computes behavioral patterns and rules of a given business/organization, applying different mathematical techniques. Data Mart collects knowledge applied by a specific user, and Knowledge Base stores all defined business/organization rules and behavioral patterns of stakeholders. The results are visualized, mostly graphically, to end-users via a Graphic User Interface (GUI).

The present state of KMS does not permit its operations without a considerable human intervention. One of the new positions that steers the development of KMS is a Chief Knowledge Officer (CKO). Appointment of

Figure 4-12: The Generic Architecture of Knowledge Management System

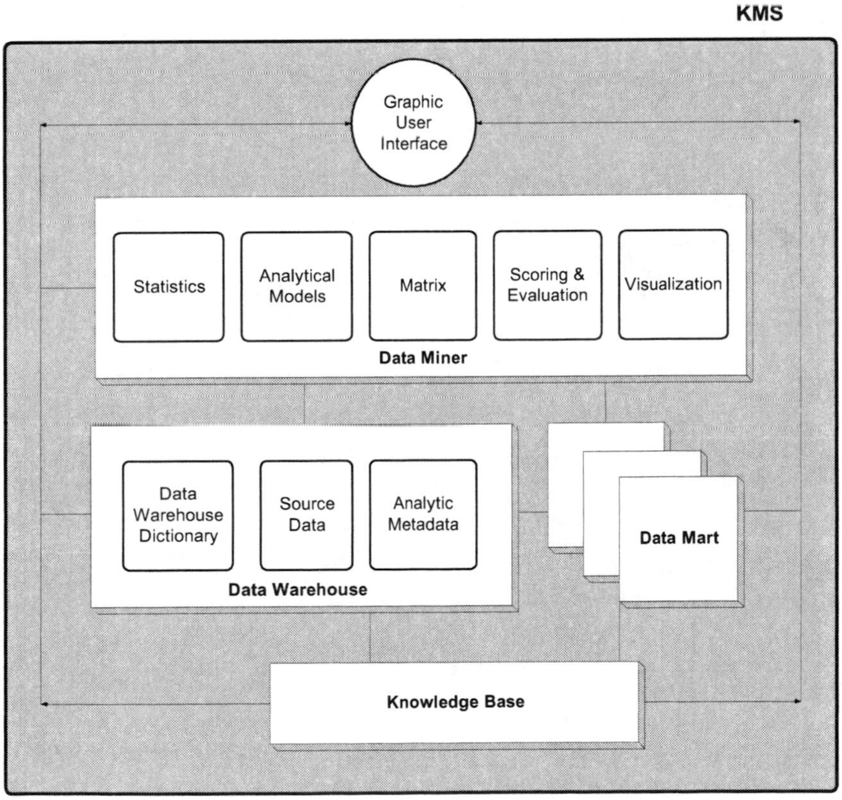

a CKO provides a focus on the knowledge development strategy within the organization.

A KMS is evolving in an Enterprise Information Portal[5] which is described in the next section. EIP's are one way of disseminating knowledge through an organization, Internet-based training, and what is now called e-Learning. Many companies combine their portal strategies with their online courses and make courses available through portals. Since 1999, the rise of EIP's (from enterprise home pages) has been a noteworthy trend in knowledge management. EIP's are also called corporate portals, enterprise knowledge portals, and collaborative portals. They give users one-point access to knowledge and application resources through the Web browser.

The outlook for KMS is upbeat, as EIP's provide information outside traditional organizational bounds and collaboration work (via an EIP) calls for higher levels of knowledge sharing. The adoption of EIP's will accelerate the establishment of KMS within organizations. Because of the widespread familiarity with Yahoo! and other consumer portals, more users will expect their corporate intranets to offer similar capabilities (such as search engines and automatic document summaries) across the enterprise-wide collection of structured and unstructured documents. Along the way, this trend will help organizations to transform from unwieldy corporate intranets into KMS.

EIP-ENTERPRISE INFORMATION PORTAL – *INTRA-OFFICE AUTOMATION*

EIP is an info-communication system which applies Web technology (on the intranets and extranets) to create a single place where one could start a search for information and knowledge using a search engine, data mining, On Line Analytical Processing (OLAP), and query and reporting techniques. The model for this type of a system comes from the successful Internet portal such as *Yahoo!* which is used by both consumers and business people.

The architecture of EIP is provided in Figure 4-13. EIP's are now being constructed to help knowledge workers locate, manage, and use all this information/knowledge within the context of their jobs' informated decision making.

Some software companies offer toolkits to help develop this read-only software. For instance, Microsoft has launched a toolkit – Microsoft Nuggets – which is a part of its Digital Dashboard strategy.

For those companies that prefer to have their portals maintained and managed by a third party, outsourcing options are becoming more widely available. For example, CoVia, Epicentric, and Netscape are among the companies that build and host specific company/industry-oriented portals.

Generic portal software packages are available in the market, such as IBM/Lotus' Knowledge Management Suite, Oracle's Portal Framework, Viador's E-Portal Suite, and others.

The adaptation of EIP's will accelerate the penetration of KMS within organizations. Because of the widespread familiarity with Yahoo! and other consumer portals, a great number of users now expect their corporate Intranet to offer similar capabilities. In such a manner, Intranets can be transformed into true Knowledge Management Systems.

The EIP is characterized by the following attributes:

- "Push" and "Pull" technologies are applied to transmit information to users through a Web-based interface with a very user-friendly GUI (Graphic User Interface),
- The interactive ability allows the users to communicate with EIP through e-mail, chat rooms, bulletin boards, etc.,
- Technologies such as Content Management, Business Intelligence (OLAP), Data Warehousing, Data Marting, and Data Mining are integrated into a single system that can handle information from one user browser,
- The ability to access external and internal sources of data, information, and knowledge.

The success of portals leads toward the development of many types of portals that at the present time can be recognized as:

- Enterprise Information Portals (EIP) – displayed on the Internet for visitors and potential customers ("data-centric"),
- Business-to-Employee Portals (BEP) – for internal way of communicating and information handling in inter-office applications ("information-centric")
  - Filing expenses reports,
  - Selecting training and participating in Web-based classrooms,

- Requesting supplies and computer maintenance,
- Managing medical insurance and retirement funds,
- Other.

Figure 4-13: The Architecture of Enterprise Information Portal (The Targowski Model)

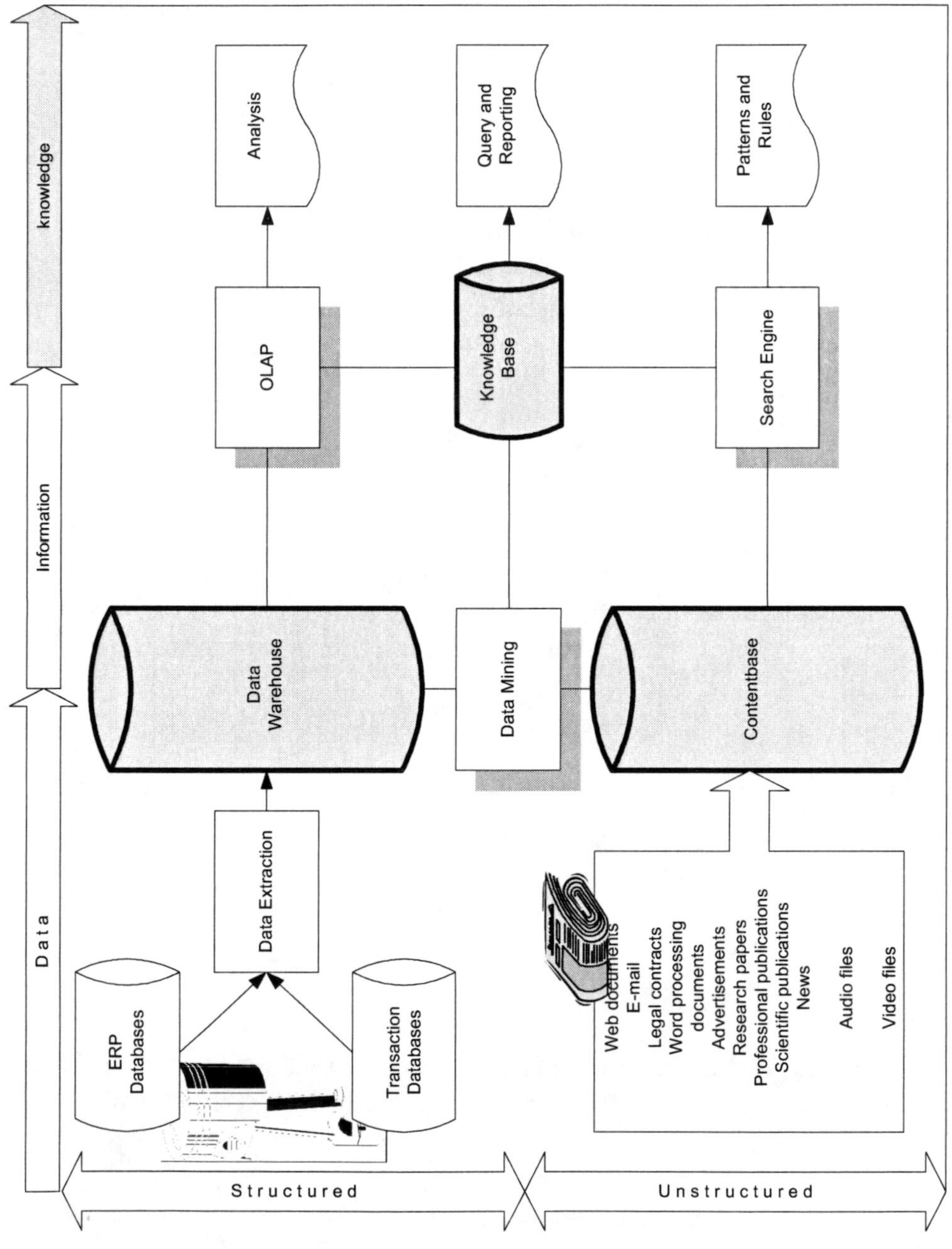

- Application Enterprise Portals (AEP) to integrate different applications via Web technologies in a mode of "process-centric."
- Vortals – vertically oriented portals oriented toward a given industry/ business which contain industry news, articles, white papers, lists of recommended books, advertisements, and even e-commerce,
- Other, such as consumer portals.

In general, one can say that these portals serve as the presentation layer (a single gateway) for business key information, business intelligence, human resources, e-business, CRM, SCM, and other systems and their components.

The EIP provides the following capabilities:

- Text retrieval for relevance with queries;
- Personalization allows users to see information related to their activities;
- Knowledge classification to summarize available scientific data and rules;
- Document management is applied for unstructured and semistructured documents;
- Collaboration tools permit co-creation and sharing of common documents, and discussions in synchronous and asynchronous modes.

DMS-DOCUMENT MANAGEMENT SYSTEM

In the shift from paper-based commerce to e-business, documents do not go away and the new challenge is how to incorporate paper's digital documents into e-enterprise's applications. Here are some examples of document handling challenges (Bruce Silver, www.eBiz.com):

- Customer Relationship Management
    - A customer sends a letter to request a new service from the power or telephone utility and does not have any response in the next few days. Then the customer phones the call center where the agent does not know about the customer's letter and the former is unhappy.

After implementing the integrated document system, the agent knows about the customer's letter and the latter is satisfied.

  - Fortune 1000 companies receive many calls from their employees about retirement plans and their statuses; however, the help desks do not know in time about an employee's recent document submission, so the employee is unsatisfied.
  - Credit card companies use the call centers to resolve disputes about payments, but if all documents are digitized, then the agent knows how to solve the customer's problem.
  - Financial services, utilities, and other organizations can use the call centers to smoothly solve the customers' problems if appropriate documents are in a digital format.

- Human Resources Self-Service
  - Employees can online update and query all personnel files, especially those associated with benefits and expenses, if all appropriate documents are digitized. Many documents require a signature or must be original, like birth certificates or physician statements; in such a case these documents must be stored in an image format.

- E-Bill Presentation and Payment (EBPP)
  - The most common way of communicating with customers is in the form of the bills and statements that the service providers send each month. The EBPP system allows the customer to pay bills and receive the account's status through Web technology via the Internet. Because all documents are in digital format, it ensures that the payees obtain superior customer services, and vice versa; the service providers can exercise marketing technique 1-to-1 and apply data mining to discover the customers' behavioral patterns.

- ERP/Financials
  - Accounts payable is a paper-intensive process that must match received invoices with delivery receipts, purchase orders, and other documents in order to be paid. Timely processing is critical to receive discounts or avoid penalties. With Web access to these digitized documents, the accountants can close transactions quite easily and quickly.

Some enterprises such as hospitals are a huge factory of documents[6]. For example a hospital with 400 beds processes the following volumes of documents:

- 8,000 payors remittances per month,
- 150 physician completing records electronically,
- 6,000 medical records per month,
- 15,000 pages faxed per month automatically,
- 2,000 pages faxed ad hoc,
- 13,500 documents signed with an electronic signature

Other types of documents include (in thousands):

- Outpatient lab results,
- Outpatient radiology results,
- Dictated reports,
- Coding verification worksheets,
- Miscellaneous documents

Some financial institutions process even more documents, and in order to do so, an e-Document Management System has to be applied, as is illustrated in Figure 4-14.

For example, IBM's approach for the e-Document Management System has the following stages:

1. Creating the e-Document Repository, called a "CommonStore-Info-Visual Archive," where three subsystems create e-folders of documents that can be routed through a workflow process and where they are specialized in different categories of documents:

- IBM Content Manager subsystem digitizes and stores images, faxes, and final form documents,
- IBM Content Manager OnDemand hosts other systems' outputs, such as statements, invoices, and reports,
- Lotus Domino.Doc stores revisable-form desktop documents and e-mail.

Figure 4-14: The Architecture of e-Document Management System

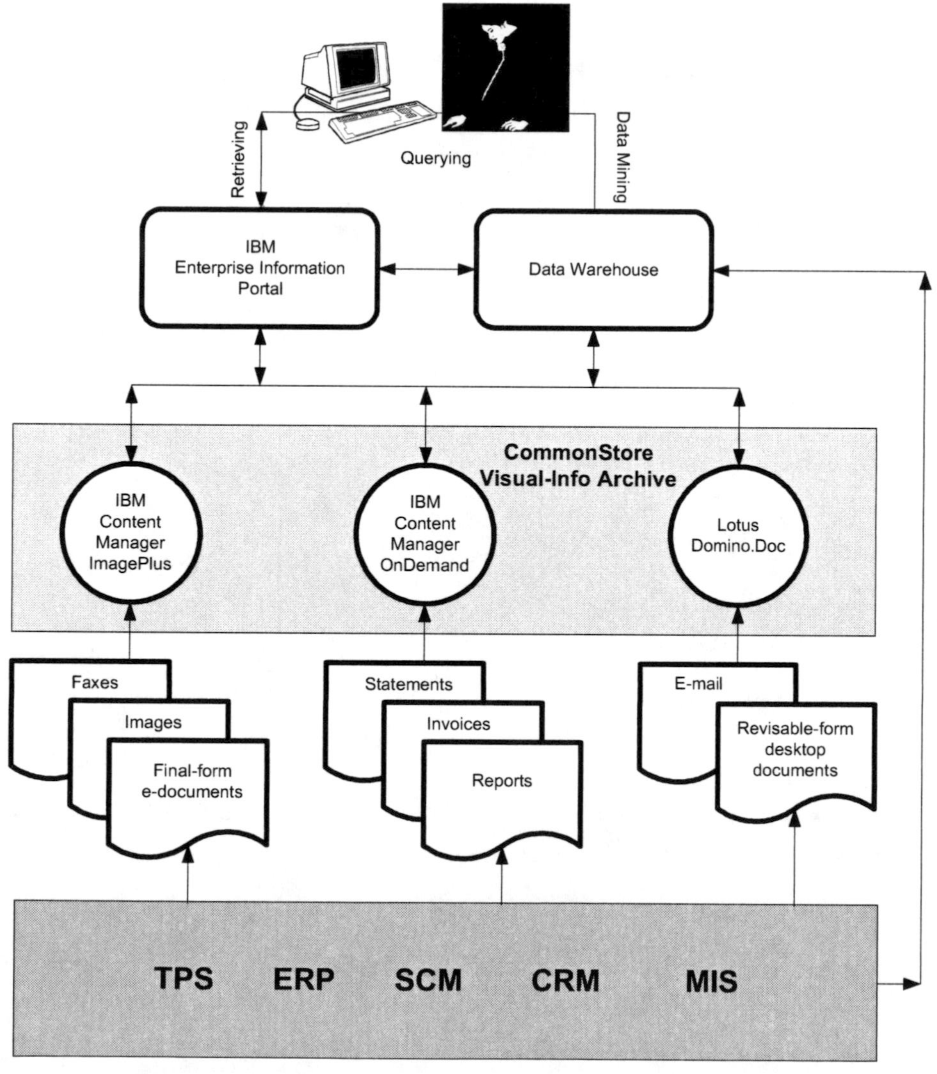

2. Providing an integrated search and retrieval capability spanning all three e-document repositories through the IBM Enterprise Information Portal. It defines search templates that translate the index fields of each repository into a common vocabulary used in the query screens.

3. Each e-document repository is Web-oriented and can be searched individually or through EIS that is also Web-oriented. In addition, by using a Java servlet on a Web application server such as IBM Webshare, Enterprise Information Portal can provide an "ultra" client that communicates to the Web browser in plain HTML script.

4. Automating business processes that use e-documents through IBM MQSeries Workflow. Workflow makes e-documents accessible and transforms them into key components of e-business transactions.

At Hewitt Associates (12,000 consultants in Human Resources services in 75 locations in 35 countries) all clients' papers such as birth certificates, benefits election forms, and others are scanned into Content Manager and indexed by the company's and employee's Social Security Number. When a client phones the call center and provides the unique PIN, then the agent can access all e-documents and answers the question or solves the problem. Also, the employees can access their own e-documents via the Internet.

The next expected solution in e-Document Management System is the ability to handle audio-visual documents for more comprehensive informing and for knowledge discovery processes. IBM DB2 Universal Database is ready to handle such documents, and IBM Intelligent Miner for text is the first step to support broad searches of all types of documents.

INFORMATION SERVICES

Information services have emerged together with the broader application of the Internet as an external information source. They are delivered free or on pay basis through the Internet. Among such services one can mention the following financial news:

- *Electronic Yellow Pages* - a well organized data collection of business and community services. This is a dynamic database which interactively can be retrieved by the user. The best known yellow pages are the French Minitel services.

- *Financial News* provided by such companies as Dow Jones, Reuters, Knight-Ridder, Associated press, McGraw-Hill, Financial News network, and market News Service.

- Stock Quotations are provided by Reuters, Holdings PLC, Quatron Systems, and Telerate. They provide information about most stocks, all commodity and financial features, and the market data: bids, offers, last-sale prices, and stock volume information.

- *Value-Added Products* - provided under the form of historical information, research information, and customized information. Companies providing such information are Quatron, Reuters, Bridge Brokerage Systems, Morningstar, and so forth.

- Foreign Exchange Data - this service is provided by Reuters, which launched the Monitor Dealing Service, allowing traders to negotiate transactions over their terminals instead of telephones. Other competing companies are Reuters, Telerate, and AP-Dow Jones.

- U.S. Government Bond Data are provided by Telerate.

Database and information retrieval services offer subscribers the ability to tap into more than 5000 commercial databases covering thousands of subjects provided by hundreds of companies. They are organized into six functional levels:

1. The information originator, a publication like *The Washington Post*, *The Wall Street Journal,* or *The New York Times*.

2. The database maintainer; an agency, company, or private individual in charge of loading and updating a computer-based database system and leasing telecommunication lines to end users.

3. Service vendor; a company or agency that provides marketing and sales of a database to information consumers (e.g., Lockheed, with some hundreds of databases).

4. Packaged analysis creator who provides analysis of raw data.

5. Search services; intermediary information brokers who provide industry-wide searches of all electronic commercial storages and sites.

6. Information consumer.

Among those companies one can recognize the following information service providers: Knowledge Index, Dow Jones news, Datatimes, NEWSNET, BRS/After dark, EASYNET, and Lexis and Nexis (legal information).

Among consumer information services providers one can mention Internet Portals such Yahoo! and America Online (AOL) with 30+ million users. Their menus are similar. For example, some of AOL's categories are as follows:

Mail	Stock Quotes Area
News & Finance	Top News of the Day
People Connection	Directory of Services
Lifestyles & Interests	What is New Area
Entertainment	Download Manager
Learning & Reference	File Search/Software
Travel & Shopping	Forums
Computing & Software	Members' On-line Support

The most popular service is "Forums," which provides message-based and real-time conference areas for the special-interest groups.

SCM-SUPPLY CHAIN MANAGEMENT – *INTER-OFFICE AUTOMATION*

The supply chain includes all functions involved in filling a customer request. These functions include: suppliers, transportation, distributors, new product development, manufacturing, marketing, finance, accounting, retailers, customers, customer service, etc. For example, when a customer buys online a Dell computer, the supply chain embraces the customer, the Web page that acquires the customer's order, Dell's manufacturing plant, and, going backwards, all of the seller's suppliers and their suppliers and distributors.

A set of involved companies in fulfilling the customer's order creates a supply chain management system (SCM) that operates as a single company. The SCM system coordinates the smooth flow of information, materials, and money among all the participating companies. This integrational, inter-enterprise effort aims at:

1. The improved production and delivery efficiency and effectiveness, leading to higher profitability through revenue growth and cost reduction (greater volumes from increased scope and enhanced sales capabilities leverage scale economies),

2. Better competitive advantage, which requires proactive management and rapid competitive responsiveness,

3. Better customer responsiveness through smooth service delivery, customer service, and data management (improved data gathering, warehousing, data mining, and lower transaction costs),

4. Improved organizational effectiveness that can be achieved if finite resources are better allocated toward high-value activities. It allows companies to pursue their most profitable customer segments. With well-defined SCM strategy, individual employees have a better understanding of their acquisition-transaction-servicing responsibilities. Properly designed incentive and performance indicators should substantially improve organizational effectiveness.

Typical quantified improvement benefits from integrating the Supply Chain, according to PRITIVIS C Benchmark Study (www.supplychain.org/html/slide1.cfm?SR=30), are as follows:

- Delivery performance 16%-28% improvement
- Inventory reduction 25%-60% improvement
- Fulfillment cycle time 30%-50% improvement
- Forecast accuracy 25%-80% improvement
- Overall productivity 19%-16% improvement
- Lower SCM costs 25%-50% improvement
- Fill rates 20%-30% improvement
- Improved capacity realization 10%-20% improvement

Companies are forced to create SCM systems since they are under pressure from the marketplace, where:

- Customers increasingly demand anytime, anyplace access to products and services,
- Customers are conducting significantly more transactions across a wider variety of channels,
- Increasingly knowledgeable customers demand higher value for the cost,
- Dichotomy grows between advice-oriented and self-directed customers; the latter are more sophisticated who seek the best value from the transaction.

A typical integrated SCM system has two components:

- Supply Chain Management (SCM I), which operates at the input (backward chaining) stage (called also *procurement*) and includes all incoming materials, and information and money flows among suppliers, distributors, producers, and transporters,
- Selling Chain Management (SCM II), which operates at the output (forward chaining) stage and includes all outcoming materials, information, and money flows among producers, distributors, retailers, transporters, and customers.

The SCM systems interact informationally with the ERP system, Enterprise Information Portal (EIP), and Customer Service Management system as is shown in Figure 4-15. The information flow is supported by the Extranet, which authorizes all stakeholders to access and process information about customers, their related orders, and their conditions leading to a successful fulfillment through all stages of logistic processes. The focal point of information gathering and sharing among SCM's stakeholders is the Enterprise Information Portal.

The functional integration of SCM I and II and ERP systems is illustrated in Figure 4-16.

Most of the buzz around e-commerce focuses on the transaction itself, when the buyer clicks through the seller's checkout process. But what happens

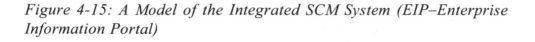

Figure 4-15: A Model of the Integrated SCM System (EIP–Enterprise Information Portal)

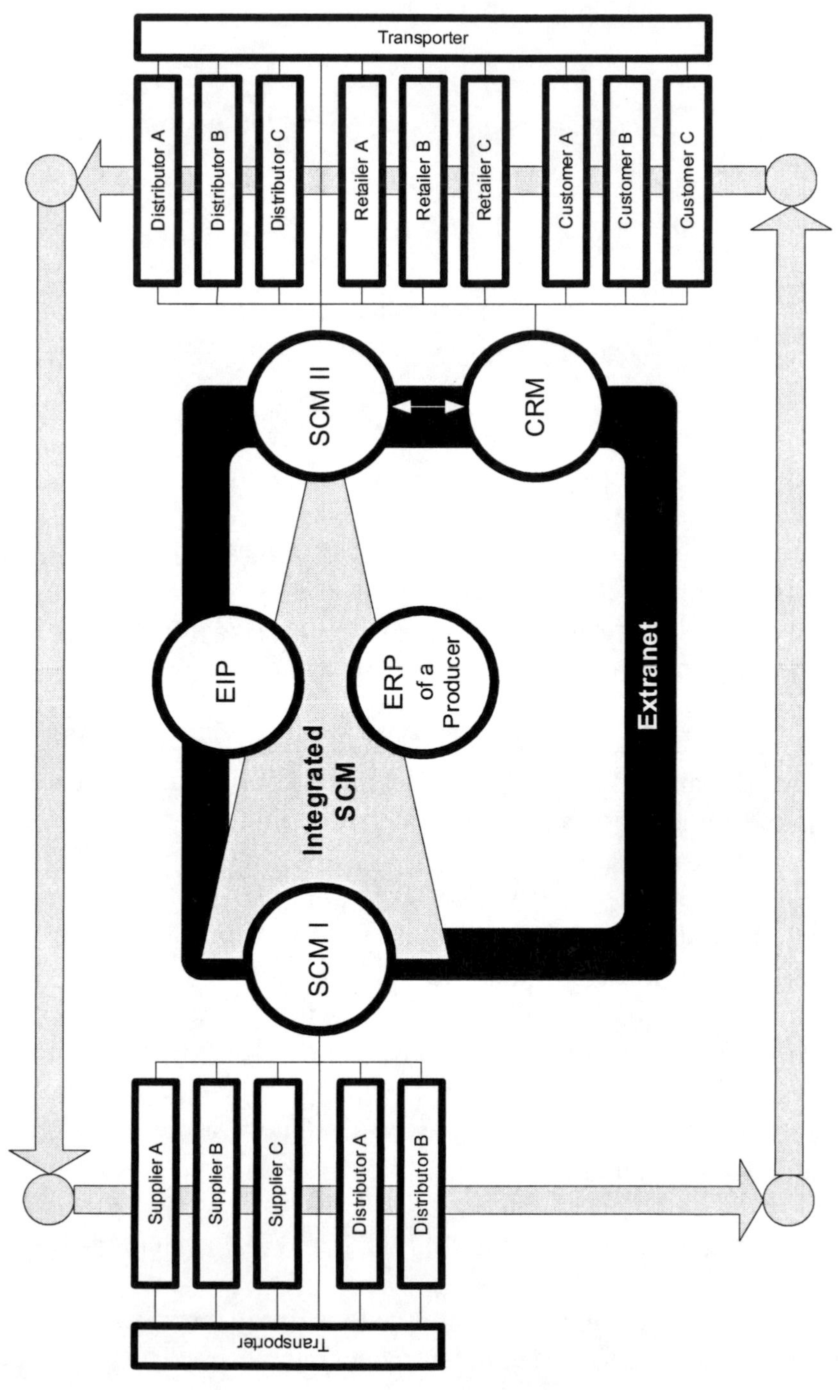

Figure 4-16: The Functional Integration of SCM and ERP Systems

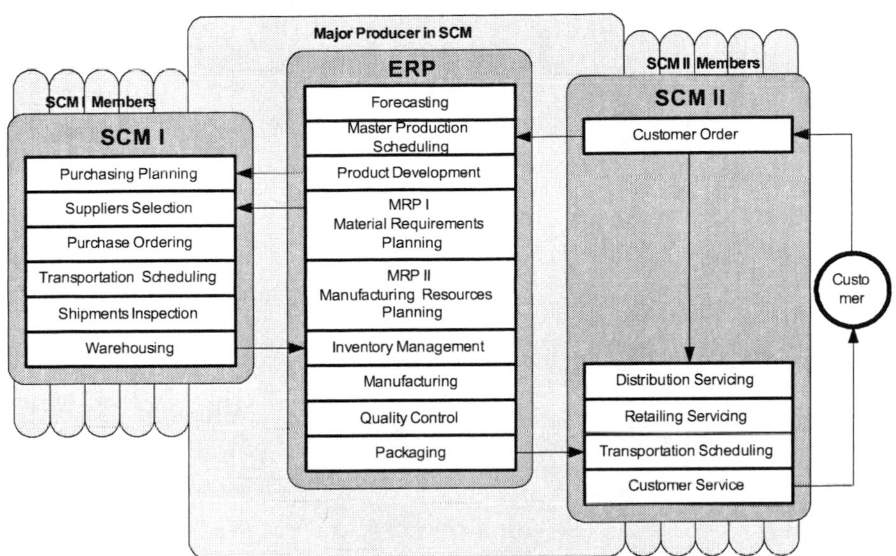

before and after that transaction has more impact on the way work is done. Businesses are tearing down the walls of communication that separate their employees from partners, customers, and suppliers to provide an environment in which all can collaborate and share. A digital workplace can complement an enterprise's investment in transaction systems by providing a place where functions such as product development, requirements planning, and contract negotiations can occur. An e-Room allows for team members to communicate in real-time online conferences. Everyone in the supply chain can meet in an e-room using a browser and Web technology. Ford Motor Co. is using e-Room to work closely with suppliers, partners, and customers. Any team can create an e-Room to share documents, hold online discussions and vote on a proposal. Participants are selected from Ford's intranet or extranet directories, so every e-Room is B2B ready. In addition, every intranet user receives his/her own personal e-Room that is intended to facilitate ad hoc collaboration.

Internet-based logistic systems offer several compelling sources of value. In particular, electronic capabilities make it possible to integrate logistic processes and deliver them in new ways. They facilitate information searches and comparison shopping, they allow electronic payments and software-based advisory services, and they make possible customizing services down to segments of one.

SCM systems are based on the Business Process Integration (BPRI) architecture (described in Chapter 7) and B2B model as is illustrated in Figure 4-17.

The SCM system can be electronically integrated at the two following levels:

1. Cross-enterprise logistic process application integration through middleware software which connects companies' ERP's with SCM's and SCM's of collaborating companies,

2. Cross-enterprise process data integration via such standards as XML.

In practice, different industries develop specific solutions of SCM; for example:

- The High-Tech industry – implements the SCM *build-to-order* model which supports mass-customization and the customer's ability to customize the ordered configuration of a product such as a computer (a case of Dell, Compaq, HP, Intel),

Figure 4-17: BPRI and B2B Application Integration Create the Inter-enterprise Infrastructure that Supports SCM to Work in the Integrated Environment

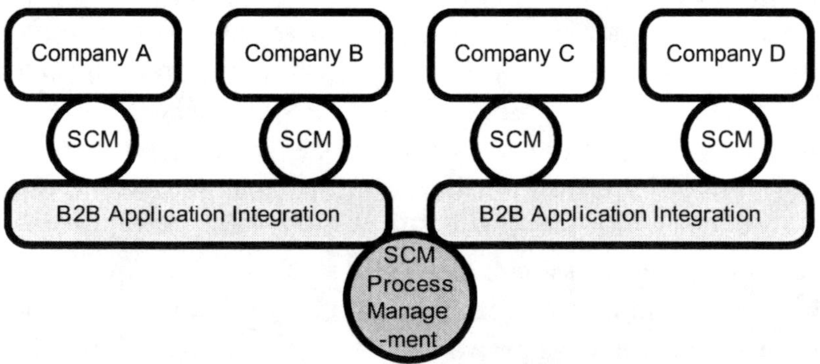

- The consumer packaged goods industry – applies the SCM *continuous replenishment* model which supports collaboration of all SCM members (such as Proctor & Gamble and Wal-Mart) to optimize the stores' stocks,

- The food processing industry – develops the SCM *make-to-stock* model which is enterprise-centric (e.g., Kellogg, Nabisco, Coca-Cola, General Mills) to speed up the delivery of products (based on forecasts, not customer orders), better utilize plants, and minimize their own inventories of raw materials, semi-products, and products.

A good example of SCM systems is provided by Covisint, which is the automotive industry exchange where OEM's and suppliers of all sizes come together to do business in a single business environment using the same tools and user interface, plus one user id and password. Among funding companies are GM, DaimlerChrysler, Ford, Renault, and Nissan. Covisint's infrastructure provides a basis for industry connectivity, as is shown in Figure 4-18.

Figure 4-18: Covisint's Information Infrastructure

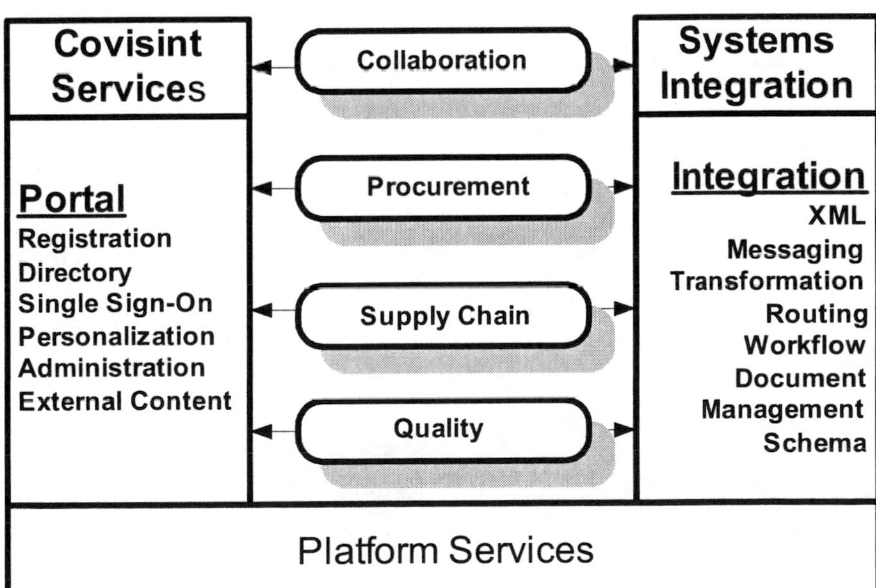

The application of Covisint's services secures effects presented in Table 4-2.

Table 4-2: The Effects of Covisint's Services

SERVICES	ROI	BUYER VALUE	SELLER VALUE
Collaboration Manager	ROI<2 months 15% time savings	Reduce non-value added work Eliminate disparate system friction	Customer information visibility Improve quality of decisions
Quote Manager	ROI<2 quotes	Accelerate supplier selection Reduce the cost of bidding process	Accelerate the FRQ cycle Reduce the cost of RFQ responses
Auctions	+400% ROI 70% process savings	Reduce negotiation time Improved decision-making	Access to true market data
Catalog	100% ROI 73% process savings	Controlled buying Reduced purchasing costs	Real-time content management
Supplier Fulfillment	<6 months Avg 1st year 166%	Multi-tier visibility	Inventory reductions Premium freight cost reduction
Problem Solver		Increased speed to closure Track cost of quality	Standard response format Systemic problem solving method

Covinst's global metrics is as follows (on September 21, 2001):

- Auctions: More than 1,000 online bidding events and over $45 billion in transactions;
- Catalogs: More than 250 catalogs, more than 2.5 million individual items, more than 61,000 transactions;
- Quote Manager/Virtual Project Workspace: more than 500 seats sold and in use;
- Supply Chain: More than 2,300 seats sold and in use by 1,500 companies;
- Registration: More than 2,600 companies registered.

Today's supply chain practice can be characterized as follows:

- Out-of-date information flow from thousands of companies in multiple formats;
- Missed sales trends or profit eating rebates;
- Overstocked inventories;
- Half-empty loads;
- Fax and phone-based communication.

These negative practices are a target for Covinst's solutions. Covinst provides the information infrastructure, which enables:

- Electronic connections between users and systems with secure and scalable technology, enabling common communications and processes via a portal as a single integration point to partners' ERP systems;
- Integration and optimization of automotive product development such as design, sourcing, production, and fulfillment;
- Real-time access to partners' information which triggers their visibility;
- Gaining advantage by smooth execution.

According to Covinst's data, North American motor OEM's spend on IT per car about \$650, European OEM's spend about \$400, and Asian OEM's spend only \$150. Today, North American OEM's still focus on cost and in the future will focus on cost and response time.

Covinst aims at the optimization of the sourcing lead-time for suppliers, which has some room for improvements, according to the following data (*www.amrresearch.com*):

- Sales – 14%
- Supply Chain – 25%

- Manufacturing – 13%
- Rework and Analysis – 32%
- Queuing – 16%

CRM-CUSTOMER RELATION MANAGEMENT – *FRONT-OFFICE AUTOMATION*

In business, success is about customers. It is about fully understanding and anticipating what they need, and meeting those needs in ways that keep your company profitable. From local shop owners using grass-roots efforts to connect suppliers with customers, to global companies using sophisticated applications, the momentum to win customers and profits continues into the 21st century.

Customer Relationship Management (CRM) software plays a large role in retaining profitable customers, and it is a hot ROI (*return-on-investment*) concept. According to recent studies, companies can expect an average revenue boost of 8% after implementing a CRM system. Between 1996 and 2000, according to Forrester Research, corporate investment in CRM technology grew at a compound annual rate of 54%. The Gartner Group projected the total CRM market for 2000 at nearly $13 billion, rising to $40 billion in 2004.

CRM evolves through the following stages:

- 1980's – "*point solutions*" identified the buyers-centric approach for specific departments, which aimed at adaptive selling and building long-term relationships with customers through "account executives." At this stage, the first specialized software was called SFA (Sales Force Automation) which included stand-alone, task-oriented tools, such as personal organizers, appointment calendars, and address/telephone directories, which were user-friendly, particularly on Apple computers,

- 1990's – "*enterprise CRM*" identified the ERP approach to capture customer information across marketing, sales, service, and support functions. This is also referred to as "*collaborative CRM,*" where your company and your customers work together to resolve their needs. At this stage the strategy was to collaborate and consult with the customers about how to solve problems and guide them about how to grow with vendors' products and services. This second evolutionary stage trapped most SFA vendors. Their packages were second-generation SFA software which focused on enhancing the office productivity of salespersons by automating such activities as contact management, opportunity management, sales forecasting, commission tracking, and teleselling management. SFA software, at this stage, could analyze, "How long it takes to answer support calls," or, "How long it takes to close the contract," but that is not something a company could turn into profitable transactions and loyal relationships.

- 2000's – "*e-CRM*" combines traditional and collaborative CRM approaches with analysis to provide accurate insights into the wants and preferences of the customer, supplier, or employee. SFA software transforms into a true CRM software, which draws from the enterprise data warehouse, the repository of organizational memory, raw company data and transforms this input into business intelligence.

Nowadays, in the new e-business world-wide practice, the extended enterprise is composed of employees, suppliers, partners, and customers collaborating as a team of stakeholders. This means that customers are transforming into commissioned salespersons through bonuses, rebates, or credit programs. On the other hand, employees are becoming customers and competitors are turning into partners.

Appropriate customer relationships are key factors to any good business. According to Sybase Customer Asset Management Solution (www.sybase.com), the following data illustrate this premise[7]:

- It costs six times more to sell to a new customer than to sell to an existing one,

- A typical dissatisfied customer will tell eight to ten people about his/her experience,

- A company can boost its profits by 85% by increasing its annual customer retention by only 5%,

- The odds of selling a product to a new customer are 15%, whereas the odds of selling a product to an existing customer are 50%,

- 70% of complaining customers will do business with the company again if it quickly takes care of a service,
- More than 90% of existing companies don't have the necessary sales and service integration to support e-commerce.

CRM is about automating and informating the customer-centric business processes of Marketing, Sales, and Service. A CRM system ensures that front-office applications improve:

1. Customer satisfaction, resulting in added customer loyalty and retention through better identification of the most profitable customers and treating them accordingly (20-80 rule), and better understanding their needs, which can be satisfied by more efficient coordination of activities of all stakeholders of a business (*integrating back-office* with *front-office* and *inter-enterprise offices*),
2. Profitability by increasing profits per sale through offering the correct products (cross-sell/up-sell),
3. Reducing marketing costs by developing effective, targeted campaigns,
4. Reducing selling costs by improved control of a sales cycle and workflow,
5. Leveraging on previous contracts with other customers for the current interaction,
6. Estimating future sales, marketing, and service activities based on analysis and customer data sharing among all stakeholders of a business (*integrating back-office* with *front-office* and *inter-enterprise offices*),
7. Other.

There is almost uniform agreement among industry analysts that CRM includes: Marketing, Sales, Marketing, where the customer makes contacts with the business, either in the pre-sale, sale, or post-sale situation. However, many software companies add mission-critical repositories, such as Customer Repository, Products and Services Repository, and Competition Repository and Analysis, which help to informate the decision-making process about

Figure 4-19: The Generic Model of Customer Relationship Management – CRM System (EIP–Enterprise Information Portal)

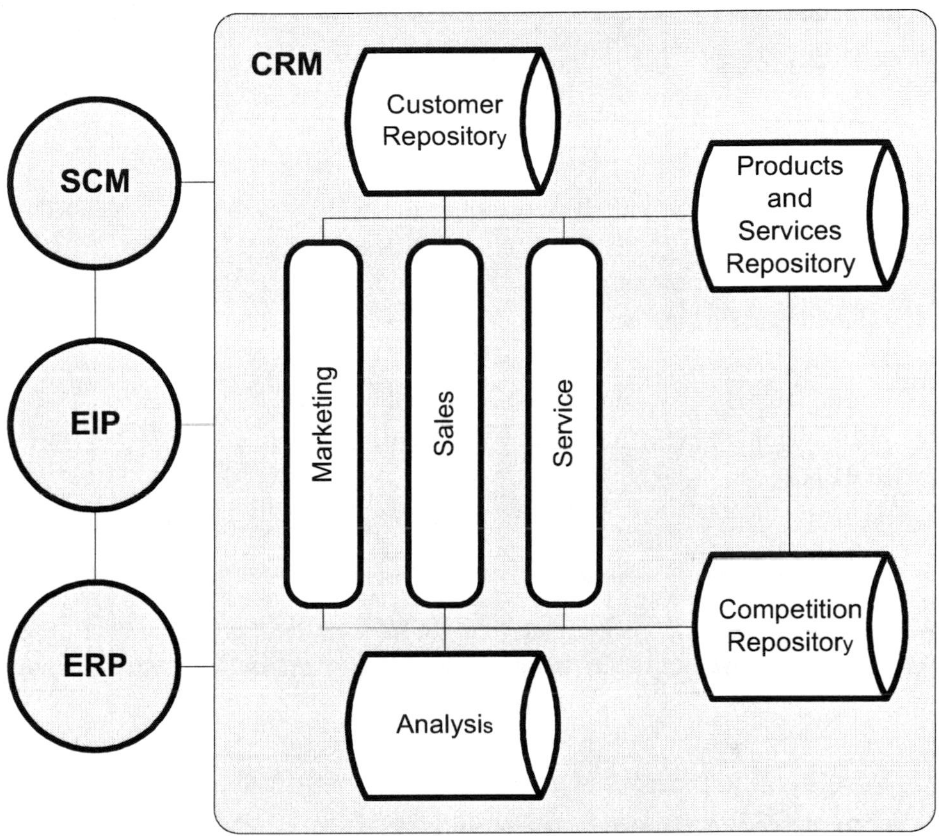

customers. These inter-linked generic areas of functionality are illustrated in Figure 4-19. The Repository of Products and Services is linked with the Competitor's Repository, so that if a company is not offering specific products and services to a given client, then this company knows who does. Also, if a company hears in the news that competitor X is either going out of business or was fired by the client, then it is time for that company to move in with a new offer.

Marketing is that business function which identifies a relationship between a product and customer which triggers the whole business process. Marketing activities are quickly evolving from traditional telemarketing to Web and e-mail campaigns. These Web-based marketing activities give prospects for the better customer experience, allowing the relevant information to be retrieved by the prospects on their own terms and their own time.

Sales is the fastest growing component of CRM. The interaction of the sales force with the prospect, turning the prospect into a customer and then maintaining a loyal relationship, is a core business concern for the business' success. The sales process must be coordinated across business functions through such systems as ERP and SCM.

Service is probably the most crucial element when it comes to customer relationship management. The quality of customer service that an enterprise provides is key to its ability to maintain satisfied and loyal customers. Today's call centers are evolving into contact centers handling an assortment of communication media. Telephone interaction must be coordinated with e-mail, fax, Web, and any other communication media. Self-service is a fast growing requirement, as more customers are making their way to the Web and want to look up their order status or make queries via their browsers. Customer service undoubtedly reaches beyond the traditional help desk. The term "Customer Care" is being used today to broaden the business' responsibility toward the customer.

Customer Repository is absolutely critical for a CRM system to have the customer data available to all customer-centric business functions of an enterprise (ERP, SCM) and also for its stakeholders. This database eliminates duplication, and conflicting or out-of-date information. Consistency in addressing the customer across all business functions is important in the following domains:

- Customer data – should include business profile, financial and demographic information, and outstanding issues with the customer, because the customer should not have to repeat a story or supply answers previously given to another representative.

- Business rules – should include policies that are applied to customers in their different aggregations in order to eliminate inconsistency in treating the same types of customers with different rules.

- News – about customers.

Products and Services Repository should include:

- Company and product/service information – should include product/service catalogues, marketing campaigns, press releases, company's history, etc. It is inconceivable that the website will offer a product that customer service knows nothing about, or that a price quote given by a sales-person contradicts a special offer advertised on the Web.

Competition Repository should include:

- Intelligence data about competitors, including their products/services offerings, market analysis, news, business performance reports, customer satisfaction reports, etc.

Analysis is a module which informates CRM in real-time evaluation of sales, applying quantitative and qualitative techniques. Particularly, win/loss analysis and customer retention analysis are performed based on data mining of a data warehouse and are associated with ERP and SCM. Data mining is one example of methods that are applied by Decision Support Systems (DSS) for this purpose.

The functional model of CRM is depicted in Figure 4-20. The CRM functions have been defined within software packages as a result of the Internet and in general Web/extranet technology applications. Among electronic solutions one can mention the following:

- e-Service – enables the customer to search databases to report and solve problems, view their pricing and ordering information, subscribe to product-related information such as white papers, and review status of warranty claims. A business can communicate with the customers via text chats, the Internet-driven telephone, and Web pages. Customers' questions, problems, and requests are automatically routed to the right source for a quick and accurate response.

- e-Store –provides an online catalog personalized for business customers (e.g., Amazon.com). Customers can maintain a list of favorite products, check the business' inventory in real-time, and check the status of their orders.

- e-Payment – allows a business to track the status of an outstanding invoice and chat online with its customer regarding the invoice.

The scope of the business internetization may be expanded into a company's information portal, which can offer e-mail, discussion boards, and up-to-date content. The goal of the internetization should be to translate customer contact

Figure 4-20: The Functional Model of CRM System

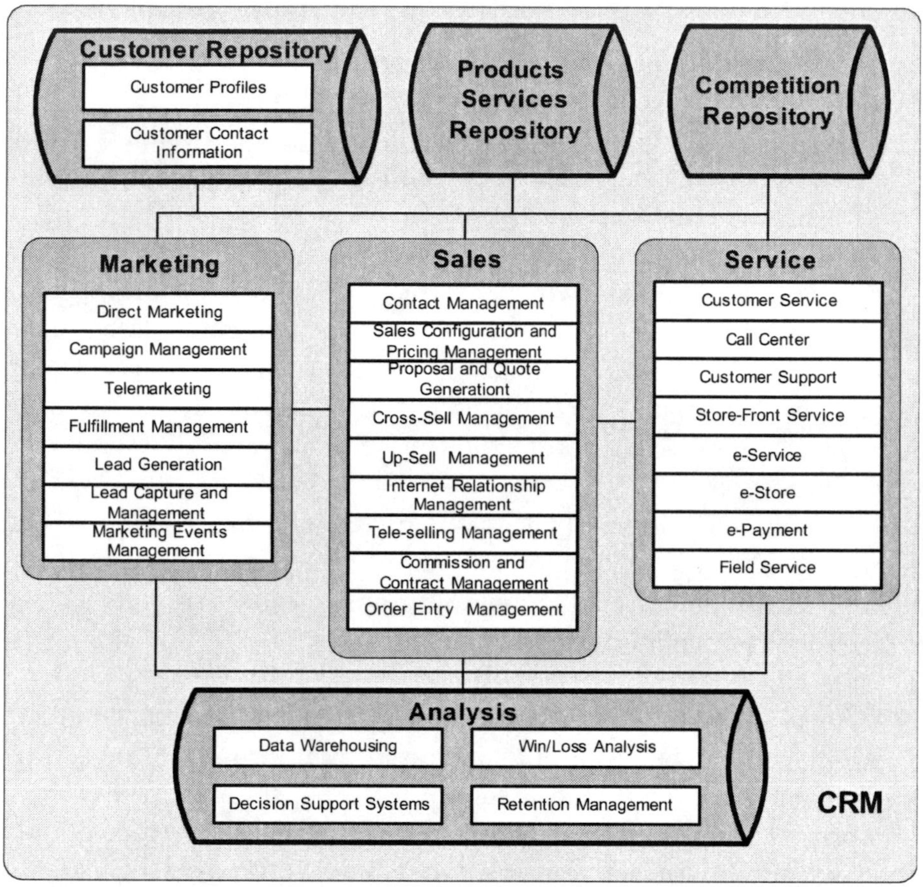

into sales. The latter should provide a more satisfying buying experience than in the physical world.

CRM is becoming a very popular software solution that perhaps will surpass ERP popularity and will become one of the largest application segments ever. This trend should change the business models of the enterprise. As products become commodities, and all other things being equal, the added value provided by CRM will define the success or failure of one business player over another.

ERP vendors such as SAP, Peoplesoft, Oracle, Baan, and others are attempting to expand their software packages as saturation is reached in the back-office applications. These vendors merge or acquire CRM vendors, as evidenced in these some examples: Siebel & IBM, Peoplesoft & Vantive, Nortell & Clarify, HP & Oracle. Systems Integrators (e.g., KPMG, E & Y) are offering their services to integrate CRM with other enterprise applications. The hardware and networking infrastructure, particularly in the area of extranets, mobilized such companies as CTI, Cisco, HP, IBM, Lucenet, Nortell, Geneysis, and Quintus towards the development of solutions for CRM.

WFS-WORKFLOW SYSTEMS

Workflow systems have evolved to integrate the applications and tools being used in workgroup environments on networked enterprise information infrastructures. Their purpose is to speed up a task's completion through the collaboration of several workers. A workflow system is composed of:

- business processes; e.g., loan approval,
- cases; e.g., a customer application for a car loan,
- folders; e.g., a customer's e-folder, containing documents from different sources, including text and images,
- rules; e.g., about size of collateral for a loan,
- definitions; e.g., descriptions of participants in terms of locations, job function, supervisor, and security level,
- routing; e.g., sequential, parallel (with rendezvous point), or dynamic/ conditional, depending upon dynamically occurring conditions.

The core component of a WFS is the workflow engine. It is a software responsible for process creation and control of the activity scheduling in an operational process and interaction with tools or human resources. WFS very often operates across many computer platforms and applications over wide geographic areas. The workflow engine exchanges controls among different applications via COBRA, Dynamic Data Exchange (DDE), OLE, or R/3's Business Application Programming Interfaces (BAPI's) standards. A good example of WFS is Lotus Notes for a groupware environment.

On the rise are Web-enabled workflow systems to support inter-enterprise activities, such as those occurring in SCM systems and inter-trading systems. Of course, e-Document Management Systems expand the potential of WFS. The next step in this system development is the inclusion of mobile workers into the workflow process.

The architecture of a WFS is provided in Figure 4-21. The WFS contains workflow engines, administration and monitoring tools, business process integration tools, client subset of WFS, and interfaces to other workflow services, applications, API, and others.

The WFS' are applied mostly in financial institutions, hospitals, public administration, college admission offices, SCM environments, and so forth, and everywhere the process is well defined and time-sensitive.

Figure 4-21: The Architecture of a Workflow System

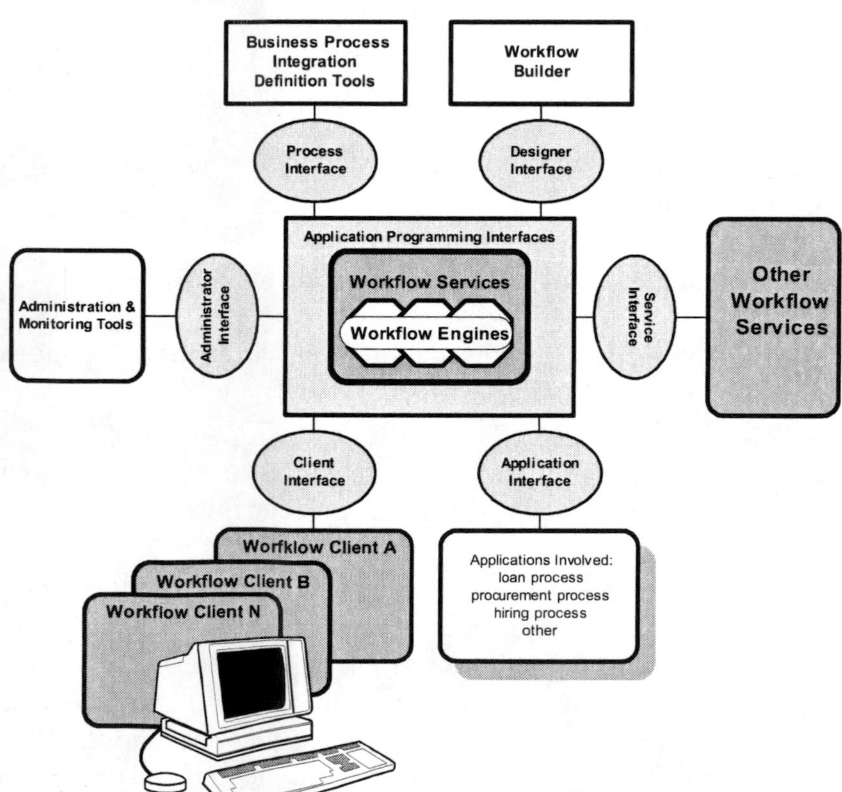

m-MOBILE APPLICATIONS

Mobile business nowadays is driven by the applications of wireless communications. The Wireless Application Protocol (WAP) has emerged, which allows workers on the road to have immediate access to information and transactional services in such areas as e-mail, customer care, call management, information services, e-commerce, online address book and directory services, as well as corporate intranet applications.

m-Mobile access is necessary, not only for sales "road warriors," but also for executives, filed support staff, knowledge workers, and potentially, all workers. This is driven by the need for organizations to create a workforce that is more productive, responsive, and connected, with improved support for virtual teams, and the ability of management to have their finger on the pulse of the business at all times. New sources of competitive advantage will be created for visionary enterprises prepared to take advantage of the merging opportunities (www.magic.com). The common goal of this application is to keep employees out of the office, yet connected to needed information.

FedEx, the global delivery giant increased productivity 30% in the early 1980's when it launched its Digital Assisted Dispatch System. The company was able to more efficiently route pick up and deliveries, keeping couriers on the road instead of back at the water cooler. Coupled with the SuperTracker, a handheld device that communicates location, shipping, and other information about deliveries to customers and the FedEx headquarters, the company was able to pick up and deliver packages in real time after 1986. Its wireless system eliminated the need to write down a million addresses a day, saving time, money, and a lot of ink.

Office Depot teamed with Aether Systems to develop a way to track the retailer's vehicle fleet and to capture customer signatures via a Palm or Pocket PC-based handheld from Symbol Technologies. Office Depot cannot charge a customer until a signed bill is logged in the system. With the mobile device, the signature and bill are shipped to the Web and delivered, in real time, back to the customer. By speeding billing delivery, the company accelerates cash flow and brings an additional value to its business.

Networkcar sells a plug-in device that connects to computer diagnostic ports that are standard-issue in cars made after 1996. The device beams vital signs to a dealer, who can remotely diagnose or spot trouble. In such a manner, dealerships can achieve competitive advantage by maintaining a closer bond with their customers.

California utility firm Sempra Energy's engineers had to return to an office to enter data about heating, ventilation, and air conditioning units run by big users such as hotels. The mobile computers allow engineers to transmit and receive data and to make necessary equipment adjustments without leaving rooftops. This application should save a lot of time and cost.

iMeritikus allows doctors and patients wireless-online access to medical records. Patients can report any medical problems and update their health-care provider on what type and quantity of drugs they are taking, information that physicians can routinely monitor. For example, a patient can check his blood-sugar level as many as eight times a day, regularly uploading results onto the Web so his health-care provider can monitor his status. That patient complained about the trouble he has maintaining a virtual link to his physician when on the road--a link that grows more tenuous the deeper he goes into the back roads. With the wireless connection the patient solved his problem.

Research survey (www.indiqu.com) shows that 40% of the Fortune 2,500 businesses in the United States have equipped or are equipping their work forces with wireless tools. Another 30% "are considering" rolling out wireless systems.

So-called third-generation or 3G wireless networks promise super-fast mobile Internet-connectivity, real-time video, and streaming audio. This technology will support the development of m-commerce (mobile commerce for consumers).

Table 4-3: Types of Wireless Access Requirements for Mobile Workers

USERS	APPLICATIONS & CONTENT	USAGE PATTERNS
Mobile professionals	• E-mail and Personal Information Manager (PIM) • Corporate intranet • Real-time access to information (such as inventory numbers and sales)	• Significant travel and time in airports, taxis, and meetings • Outside of office more than 50 percent of time
Customer-facing employees	• E-mail • Corporate intranet	Outside office more than 20 percent of time
Sales forces	• E-mail and PIM • Corporate intranet • CRN • ERP for status and fulfillment	• Significant travel and time in airports, taxis and meetings • Outside of office more than 50 percent of time
Field service technicians	• Access to job dispatcher services • Access to parts database	• Varied locations, not always within wireless network coverage • May require ruggedized mobile device

Source: PriceWaterhouseCoopers, Technology Forecast: 2001-2003, Melno Park, CA 2001

Table 4-3 identifies mobile applications.

The following strategies can facilitate the company's transition to wireless applications (www.stellcom.com):

1. Keep it simple – begin with e-mail and later with the Web applications,

2. Customization is key – keep the information targeted, concise, and easy to access, eliminate multiple screens,

3. Find partners – to help the company in the correct implementation process,

4. Cater to customers – not just employees – provide information for customer and later for employees to achieve a new value for the business,

5. Become device-agnostic – find a right e-mobile application for a particular device, such as PC's, laptops, PDA's, pagers, cell phones, and voice mail. You won't ever book your flights on a cell phone. You'll book either by a phone or online. But when a flight is delayed, you expect to get a message on a cell phone.

EUC-END-USER COMPUTING

The end-user computing is a result of the rapid explosion of personal computers and the information centers in the 1980's when the latter supported that type of computing. From the 1960's to the 1980's computers were applied by the users of enterprise computing (ERC) which was composed of data processing applications. In the 1900's-2000's these applications evolved into a complex of ERP, SCM, CRM, e-DM, and WFS systems with very user-friendly Graphic User Interfaces (GUI). Those users were mostly engineers and "leading edge" managers and professionals. Nowadays, computers are applied by the majority of office workers under the form of end-user computing. Even workers at the shop level use computers either as a part of enterprise computing (e.g., Computer-Aided Manufacturing) or at home, just to send e-mail or browse through the Internet. Figure 4-22 illustrates the relationship among enterprise computing, hybrid computing, and end-user computing.

The end-user applications fall into two major categories:

1. Hybrid applications (HBA) that interface between (ERC) and EUC, such EIS, EPM, DSS, Data Mart, Data Mining, Data Retrieval from databases through a common language – SQL, and small applications that are written in the user-friendly languages of 4th generation (e.g., Visual Basic). Those applications are equipped with a GUI that is very user-friendly.

2. End-user computing that steadily expands its scope from office automation (word processing, spreadsheet, small database, e-mail) to graphics, desktop publishing (e.g., newsletters), calendaring, project management, home page design, browsing of the Internet, and so forth.

Figure 4-22: The Relationship of End-User Computing (EUC) with Enterprise Computing (EC)

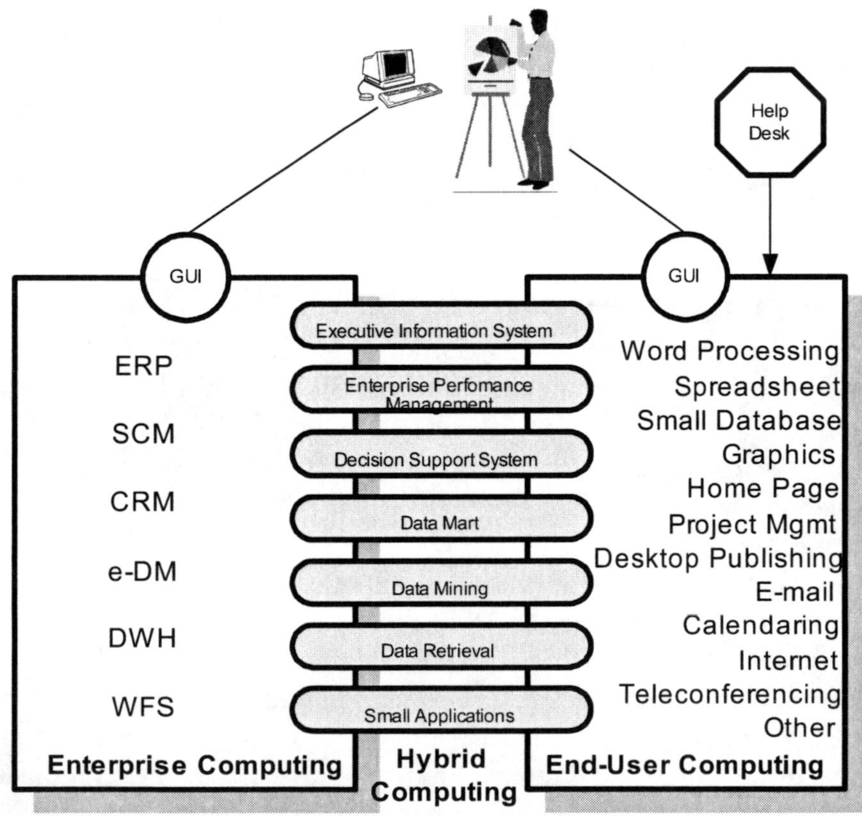

The end-users in the 2000's are recruited from:

- Managers, who on average constitute 28% of the office workforce and who spend 50% of their time in face-to-face communication. In general they are involved in analysis, searching for information, and managing activities (controlling and communicating). Hence, managers will mostly apply office automation and project management tools along with hybrid applications (EIS and EPM) on top of enterprise computing applications.

- Professionals (engineers, accountants, marketing and sales representatives, planners, etc.) must have a high degree of product/service knowledge. They spend about 30% of their day in face-to-face communication and about 40% of their day in problem-solving activities. They apply all types of end-user applications and more analytical hybrid applications along with enterprise computing applications. These types of users are very demanding and they lead other users in computer applications.

- Secretaries are very important workers of the enterprise and with the advent of computers they become even critical. The lead secretary in an office is rapidly becoming an office manager who is handling electronic files and all-office e-communications.

The EUC activities are supported by an information center (a term coined by IBM in the 1980's) which in the 2000's transformed into a help desk. Very often companies treat EUC as a tactical issue, while it should be treated as a strategic one. If end-users are at a competent level of computing skills they will strongly support the development of enterprise computing and make the business more effective. On the other hand, EUC cannot be a substitute for ERC, but just reflects about 10% to 20% of the enterprise's whole needs for computing, according to the author's estimation.

ENTERPRISE APPLICATIONS GRID

Figure 4-23 identifies a complex of enterprise applications. The enterprise application complex is characterized by the following system interactions:

- **Supervising Systems** such as MIS (Management Information System) and KMS (Knowledge Management System) help management in big-picture managing of the whole enterprise,

- **Integrating Systems** such as those which are operating via Web. These systems are mostly operational "processors" that facilitate handling components, queries, GUI, and security and include an Enterprise Information Portal too,

- **Fulfillment Systems** such as SCM (Supply Chain Management), ERP (Enterprise Resource Planning), and CRM (Customer Relationship Management) take care of mission-critical information processing of the enterprise,

Figure 4-23: The Architecture of e-Enterprise's Applications

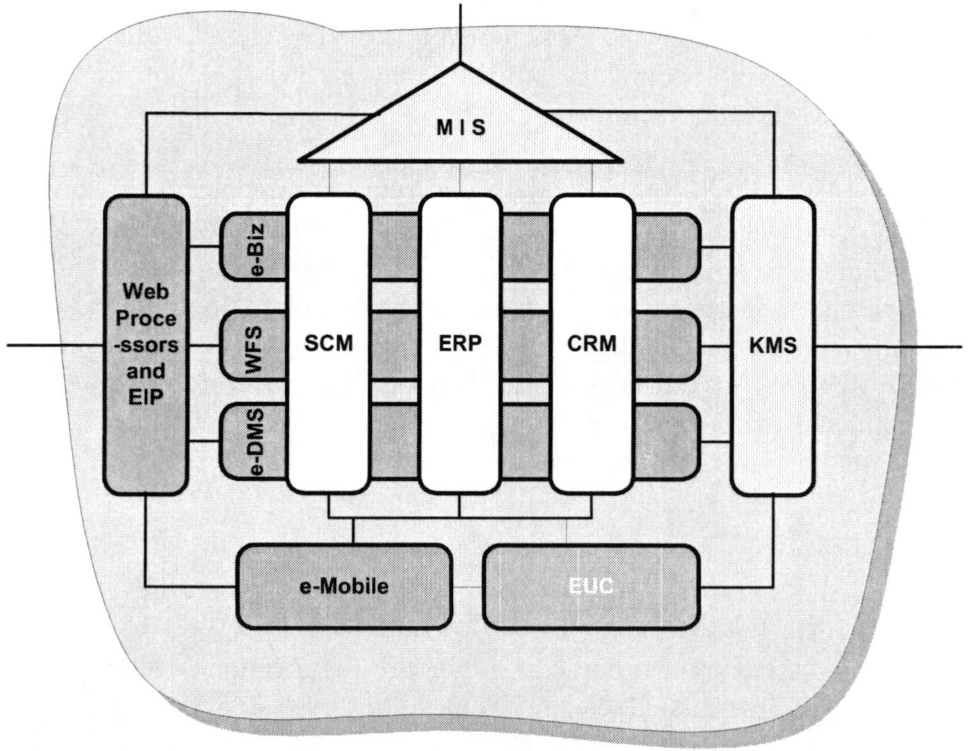

- **Electronizing Systems** such a e-DMS (e-Document Management System), WFS (Workflow System), e-Biz, and e-Mobil support the above systems in fulfilling their missions (in shadowed area),
- **Independent System** such as EUC (End User Computing).

FURTHER TRENDS

The further development of enterprise computing, at the Application Layer, will lead to steady growth of applications integration (EAI) within the framework of Business Process Integration (BPI), which is described in Chapter 7.

One of the forms of the application integration will be the evolution from e-business to m-business based on total mobility (look at Chapter 5).

The future of end-user computing is in improvements of application sophistication (e.g., use of intelligent agents) and in desk-top conferencing, perhaps with broader applications of telecommuting.

EUC becomes the second "driver's license" in human civilization that has entered the Information Wave phase. Those who neglect this license will be victims of human development, at least in terms of monetary values. However, monetary values may not necessarily be the most important to everybody.

CONCLUSION

The Application Layer becomes a very complex set of system federations at the level of business, product, operation, inter-organizational, and management processes. For example, the SAP ERP software package contains 0.5 billion lines of code, and the package does not include all business processes of an enterprise, it takes care of just 800 business processes.

Every year brings new applications and new ways of integrating them. The smooth integration of applications and technological solutions coming from different vendors requires their better standardization and electronization to facilitate development and operations of IT-driven enterprise. This issue will be discussed in Chapter 5.

BIBLIOGRAPHY

Akerlof, G.A. (1984). *An Economic Theorist's Book of Tales*. New York: Cambridge University Press.

Bertalanffy, L. (1968). *General System Theory.* New York: George Braziller.

Brobst, S. and Rarey, J. (2001). The five stages of an active data warehouse evolution. *Teradata*, Spring, p. 38-44.

Brunnermeier, M.K. (2001). *Asset Pricing under Asymmetric Information.* New York: Oxford University Press.

Chopra, S. & Meindl, P. (2001). *Supply Chain Management, Strategy, Planning, and Operations*. Upper Saddle River, NJ: Prentice Hall.

The CRM Phenomenon, White Paper, (2001). www.magic-sw.com.

Growth, R. (1998). *Data Mining.* Upper Saddle River, NJ: Prentice Hall PTR.

Harvard Business Review on Measuring Corporate Performance. (1998). Boston: Harvard Business School Press.

Hillier, B. (1997). *The Economics of Asymmetric Information*. New York: St. Martin's Press.

Kalakota, R. & Robinson, M. (2000). *e-Business, Roadmap for Success*. Reading, MA: Addison-Wesley.

Kalakota, R. & Robinson, M. (2001). *e-Business 2.0, Roadmap for Success.* Reading, MA: Addison-Wesley.

Kaplan, R. S. & Norton, D.P. (1996). *The Balanced Scorecard.* Boston: Harvard Business School Press.

Mattesini, F. (1993). *Financial Markets, Asymmetric Information and Macroeconomic Equilibrium*. Brookfield: Dartmouth.

Nonaka, I. & Takeuchi, H. (1995). *The Knowledge-Creating Company*. New York: Oxford Press.

Pollard, D. (2000). Becoming Knowledge-powered: Planning the Transformation. In *Knowledge Management and Virtual Organization*. Harrisburg, PA: Idea Group Publishing.

Saint-Onge, H. (199%). *Taping into the Tacit Knowledge of the Organization.* Toronto: CIBC Leadership Centre (unpublished).

Silver, B. (2000). *E-Documents for E-Business, IBM's Enterprise Information Portal Takes Aim at E-Business*. www.bsilver.com.

Targowski, A. (1990). *The Architecture and Planning of Enterprise-wide Information Management Systems*. Harrisburg, PA: Idea Group Publishing.

Targowski, A. (1999). *Enterprise Information Infrastructure.* Boston: Pearson.

Wiener, N. (1948). *Cybernetics: Or Control and Communication in the Animal and the Machine.* New York: Wiley.

ENDNOTES

1 Other 5 layers of EII have been presented in Chapter 3.

2 Depending on a type of industry.

3 In the past RMS stored and retrieved archived documents, which is now a subject of DMS.

4 In the SAP environment there is the EIS, which belongs to Financial Accounting – Controlling. Its mission is to control cost and revenue; as such it is an equivalent of the tactical EPM system.

5 One can mention a concept of an Enterprise Application Portal (EAP), which includes EIP and Application Integration via application servers and middleware.

6 Source: A student project at Western Michigan University, 2000.

7 It is necessary to notice that these data about improvements come from a vendor of CRM software.

Chapter V

Enterprise Electronization and Integration

STRATEGY AND RATIONALE

The goal of the electronic enterprise is to implement all major applications to build the extended enterprise that functions as a paperless organization, whose units and workers process information and communicate via all layers of the Enterprise Information Infrastructure (look at Chapter 3).

The strategy of the e-enterprise development is the integration of all business and application components via the Internet or intranet/extranet environment ("electronization"). The e-enterprise evolves from the net-commerce, based on EDI (1980's/1990's), the e-commerce stage (1997) and its follower - the e-business stage (1999), as a result of the electronization and integration of all enterprise applications.

The development of the e-enterprise began in the 2000's with the re-engineering of ERP systems in two directions:

- The expansion of ERP into links with SCM and CRM systems,
- The application of the four-tier IT architecture, where the Web-driven server integrates all components of the above systems.

Of course, the development of a complete e-enterprise will take decades, if not the whole 21st century, having in mind the whole economy. This process involves about 15% of the American GDP, which means that spending on information management exceeds $1 trillion. This sum can transform the industrial model of the enterprise into the information model quite effectively.

The annual productivity growth in the American Economy in the 1990's was at the level of 3% to 5% and was mostly influenced by information technology. As a result, almost each American business is almost transforming itself into the advanced computerization stage, which is reflected in 400,000 IT jobs vacancies in 2000/2001. Another result of this trend is the restructuring process of many corporations, which in the 2000's is reducing employment by thousands of workers, who in most cases are being replaced by the job automation and informatization.

The e-enterprise is not longer *science fiction* but the reality of the American business landscape.

SYSTEMS ELECTRONIZATION

The rapid electronization of an enterprise's applications in the 2000's is triggered by the application of the Internet, extranets, and intranets' capabilities, and particularly by their Web technology. The latter provides the following solutions:

- World Wide Web (WWW), whose heart is hypertext, by which information is organized as a series of documents with links for search and retrieval of text, images, sound, and video,
- Graphic User Interface (GUI), which is based on home pages whose users are impressed by its friendliness and ease of use,
- Web browsers that are powerful tools in searching information and fulfilling computing tasks,
- Web software servers that are computer language independent to allow for the integration of different applications that up until now have been isolated and have created the so-called "island of automation,"
- Enterprise Information Portals that integrate the user's community with a variety of shared information and applications,

- Easy and rapid connectivity among users and applications through the Internet and its derivatives, such as extranets and intranets,

- Internet Service Providers (ISP) that provide access to the Internet in almost every city and town, allowing a user paying a monthly fee to access the Web and enjoy a sophisticated e-mail system and plenty of other services.

Discussions about internet (Web) technologies typically focus their attention on end-user access; however, system-to-system integration is equally important and often considerably more complicated and costly. Fundamentally, internet computing is a platform that supports the open flow of information between systems. By leveraging ubiquitous technologies such as HyperText Transfer Protocol (HTTP), Hypertext Markup Language (HTML), Extensible Markup Language (XML), and JavaScript, that is a foundation for creating and transferring structurally complex documents across the Internet - the electronic (the Web-based) architecture delivers a set of server-based systems and services that support the true electronic systems integration.

A good example of the system electronization is the *PeopleSoft* Internet Architecture illustrated in Figure 5-1. It is a Four-Tier Architecture composed of the following levels:

1. Client Access – it can be a Web browser, a cell phone, or any external system,

2. Web Server – composed of the following services:
   - Portal Servlet[1] – based on JavaServlet that handles all inbound markup language and outbound requests for the Portal. It also manages all aspects of the *PeopleSoft* Portal such as search, content management, and home page personalization. It communicates with this back-end service via BEA System's JOLT,
   - Presentation Relay Servlet – based on JavaServlet that handles all inbound and outbound HTTP requests for *PeopleSoft* transactions and queries. This very thin servlet acts as a relay between the client device and the core back-end services. It receives and serves HTML, XML, and WML (wireless) requests over HTTP and maps the data in these requests to the Component Processor and Query Processor application services that execute under Tuxedo (Trans-

Figure 5-1: The PeopleSoft Internet Architecture

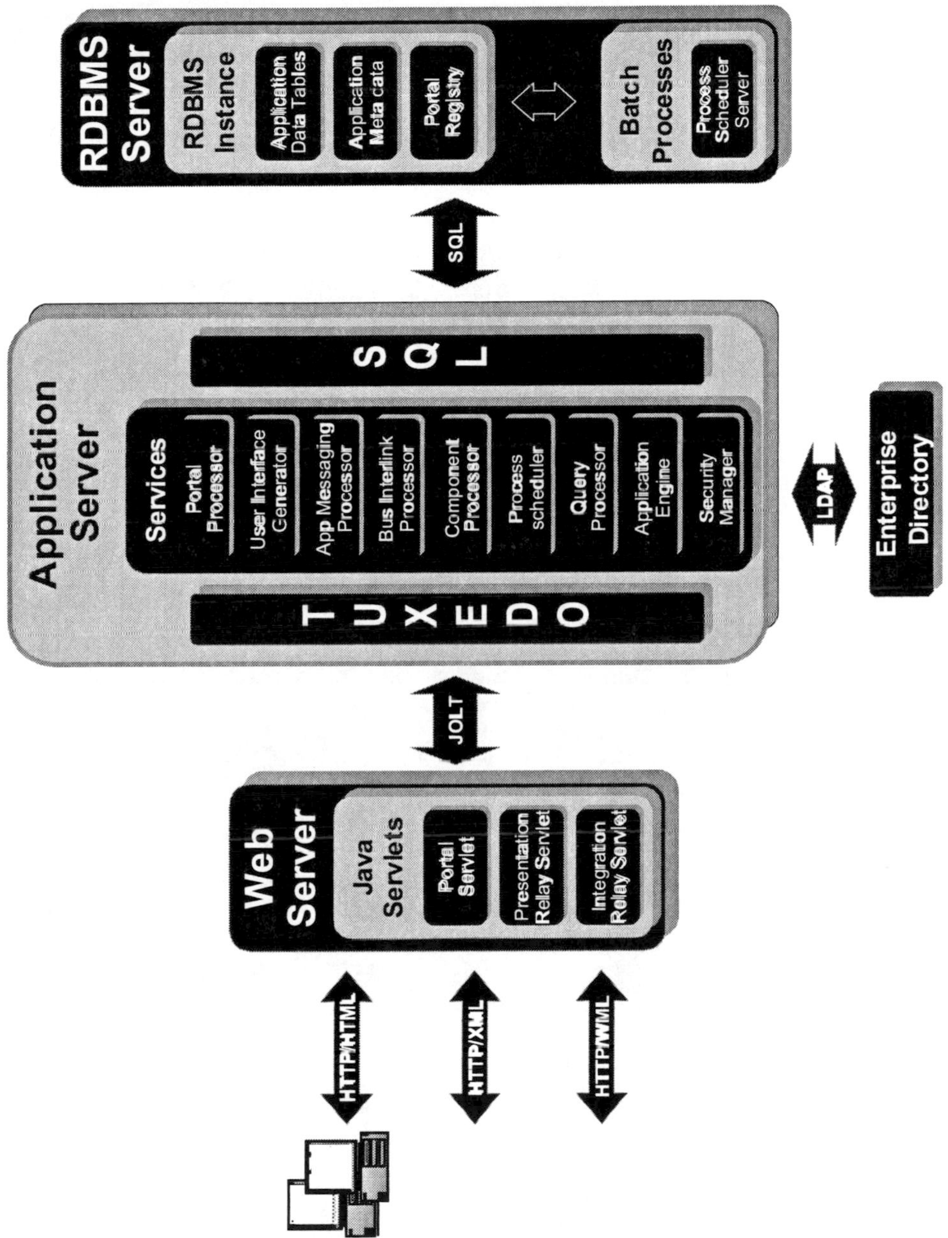

action Processing Monitor). It communicates with this back-end service via BEA System's JOLT,

- Integration Relay Servlet – based on JavaServlet that handles all inbound and outbound HTTP/XML requests for the third party system integration. This is also a very thin servlet that acts as a relay between the external or third-party system and the core back-end integration services. It receives and serves XML requests over HTTP and maps the data in these requests to the integration services – Application Messaging Processor, Business Interlink Processor, Component Processor – that execute under Tuxedo. This component communicates with this back-end service via BEA System's JOLT.

3. Application Server – applies Tuxedo – Transaction Processing Monitor (delivered by BEA Systems) to manage the following services:
   - Portal Processor – provides personalized and secured access to any system on the enterprise's internal and external network,
   - User Interface Generator – it dynamically generates the user interface based on the Component or Query definition and generates the appropriate markup language (HTML, XML, or WML) and scripting language (JavaScript, WMLScript) based on the client accessing the application,
   - Application Messaging Processor – manages the publishing, subscribing, and delivery of Application messages in a *PeopleSoft* system environment,
   - Business Interlink Processor – manages the execution of Business Interlink Plug-ins and their interaction with third-party systems, which for example have been acquired after the merger or in B2B inter-operations involving different platforms, such as UNIX and Windows NT,
   - Component Processor – is a key part of the Application Server; this processor executes *PeopleSoft*'s business application components,
   - Process Scheduler – executes reports and batch processes and registers the reports in the Portal's Content Registry,
   - Query Processor – executes queries defined using the *PeopleSoft* Query Tool,
   - Application Engine – Executes *PeopleSoft* application processes such as billing, loan handling, etc.,

- Security Manager – interfaces with the Enterprise Directory Server using Lightweight Directory Access Protocol (LDAP) to authenticate end users and manage their system access privileges,
- SQL Access Manager – manages all interactions with the Relational Database Management System (RDBMS) on its server.

4. RDBMS Server is the repository for all information managed by *PeopleSoft*'s enterprise applications. All *PeopleSoft* internet applications support industry-leading database management systems, including Oracle, Informix, IBM DB2, Sybase, and Microsoft SQL Server. Not only are application data stored in the database, but *PeopleSoft* metadata are also maintained in the database. The *PeopleSoft* Tools Application Designer development tools maintain this metadata which is then used to drive the runtime architecture. The *PeopleSoft* Application Server executes business applications based on this *PeopleSoft* metadata. Examples of common application objects are Fields, Records, Pages, Components, Application Messages, and Business Interlinks. When an application developer saves an application object, the Application Designer saves this definition to the PeopleTools metadata Repository. At execution time, the Application Server fetches the most recent application object definition from the Metadata Repository. It then compiles and caches in memory the application object definition and then executes the business application based on the definition. For example, when a Home Page is executed by the Application Server, the metadata definition is fetched, compiled, and cached. The page layout is generated based on this definition.

It is worthy to notice that using *PeopleSoft* Component Interfaces, third-party systems can synchronously invoke *PeopleSoft* business applications using COM, CORBA, EJB, or XML bindings, which will be described in the following sections.

PeopleSoft Portal is an important systems integration technology since it ties together content from a wide variety of data sources and delivers this content to end-users in the central User Interface Generator. Figure 5-2 depicts the architecture of *PeopleSoft*'s Portal. Its functions include:

- Personalized Homepage,

- Content Management,

- Web Publishing,
- Search,
- Workflow,
- Rule-based Access and Security,

Figure 5-2: The Architecture of PeopleSoft Portal

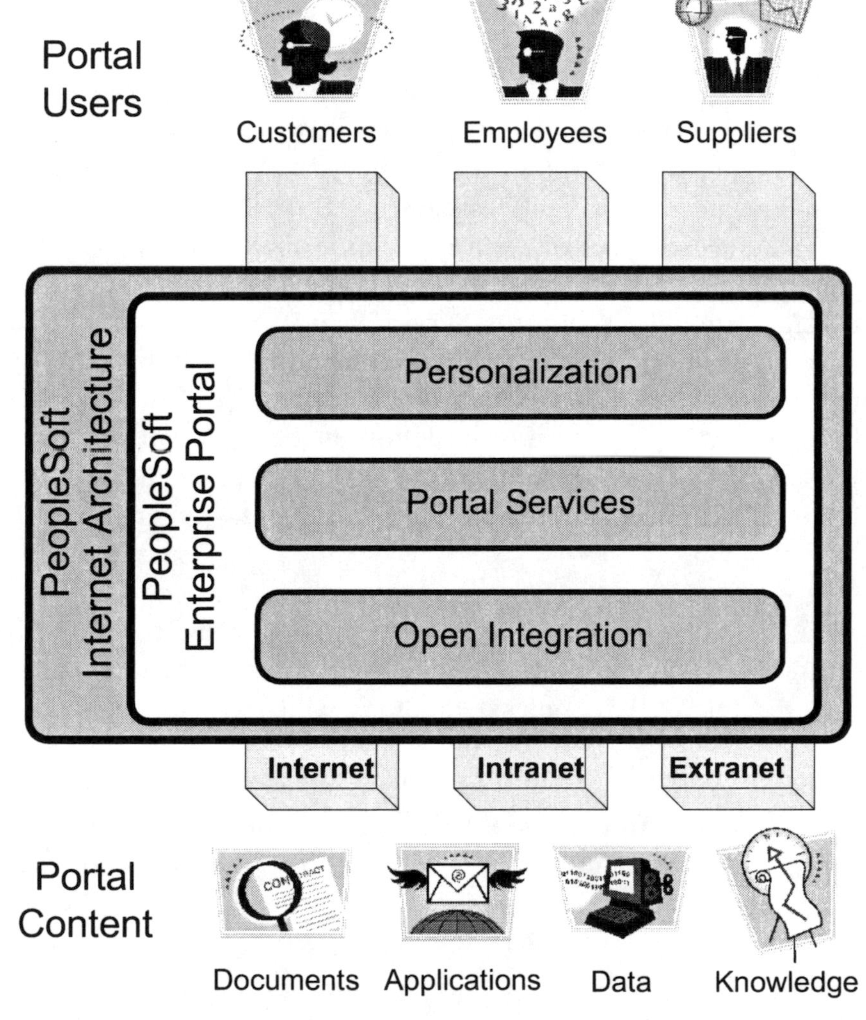

- XML Integration,
- LDAP Interface,
- Register new content,
- Upgrading,
- Metadata-driving,
- Multi-lingual,
- Multi-currency,
- Other.

SYSTEMS STANDARDIZATION

Distributing an application within a networked enterprise is not an end in itself. Distributed applications introduce a whole new kind of design and deployment issues. For this added complexity to be worthwhile, there has to be a significant payback. Some applications are inherently distributed: multi-user games, chat, and teleconferencing applications are examples of such applications. For these, the benefits of a robust infrastructure for distributed computing are obvious.

Many other applications are also distributed, in the sense that they have at least two components running on different machines. But because these applications were not designed to be distributed, they are limited in scalability and ease of deployment. Any kind of workflow or groupware application, most client/server applications, and even some desktop productivity applications essentially control the way their users communicate and cooperate. Thinking of these applications as distributed applications and running the right components in the right places benefits the user and optimizes the use of network and computer resources. The application designed with distribution in mind can accommodate different clients with different capabilities by running components on the client side when possible and running them on the server side when necessary.

Designing applications for distribution gives the system manager a great deal of flexibility in deployment. Distributed applications are also much more scalable than their monolithic counterparts. If all the logic of a complex application is contained in a single module, there is only one way to increase the throughput without tuning the application itself: faster hardware. Today's servers and operating systems scale very well but it is often cheaper to buy another identical machine than to upgrade to a server that is twice as fast. With a properly designed distributed application, a single server can start out running all the components. When the load increases, some of the components can be deployed to additional lower-cost machines.

With the advent of the Java programming language and the growth of the Internet, information technology (IT) managers are again excited at the prospect of using component software technology—the idea of breaking large, complex software applications into a series of prebuilt and easily developed, understood, and changed software modules called components—to deliver software solutions much more quickly and at a lower cost.

A component architecture for building software applications will enable the software provider to achieve economies of scale for software deployment by:

- **Speeding development**—enabling programmers to build solutions faster by assembling software from prebuilt parts.

- **Lowering integration costs**—providing a common set of interfaces for software programs from different vendors means less custom work is required to integrate components into complete solutions.

- **Improving deployment flexibility**—making it easier to customize a software solution for different areas of a company by simply changing some of the components in the application.

- **Lowering maintenance costs**—isolating software function into discrete components provides a low-cost, efficient mechanism to upgrade a component without having to retrofit the entire application.

A key goal of any component software architecture is to separate business logic—how a tax component calculates tax rates—from execution logic—whether the tax component runs in a browser or on a multiprocessor server. The following standards extend this separation even further because the same components can communicate with each other across processes in a single computer or between computers over the Internet.

However, components by themselves do not solve all of the issues of enterprise application complexity. For example, suppose a business wants to rapidly build and deploy a customer order entry application that involves five different areas of functionality: tax calculation, customer credit verification, inventory management, warranty update, and order entry. The application will be built from five separate components and will operate on a Web server. How does the developer handle exceptions? System failures? Network outages? Peaks in performance load? Must these be hand-coded into the application? It defeats the two main goals of component-based development—fast time to market and lower development costs—if companies are forced to hand-code the mission-critical services that are required for online production systems.

To address enterprise requirements for a distributed component architecture without sacrificing rapid development and cost effectiveness, the following standardized architectures support this requirement.

Hundreds of applications and thousands of their objects (components) are distributed through the e-enterprise environment. To facilitate this distribution, particularly among objects (components) from software developed by different programmers and vendors, standards have been offered by some developers, such as OMG (CORBA), Sun Microsystems (EJB), Microsoft (COM), and others.

CORBA STANDARD

CORBA, which stands for Common Object Request Broker Architecture, is an industry standard developed by the OMG (Object Management Architecture Guide, a consortium of about 800 companies organized in 1989). CORBA is open, vendor-independent architecture and infrastructure that computer applications use to work together over networks. Using the standard protocol IIOP, a CORBA-based program from any vendor, on almost any computer, operating system, programming language, and network, can interoperate with a CORBA-based program from the same or another vendor, on almost any other computer, operating system, programming language, and network. Some large companies are embedding CORBA in networked devices for finance and medical applications.

CORBA is useful in many situations. Because of the easy way that CORBA integrates machines from so many vendors, with sizes ranging from mainframes through minis and desktops to hand-held and embedded systems, it is the middleware of choice for large (and even not-so-large) enterprises. One of its most important, as well most frequent, uses is in servers that must handle large numbers of clients, at high hit rates, with high reliability. CORBA works behind the scenes in the computer rooms of many of the world's largest Websites, ones that you probably use every day. Specializations for scalability and fault-tolerance support these systems. But it is not used just for large applications; specialized versions of CORBA run real-time systems and small embedded systems. In CORBA, client and object may be written in different programming languages.

CORBA's architecture is based on *Object Orientation,* and built around seven key building blocks (www.omg.org):

- OMG Interface Definition Language, OMG IDL – defines the types of objects by defining their interfaces. An interface consists of a set of named operations and the parameters to those operations. Despite the fact that IDL is similar to C++ and Java, IDL is not a programming language. Through IDL, a particular object implementation tells its potential clients what operations are available and how they should be invoked. From IDL definitions, the CORBA objects are mapped into different programming languages, such as C, C++, Java, Smalltalk, LISP, and Python,

- Dynamic Invocation Interface (DII) – it allows client applications to use server objects without knowing the type of those objects at compile time,

- Dynamic Skeleton Interface (DSI) – it is a gateway to a server,

- Interface Repository (IR) – it provides another way to specify the interfaces to objects. Interfaces can be added to the interface repository service. Using the IR, a client should be able to locate an object that is unknown at the compile time, find information about its interface, then build a request to be forwarded through the OBR,

- Object Adapters (OA) – it is the primary way that object implementation access services are provided by the ORB. Such services include: object reference generation and interpretation, invocation method, security of interaction, and object implementation activation and deactivation,

- The Object Request Broker or ORB is a software responsible for: 1) finding the object implementation for the request, 2) preparing the object implementation to receive the request, and 3) communicating the data making up the request. A number of implementations exist in the market today, including ORBIX from IONA Technologies (*www.iona.ie*), VisiBroker from Inprise (*www.inprise.com*), and JavaIDL from JavaSoft (*www.java.sun.com/products/jdk.idl*),

- The standard protocol IIOP (The Internet Inter-ORB Protocol) makes sure that a client will be able to communicate with a server written for a different ORB from a different vendor.

CORBA applications are composed of *objects*, individual units of running software that combine functionality and data, and that frequently (but not always) represent something in the real world. Typically, there are many *instances* of an object of a single *type* - for example, your e-commerce website would have many shopping cart object instances, all identical in functionality but differing in that each is assigned to a different customer, and contains data representing the merchandise that its particular customer has selected. For each object type, such as your shopping cart, you define its interface in OMG IDL.

Figure 5-3: A Request Passing from a Client to an Object's Implementation

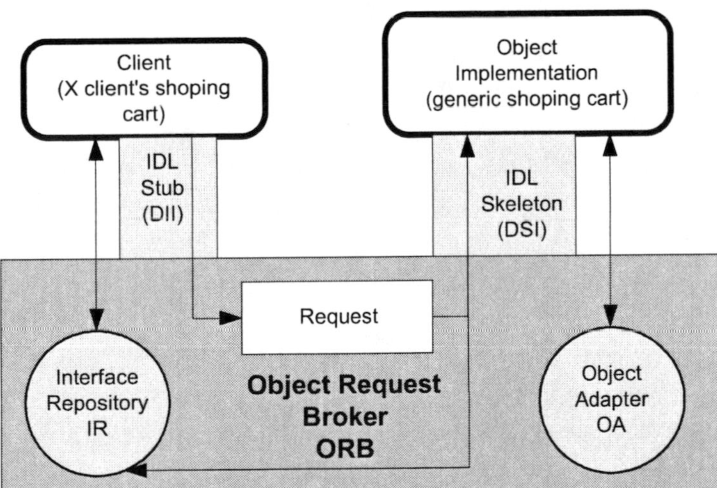

This fixes the operations it will perform and the parameters (input and output) for each. This interface definition is independent of your programming language, but *maps* to all of the popular programming languages via a set of OMG standards: OMG has standardized mappings for C, C++, Java, COBOL, Smalltalk, Ada, Lisp, Python, and IDLscript.

This is the essence of CORBA - how it enables interoperability, with all of the transparencies we have claimed. The *interface* to each object is defined very strictly. But, in contrast, the *implementation* of an object - its running code, and its data - is hidden from the rest of the system (that is, *encapsulated*) behind a boundary that the client may not cross. Clients access objects only through their advertised interface, invoking only those operations which that object chooses to expose, with only those parameters (input and output) that are included in the invocation.

Figure 5-3 shows how everything fits together, at least within a single process: You compile your IDL into client stubs as a Dynamic Invocation Interface (DII) and object Dynamic Skeleton Interface (DSI) and write your object (shown on the right) and a client for it (on the left). DII uses the Interface Repository (IR) to validate and retrieve the signature of the operations on which a request is made. Stubs and skeletons serve as proxies for clients and servers, respectively. Because IDL defines interfaces so strictly, the stub on the client side has no trouble meshing perfectly with the skeleton on the server side, even if the two are compiled into different programming languages, or even running on different ORB's from different vendors.

In CORBA, every object instance has its own unique *object reference*, an identifying electronic token. Clients use the object references to direct their invocations, identifying to the ORB the exact instance they want to invoke (ensuring, for example, that the books you select go into your own shopping cart, and not into your neighbor's). The client acts as if it's invoking an operation on the object instance, but it's actually invoking on the IDL stub which acts as a proxy. Passing through the stub on the client side, the invocation continues through the ORB (Object Request Broker) and the skeleton on the implementation side to get to the object where it is executed.

How do remote invocations work? Figure 5-4 diagrams a remote invocation. In order to invoke the remote object instance, the client first obtains its object reference. (There are many ways to do this, but we will not detail any of them here.) To make the remote invocation, the client uses the same code that it used in the local invocation we just described, but substitutes the object reference for the remote instance. When the ORB examines the object reference and discovers that the target object is remote, it marshals the

Figure 5-4: Inter-operability uses ORB-to-ORB Communication

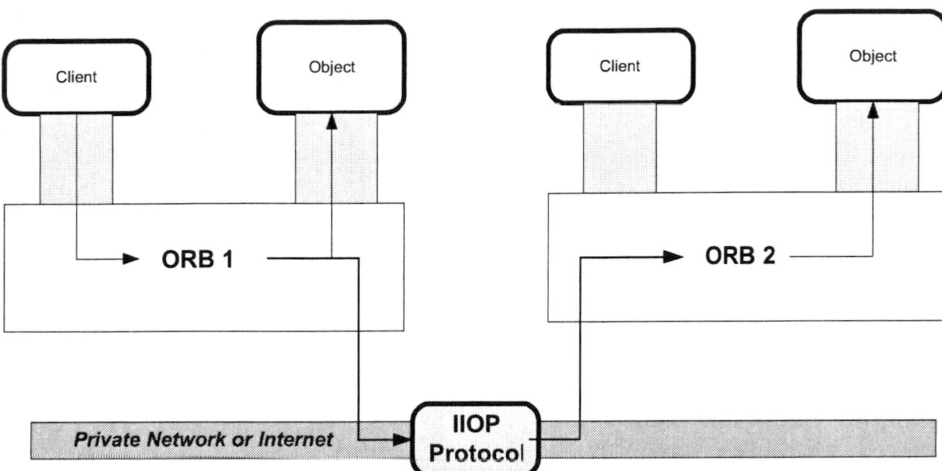

arguments and routes the invocation out over the network to the remote object's ORB.

Why does this work? OMG has standardized this process at two key levels: first, the client knows the type of object it is invoking (that it is a shopping cart object, for instance), and the client stub and object skeleton are generated from the *same IDL*. This means that the client knows exactly which operations it may invoke, what the input parameters are, and where they have to go in the invocation; when the invocation reaches the target, everything is there and in the right place. We have already seen how OMG has defined this. Second, the client's ORB and object's ORB must agree on a *common protocol* - that is, a representation to specify the target object, operation, and all parameters (input and output) of every type that they may use. OMG has defined this also - it's the standard protocol IIOP. (ORB's may use other protocols besides IIOP, and many do for various reasons. But virtually all speak the standard protocol IIOP for reasons of interoperability because it is required by OMG for compliance.)

Although the ORB can tell from the object reference that the target object is remote, the client cannot. (The user may know this also because of other knowledge - for instance, that all accounting objects run on the mainframe at the main office in Tulsa.) There is nothing in the object reference token that the client holds and uses at invocation time that identifies the location of the target object. This ensures *location transparency* - the CORBA principle[2] that simplifies the design of distributed object computing applications.

Use of CORBA and UML (Universal Modeling Language) pays off in many types of applications, but here is where the benefits compound:

- If you use CORBA in a small client-server type of application, you will get the benefits of a sound, standard infrastructure, and if you use UML to design before you start to code, you will be much more likely to get a final application with the structure and functionality that you had in mind (or would have asked for!) when you started. CORBA lets you build and run client and server sides on different platforms and in different programming languages, so there are a number of benefits that we can list even for small applications run alone on a network. But these are purely computer-domain benefits; the business functionality of this type of application is the same as if it had been written to sockets, or a proprietary call mechanism.

- Businesses benefit when all of their applications, with their diverse functionality and data, work together. For example, a salesman on the road in a customer's office may need access to product description information (from the catalog), product technical data (from engineering), pricing (from the back office), stock (from the warehouse), production schedule if there are not enough in stock (from the plant), order placement, customer credit data, sales department totals and his own totals, and more. In the old days, he used to collect this by telephone and memo, moving to FAX as technology advanced, but now computer networks give you an opportunity to make the diverse systems in all of these departments work together to support your salesman as he generates the income that, after all, keeps your company in business. So you wrap these legacy applications with OMG IDL interfaces and put them all onto your network, accessible via CORBA object references. This lets your IT department build a client that integrates information from all of them into a sales application. Your salespeople, online in their customers' offices via modem or wireless connection, can answer questions immediately and make more sales. Orders enter into your fulfillment system as they are taken, allowing you to schedule shipping (and production, if you need to) and billing automatically and immediately.

- The sales-peoples' application could become a Web sales site, allowing any potential customer with a browser to find and order your products themselves. Because all of your supporting applications are available via CORBA, it is easy to generate the application that drives the website, so you do this, and the sales start rolling in.

- With so many customers out there, the load of product support and repair calls increase and, since support has always been a cost center, you brainstorm to figure out a way to deal with it. You finally decide to design a call-center support application around your CORBA enterprise infrastructure. By standardizing response to trouble calls, you deal with these in less time, but the real benefit comes in parts and repair: with all of the engineering diagrams online, your telephone staff can sell and ship parts to customers with one or two clicks of a mouse, and with another click or two, can dispatch contracted repair vans to take care of the installation. Income from parts and commission on repair calls turn this cost center into a profit center, and customers' satisfaction increases at the same time. Integration of many applications around your enterprise that connect to the call-center application, a potential nightmare, is straightforward because they all have CORBA wrappers already.

- With success, the load on your e-commerce website increases until it outgrows the capacity of the mainframe applications that supported it at start-up. Since CORBA has been so successful for you on your network, you decide to build your server's replacement object-oriented in CORBA from the ground up. To start, you use UML for your analysis and design: it helps you gather requirements, work through use-cases, and set down the functionality that the new server will provide. Then, class diagrams, object diagrams, and action diagrams let you picture how it will work. By the time you're done, the UML diagrams that you have generated dictate most of your OMG IDL and language code. To take care of both current and anticipated load, you decide to buy an ORB that runs load-balanced on a roomful of server machines. It is based on OMG's Portable Object Adapter or POA, which helps you take the best advantage of your hardware when you run heavy loads, like the ones that Web-based applications generate. If your application needs to stay up reliably (as it would if you are running stock or bond trades, for example), you may decide to use CORBA Fault Tolerance also. More than just load-balancing, fault tolerance runs every object on two or more separate machines at the same time and automatically switches to the good one if one fails. If you duplicate your hardware (computers, networks, even power sources) also, you can set up a very reliable server indeed. By the way, you have not replaced all of your legacy systems (that is, the functional systems that run your business!), and this server still needs to access the ones that are still around. Since they all retain their CORBA wrappers, of course, this is routine. To maximize sales, you design the front-end for this server to be accessible from as many customer client types as possible: some customers come in via Web browsers, using HTTP which your Web server translates into CGI invocations of your CORBA front end. Others use Java/CORBA clients for more sophisticated programmatic access, while some users with direct network connections use OMG's standard COM/CORBA bridge to come in straight from a Microsoft desktop. Type-specific adapters condense your screens, eliminating graphics and isolating key lines of text, enabling digital PDA's, pagers, and browser-capable cell phones to place orders using your same business-logic architecture and implementation.

- To keep up with demand, you decide to automate your plant. Because of the speed that parts travel around the assembly line, the control program must run in real-time, so you build this system on an ORB and operating system that conform to the CORBA real-time specification. Computers on your shop-floor equipment also run CORBA (in real-time where needed here too), so your plant hums smoothly along; in fact, some of the processors on your shop floor run minimal CORBA, OMG's standard for embedded ORB's. Of course the plant doesn't run in isolation: it needs stock, which needs to be bought, which costs money, and needs to be brought to the plant, which needs logistical coordination, so your automation system also talks to your supply and logistics applications over CORBA interfaces, of course.

- The next addition would be CORBA-based interfaces to your suppliers, automating your logistics out to their warehouse (and, within their enterprise, hopefully to their plant as well). This is not a purely hypothetical example; Boeing Aircraft automates its manufacturing system from order entry through production and delivery, to maintenance, using CORBA.

So where's the payoff? Just as the different departments and divisions that make up your enterprise need to work together in order to maximize profit, their computing applications also need to work together. CORBA lets you do this, and that is where standards pay off in a big way: you cannot limit the diversity of computers in your enterprise - you need to pick different computers for different uses. This is clear on the shop floor, where equipment may come with a processor built-in, or in the call center, where machines need to link up to the telephone system computer for both voice and data to take advantage of ID information that comes with incoming calls. So, you pick a *standard interoperability infrastructure* - CORBA! - to tie your applications together. You would like to use it for *all* of your applications, but sometimes this just is not possible. For these cases, CORBA gives you the couplings you need: the COM/CORBA interoperability standard to connect to the desktop that everyone uses (and to Microsoft servers, too, if you have them); the reverse Java-to-IDL language mapping and RMI/IIOP to connect to Java RMI objects and EJB's, and the mapping from XML to OMG IDL.

How do they work together? You'll want (and need, actually) to perform an analysis and design before starting any substantial software development project. For this, you buy and use a tool based on UML, the Unified Modeling Language. Using XML Metadata Interchange or XMI, you transfer your model - which is the *metadata* for your application - into a standardized repository based on the MOF, or Meta-Object Facility. Using XMI again, you transfer your model from your MOF into a development environment that lets you implement it as a CORBA application. You will generate OMG IDL interfaces, which will map into the programming languages that you choose for your clients and objects, using the OMG-standard language mappings. You may design a scalable server-side architecture using features of the Portable Object Adapter or POA, and augment CORBA's support for load-balancing with a standard Fault Tolerant infrastructure. You will surely want to design your overall application around the CORBA services and possibly the Domain CORBA facilities to reap the major gains possible from the buy-vs.-build philosophy.

Who is using them, and what for? OMG has collected hundreds of design wins and success stories from companies that use CORBA, and posted them on our Website at *http://www.corba.org*. For readers who do not want to surf to that page now and get totally sidetracked, here are summaries of a few big CORBA users' applications:

- CNN uses an application based on the CORBA event service to distribute news material that comes in from hundreds of sources, in many formats, from many different machine types, to all of their news editors who run automated filter programs that audit the incoming events and flag the stories that qualify as important to each editor's individual preferences.

- Boeing integrated four "best of breed" manufacturing applications into a comprehensive infrastructure that takes care of airplane configuration from ordering, through manufacture, to maintenance.

- Charles Schwab and Company built a CORBA-based trading application that they use for their 5,000 best customers, handling accounts worth multiple billions of dollars.

ENTERPRISE JAVABEANS (EJB) STANDARD

The application of the Internet and its Web technology has changed the traditional client-server two-tier architecture into the four-tier architecture. Sun Microsystems, which developed the Java language, supports this architecture on its servers. Web-driven applications use various plug-in extensions to Web servers. These extensions invoke programs on the server that dynamically construct HTML documents ("home pages") from information stored in corporate databases and vice versa, the Web server extensions also enter information submitted in HTML forms into the corporate databases. An example of such extensions is CGI-bin scripts, which stands for Common Gateway Interface, and interface for developing HTML pages and Web applications.

Figure 5-5 illustrates the so-called J2EE (Java 2 Enterprise Edition) architecture which allows for the development and implementation of enterprise Web-oriented applications using the Java programming language.

Figure 5-5: The Four-Tier J2EE Architecture for Web-based Applications

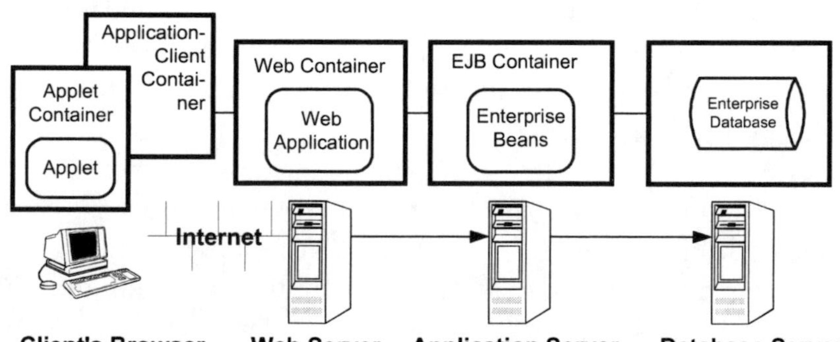

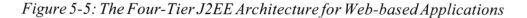

The J2EE platforms consist of four programming environments, called containers:

- The EJB Container – provides the environment for the development, deployment, and runtime management of enterprise beans. Enterprise beans are components that implement the business processes and entities under the form of applications.

- The Web Container – provides the environment for the development, deployment, and runtime management of servlets and JavaServer Pages. Servlets are specialized programs called pseudo applets (mini applications) that run on the server side. Java Servlets are a popular choice for building interactive Web applications, replacing the use of CGI scripts. Servlets are similar to applets (generated from the browser) in that they are runtime extensions of applications. Instead of working in browsers (like applets), servlets run with Java Web servers, configuring or tailoring the server.

- The Application-Client Container – provides the environment for executing J2EE application clients. This environment is essentially the Java 2 platform, Standard Edition.

- The Applet Container – provides the environment for executing Java applets. This environment is typically embedded in a Web browser.

The J2EE Platform embraces the Common Object Request Broker Architecture (CORBA). All J2EE Containers include a COBRA-compliant Object Request Broker (ORB) module. The inter-operability protocol between EJB Containers from multiple vendors is based on COBRA standards, such as Remote Method Interaction over the Internet Inter-ORB protocol (RMI-IIOP) and the Object Transaction Service (OTS).

The EJB architecture requires six roles of professionals:

1. Bean Developer – develops the enterprise applications' components (beans),

2. Application Assembler – puts together different, but logically interrelated beans into a larger unit such as a subsystem or a system,

3. Deployer – deploys the application within a particular computer operated environment,

4. System Administrator – configurates and administers the Enterprise Information Infrastructure,

5. EJB Container Provider and EJB Server Provider – a vendor specializing in transactions and application management.

DNA - DCOM STANDARD[3]

The Distributed Component Object Model (DCOM) developed by Microsoft has three strengths that make it a key technology (*www.msdn.microsoft/library.com*):

- DCOM is based on the most widely-used component technology today. DCOM is simply "COM[4] with a longer wire"—a low-level extension of the Component Object Model, the core object technology within Microsoft® ActiveX® (COM enabled for the Internet). Major development tools vendors—including Microsoft, Borland, Powersoft/Sybase, Symantec, ORACLE, IBM, and Micro Focus—already sell software development tools that produce ActiveX components. These tools and the applications they produce automatically support DCOM, providing the broadest possible industry support. Additionally, over 1,000 existing commercial software components that will work with DCOM are already available for use by developers.

- DCOM extends component applications across the Internet. Because it is an ActiveX technology, DCOM works natively with Internet technologies like TCP/IP, Java, and HTTP, enabling business applications to work across the Web. DCOM enables distributed Java today without requiring any communications-specific code or add-ons.

- DCOM is an open technology that runs on multiple platforms. Microsoft is openly licensing DCOM technology to other software companies to run on all of the major operating systems, including multiple implementations of UNIX-based systems. Software AG has DCOM running on the Solaris-based operating system today. Additionally, Microsoft is handing over DCOM technology with other core ActiveX technologies to The Open Group. The Internet Draft technical publication that contains a publicly available description of the DCOM network protocol can be found at *http://www.dc.luth.se/doc/id/draft-brown-dcom-v1-spec-00.txt*.

The combination of these three factors—the largest installed base, native support for Internet protocols, and open support for multiple platforms—means that businesses can gain the benefits of a modern component application architecture without having to replace investments in existing systems, staff, or infrastructure.

DCOM Architecture

DCOM is an extension of the Component Object Model (COM). COM defines how components and their clients interact. This interaction is defined such that the client and the component can connect without the need of any intermediary system component. The client calls methods in the component without any overhead whatsoever.

In today's operating systems, processes are shielded from each other. A client that needs to communicate with a component in another process cannot call the component directly, but has to use some form of inter-process communication provided by the operating system. COM provides this communication in a completely transparent fashion: it intercepts calls from the client and forwards them to the component in another process. Figure 5-6 illustrates how the COM/DCOM run-time libraries provide the link between client and component.

Figure 5-6: DCOM: COM Components in Different Processes (DCE–Distributed Computing Environment, RPC–Remote Procedure Call, LPC–Local Procedure Call)

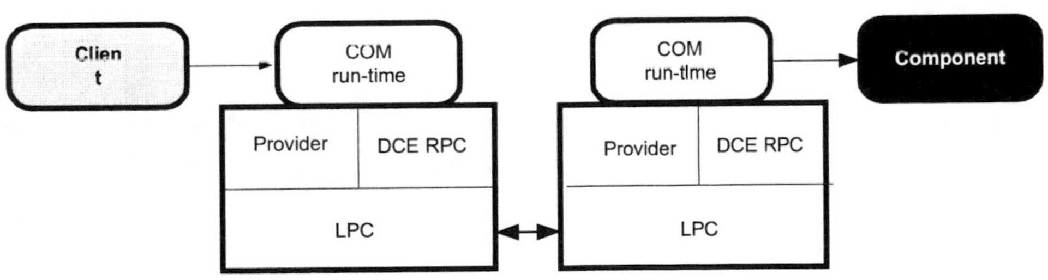

Figure 5-7: DCOM: COM Components on Different Machines

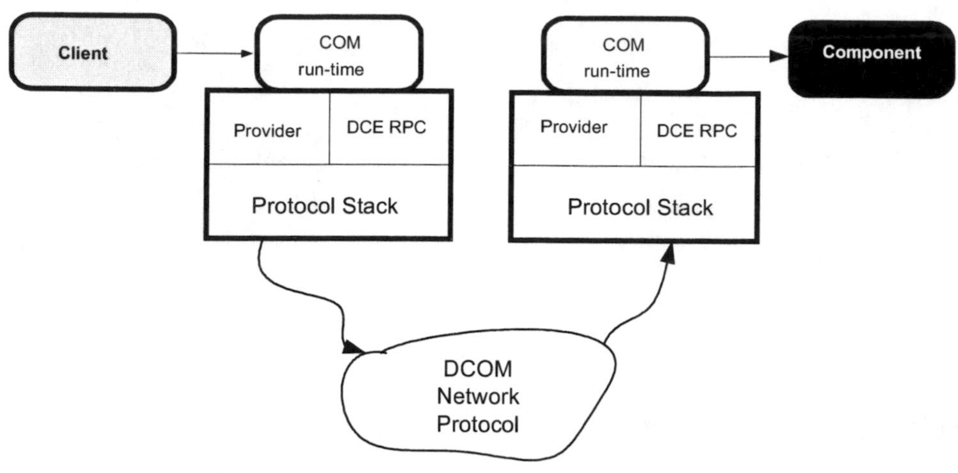

When client and component reside on different machines, DCOM simply replaces the local inter-process communication with a network protocol. Neither the client nor the component is aware that the wire that connects them has just become a little longer. Figure 5-7 shows the overall DCOM architecture: the COM run-time provides object-oriented services to clients and components and uses RPC and the security provider to generate standard network packets that conform to the DCOM wire-protocol standard.

Components and Reuse

Most distributed applications are not developed from scratch and in a vacuum. Existing hardware infrastructure, existing software, and existing components, as well as existing tools, need to be integrated and leveraged to reduce development and deployment time and cost. DCOM directly and transparently takes advantage of any existing investment in COM components and tools. A huge market for off-the-shelf components makes it possible to reduce development time by integrating standardized solutions into a custom application.

Components and the Enterprise

As distributed applications are built from simple components and Internet protocols emerged, a new set of enterprise platform services for component applications will be required. To address enterprise requirements for distributed component architecture without sacrificing rapid development and cost effectiveness, Microsoft is integrating DCOM into the Active Server. The Active Server is a series of technology services that speed deployment of component-based applications for the Internet and corporate intranets. These services include:

- **Transactions**—traditional rollback and recovery for component-based applications in the event of system failure.
- **Queuing**—integration of component communication with reliable store-and-forward queues, which enables component applications to operate on networks that are occasionally unavailable.
- **Server scripting**—easy integration of component applications on the server with HTML-based Internet applications.
- **Legacy access**—integration of component applications with legacy production systems, including mainframe systems running CICS and IMS.

The Active Server technologies use publicly obtainable Internet protocols and are currently available[5].

MICROSOFT .NET FRAMEWORK[6]

Microsoft evolves from the COM-DNA platform to the new .NET platform designed to simplify application development in the highly distributed environment of the Internet. This is a transformation from desktop applications to the distributed GUI-based .NET applications. The .NET Framework affects all of Microsoft's products, from operating systems, servers, and middleware to applications. All these products are capable of handling and processing .NET traffic and leveraging the .NET infrastructure. These products will transform to Windows.NET, Office.NET, MSN.NET, and so forth.

The .NET Framework is aimed to develop a new software platform that is independent of an operating system, components, and applications that are written to run on the virtual machine. The .NET virtual machine is Common Language Runtime (CLR), which can be a platform for applications written in any language, unlike JVM (Java Virtual Machine) which accepts applications written only in Java. Micosoft designed .NET to be a very friendly environment for applications, particularly those written in Visual Basic and C#. The .NET Framework supports any of a variety of languages. It also relies on XML coupled with SOAP (Simple Object Access Protocol) to link components running on distributed .NET platforms.

Since COM is too embedded in Windows, Microsoft is replacing DCOM with XML and SOAP while transforming from Windows to the .NET Framework[7].

The architecture of the .NET Framework is shown in Figure 5-8.

The .NET Framework has four main components:

1. The Common Language Runtime (CLR)

2. The .NET Framework Class Library

3. Communication Protocols

4. Visual Studio .NET

Common Language Runtime (CLR)

The Common Language Runtime is the foundation of the .NET Framework. You can think of the runtime as an agent that manages code at execution time, providing core services such as memory management, thread management, and remoting, while also enforcing strict safety and accuracy of the code. In fact, the concept of code management is a fundamental principle of the runtime. Code that targets the runtime is known as managed code; code that does not target the runtime is known as unmanaged code.

Managed components are awarded varying degrees of trust, depending on a number of factors that include their origin (such as the Internet, enterprise network, or local computer). This means that a managed component might or might not be able to perform file-access operations, registry-access operations, or other sensitive functions, even being used in the same active application.

The runtime enforces security in a way that enables users to trust that although an executable attached to an e-mail can play an animation on screen or sing a song, it cannot access their personal data, file system, or network. The security features of the runtime thus enable legitimate Internet-deployed software to be exceptionally feature-rich. The runtime also enforces code robustness by implementing a strict type- and code-verification infrastructure called the common type system (CTS). The CTS ensures that all managed code is self-describing. The various Microsoft and third-party language compilers generate managed code that conforms to the CTS. This means that

Figure 5-8: The Architecture of Microsoft .NET Framework within the Microsoft Software Tools Environment (The Targowski Model)

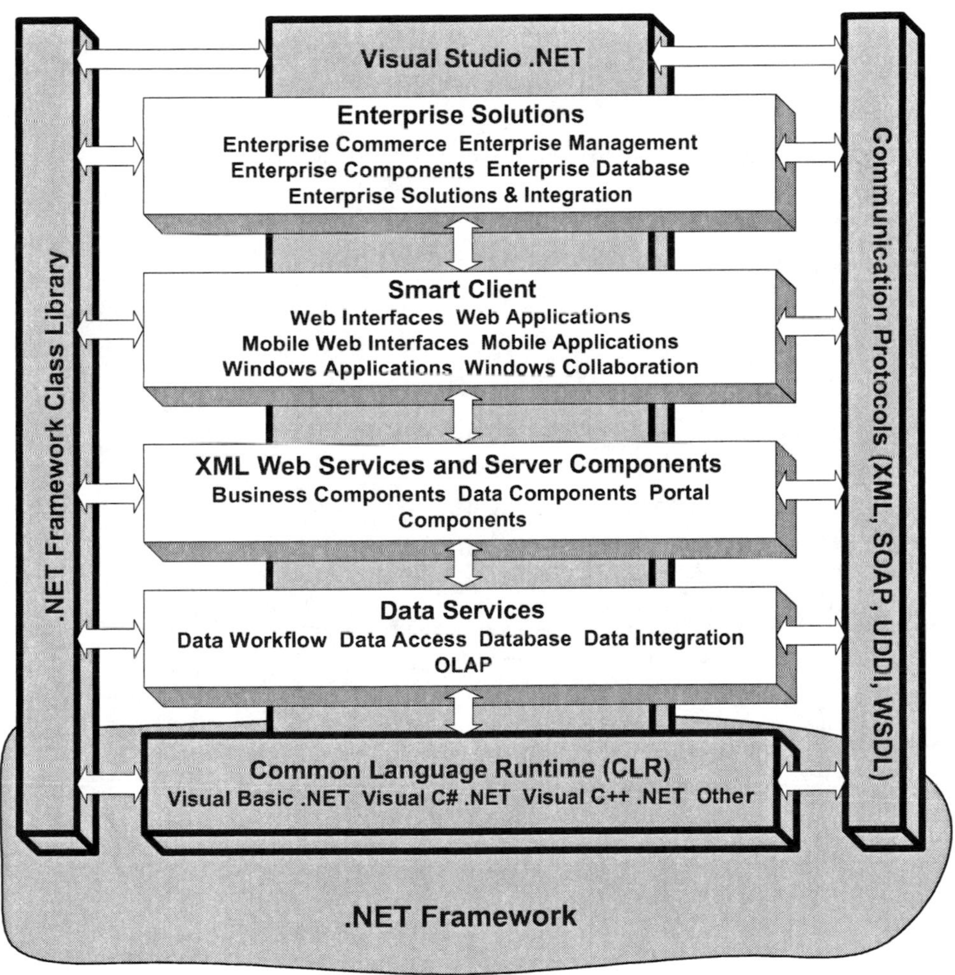

managed code can consume other managed classes, types, and objects, while strictly enforcing type fidelity and type safety.

The runtime, coupled with the CTS, also accelerates developer productivity. For example, programmers can use their favorite development language, being absolutely assured that they can still take full advantage of the runtime, the class library, and components written in other languages by other developers. Any compiler vendor who chooses to target the runtime can do so. Language compilers that target the .NET Framework make the features of the .NET Framework available to existing code written in that language, thus greatly easing the migration process for existing applications.

Although the runtime is designed for the software of the future, it also supports software of today and yesterday. Interoperability between managed and unmanaged code enables developers to continue to use necessary COM components and DLL's. The runtime is designed to enhance performance. A feature called Just-In-Time (JIT) compiling enables all managed code to run in the native machine language of the system on which it is executing.

Finally, the runtime can be hosted by high-performance, server-side applications, such as Internet Information Services (IIS) and Microsoft® SQL Server. (www.microsoft.com).

.NET Framework Class Library

The .NET Framework class library is a comprehensive, object-oriented collection of reusable classes that you can use to develop applications ranging from traditional command-line or graphical user interface (GUI) applications to applications based on the latest innovations provided by ASP.NET and Web Services. The class library builds on the object-oriented nature of the runtime, providing types from which your own managed code can derive functionality. This not only makes the .NET Framework types easy to use, but also reduces the learning curve associated with using a new piece of code. In addition, third-party components can integrate seamlessly with the classes in the .NET Framework.

As you would expect from an object-oriented class library, the .NET Framework types enable you to accomplish a range of common programming tasks, including tasks such as string management, data collection, database connectivity, and file access. In addition to these common tasks, the class library includes types that support a variety of specialized development scenarios.

For example, you can use the .NET Framework to develop the following types of applications and services:

- Console applications
- Scripted or hosted applications
- Windows GUI applications (Windows Forms)
- ASP.NET applications (Active Server Pages)
- Web Services
- Windows 2000 and Windows NT services

For example, the Windows Forms classes are a comprehensive set of reusable types that vastly simplify Windows GUI development. If you are writing an ASP.NET application or Web Service, on the other hand, you use different classes, such as the Web Forms classes (www.microsoft.com).

Communication Protocols

The communication protocols form the foundation of the .NET Framework, which develops distributed applications that inter-operate through the Internet; therefore they must do this by complying with a common communication protocol. The current practice with the set of Remote Procedure Call (RPC) technologies has too many limitations that make an application not fully inter-operational. Rather than develop a brand-new protocol to overcome the shortcomings of COM/DCOM and CORBA, Microsoft decided to build the .NET Framework on top of a set of standard, open, XML-based protocol such as Simple Object Access Protocol (SOAP), Universal Discovery, Description and Integration (UDDI), and Web Service Definition Language (WSDL).

This protocol transmits SOAP, UDDI, and WSDL messages as a plain text, so it is platform neutral. There is no need to write a bridge to translate a method call from one Object RPC to another. A SOAP message looks the same on Linux as it does on Windows as it does on AS/400. Since these protocols are open standards, they can be implemented anywhere in the manner that is most appropriate for the platform. On the Microsoft platform, a SOAP server is targeted at IIS and written in either ASP or ISAPI (www.microsoft.com).

Visual Studio .NET

To succeed in today's business environment, applications must be more scalable, reliable, and flexible than ever before. At the same time, the fast pace of business change means that developers must design and launch enterprise applications in days or weeks rather than months or years. Microsoft Visual Studio is a complete enterprise-class development system that helps developers meet those demands by providing the tools to create powerful, mission-critical applications—quickly and efficiently.

Visual Studio offers a wide range of features and tools designed specifically to support team-based application development efforts, including teams that are geographically dispersed. The distributed Web project model uses HTTP for all authoring operations, so that developers working in different locations can collaborate on the creation of sophisticated Web applications. With a Visual Component Manager, developers can find, track, catalog, and reuse components easily. For better version control, Microsoft Visual SourceSafe® provides complete code source control and file-locking features for team development projects from any tool within the Visual Studio development suite.

Developers can use a familiar, shared development environment and the programming languages they already know. Pre-built components, programming wizards, and the ability to reuse components written in any language can cut the development cycle time significantly. IntelliSense®-based code completion enables developers to produce accurate code more quickly. Finally, powerful end-to-end, cross-language debugging support, coupled with cross-language debugging, helps development teams get applications up and running more rapidly.

Increasingly, all business is e-business. Enterprises look to the Internet as an essential medium not only for communications but also for commerce and operational efficiency. The Visual Studio delivers highly scalable, data-driven websites and applications. Its wide range of database programming and design tools utilize the Microsoft Universal Data Access technology. Developers can use powerful point-and-click database diagrams and graphical tools for creating tables, relationships, stored procedures, and database functions for Microsoft SQL Server™ and Oracle databases. ActiveX® Data Objects enable easy access to information from all industry-leading data sources, including Microsoft SQL Server, Microsoft Access, Microsoft FoxPro®, Oracle, and IBM mainframe and AS/400 databases. The Microsoft Data Engine ensures full compatibility with large SQL Server databases.

Developers can also choose the programming language they know best—and the language that is best suited to the solution, including Microsoft Visual Basic®, Visual C++®, Visual J++®, and Visual FoxPro®.

Thin-client, HTML-based front ends make it easy to deploy the results to any desktops running virtually any operating system (www.microsoft.com).

Client Application Development in .NET

Client applications are the closest to a traditional style of application in Windows-based programming. These are the types of applications that bring up Windows or Forms on the desktop and which you use to perform a task. Client applications include applications such as word-processors and spreadsheets, as well as custom business applications such as data-entry tools, reporting tools, and so on. Client applications usually employ windows, menus, buttons, and other GUI elements, and they likely access local resources such as the file system and peripherals such as printers.

Another kind of client application is the traditional ActiveX control (now replaced by the managed Windows Forms control) deployed over the Internet as a Web page. These types of applications are much like other client applications, in that they are executed natively, have access to local resources, and include graphical elements.

In the past, developers created such applications using C/C++ in conjunction with the Microsoft Foundation Classes (MFC) or with a rapid application development (RAD) environment such as Microsoft® Visual Basic®. The .NET Framework incorporates aspects of existing products into a single, consistent development environment that simplifies the development of client applications.

The Windows Forms classes contained in the .NET Framework are designed to be used for GUI development. You can easily create command windows, buttons, menus, toolbars, and other screen elements with the flexibility necessary to accommodate shifting business needs.

For example, the visual attributes of forms often need to be modified during the life of an application. Forms are implemented using a window from the underlying operating system. However, some visual changes might not be supported by the underlying operating system for existing windows. Changes to visual features of that type can require the creation of an entirely new window. In unmanaged applications, such a visual feature would probably be discarded, due to the complexity of updating it. In managed code, however, when you change a Windows Form object, the framework creates a new operating system window object and automatically moves the relevant state from the old window to the new window. This is just one of many examples of the ways in which the framework homogenizes the developer interface, thus making coding simpler and more consistent.

The runtime's built-in security and deployment features can revive the client application in some innovative ways. For example, many applications that once needed to be installed on a user's system can now be deployed through the Web. This is possible because code-access security limits what a piece of software can do, even though the software is running in native machine language. In fact, a single Web-deployed application can comprise various components distributed from any number of different websites. In such a case, object methods provided by one vendor can have different security rights than object methods provided by a second vendor, even though they are used together to create a single application running in a single system process.

Unlike ActiveX controls, Windows Forms controls enjoy semi-trusted access to a user's machine. This means that binary or natively executing code can access some of the resources on the user's system (such as GUI elements and limited file access), without being able to undermine a user's system (www.microsoft.com).

Server Application Development in .NET

Web Services, an important evolution in Web-based technology, are distributed, server-side application components similar to common websites. However, unlike Web-based applications, Web Services components have no UI and are not targeted for browsers such as Internet Explorer and Netscape Navigator. Instead, Web Services consist of reusable software components designed to be consumed by other applications, such as traditional client applications, Web-based applications, or even other Web Services. As a result, Web Services technology is rapidly moving application development and deployment into the highly distributed environment of the Internet.

ASP.NET (Active Server Pages) is the hosting environment that enables developers to use the .NET Framework to target Web Services applications. Both Web Forms and Web Services use Internet Information Server (IIS) as the publishing mechanism for applications, and both have a collection of supporting classes in the .NET Framework. ASP.NET is more than the next version of Active Server Pages (ASP); it is a unified Web development platform that provides the services necessary for developers to build enterprise-class Web applications. While ASP.NET is largely syntax compatible with ASP, it also provides a new programming model and infrastructure that enables a powerful new class of applications.

ASP.NET has been designed to work seamlessly with WYSIWYG HTML editors and other programming tools, including Microsoft Visual Studio.NET. This makes Web development easier, but it also provides the benefits that these tools have to offer, including a GUI that developers can use to drop server controls onto a Web page, as well as fully integrated debugging support.

Developers can choose from two programming models when creating an ASP.NET application, or combine these in any way they see fit:

- Web Forms allows you to build powerful forms-based Web pages. When building these pages, you can use ASP.NET server controls to create common UI elements and program them for common tasks. These controls allow you to rapidly build up a Web Form out of reusable built-in or custom components, simplifying the code of a page.

- A Web service is a way to access server functionality remotely. Using services, businesses can expose programmatic interfaces to their data or business logic, which in turn can be obtained and manipulated by client and server applications. Web services enable the exchange of data in client-server or server-server scenarios, using standards like HTTP and XML messaging to move data across firewalls. Web services are not tied to a particular component technology or object-calling convention. As a result, programs written in any language, using any component model, and running on any operating system can access Web services.

ASP.NET takes advantage of performance enhancements found in the .NET Framework and runtime, and it has also been designed to offer performance improvements over ASP and other Web development platforms. All ASP.NET code is compiled rather than interpreted, which allows early binding, strong typing, and just-in-time (JIT) compiling to native code, to name only a few of its benefits. ASP.NET is also easily factorable, meaning that developers can remove modules (a session module, for instance) that are not relevant to the application they are developing. ASP.NET configuration settings are stored in XML-based files, which are human readable and writable. Each of your applications can have a distinct configuration file and you can extend the configuration scheme to suit your requirements. ASP.NET provides easy-to-use Application and Session state facilities that are familiar to ASP developers and are readily compatible with all other .NET Framework API's.

If you have used earlier versions of ASP technology, you will immediately notice the improvements in Web Forms. For one thing, you can develop your Web Forms pages in any language that supports the .NET Framework. In addition, your code no longer needs to share the same file with your HTTP text (although it can continue to do so if you prefer that structure). Web Forms pages execute in native machine language because they take full advantage of the runtime like any other managed application. Unmanaged ASP pages were always scripted. In short, ASP.NET pages are faster, more functional, and easier to develop because they interact with the runtime like any managed application.

The .NET Framework also provides a collection of classes and tools to aid in development and consumption of Web Services applications. Web Services are built on standards such as SOAP (a remote procedure-call protocol), XML (an extensible data format), and WSDL (Web Service Description Language). The .NET Framework conforms to these standards to promote interoperability with non-Microsoft solutions.

If you develop and publish your own Web Service, the .NET Framework provides a set of classes that conform to all of the underlying communication standards, such as SOAP, WSDL, and XML. Using those classes enables you to focus on the logic of your service, without worrying about the communications infrastructure required by distributed software development.

Finally, like Web Forms pages in the managed environment, your Web Services will run with the speed of native machine language using the scalable communication of IIS (www.microsoft.com).

XML STANDARD

When not pursuing wholly new application development, organizations can be found attempting to create applications that aggregate several traditional, task-oriented applications into a single, composite application. This sometimes includes integrating applications that exist within the boundaries of a separate entity, such as another company or a service provider. However, a still greater dilemma arises when attempting to integrate legacy applications built using an assortment of technologies, object models, operating systems and programming languages. How do you make them all work together? The answer is the programmable Web.

XML (eXtensible Markup Language) as an open data description format has given rise to the reality of a programmable Web. Just as TCP/IP provided universal connectivity for the Internet and HTML provided a standardized language to display information on a wide variety of platforms for human consumption, XML provides a standardized language to exchange data for automated consumption. This makes it possible to represent data in a widely accepted format that enables computers to send and receive data in a predictable style that enables programmability that extends beyond closed, controlled systems. XML is liberating because its simplicity and extensibility lets you define just about anything with room to expand later. One of the fundamental building blocks of the programmable Web is Web Services.

XML is for documents containing structured information. Structured information contains both content (words, pictures, etc.) and some indication of what role that content plays (e.g., content in a section heading has a different meaning from content in a footnote, which means something different than content in a figure caption or content in a database table, etc.). Almost all corporate documents have some structure. A markup language is a mechanism to identify structures in a document. The XML specification defines a standard way to add markup to documents. Among documents one can mention those such as word processing, vector graphics, e-commerce transactions, mathematical equations, object metadata, and so forth.

XML was created so that richly structured documents could be used over the Web. Its predecessor HTML, for the creation of homepages, does not provide a way to define a structured document. The term markup comes from the print profession where electronic documents are "marked up" with tags that tell a computer what to do. It serves two purposes; to determine the formatting and to define a document's structure and meaning. XML is a standardized set of markup tags that conform to a defined syntax (grammar).

Every XML document has logical and physical structures. The former defines a document's framework and the latter contains the actual data that fills a document. In order to publish a document's "data" on a Web it is necessary first to define its logical structure.

The main advantage of XML documents is their ability to be processed by different enterprise-wide applications that are XML ready. XML documents are particularly suitable for e-Document Management Systems, portals, call centers, and so forth.

SOAP STANDARD

The Single Object Application Protocol (SOAP) is a XML-based protocol for information exchange in a decentralized, distributed environment. It consists of the following components:

- Envelop –defining a framework for describing a message's content and how to process it
- Set of encoding rules for expressing instances of application-defined data types
- Convention for representing responses and remote procedure calls

Microsoft, IBM and other IT firms proposed SOAP to World Wide Web Consortium as one of middleware transport standard based on XML. Microsoft applies SOAP in its BizTalk framework (a software platform which supports XML applications), and IBM, Oracle and Sun Microsystems have also incorporated SOAP into their Universal Description, Discovery Integration (UDDI) registry.

UDDI STANDARD

Universal Description, Discovery Integration (UDDI) – any company that wants to locate a component to provide some specific service will be able to send a description of the desired component to the UDDI registry and find out if such a service exists and where. The Microsoft .NET Framework relies on the UDDI registry, providing the example for other companies to follow the software giant.

For example, a customer of an e-retail business can trace its delivery through a link to a transportation firm. This link is provided by the latter to the e-retailer. In the future, the e-retailer will look to the UDDI registry for that component and link.

WSDL STANDARD

WSDL (Web Service Description Language) – specifies a common XML framework for describing a network service. A network service is a software component that performs a specific function and can be accessed by another application (a client, a server or another network service) over the Internet using ubiquitous protocols. The network service is delivered on demand through a well defined interface.

A network service usually is hosted in a central location and as a shared service is delivered to different devices and users. It is accessible through the Internet as an XML interface via a communication protocol SOAP, being listed by the UDDI registry, and delivered as an XML message.

Several vendors offer their version of network services; for example, IBM's Web Application Framework for e-business, Microsoft's .NET, HP's NetAction, Oracle's Dynamic Service Framework, and Sun Microsystems' Open Net Environment (ONE). Each vendor provides its software tools to pursue a stronger grip on proprietary technology; Sun Microsystems on Java and Microsoft on Windows. A developer's tools include common features:

- Programming environment, including a set of API's (Application Programming Interface) that integrate service components as a part of network services
- Server infrastructure for operating network services
- Interfaces to different devices on the Internet

BASIC WEB SERVICES PROTOCOLS

The XML standard was designed to facilitate exchange between multiple systems. It is a framework for data description. However, it needs another three standards such SOAP, WSDL and UDDI (described above) to make Web services effective. Figure 5-9 depicts a relationship among these standards. Only Microsoft and IBM have led the development of all three. In fact, SOAP, WSDL, and UDDI are the foundation of Microsoft's .NET initiative, which is based on Web services.

All these three standards are multi-vendor specifications, allowing each of them to develop their Web service framework. A Web service applying these standards may be written in any language and run on any platform, as long it has an XML wrapper that conforms to these basic Web services standards (PriceWaterhouseCoopers, 2002).

Figure 5-9: A Stack of Web Services

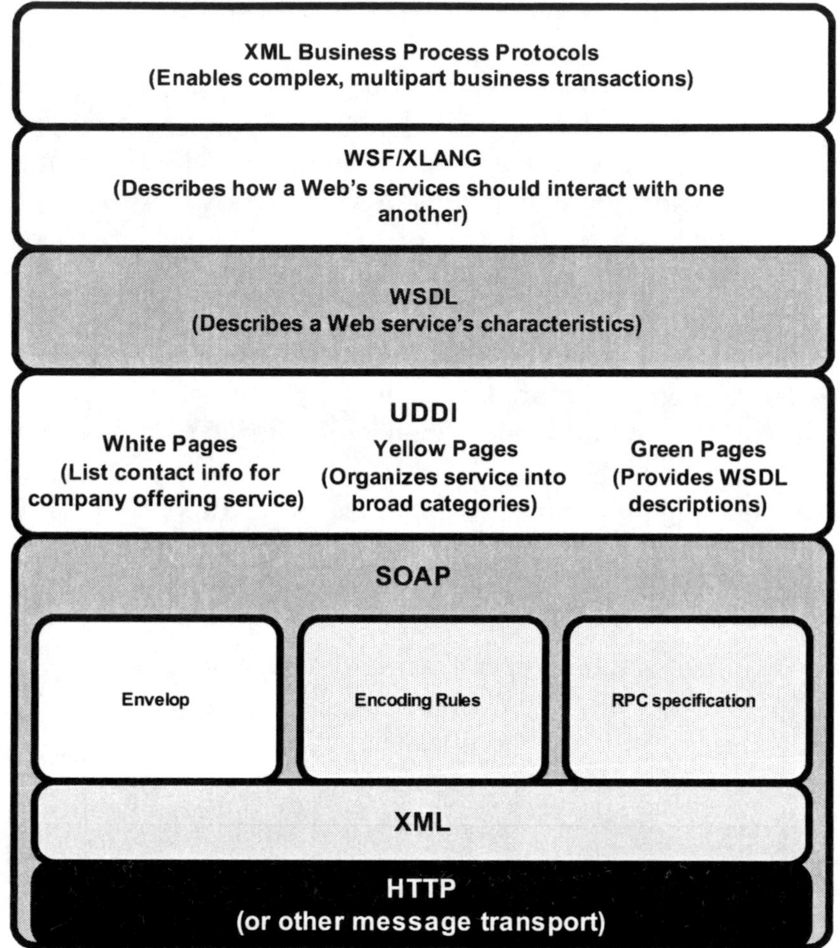

APPLICATIONS INTEGRATION

The emergence of a digital marketplace has impacted the traditional business landscape much like the fall of the Berlin Wall on foreign policy. The traditional "brick-and-mortar" structures of the past are evolving into a whole new way of conducting business. The new business structure evolves into the "brick-and-click" way of doing business. It means that the Application Layer of the Enterprise Information Infrastructure must be integrated into one electronic environment.

Figure 5-10 illustrates such an integration that is characterized by the following system interactions:

- Interactions of fulfillment systems such as SCM (Supply Chain Management), ERP (Enterprise Resource Planning), CRM (Customer Relationship Management), MIS (Management Information Systems, including MKS [Management Knowledge Systems]) which take care of mission-critical information processing of the enterprise is secured by the application logic INTEGRATION,

- Interactions of facilitating systems such an Enterprise Information Portal (EIP), e-DMS (e-Document Management System), WFS (Workflow System), e-Biz, EUC (End User Computing) which support the above systems in fulfilling their missions is secured by the ELECTRONIZATION through the application of the Web technology,

- Interactions of mobile applications is provided by wireless networks and gateways (MOBILIZATION) to enterprise networks,

- All the above applications can interact and be integrated through enterprise networks (LAN, WAN, GAN, and Intranet and Extranet) and the Internet,

- All the above interactions and integration are possible through the applications and communications STANDARDIZATION.

The integration of these applications takes place nowadays through their decomposition into components that are handled according to such standards as CORBA, EJB, DCOM, or .NET. These standards require that a business process must be broken down into a set of components that communicate with one another through various *integration points*. Determining the best implementation for a specific integration point requires that the enterprise's Application Layer defines several functional and system-level attributes of communication.

Functional attributes of applications integration, according to *PeopleSoft*'s framework, include:

- Direction of the processing (that is, inbound and/or outbound). Does the integration point accept data (inbound direction) or does it transmit information (outbound direction)?

Figure 5-10: Applications Integration

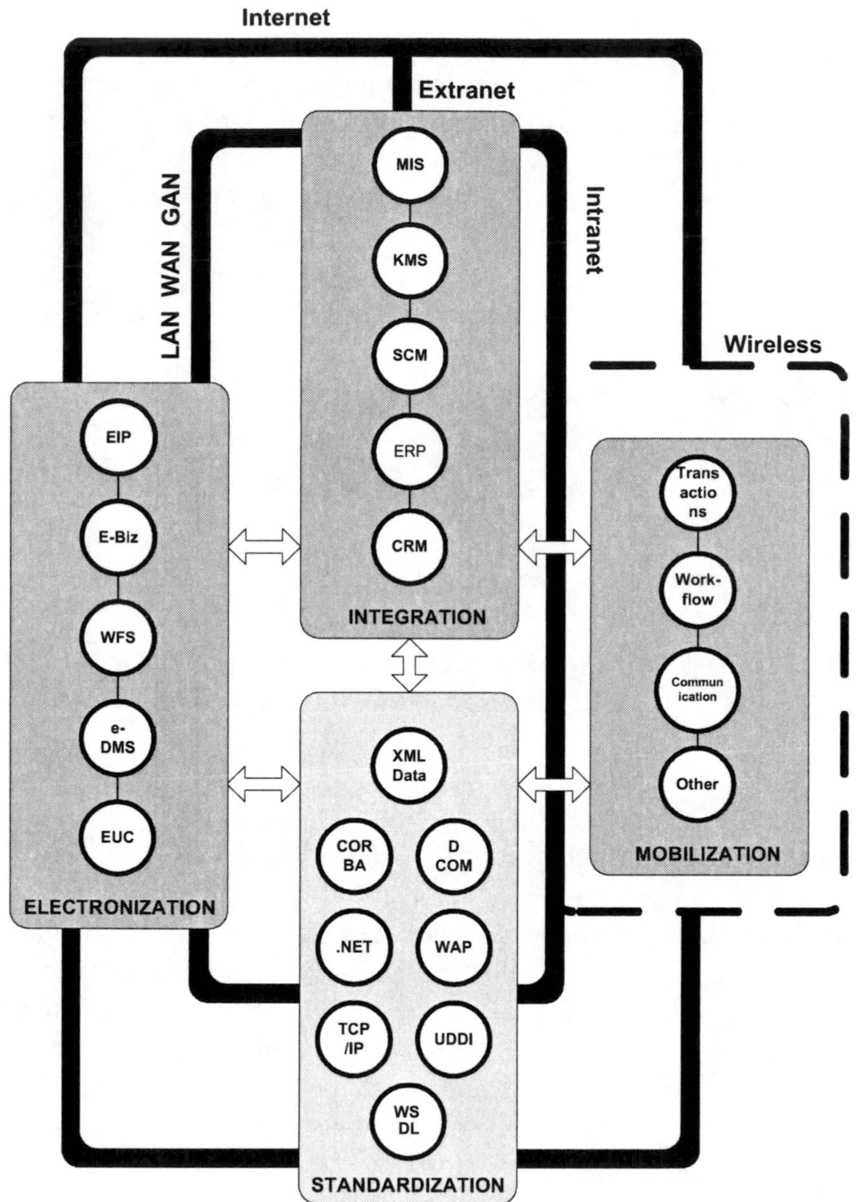

- Expected application behavior and performance. What is the timing of the integration? Does it happen right away? Is a response required to complete a business transaction? If there is no real-time link between the components, what is the latency between when the sending components send information and when the receiving components process it?

- Volume required to support inbound and/or outbound processing. In today's integration landscape, data volume is an issue. Usually, a large volume of data requires a different type of communication than smaller-volume integration.

System attributes, according to *PeopleSoft* framework, include:

- Available formats. What formats are the sending components capable of producing? Can the receiving components accept that format? Is some sort of transformation required to migrate the data from one format to another?

- Low-level interfaces available to implement the *integration point*. Application Programming Interface (API) is another term that gets wide use and whose meaning changes depending on context. Some people refer to the *entire integration point* as an API. For the context of this consideration, API will refer to the more technical layer that allows the communication between applications. *Integration point* will refer to the higher-level interface exposing the application component. An application programmer should deal with the *integration point,* not the lower level API.

Application integration is an important, but complex undertaking. There are several major types of application integration points that must be addressed well to deliver a comprehensive, powerful integration environment. Current application integration solutions do not support the breadth of application integration required by organizations today.

Most solutions consist primarily of something between integration points and more low-level API's that are packaged with an application or application suite. They are designed to allow third-party applications to initiate communication through a standard synchronous mechanism. They are not a complete solution. They do not represent easily identifiable business entities. Other integration methods include: tightly coupled integration and loosely coupled integration.

Tightly Coupled Logic Integration[8]

When components are tightly coupled, the two parts are linked in real-time. The called component must return some type of information before the initiating component can complete its transaction. Tightly coupled integration is sometimes referred to as synchronous processing, or request/reply. For example, when a Billing application is calculating a customer bill online, it needs tax information. Assume that the Billing application developer decides that rather than maintaining tax rules, rates, and tax algorithms within their Billing application, they wish to leverage a tax application. In this case, a component in the Bill application requests processing from a component in the Tax application. To get an accurate tax calculation, the Billing application may also

Figure 5-11: The Tightly Coupled Integration (The Database Server is not shown)

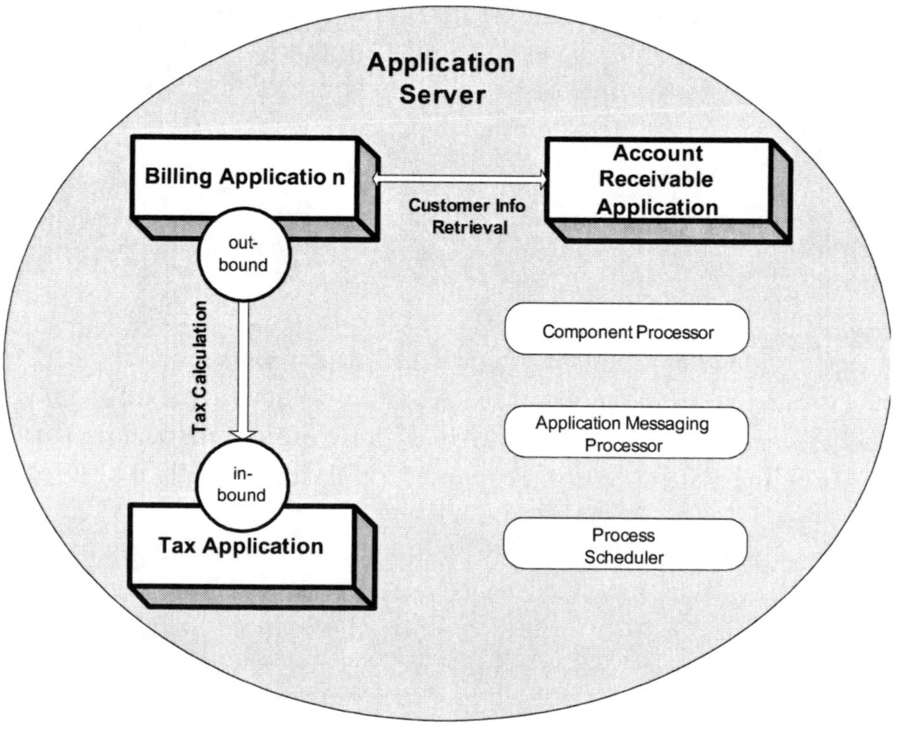

need to retrieve customer information from the accounts Receivable application, as illustrated in Figure 5-11.

From the standpoint of the Billing application, it is initiating the communication, so there must be an outbound integration point to retrieve the tax information. Correspondingly, there must be an inbound integration point in the Tax application to accept the information necessary to produce an accurate tax calculation. Since the final bill amounts include tax, the Billing user must wait while the tax application processes the request and replies with the tax amount. This integration requires tight coupling to deliver the required performance. Tight coupling would be accomplished by providing an integration point in the tax calculation component, which performs the tax calculation and returns the desired data via a reply when synchronously called.

The volume of data transmitted is of low to medium volume, consisting of detailed bill information, such as customer location and product information. The volume of information received is low, consisting of the calculated tax amount for the bill. The big advantage to tight coupling in this instance is the real-time link it provides, since the Billing application needs the tax amount to calculate the bill. However, in order for Billing to call a different calculation component, it either would need to be modified for each new tax calculation routine it was interfaced with, or it would require a flexible mechanism for calling out. The second option is more difficult, but can maximize options across multiple organizations with varying requirements for tax services.

Loosely Coupled Logic Integration[9]

Not all integration is best achieved through tightly coupling applications integration. The benefits from that type of integration can easily be seen when the required integration engages communications among several components. Let's take an example of hiring a new employee that requires the interaction of the following applications (Figure 5-12):

- Human Resources – enters the new employee's personal information and job information,
- Enterprise Directory – assigns the new employee a network ID and appropriate security access to other company information resources based on the employee's job code and department,

- Access ID Card Application – adds the employee to a database to track building clearance and generates a security card to allow entry to appropriate buildings,

- Computer Service Application – creates a work order to build a computer for the new employee, based on the appropriate configuration for the employee's department,

- Purchasing – enters requisitions for purchasing standard documentation and office supplies on behalf of the new employee.

The business requirement is that the business event of hiring an employee in the Human Resources application automatically triggers the appropriate processing in the other applications. The overall process is actually more complex at most enterprises, which typically have more applications involved

Figure 5-12: The Loosely Coupled Integration (The Database Server is not shown)

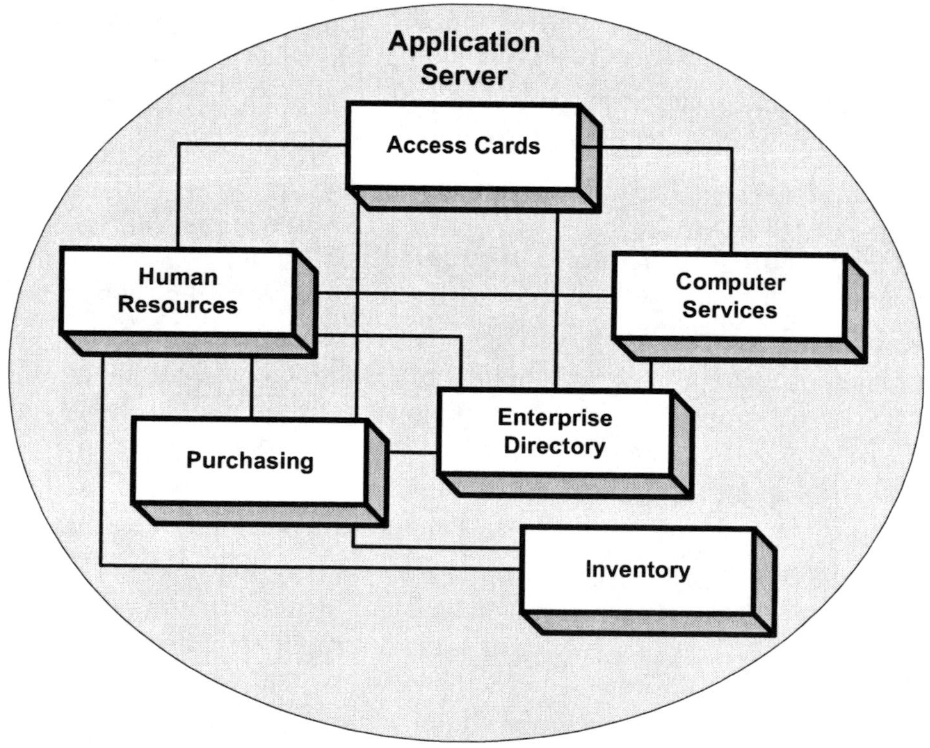

and require follow-up processing steps for each component, as well as other related communications between the other components.

Since Human Resources does not require information from the other components in order to complete its unit of work, loosely coupled integration is the preferred integration approach. Thc HR application can publish an electronic Employee Hire message, and all the components needing that information can subscribe to the message. Besides this first step, the task integration requires interactions among remaining components. Rather than integrating the business process components through separate synchronous connections, it would be better to define a single outbound integration point for the HR application through which data would be published in loosely coupled configuration. The format of such an integration point in this case would be a message, as shown in Figure 5-13.

In practice, a collaboration among different components takes place among different vendors' software. This collaboration changes according to

Figure 5-13: The Integration Point's Message

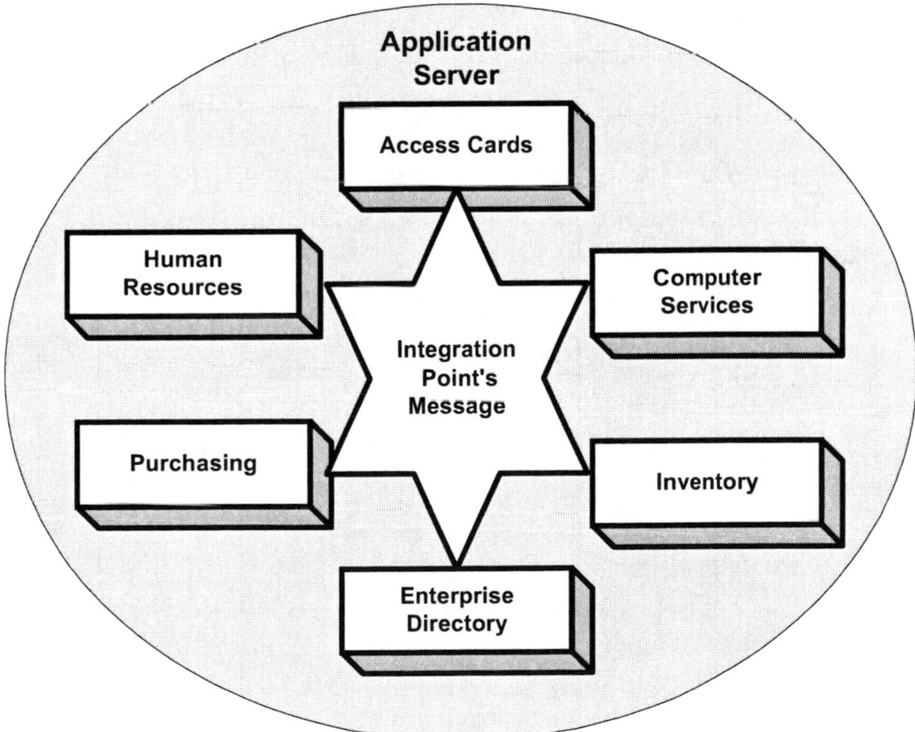

the enterprise's evolution of practice. However, this simple HR example indicates how many different components are usually involved in a complex procedure.

In a loosely coupled messaging system, the other involved components would subscribe to the HR application's message to a relevant form for their individual applications. In other words, each receiving component takes what it needs from the HR application's message, and converts it to a meaningful form for its application. To do so, an application messaging system will deliver messages to the appropriate components (look at the Application Messaging Processor in the *PeopleSoft* Internet Architecture on Figure 5-1).

When possible, applications should communicate in loosely coupled fashion. If a transaction needs data from another system to continue, or if an end user is waiting for a response, the integration point will tend to require tight coupling. For the broader range of application integration, including most system-to-system or business-to-business communication, loosely coupled integration based on messaging is sufficient.

MOBILE INTEGRATION

Wireless networks transport information between thin clients and content providers. Mobile clients have limited screen, keyboards, and storage; therefore servers must play a strong role in solving these problems. Other problems are caused by the small bandwidth, usually between 9,600 and 19,200 bps, which is responsible for slow data transfer and long delays, and higher latencies of responses to users.

To minimize these problems, some standards are evolving, such as:

- Wireless Application Protocol (WAP) for mobile Internet applications
- NTT DoCoMo's i-mode protocol (Japan) widespread in the market-place

WAP was developed by Ericsson, Nokia, Motorola and UP (now Openwave) in September 1997. WAP applies Internet protocols when possible but departs from them to address limits of wireless communication. Because the wireless provider may be dropped by the end-user, WAP orients a Wireless Session Protocol to a content provider. It means that an enterprise may have its own WAP gateway which is partially in a firewall and is accessible also from a LAN environment.

The browser-based clients are of the following types:

- WAP-enable phones and Personal Digital Assistants (PDA)
- Smart phones
- Mobile e-mail devices

Each of these devises handles information programmed in one of the following languages:

- HTML (Hyper Text Markup Language) - most of Web-based home pages are coded in it, applied by MS Windows CE
- HDML (Handheld Device Markup Language) designed mostly for cell phones to receive stock quotes, news headlines, and e-mail
- cHTML is applied by cell phones and PDA's made by Japanese firms
- WML (Wireless Markup Language) is based on XML and supports both text and images, including formatting, layout commands, and navigation through stored home pages

Because many companies invested in the Web infrastructure, they want to transmit HTML-based information to mobile devices. There are two ways of delivering an enterprise-based HTML content to mobile devices through the application of:

- Transcoders which translate an enterprise's HTML/XML content to mobile devices that are driven by their own data protocols and network constraints,
- Wireless Server (a gateway from a carrier to an enterprise) and Wireless Application Server, which is specialized in mobile applications and is also a link to an Enterprise Application Server, as it is shown in Figure 5-14.

Figure 5-14: The Architecture of Electronic and Mobile Enterprise

Tier 1
e-Client
Internet Service Provider
Intranet
Tier 2
Web Server
Tier 3
Application Server
E-Mail
E R P
S C M
C R M
Legacy
Other
Tier 4
Database Server
Tier 5
Wireless m-Client
Wireless Service Provider
Tier 6
Wireless Server (gateway)
Tier 7
Wireless Application Server
Transactions
Workflow
Communication
Naming
Other

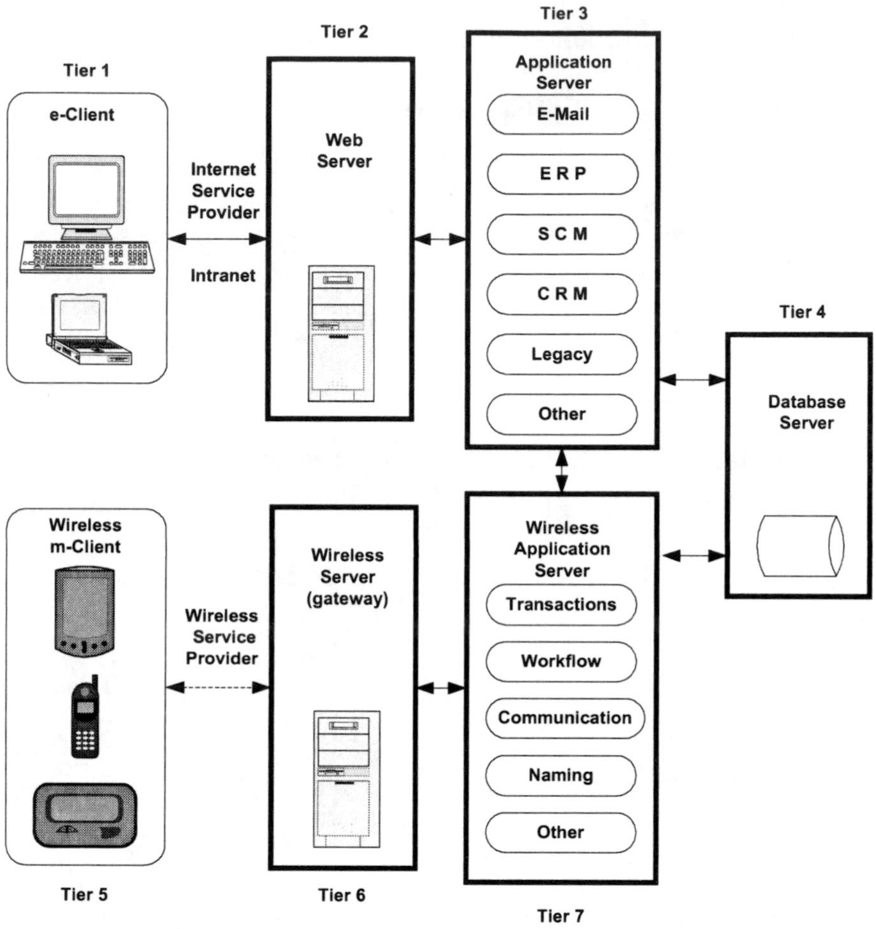

The electronic and mobile enterprise needs the information infrastructure to be composed of seven tiers. This infrastructure should secure the following situations (PriceWaterhouseCoopers, 2001):

- An employee within an office building uses a mobile device over the wireless 802.11 LAN.
- As the employee walks out of the building, the device automatically switches to a cellular/packet data network.

- As the employee enters the airport, the device communicates with an access node to get a high-speed network connection.

- After boarding the plane, the employee uses the onboard phone system, LAN or wireless LAN to achieve network connection.

- While the employee is driving in areas with weak wireless cellular/packet networks coverage, the mobile device interfaces with the employee's network-enable phone, using it as a modem to get a network connection via circuit-switched cellular.

ENTERPRISE INTEGRATION

The enterprise integration means that multiple applications are deployed in different countries, on different platforms, and even on different releases of the same technology. At the same time enterprises are dynamic, as they grow, shrink, reconstruct and improve, and as a result their systems are subject to constant change. Enterprises are also diverse, since their large organizations are sets of smaller groups – each with its own priorities, culture, and degree of autonomy.

Enterprise-wide applications, even standing alone, are expensive and difficult to implement. Connecting them together is also expensive, and the expense increases exponentially as more applications come together through more expanded networks. The better the integration of applications, the more money it saves for the enterprise.

At one time, it was a popular idea that the application integration could be done through the replication and distribution of databases. However, it was found also that applications are too complex for database replication to satisfy the users' requirements. Database technology provides only a partial solution to the problem of integrated applications. The correct solution is the solution exemplified by *PeopleSoft*'s Internet Architecture, which integrates enterprise components through the four-tier computing environment of the extended enterprise.

From the extended enterprise point of view, its applications provide the following opportunities:

- SCM – optimizes relationships with business partners and reduces costs of goods sold,

- ERP – facilitates internal operations and increases productivity,
- CRM – optimizes business relationships with customers and increases service effectiveness,
- MIS – supports executives in making satisfactory decisions,
- KMS – supports executives in making optimal decisions,
- E-Biz – optimizes commercial transactions,
- WFS – streamlines internal operations, shortening the fulfillment time,
- E-DMS – optimizes the use of information content in decision-making,
- E-Mobile – allows for fulfilling tasks anytime, anywhere,
- EUC – allows the end-users to be more productive and better informed.

The first step in enterprise integration and moving towards the extended enterprise is to understand that all the above applications should be integrated. The first who have understood this premise have been ERP vendors, who expanded their software packages into new applications.

Oracle and *J.D. Edwards* have been the most aggressive vendors in this regard, adding capabilities in both SCM and CRM in 1999. Focusing on customer management, Oracle has launched a front-office suite offering functionality in all three CRM segments as well as integration with the company's ERP applications. The company has also launched a Supply Chain Planning application targeted at the manufacturing industry, and has entered into partnerships with EAI vendors *TSI* and *TIBCO*.

J.D. Edwards has focused on adding supply chain capabilities to its ERP suite, agreeing to acquire a major SCM vendor *Numetrix* and entering into a partnership with *IBM* and *SynQuest* to develop supply chain solutions for the manufacturing industry.

SAP has moved into the extended enterprise application space, partnering with SCM software vendor *Aspect Development* and launching a Web-based sales configuration engine. SAP also acquired a 9.7% stake in *Catalyst International* and announced that the two companies have entered into a strategic alliance to develop Supply Chain Execution solutions for mySAP.com.

PeopleSoft has also begun to move aggressively in 1999, agreeing to acquire CRM vendor *Vantive* and partnering with Supply Chain Execution vendors *Optum* and *McHugh*.

The second step in developing the extended enterprise is to understand which technology one must use to integrate applications from different vendors. The following architecture levels of the integration strategy provide these technologies (described in detail in Chapter 7):

- Business Architecture:
  - BPI – Business Process Integration,
  - B2B, *e.g.,* e-commerce,
  - e-Market Integration

- Application Architecture:
  - Legacy systems integration,
  - Middleware software,
  - EAI – Enterprise Application Integration,
  - Workflow-driven integration,
  - e-Mobile integration

- Network Architecture:
  - LAN,
  - MAN,
  - WAN,
  - GAN

- Technology Architecture
  - Development tools,
  - Server architecture,
  - Transaction management,
  - Database gateways,
  - Messaging integration points,
  - Messaging services, e.g., IBM MQSeries, Microsoft Message Queuing Services (MSMQ), SAP's Application Linking, IBM CICS transient data queues, etc.,
  - Object models,
  - Object Request Brokers,
  - Web processors,
  - Interfaces,

- Standards; CORBA, EJB, DCOM, BizTalk, .NET,
- Other.

It is not surprising that when "Extended Enterprise" software vendors accelerated efforts to introduce new software packages, they selected acquisition or partnering strategies rather than internal development as the preferred means of obtaining the necessary intellectual capital and technological infrastructure. For example, EAI software vendors first acquired smaller technology leaders, e.g., EAI vendor *New Era of Networks (NEON)* acquired five integration technology vendors and entered into an alliance with *BEA Systems*, a provider of integration and networking software. In consequence, SCM and CRM vendors have also been active in expanding their product offerings via acquisitions and strategic alliances. For example, SCM vendor *Aspect Development* is in a partnership with i2 technologies. The same consolidation process takes place among consulting firms, which in order to provide the integrated services on the extended enterprise merge with the niche firms, e.g., CIBER – a management consulting firm acquired by Waterstone Consulting, specializing in SCM and CRM solutions.

WEB-DRIVEN INTEGRATION

The Web technology allows the transformation of the IT strategy from a proprietary to outsourcing solution. The model of the Web out-sourced services architecture is shown in Figure 5-15. The Web is the mechanism of integrating out-sourced and in-house applications and services.

The Web Outsourced Services Architecture has three layers (Hagel and Brown, 2001):

1. The Standards and Protocol Layer is composed of software and communication standards including UDDI, which is an XML-based registry for businesses worldwide to list themselves on the Internet. Its ultimate goal is to streamline online transactions by enabling companies to find one another. Included is also SOAP, which supports a program running on one kind of operating system to communicate with a program running on another kind of operating system;

Figure 5-15: The Web Outsourced Services Architecture

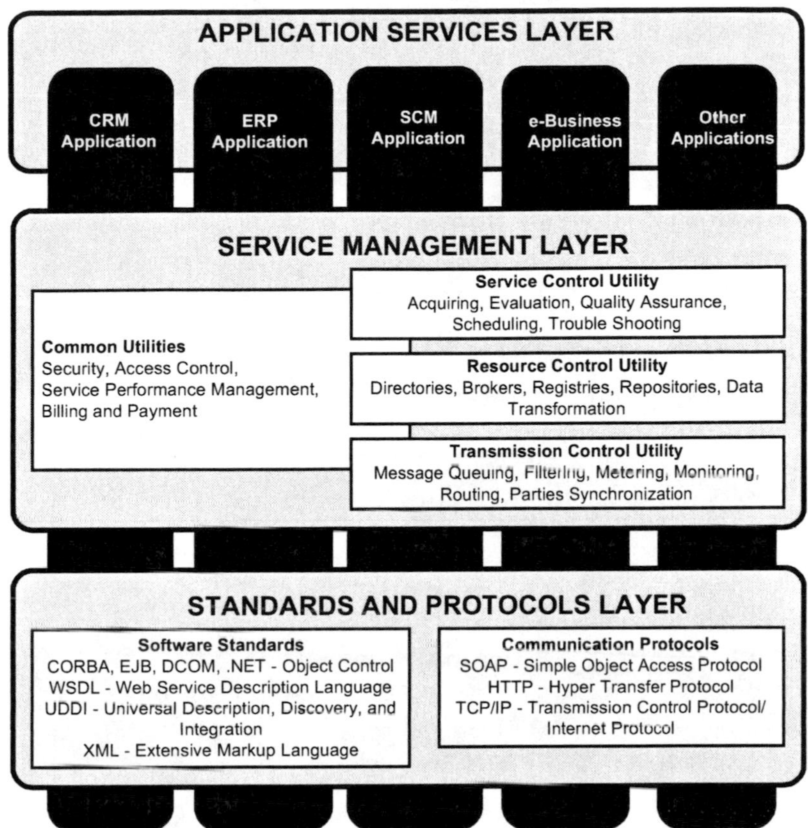

2. The Service Management Layer provides key supervising services allowing the access, transfer and quality control of outsourced applications through the enterprise's Web;

3. The Application Services Layer integrates a mix of proprietary and outsourced applications (SCM, ERP, CRM, and others) for day-to-day operations supporting end-users' business processes.

INTEGRATION COMPLEXITY

Attention to each of the EII's layers and the integration strategy's architecture levels reveals the complexity of the integration approach towards the enterprise. Figure 5-16 illustrates this complexity. The following analysis highlights some issues of this complexity.

- Business Architecture
  Assume that number of business processes in an average enterprise is about 100 and each one can interact with each other. It means that the number of interactions is i = (100 - 1)100 : 2 = 4950. The number of states of each interaction, assuming only two (*on* and *off*) is $s = 2^n$, where n=100, and s=infinite.

Figure 5-16: The Matrix of e-Enterprise's Integration Strategy

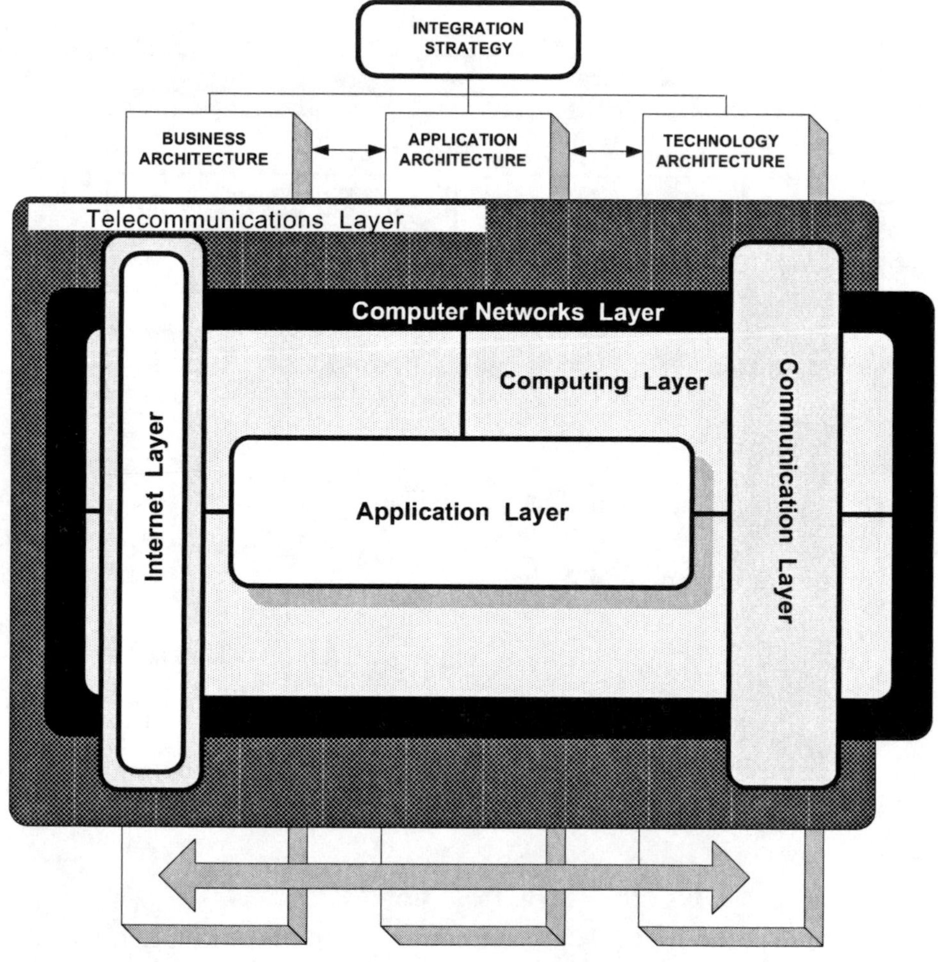

Figure 5-16 The Matrix of e-Enterprise's Integration Strategy

- Application Architecture
  The number of major applications (Figure 6-9) is 8 (we exclude EUC and e-Mobile) and each one can have about 1000 components. In every application the number of interactions among components is $i = (1000 - 1)1000 : 2 = 499{,}500$. The number of states of these interactions is infinite. However, applications can interact between each other, so their number of interactions at the very aggregated manner is $i = (8 - 1)8 = 56$.

- Technology Architecture
  Assume that number of major involved technologies is about 20, hence, their number of interaction $i = (20 - 1)20 = 380$.

The number of elements in the extended enterprise is about 1000+ and the number of their interactions is at the level of 500,000+, which means that such an enterprise becomes very complex. It is difficult to conceptualize such an entity, even more difficult to design such an organization, and it is extremely difficult to operate and maintain such an enterprise.

This analysis indicates that integration issues cannot be identified only with the technology architecture, but should also be reflected in the business and application architectures.

The integration project should solve the following issues:

1. The integration solutions should be planned in-house, but some of their systems can be outsourced,

2. The development of all harmonized layers of the EII,

3. The Application Architecture should support the Business Architecture,

4. The Technology Architecture should support the Application Architecture,

5. The selection of component standards between CORBA, EJB, DCOM or .NET should begin all development tasks.

It is important to notice that some major problems can be associated with the integration:

1. Integration may solve some current problems, but what about the next generation of the extended enterprise's growth's requirements?

2. The Application Architecture may work fine in the online mode but may trigger some problems in real-time operations.

3. There is confusion in choosing the correct development tools since none can fit all needs.

4. The development of the integrated enterprise can be relatively easy for an experienced staff, but major problems may occur during the systems testing and operations phases.

It is also important for leaders of the extended enterprise to take the broader approach towards the integration by considering the following challenges:

1. Choose which is more strategic for your company: the internal integration of systems or the external integration with stakeholders?

2. Choose between re-engineering of the enterprise's business processes and outsourcing those processes, e.g., human resources process.

3. Choose between re-engineering business processes and the re-use of some existing solutions in order to avoid the development process of new solutions.

4. In the case of mergers and acquisitions, choose between integrating all sources of the same information and selecting one source as the common solution for all users.

The enterprise integration by IT is a business process itself. It usually takes place at the following levels (*www.butlergroup.com.uk*):

- Plug-and-Play – integration between applications that share common business components, business interface, and technology,

- Well-Defined – integration between applications with well-defined, but incompatible components and interfaces, for example package-to-package from different vendors,
- Undefined – integration of in-house legacy, and new in-house built with each other or with a package application,
- Complex – multiplexed integration of multiple sources with complex rule-driven integration.

Based on the presented analysis, companies should balance immediate requirements with long-term integration needs. As there are thousands of ERP implementation projects and hundreds of EAI implementation projects – it is not hard to notice that the opportunity for growth in this lucrative area exists.

FURTHER TRENDS

Modern enterprise is about 400 years old, but its information model or more specific – electronic model – is just emerging in the 2000's. Perhaps it will take another century to conclude its theory and practical solutions.

The framework of such an electronic enterprise is sketched in this book; however, its implementation will require wise leadership, skillful staff members, abundant resources, and the will to take the risk with such an undertaking. The benefits should be realized in the areas of the company's improved competitive position, better profitability and productivity. On the other hand, the complexity of the e-enterprise will require mature management supported by the skillful "IT back-office" and a healthy balance between the range of outsourcing and in-house IT services.

CONCLUSION

The progress in the enterprise evolution is driven by the goal of integrating all applications into one coherent complex, operating in real-time. This is gradually achievable through the application of:

- Web technologies which electronize the Enterprise Information Infrastructure,

- Mobile connectivity and applications which make an enterprise operating in real-time,

- Standards for information processing in a distributed environment through the Web,

- Integration techniques at the level of computerized business processes' components (tightly and loosely coupled integrations) which also apply Web services to accelerate the information flow among multi-vendor information technologies in different locations,

- Integration strategy which has to design plans for the integration of business, application, and technology architectures.

The goal of integrating the EII is the greatest challenge for most large organizations. The majority of these organizations which acquired a variety of IT solutions (software and hardware) along with in-house developments created a diverse portfolio of disconnected solutions.

During the mid 1990's, specialized middleware products were developed to meet the increased demand for the EII integration. This topic will be discussed in Chapter 7.

BIBLIOGRAPHY

Application Integration, Management Guide. (2000). *www.butlergroup.com.uk*. Baartse, M. et al. (2000). *Professional ASP XML*. Birmingham, UK: Wrox Press Ltd.

Cherry Tree & Co. (2000). Extended enterprise applications, Spotlight Report. *www.cherrytreeco.com.*

Hagel, J., III & Brown, J.S. (2001). Your next IT strategy. *Harvard Business Review*, October, p. 105-115.

Hoque, F. (2000). *E-Enterprise, Business Models, Architecture, And Components*. Cambridge, UK: Cambridge University Press.

May, P. (2000). *The Business Of Ecommerce, From Corporate Strategy To Technology*. Cambridge, UK: Cambridge University Press.

Open Integration Framework. *PeopleSoft*'s Approach to Enterprise Application Integration. (2000). *www.PeopleSoft.com*.

PriceWaterhouseCoopers. (2001). *Technology Forecast: 2001-2003*. Menlo Park, CA.

PriceWaterhouseCoopers. (2002). *Technology Forecast: 2002-2004*. Menlo Park, CA.

Targowski, A. & Rienzo, T.H. (2002). *Enterprise Information Infrastructure*. Kalamazoo: Paradox Associates.

ENDNOTES

1 Java servlets are essentially server-side applets (mini applications) which enable Web servers to communicate with back-end systems. Introduced in 1997, servlets can provide Web-based access to data; for instance, processing data from an HTML form and returning a response. Several servlets can be chained together to handle requests that may involve a series of steps. On the client side, a new extension to the servlet technology are JavaServer Pages (JSP) – allows Java business applications to be inserted into HTML or XML pages. At run-time JSP's are compiled into servlets for execution.

2 Location transparency is a general principle of distributed systems; it is not only CORBAS' unique principle.

3 Microsoft identifies the application of COM and DCOM embedded in Windows as DNA – Distributed Network Architecture or COM-DNA.

4 COM – a model for binary code developed by Microsoft. It enables programmers to develop objects that can be accessible by any COM-compliant applications. Both OLE and Active X are based on COM. OLE – Object Linking and Embedding is a compound document standard developed by Microsoft. It enables programmers to create objects with one application and then link or embed them in a second application. Embedded objects retain their original format and links to the application that created them. Support for OLE is built into Windows and Macintosh Operating System. The description of DCOM is based on the vendor's documentation available on the Internet.

5 In 2000 Microsoft introduced the Windows 2000 DNA standard which very soon was replaced by .NET standard.

6 Microsoft's approach towards network services is described in more detail; however, one must mention that other vendors such as IBM, Sun Microsystems, Oracle and others provide similar solutions, embedded in

their proprietary technologies. Due to Microsoft's Windows and Internet Explorer popularity, its solutions deserve good attention.

7 Perhaps this strategy has something to do with the threat of breaking Microsoft into two separate companies.

8 This is an example of PeopleSoft's solution.

9 This is an example of PeopleSoft's solution.

Part III

The Internet Ecosystem

Chapter VI

The Internet Applications and Business

THE INTERNET ECONOMY

The Internet Economy is an ecosystem of producing, distributing, and consuming wealth. This ecosystem is made up of companies directly generating all or some part of their revenues from Internet or Internet-related products and services. The economy includes not only "high-tech" companies but any company that generates revenue from the Internet.

Internet Usage

The Internet landscape of the United States will undergo a profound change from 2002 to 2003. The United States will lose the distinction of having the largest number of Internet users worldwide. However, the loss of this distinction is not without an up-side. Eighty-four percent of U.S. PC's access the Internet today, and this will grow to 88% by 2003. The Internet has become part of U.S. culture — approximately 71% of the population will use the Internet at least once per month by 2003. The United States will maintain its leadership role as the biggest e-commerce generator of all regions. The maturity of the e-commerce market in the United States is responsible for the erosion of the United States' standing as the world leader in terms of Internet users. Other regions with larger populations are becoming increasingly connected. Alternatively, it is the maturity of the U.S. market that has driven the United States to dominate e-commerce spending worldwide (www.idc.com).

However, not every Internet user shops online; only 17 million households (17% or every 5th) do it (NUA/Forrester Research). In 2000 about 56% of U.S. companies were selling their products and services online, up 24% from 1998 (NUA).

Economic Impact

The Internet Economy force has become a more integral part of the U.S. economy than ever before, creating jobs and increasing productivity in companies across the economy. The impact goes far beyond dot coms, as Internet Economy forces are transforming traditional companies and jobs. Seven of every 10 of these jobs are traditional rather than high-tech jobs, according to a new study by the University of Texas' Center for Research in Electronic Commerce. Of the Internet-related jobs, only 28% are in Information Technology, which ranks below sales and marketing (33%) as the job function generating the most Internet-related employment. Dot com companies are a very small part (about 9.6%) of the overall Internet Economy.

The research is contained in the fourth report measuring the Internet Economy commissioned by Cisco Systems and covers the first half of 2000. It shows the Internet is transforming the economy and the way people work, to an extent few people would have imagined just a few years ago.

According to the study, the Internet Economy now directly supports more than 3.088 million workers, including an additional 600,000 in the first half of 2000. This is about 60,000 more than the number employed in the insurance industry and double the real estate industry. These jobs were created both by the explosion of the Internet and by companies shifting workers to take advantage of the benefits created by embracing the Internet. Employment in Internet Economy companies is growing much faster than employment in the overall economy. Total employment at Internet Economy companies grew 10% between the first quarter of 1999 and the first quarter of 2000. Internet-related jobs at Internet Economy companies grew 29% during the same period. Both of these figures far exceed the growth of non-Internet related jobs in these same Internet Economy companies, which grew 6.9% during the same period.

The Internet Economy generated an estimated $830 billion in revenues in 2000, a 58% increase over 1999. The $830 billion in revenues is a 156% increase from 1998, when the Internet accounted for $323 billion in revenues. Internet economy revenue is growing twice as fast as Internet Economy employment. In 2000, for example, second quarter revenue grew 58.8% over the second quarter of 1999. Meanwhile, second quarter employment grew

22.6% over 1999. Internet-related revenue is a growing piece of corporate revenue as a whole. For Internet Economy companies, Internet revenue is one-fifth the size of non-Internet revenue – but growing three times as fast as corporate revenue as a whole. Revenue grew by $23 billion between the first quarter of 1999 and first quarter of 2000. Internet-related revenue grew $68 billion during the same period.

Internet Economy employees are increasingly productive employees. Revenue per employee increased an estimated 11.5% in the first half of 2000 – a key indication of the productivity gains generated by the Internet. In the first half of 2000, Internet Economy companies generated $1 of every $5 in revenue from the Internet. Even as the overall economy experiences fluctuations, Internet Economy forces continue to reshape the economy in unprecedented ways, producing savings for businesses and consumers alike. And reports of strong online holiday spending levels in 2000 (a study by Goldman Sachs and PC Data, for example, said total Internet holiday spending rose to $8.7 billion from $4.2 billion in 1999) provide yet another sign of the way customers and retailers now routinely use the Internet.

The Internet is increasingly becoming part of the basic business model for many companies, laying the groundwork for even more impressive growth during strong economic conditions. The Internet is rapidly becoming an integral part of the traditional economy – like telephones, elevators and personal computers over the years – leading to the day when there will be no separate measure of the Internet Economy[1].

That makes the United State's Internet Economy by itself the 10th largest economy in the world, greater than South Korea's and equal to Spain's. The Internet jobs exceed employment in the insurance, telecommunications, real estate, public utilities industries and twice as many as the airline, chemical, and allied products, legal and real estates industries. As an example of its growing role in the economy, the Internet Economy now employs more workers than the insurance industry (2.36 million workers) and the real estate industry (1.5 million).

The Internet sector rivals the automobile and telecommunications industries which have been in existence for nearly a century. The planned speed for the Internet communications is about three Terabits per second which is an equivalent of sending the Encyclopedia Britannica within 1 second. The Internet infrastructure is built of components that cost about $1 trillion and the development process is still taking place at the rate of $200-300 billion spent per year.

The Internet Economy started about 1994 when the first browser Mosaic was available. Ever since, its growth has been much faster than the Industrial Revolution's that began in the 18th century. The latter economy was based on physical assets to create value, while the former economy is based on instantly communicated information and discovered knowledge (patterns and rules) about customers and potential ones. This knowledge leads to better customer relationships and more opportunities for all stakeholders.

THE INTERNET ECOSYSTEM

The Internet Ecosystem is a business model made up of a community of users, customers, technological infrastructure, support solutions providers, and product and services producers and suppliers.

The Internet Ecosystem can be organized in the following layers (The University of Texas's Center for Research in Electronic Commerce in Austin):

1. **Infrastructure Layer** – companies that manufacture or provide products and services that make up the I-infrastructure which is being built of telecommunications and computer networks, dial up access, PC's, servers, modems, and other components necessary for the Internet to function. Such companies can be considered here: AT&T, Cisco, Dell, IBM, HP, Compaq, Sun, Oracle, and others.

2. **Application Layer** – companies that provide e-commerce application software and tools. For example: applications (e.g., Netscape, IBM, Microsoft, Sun), multimedia applications (e.g., Macromedia), Web development software (e.g., NetObjects, Allaire, Vignette), search engine software (e.g., Inktomi, Verity), Web-enable databases (e.g., Oracle, IBM DB2, Micosoft SQL Server, Sybase, Informix), Internet consulting services (e.g., USWeb/CKS, Scient, EDS, Ernst & Young), training services (e.g., Sylvan Prometric, Assymetrix). Products and services in this layer make it technologically possible to perform business activities online.

3. **Intermediary Layer** – companies that increase the efficiency of e-markets as Internet middlemen by facilitating the meeting and interaction of buyers and sellers via the World Wide Web. For example: online

brokerages, Internet ad brokers (e.g., Yahoo!, Geocities), market makers in vertical industries (e.g., VerticalNet, PCOrder), content aggregators (e.g., Cnet, ZDnet, Broadcast.com), and online travel agencies (Priceline.com).

4. **Commerce Layer** – companies that generate product and service sales to consumers (B2C) or businesses (B2B) over the Internet. For example: eBay, VerticalNet, Amazon, Toysrus, AmericanAirlines, and others.

The model of The Internet Ecosystem is illustrated in Figure 6-1.

The 1999 Internet Economic Indicators are provided in Table 6-1.

The largest subsector of the Internet Economy is the 1-Infrastructure Layer which employs the largest number of workers who produce endless

Figure 6-1: The Internet Ecosystem Model

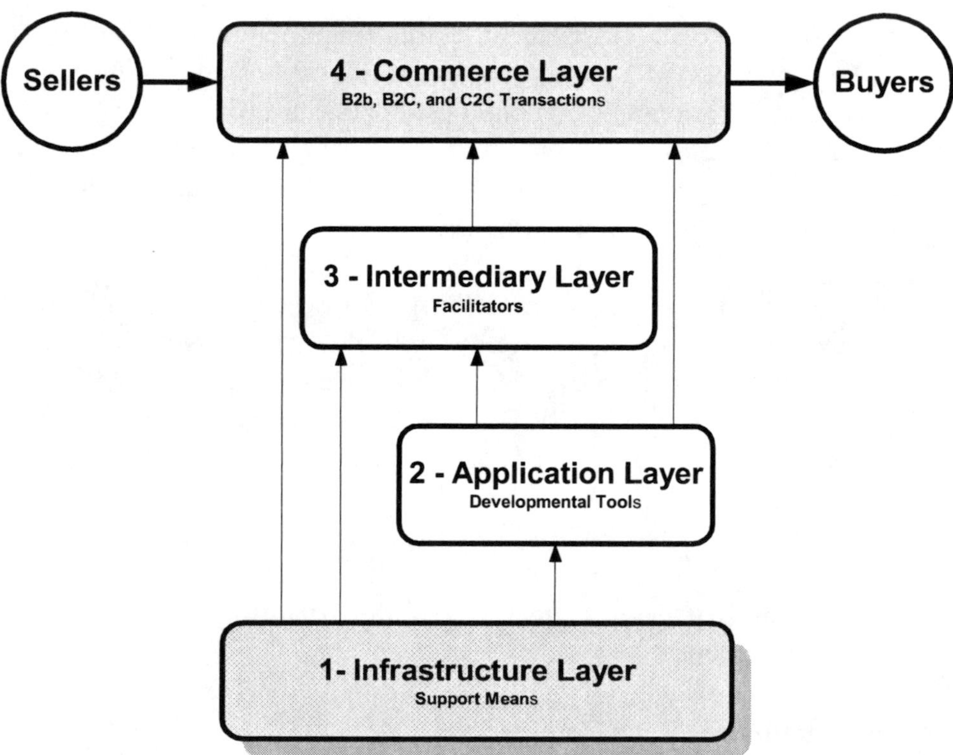

Table 6-1

Layer	Revenues in $Billion	Employment	Revenues Per Employee in $	Percentage of Revenues
4-Commerce	171	726,000	253,987	30%
3-Intermediary	96.81	340,600	284,143	17%
2-Application	101	681,568	148,628	18%
1-Infrastructure	200	778,602	254,174	35%
Total	568.81	2,189,576	259,780	100

numbers of hardware, software, telecommunications components and services. However, the largest revenue per employee (productivity) generates the 3-Intermediary Layer, which according to the trade tradition of a middleman makes the most money. Productivity of Information Economy is about two times higher than productivity of The Industrial Economy.

The Internet Ecosystem has evolved from an alternative marketing channel and 4th medium to a complete economic system consisting of (The University of Texas's Center for Research in Electronic Commerce in Austin):

1. Communication networks using the Internet technologies and standards (L1);

2. Applications and human capital that enable business to be conducted over this network infrastructure (L2);

3. Interconnected electronic markets that operate over the network (L4);

4. Producers (L4) and intermediaries (L3) providing a variety of digital products and services to facilitate market efficiency and liquidity; and

5. Emerging policy and legal frameworks for conducting business over the Internet.

The prevailing model of competition in the Internet Economy is more like a web of inter-relationships than the hierarchical, command-and-control model of the Industrial Economy. This economy is inclusive and has low barriers to entry, and possesses the ability to self-organize.

E-COMMERCE

Electronic commerce (e-commerce or EC) is a combination of EDI and EFT. It is a method to seek, manage, and operate business transactions applying computers and telecommunications networks. It provides business partners with the following advantages:

1. Price optimization,
2. Time minimization of business transactions,
3. Shorter procurement cycle,
4. Cost minimization through savings on inventory and the use of the just-in-time (JIT) technique,
5. Quick response business practice (QR),
6. Shorter product life cycle,
7. Accelerated time-to-market through the e-collaboration among the business partners,
8. Other.

E-commerce has become a buzz word for consumers and companies during the last few years of the 1990's. Increased awareness about the use of computer and telecommunications networks simplifies business procedures and increases efficiency.

E-commerce combines the following systems:

- Electronic Data Interchange (EDI)
- Electronic Fund Transfer (EFT)
- E-mail (EM)
- Web applications

E-commerce provides ways to exchange information - among individuals, companies from different countries, and among computers that support the whole system.

During the 1970's pilot systems of e-commerce were set up. Two of the most successful, DISH and SHIPNET, are applied by some sea ports (Southhampton, Felixstove, Rotterdam, and Amsterdam). They support the total set of import/export processes.

During the 1980's, a number of Value Added Networks (VAN) emerged as public telecommunications networks that began to support the first applications of e-commerce. Subsequently, smaller VAN's have emerged to cater to the requirements of specific sectors, such as education. The airline and motor industries have created networks for the transportation of EDI and e-mail messages. EDI had reached a respectable level of awareness among businesses. A few newsletters and magazines were dedicated to it. The X.400 standard for e-mail and fax was created to support the EDI systems. However, large organizations have found it difficult to extend their trading communities beyond their main business partners.

Since 1997, the term "electronic commerce" has rapidly broadened to encompass business conducted over the Internet and the World Wide Web. If EDI systems are characterized by defined relationships among business partners, the Web systems are characterized by ad hoc relations among business participants.

E-Commerce Applications

Most companies conducting Web-driven commerce are doing one or more of the following processes:

a) Selling products and services:
   i) consumer entertainment
   ii) leisure products, such as music CD's
   iii) books
   iv) airline tickets
   v) computers
   vi) other

b) Selling advertising:
   i) advertisements on the most popular home pages and application systems,

a) so-called "flat ads," and
b) dynamic ads, blinking or video type

ii) advertisements "pushed" to customers' e-mails

c) Selling fee-based information:
   i) Customized information about news and business events, trends,
   ii) E-periodics, such as Microsoft's "Slate."

The e-commerce applications are still evolving and gaining strength as the Internet applications continue to develop.

E-Commerce Business Models

E-commerce business models are still evolving; however, according to Rappa (2000) and Timmers (1998) one can distinguish their following classifications:

- The **Brokerage Model** firms act as market makers who brings buyers and sellers together and charge a fee for the transactions that they enable. They can be: B2B, B2C, C2C. For example: online travel agents (*www.priceline.com*), online brokerage firms (*www.etrade.com*), and online auction houses (*www.eBay.com*).

- In the **Advertising Model**, the owner of a website provides some content and services that attract visitors. The website owner makes money by charging advertisers for fee for banners, permanent buttons, and so forth. For example: consumer portals such as *www.Yahoo!.com* which among many services provides very popular maps and driving directions or *www.Altavista.com*.

- The **Infomediary Model** is applied by firms collecting valuable information on consumers and their buyers' habits and sells it to firms, who in turn can data mine it for important patterns and rules and other useful information to help them better serve their customers.

- The **Merchant Model** is the "e-tailer" model in which wholesalers and retailers sell goods and services over the Internet. These include a virtual merchant, catalog merchant, surf-and-turf, and bit vendor. For example: "brick & mortars"; furniture retailer - *www.ethanallen.com* and groceries retailers *www.kroger.com*, catalog merchants of everything for cooking and chefs – *www.cooking.com* or *www.tavolo.com* or a bookstore such as *www.Amazon.com*.

- In the **Manufacturing Model**, producers try to sell products directly via the Internet to end users instead of going through a wholesaler or retailer (dealer). By doing so, they can save costs and better serve customers by finding directly what they want. For example: computer manufacturers – *www.dell.com* or *www.compaq.com*.

- In the **Affiliate Model**, a merchant has affiliates whose websites have click-through to the merchant. Each time a visitor to an affiliate's site clicks through to the merchant's site and buys something, the affiliate is paid a fee, usually a percentage of the revenue. The most popular websites and portals apply this model; for example: *www.WebMED.com*, *www.MSN.com*, *www.Lycos.com*, *www.cometsystems.com*.

- The **Community Model** is based on members' loyalty rather than traffic. Users have invested in developing relationships with members of their community and are likely to visit the website frequently. Members of such a community can be very good market targets. For example: *www.iVillage.com*.

- The **Subscription Model** – members pay a subscription price and in return receive high-quality content. For example: America Online (AOL) which offers an access to the Internet but whose service is provided by the private network which is leased from the public Value Added Network service.

- The **Utility Model** – activities are metered and users pay for service that they consume.

- Other.

An Internet business model explains how a firm is going to make money using the Internet capabilities. As events in 2000 have shown, making money on the Internet is trickier than anyone suspected. We will discuss this issue later in this chapter, when we describe the nature of so-called "dot.com" business.

E-Commerce Architecture

E-commerce covers any form of computerized buying and selling, both by consumers and from company to company. There are two basic types of e-commerce modes:

- consumer-to-business (C2B)
- business-to-business (B2B)

Consumers spent $700 million online in 1996 vs. more than $7 billion in 1998, about $14 billion in 1999, and more than $20 billion in 2000. E-commerce increases sellers' ability to know their buyers, and buyers to know more than ever. Comparison shopping has never been easier, thanks to such business as *www.priceline.com* and *www.eLoan.com* and such services as *www.mySimon.com* that will crawl the Web as a robot or individualized "bot" looking for the best price for a consumer.

Consumer advocates speak cheerily of how sites that match buyers with the lowest price available are facilitating a "frictionless" economy or "perfect capitalism," where the prices are set by a perfect agreement between what a buyer wants and the seller can afford to sell for. Sounds ideal, doesn't it? Almost anything you may want to buy is available online today. The virtual auction house - *www.eBay.com* - even has a listing for people who might be interested in purchasing a best friend.

Brick-and-mortar outposts, to justify the cost of rent, salespeople and other real-world necessities, cannot afford to have people just look. They must turn mere sneaker *shoppers* into sneaker *buyers*, a conversion process that market researchers measure by calculating what percentage of people who visit a store wind up purchasing an item. This percentage is called "sell-through" rate, and most have sell-through rates around 50% (though some supermarkets have much higher rate). By contrast, the highest of any online retailer is only 7%. E-commerce B2C sites will have to address the shoppers-into-buyers problem if they want to move far beyond their current niches.

An example of a new approach to online buyers offers *www.Alloy.com* for young consumers. This site provides a virtual chat room, user home pages, and auctions to enliven shopping portal, where kids can buy anything from backpacks and miniskirts to games. A site - *www.wine.com* - offers for mature consumers e-mail service and chat boards to encourage a kind of a virtual wine-testing party.

A result of B2C is so called disintermediation – a word for direct marketing built on the idea of companies manufacturing directly and selling directly to customers out of a factory, without dealing through indirect channels.

For instance, *www.CipShot.com* is a golf-club manufacturer that takes orders on the Web. When customers go to the company's website, they describe their swing and certain proportions of their bodies. Chip Shop then builds the clubs in the factory and ships them out. Customers get their clubs within a couple of days, totally guaranteed. This method of doing business represents a very big change from the customer having to go a specialty shop, deal with a pro, which can be intimidating, and wait six to eight weeks for delivery of clubs. Chip Shot's strategy is very much like the strategy that *www.Dell.com* used to achieve its position of prominence in the PC industry.

This business model will transform other industries in the future. It can be summed up as follows:

- Configurate a product by a consumer,
- Make a product of standard, name-brand components,
- Sell by yourself online,
- Sell other manufacturers' goods as a by-product service.

E-retailers perform many of the functions of dealing directly with the consumers, such as customer service, and consumers love the virtual alternative. The Internet works not simply because producers save costs but because consumers want to make business with those manufacturers and merchants.

The e-commerce business-to-consumer architecture is depicted on Figure 6-2.

At the heart of online retail business is the electronically supported selling of goods and services by vendors to consumers. The components of the business-to-consumer e-commerce system are as follows:

Personalization. This is one part of a marketing effort to present specific contents to specific types of customers. By implementing a target marketing concept, every single customer can be provided with his/her personal scope of interest in a given product/service line. This type of information is taken from data warehouses of search engines, customer databases, and marketing research centers.

Figure 6-2: A Frontstore of E-commerce within a Business-to-Consumer (B2C) Framework

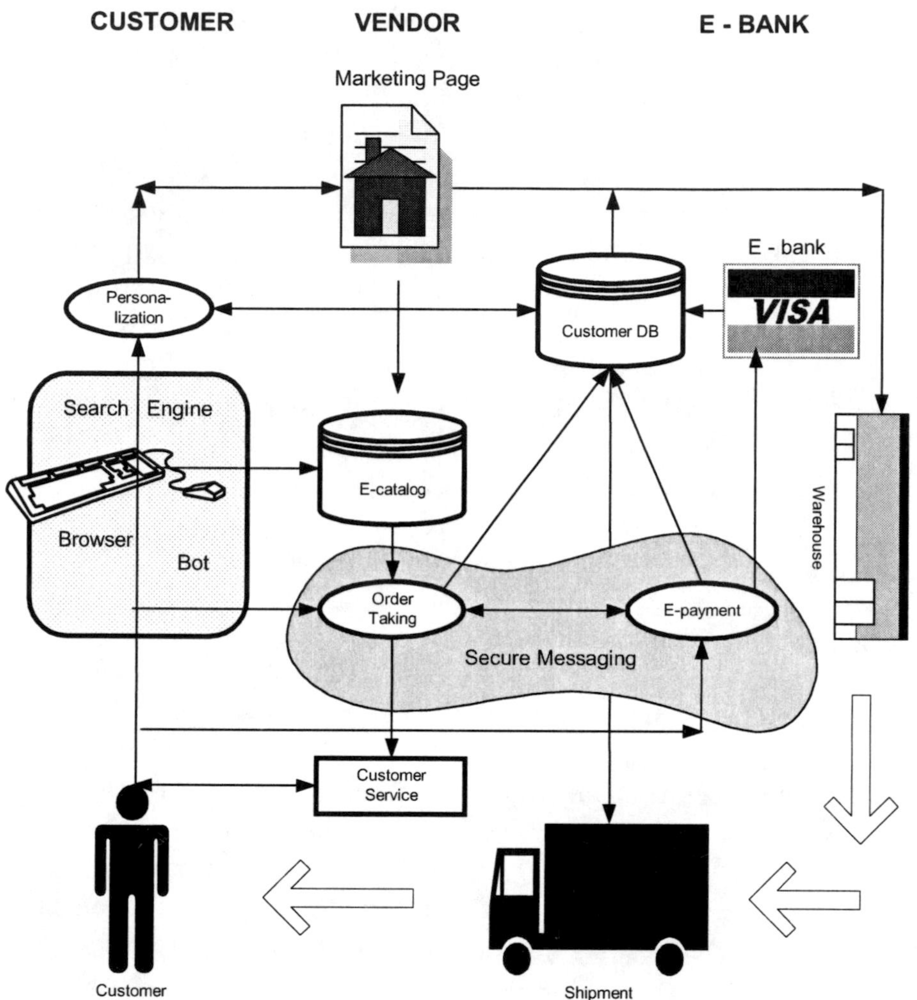

E-catalogues. Products and services are presented by way of electronic catalogs. Easily navigable, browsing-oriented graphic user interfaces, multimedia enhanced content design and support for marketing promotions are some of the key aspects in this context.

Order Taking. The subject of retail transaction can be a physical good, service or digital goods or services. Key solutions include: an e-shopping cart subsystem, a credit card-based payment, an order status traffic and notification subsystem, and so forth.

Customer Servicc. This service is provided either by e-mail to the customer or through a Bulletin Board System (BBS).

Search Engines. This includes the popular Internet search engines, such as Yahoo, Info-Seek, Altavista and others.

Bots. These components are software "robots" that do the customer's bidding. Among the more sophisticated are digital bargain-hunters.

The e-commerce business-to-business architecture is depicted on Figure 6-3.

The business-to-business sector is characterized on one hand by traditional long-term business relationships but on the other hand also by new kinds of ad hoc deals facilitated by the increased transparency in electronic markets. Thc components of such a system are as follows:

Association of Members. The association member pays a fee to enter a system of thousands of potential contractors and subcontractors in the world. The system provides global marketing for offered products and services and also facilitates the search of potential partners.

Customization. This part of the marketing effort presents specific contents to specific types of customers. By implementing a target marketing concept, every single customer/company can be provided with its customized scopc of interest in a given product/service line. This type of information is taken from data warehouses of search engines, customer databases, and marketing research centers.

Marketing/Purchasing Message. This is a given message about sought-for buyers or partners. It is distributed by the system administration.

Negotiation Message. A process of negotiation is supported by a set of interactive hypertext documents that are interexchanged forward/backwards among partners. Most negotiations take place within the first 15 minutes of the e-contact. The negotiations are about price, delivery conditions, warranty, and so forth. These negotiations can bc conducted automatically or "manually." A derivative of the negotiation message is the next level of negotiations about the transport and shipment intermediaries.

E-payment. The system administration arranges e-payments through associated electronic financial institutions.

Customer Service. This service is provided either by e-mail to the customer or through a Bulletin Board System (BBS).

Figure 6-3: E-commerce B2B in the Association Business Model

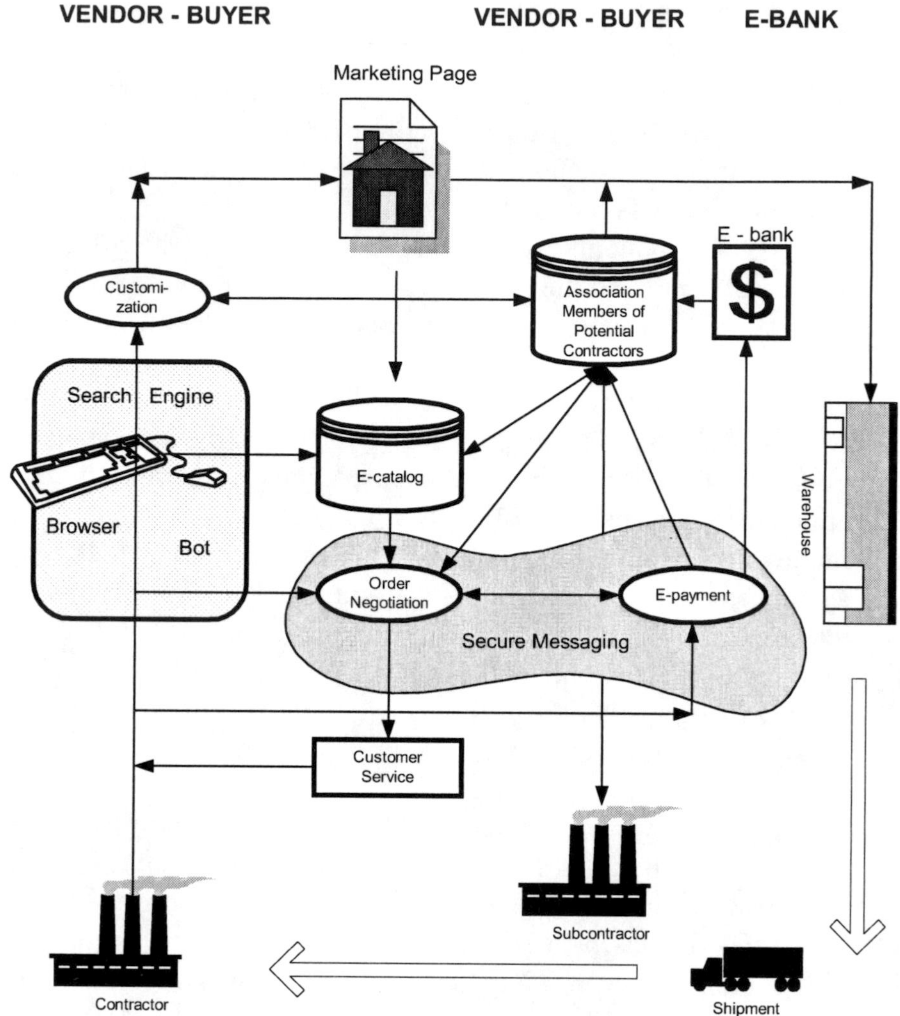

Business-to-business (B2B) e-commerce is the richest vein of commerce opportunity, accounting for more than 70% of transaction values in 2000, and in 2004 it will reach $2.2 trillion as an 87% portion of the e-commerce total.

B2B models can be classified as follows:

1. **Supplier-controlled e-commerce** – in markets dominated by brand-names, such as Cisco, that sell complex goods and services and provide

quality customer service for their customers and channel partners. They want to build websites and Extranets with subcontractors which ensure that customers return to buy goods and services. Therefore these suppliers want to maintain tight control through CRM (Customer Relation System).

2. **Buyer-controlled e-commerce (e-procurement)** – the buyer is the driving force. For example: companies such as Ford and General Motors and Wal-Mart set up e-commerce systems for their huge number of suppliers which compete for an order. In this case the buyer is the policy setter. The critical functions in this model are transaction performance and integrity.

3. **Suppliers-buyers controlled e-commerce** – is a combination of systems for big suppliers and buyers who want to reduce logistic cost and be more efficient.

4. **Digital markets** – include trading associations (third parties), exchanges, and online marketplaces for small and medium-sized buyers and suppliers. Third party associations bring buyers and suppliers to exchange information, conduct transactions, and use e-legal and e-banking services provided for association members.

The future of B2B is the interconnection among all the above models.

Person-to-person payment is a way to send money through the Web to an individual who is not set up to accept credit-card payment. This fast growing area of the Web payment systems owes its success almost entirely to *www.eBay.com*. Now that we are all buying from each other's attics, the need for a payment system that does not require credit card authorization capability has arisen. This system works like escrow accounts, but without some of protections offered by escrow, a legal term for an agreement that is put in the care of a third party and won't get executed until certain conditions are met. The sender of money sets up an account with a credit-card number attached. The recipient must "pick up" his/her money by visiting the website and giving a physical address or a bank account. PayPal, a unit of www.X.com, is by far the best-known person-to-person payment system online, with 4 million registered users. It processes about 130,000 transactions a day, with an average payment of $50. The user needs a password to collect a payment. eBay applies Billpoint solution, and Yahoo! uses Paydirect utility. This way of paying empowers the entrepreneur in all of us. Most of these systems charge no fee to users, because they make their money on the interest earned on the accounts. Some charge fees to small businesses that want to accept payments.

Virtual Escrow ensures that the buyer receives the item and that the seller receives payment. Prior to conducting the transaction, both parties agree to register the same escrow service and agree to its terms. The buyer then transmits payment via credit card, check or bank transfer to the escrow service. Once the escrow service verifies the payment, the seller sends the merchandise to the buyer for inspection. If items are acceptable to the buyer, the escrow service transmits payment to the seller. The market leader is i-Escrow, Inc. of Redwood (California) whose services are used by eBay and Amazon's auctions.

Digital Wallets are the way to speed checkout and avoid setting up separate accounts at different Web merchants. Users download software that stores their credit card numbers and personal information. Participating sites download software that enables them to receive payment from the wallet. The process is very similar to digital cash, except that the retailer actually receives a credit-card number rather than a form of the Internet currency. The wallet also stores shipping and billing addresses. Yahoo! is the leader in electronic wallets, with a roster of more than 11,000 merchants, and it accepts only one credit card number. America Online's wallet, called Quick Checkout, stores 10 credit card numbers and 15 shipping addresses but is accepted at only 30 merchants. Microsoft's wallet is called Passport, and is without any limit to the number of credit-cards.

Virtual Credit Card allows one to use a credit card online without having to disclose the actual credit-card number. A bank asks its credit card customers to download some software onto their computers. Whenever they shop, that software generates a one-time credit card number for the purchase. The merchant does not know it is not the real credit card number because when the merchant checks with the bank, the bank confirms that it is tied to the customer's account. This system applies to American Express.

Electronic Payment Systems

The Internet environment of e-commerce triggered the development of several innovative payment systems (Price Waterhouse, 1997):

1. Credit-based payments:
   a) small transactions <$5

- Visa, MasterCard, FirstVirtual, IBM InfoMarket, ClickShare

b) large transactions >$50
- CyberCash credit card, CyberFee credit card

2. Debit-based payments

a) small transactions <$5
- NetCheque, CyberCash Check, CyberCash CyberCoins
- FSTC Electronic Check

3. Digital currency

a) small transactions <$5
- DigiCash, NetCash

b) large transactions >$50
- Citibank

The most popular consumer e-payment is provided by MasterCard and Visa cards, whose ID and numbers are submitted via an e-mail or encrypted response message. The payments are also provided by trusted third parties such as the Net Banking Consortium, consisting of more than 20 large banks, using IBM's Global Network Internet Access service and website hosting capabilities to facilitate e-commerce transactions among partners associated with this Consortium.

Payment in the form of a digital check replaces a paper check with an electronic one for the same purpose of existing inter-bank clearing systems.

The digital cash is based on digital tokens that represent secure currency (without double spending) and allow direct buyer-to-seller transfer of value.

Smart cards, popular in France, Germany and Australia are another e-payment system. A memory chip is implanted into a piece of plastic that is almost indistinguishable from a credit card. The chip can store any kind of data, and can process data and execute algorithms. The Mondex card is owned by 17 major banks and organizations from several countries. Visa Cash smart cards are available in 15 American cities. The Wells Fargo Bank of San Francisco provides a VeriFone smart card, which can obtain virtual cash by the phone.

Micropayments are another kind of e-commerce payment. They provide a merchant with a mechanism to charge as little as between $0.08 to $0.30 per transaction. In this range, CyberCash and CyberCoin are applied. To use this system, a consumer must have a credit card and an account with a participating. In addition, both the vendor and consumer must have installed special software. Money can be transferred from the account to the CyberCoin "wallet" in increments of $20. To make a purchase, a consumer clicks on a Web page and is queried about the purchase and payment amount; when the customer approves the purchase, money is then transferred from the wallet to the merchant (Price Waterhouse, 1997).

E-Commerce Security

Essential security solutions are based on the following functions:

- A user authentication service which provides log-in identification (ID) and password verification
- An authorization engine which makes decisions to grant or deny access to protected resources on the net
- An administrative interface to determine the authorized association of users and protected resources on the net
- An audit service to record attempted security incidents and administrative changes
- A cryptographic service to protect the confidentiality of the user's passwords

Security of e-commerce is based on the following standards:

- RSA (named after inventors Rivest, Shamir, and Adleman from MIT) algorithm introduced in 1978 to provide public-key encryption in peer-to-peer secure transactions, authentication of user by passwords, and digital signature. This standard is widely implemented in hardware and software products. The standard is based on 129 or more digits.
- DES (Data Encryption Standard) is a private-key encryption system which is based on two keys, one to encrypt the data and another to decrypt the data.

The net security system is depicted on Figure 6-4. Its solution is based on the publicly known public key, which the sender applies to encrypt its own data, and the receiver has the private key which is applied to decrypt the received

Figure 6-4: Public-Key Encryption Architecture

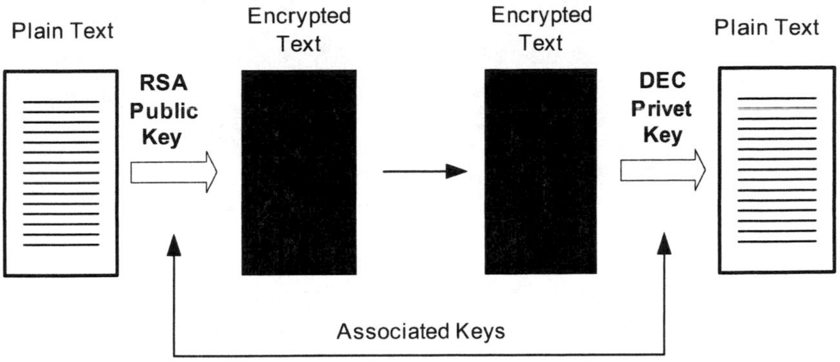

Source: SET Specification 1996

data. A public-key is distributed by the trusted third party, which certifies its authenticity.

Good-Bye to Fixed Pricing

Today, the first signs of a new fluid pricing can be found mostly on the Internet. Online auctions allow cybershoppers to bid on everything from collectibles to treadmills. Electronic exchanges, on the other hand, act as middlemen, representing a group of sellers of one type of product or service – for example, long distance service - that is matched with buyers.

The pricing revolution, though, goes beyond the Net. Companies also are creating private networks, or "extranets," that link them with their suppliers and customers. These systems make it possible to get a precise handle on inventory, costs, and demand at any given moment - and adjust prices instantly. In the past, there was a significant cost associated with changing prices, known as the "menu cost." For a company with a large product line, it could take months for price adjustments to filter down to distributors, retailers, and salespeople. Current streamlined networks reduce menu cost and time to near zero.

This will clearly benefit consumers. Already, many are finding bargains at the hundreds of online auction sites that have cropped up. And on the Net, it is a cinch to check out product information and compare prices – thanks to a growing army of shopping helpers called "bots." This shifts the bargaining power to consumers.

But that does not mean sellers get a raw deal. Businesses can gather more detailed information than ever before about their customers and run it through powerful database systems to glean insight into buying behavior. Suddenly, marketers can communicate directly with prospective buyers, offering them targeted promotions on an individual basis.

As buyers and sellers do battle in the electronic market, the struggle should result in prices that more closely reflect their true market value. The future of e-commerce is in implicit one-to-one negotiation between buyer and seller. An individual can get a spot price on everything. Some day, you may haggle over the price of just about anything, the way you would negotiate the price of a carpet in a Turkish bazaar. However, it is likely to take place on an electronic exchange, and it may be a computer bidding against another computer on your behalf.

For a preview of what is to come, let's just look to the financial markets. The NASDAQ stock market is a model for e-commerce. NASDAQ, for example, uses a system of dealers, or market makers, who trade shares of stock for brokers or individuals. The dealers are linked by computer networks that match buy orders with sell orders, and thus arrive at the value of a stock for that moment in time.

Like NASDAQ dealers, the new Internet market makers must set up mechanisms for clearing transactions and for making sure that both buyers and sellers are satisfied. As electronic exchanges are established to trade everything from advertising space to spare parts, the true market value of products should emerge.

The most widely used form of this is an online auction. In the world of virtual gavels, Onsale makes a good business. The website runs seven live options a week where people outbid one another for computer gear, electronics equipment, and even steaks. Onsale buys surplus or distressed goods from companies at fire-sale prices so they can weather low bids. And the customer loves it. He/she can buy, for example, an eight-year-old model desktop computer for his business via Onsale. They saved 40% over what they would have paid in a store. So far, the lure of a bargain has proved powerful: more than 4 million bids have been placed in the period from 1995 to 1998. It sold $115 million worth of goods in 1997, up 30% from 1996. In such a manner, customers are active participants in price-setting, so it is almost an infinity of economic Democracy.

For every couple dozen online auctions, though, there is an entrepreneur applying the Net economics in ways that will ultimately transform entire industries – from telecommunications to energy. These companies are setting an example for tracings commodities such as phone minutes, gas supplies, and clectronic components. Their approach is a departure from the old mode of commerce. This is "the third wave" of commerce on the Net – companies, which are moving beyond simple marketing and online ordering, now create an entirely new electronic marketplace.

> You might not think of a stodgy utility as being in the vanguard of cyberspace, but that is exactly where Southern California Gas is. A couple of years ago, it saw an opportunity in the dove-tailing of two sweeping trends - the deregulation of the energy industry, which lets customers shop for energy suppliers the way they shop for long-distance phone service, and the rise of the Web. So, last fall, it launched Energy Marketplace, a Web-based exchange that lets customers shop for the best gas prices.
>
> The system has something for everyone. Small and midsize gas providers list their prices on the exchange. That lowers their marketing costs and gives them access to a broader market - putting them on equal footing with big energy suppliers. Customers, mostly businesses, save money by shopping for the best price, or locking in long-term deals when prices are low. And Southern California Gas, as a distributor, increases its volume of business and collects a subscription fee from gas providers that use the exchange. Solaces offers residential customers the same opportunity and has expanded the service to include electricity.
>
> Does it work? Using Energy Marketplace, Summoned Wire Product Corporation in Stockton, California, found a new supplier, Intermarket Trading Co., and now saves \$500 a month – about 20% of its \$3,000 a month energy bill.
>
> New York-based ArbiNET (short for Arbitrage Network) is building an exchange for routing phone calls over the lowest-cost network on the fly. Most telecommunications carriers have built massive networks to handle peak loads. The problem is, much of the

capacity goes unused. AT&T, for example, typically uses just 20% of its global network capacity, in a fiercely competitive market that has seen margins erode. Unused capacity can be the difference between making money and losing money. ArbiNET's exchange lets carriers optimize their capacity by accepting lower cost calls over their networks during off-peak hours. There are other companies that broker long-distance minutes, but ArbiNet is the only one attempting it in real-time. ArbiNet Clearing Network works this way: work carriers, such as AT&T, supply information about their network ability and price at a given time. Carrier customers send calls through ArbiNet's clearing house - say, a phone call from New York to Hong Kong that must travel over secure lines. ArbiNet's powerful computers and phone switches match the request with the lowest-cost carrier for the particular call - all in milliseconds. ArbiNET plans to open service for consumers. Then, a smart phone, for example, could automatically check for the lowest carrier on each call that is placed. Naturally such a scenario is unnerving the giant phone companies, because it will undercut their prices.

Other big players are embracing the Net to dispose of surplus goods while protecting margins on their core products. Chicago-based FastParts Inc. and FairMarket Inc. in Woburn, Mass., operate thriving exchanges where computer electronics companies swap excess parts. All U.S. industries generate some $18 billion in excess inventory a year - around 10% of all finished goods. When Intel Corp.'s 386 microprocessor came out, one customer found himself with a boatload of 286 chips that were instantly obsolete. Afraid that he might have to write off the inventory as a loss, he made some calls and found a customer willing to buy the stock. Now, the same surplus customer at Mao Technologies Inc. sells a $100,000 software package to companies that want to run their own auctions to generate revenue from aging merchandise.

Internet bidding exchanges are flourishing for a wide array of products - and more are sure to come. Among the most popular are:

- **Aucnet.com** - auction of used cars. Its rating system helps buyers to judge the quality of cars.

- **Narrowline.com** - an electronic exchange for net advertisers that brings together media buyers with websites looking to sell available space.

- **Eworldauction.com** - this site holds monthly online auctions of old books, maps, and medieval manuscripts.

- **Priceline.com** - mortgages, cars, and airline tickets: provide your price and terms - and Priceline will try to find you a willing seller.

- **Energymarket.com** - lets suppliers of natural gas and electricity compete for the business of big corporate energy users.

- **eBay** - the largest on the Internet auction house that provides the market for 3+ million goods, where about 2-3 million users trade daily.

"Third Wave." These e-commerce systems pave the way for fluid pricing to reach beyond commodity products and surplus goods to popular, even premium-priced items. E-markets could be just as effective selling unique items, such as a van Gogh painting or a company's core product line. The move away from surplus goods to primary goods is the real thrust of the third wave.

There is just one snag: when anyone on the Net can easily compare prices and features, some high-margin products could fall in price. And a strong brand name alone may not be enough to make a premium price tag stick. Some branded products may even prove to be interchangeable. You might not trust your phone service to an outfit you have never heard of on the basis of price alone. But you might be willing to swap among AT&T and MCI, or Sprint for a better deal. And do you really care if your credit card is MasterCard or Visa?

One way companies can respond is by cooking up creative ploys to differentiate their products. They could include personalizing products or offering loyalty programs that reward frequent customers. Thanks to Internet brokers, trading fees are already rock-bottom. Now, companies such as E*trade, the online brokerage firm, are mulling loyalty programs that reward frequent traders.

There are other ways to side-step the effects of the ultra-efficient Net market. Just look at the airline industry. It was one of the first industries to go online, starting with American Airlines Inc.'s Sabre automated-reservation system in the 1960's. When airlines followed suit, American introduced the frequent flyer program to keep customers loyal. Three decades after Sabre, airlines still manage to get many passengers to pay rich fares. The secret:

knowing who to gouge - in this case, the business customer who also has perfected the science of yield management, concocting complicated pricing schemes that defy comparison. The price for an airline seat can change several times and a passenger is virtually certain that the person sitting in the next seat has paid a different fare.

Now, airlines are tapping into the Net - but mainly as a way to sell unfilled seats. They routinely send out e-mail alerts of last minute fare specials. And several airlines have signed up with Priceline, which lets customers specify when and where they want to travel, and name their price. Priceline then forwards the bids to participating airlines, which can choose to accept the request or not. The company makes its money on the spread between the bid and the lower airline price. It empowers the buyer and also the seller. They can plug in demand to empty flights.

Such e-markets produce a price that fairly reflects demand. Some companies may be surprised by the results. Look at AucNet, an online auction for used cars. Dealers and wholesalers flock to the AucNet's website to buy and sell some 6,000 cars a month. Surprisingly, sellers fetch more for their used cars than they might on a physical lot. That is partly because of the larger audience they have attracted on the Net.

E-BUSINESS

The e-business idea means more than simply creating a marketing "presence" on the Web. It represents a transformation of the business process itself, enabled by the Internet's unique combination of features:

- instant access to information,
- universal and global reach, and
- personalized delivery of information and services.

In e-business, critical business systems are connected directly to an enlarged community of users, including customers, trading partners, and employees. That means these users can:

- buy goods and services,

- update their own accounts,
- get up-to-the-second information, and
- resolve disputes – all electronically, immediately, with 7x24 availability.

That also means the providers of goods and services using the Internet are not bound by the constraints and delays of traditional businesses, including:

- *brick-and-mortar* facilities,
- paper-based communications with customers and suppliers, and armies of middlemen translating the external business environment into the data formats understood by internal systems.

The result is that e-business allows companies to:

- develop new products and services faster,
- increase customer loyalty through superior service, and
- integrate the supply chain more efficiently, and market more effectively to the individualized needs of their customer base.

The world of e-business is a radical departure from the models that have governed commerce for decades – and the IT systems that have served them. Profit margin is starting to take a back seat to revenue growth and market share, as whole industries consolidate through mergers and acquisitions.

The digital revolution, driven by the sudden emergence of inexpensive, standards-based communications linking all businesses and customers anywhere in the world, is transforming every industry, and no company is safe from the winds of change. For example, information about customer transactions, captured automatically on the Web, becomes almost as important as the transactions themselves. They enable companies to understand each customer's needs and preferences, and then market goods and services to each customer in an individualized way, all automatically. In e-business, marketing and service delivery blend transparently.

The need for elegant brick-and-mortar facilities or finely crafted distribution channels, critical under the old rules of commercial engagement, disappears with e-business. The Internet is enabling startup companies with almost no fixed assets to deliver goods and services faster.

For years the return on technology investment in business has been increased profits from productivity gains, largely based on cost reduction of internal processes. The focus has been on making the wheels turn more freely *inside the company*. E-business brings cost reduction, too, but that's not its key benefit. The new boardroom mantra – raise the top line, increase market share, attract and retain customers – is making e-business a strategic imperative.

E-business is *externally focused* on customers and trading partners, bringing them inside the company's business process. It is about entirely new ways of finding new customers, providing free information about goods and services, and making it as easy and convenient as possible to conduct business over the Internet. And it is also about using the knowledge of the customer acquired in the process to maximize the lifetime value of that customer through superior service and individualized attention.

One-to-one marketing is a radical innovation made possible by e-business. By capturing and analyzing the site navigation behavior, self-identified interests, and actual past purchases of its customers using their website, companies can pro-actively tailor the presentation of additional goods and services to each customer.

With e-business, companies can reach out to large numbers of potential customers through portals, information-oriented sites like Yahoo that attract millions of visitors daily, and act as hubs for connecting to a wide variety of other sites. In fact, the sheer volume of information available invites users to personalize the portal, configuring their view to show only information of particular interest. These configurations enable the portal to target advertising to user for maximum impact. Portals also enable affiliate marketing, allowing companies to offer goods and services transparently behind other companies' websites, meaning new channels to the customer.

An emerging concept from the Knowledge Management discipline is the knowledge or corporate Intranet portal, which, like the Internet portal, attempts to aggregate content relevant to the user in a single point of access. Corporate portals act as a "start page" for the knowledge worker, focusing on business data acquired from a company's Intranet, ERP applications, and relevant websites from external sources. They are personalized to the users' needs and help bring organization to the "infoglut."

Gradually, several business processes enter the Web mode of operations. Among them one can recognize the following Web-driven solutions:

- **e-Commerce** – electronic environment for transactions handling (described in the previous section)

- **Enterprise Information Portals** – Web-oriented knowledge management (described in Chapter 8)

- **e-Marketing** – besides Customer Relation Management applications, there are other solutions such as e-mail "push" marketing and e-mail discussion lists, which provide free "listservs" that convey adds for targeted audiences. One of such providers is San Francisco-based *www.eGroup.com*, or *www.jaboom.com* website that attracts people by providing free music and convey to users' adds, and with the $9,000 budget bought 300,000 impressions.

- **e-Procurement** – is a sort of e-commerce among producers and subcontractors through the Extranet.

- **e-Human Resources** – provides a facility for self-service operations in creating and updating an employee's personal records and typical routines, such as submitting travel expenses, receiving employment statements, and so forth. This function can be outsourced to companies like Hewitt Assoc.

- **e-Billing Presentment and Paying (eBPP)** – holds particular promise for industries such as telecommunications, cable, utilities, financial services, and publishing, for which billing is a big chunk of their business and huge expense. The typical cost of producing and sending a statement by snail mail is between 90 cents and $1.25, whereas an electronic bill costs only 25 to 30 cents to generate and deliver. However, more savings will be in making payments, where the average processing cost drops from $1.50 for a snail mail, paper-based payment to a mere 10 cents to pay in e-bill. Third party consolidators such as Yahoo! or CheckFree provide inter-platform computability between the biller and the payee. The customer deals with the consolidator and never goes to the biller.

- **e-Signature** – is a digitized image of a signature that is linked to a mathematical algorithm that verifies the authenticity of an e-document. If the document is altered after signing, the signature is broken and invalid. This sophisticated capability likely will be pushed to customers by the companies they do business with. The mass-market technology is on the way. In 2000 Silanis Technology Inc. spun off its software (www.onSign.com) to consumers and small businesses. The 2000 e-Sign Act opens the door for more companies to adapt e-Signature.

- **e-Content** – facilitates the collection of data and information and their transformation in knowledge (patterns and rules) that support decision-making in complex circumstances.

- **e-Document** – provides a scalable digital repository for every type of document (application reports, databases, content bases, word processing, fax, images, e-mail, video files, voice files) which is retrievable through Web browsers (IBM Content Manager OnDemand and LotusDomino.Doc are example of e-document technology and strategy). Hewitt Assoc. apply e-document system for 10,000 employees in 72 locations in 32 countries and for its Fortune 500 customers (75% of the list), who can use the Content Manager of the enterprise common digital repository to load, search and reproduce a given document either needed in intra or external operations.

- **e-Publishing** – to save costs on paper-based publishing and accelerate the content delivery to readers. By an efficient process, it may improve relationships among a company's workers and management, particularly if a feedback mechanism is in place.

- **e-Service** – transforms traditional banking into Web-driven transactions and as a by-product of it, creates inputs to warehouses for further data mining.

- **e-Communities** – are virtual gatherings of customers and potential ones who are supported by added values services.

- **e-Business Intelligence** – is a system that scales down sheer volume of collected data/information (Yahoo! collects the daily equivalent of 800,000 books; Engage Co. organized 30 million profiles for adds, [*Business Week, July 26, 1999*]) and aggregates information to define trends and determine important "personalized" details (Profile, Site Path, Preference) and instantly refresh source data. One of such systems offers *www.INFORMATICA.com.*

- **e-Learning** – is about using the Internet to revolutionize the way people learn. The reusable education content is delivered by e-Document, real-time collaboration (e.g., desktop videoconferencing, telephoning or text), virtual labs, broadcast video, or simulation. In a sort of self-service mode, an employee identifies knowledge gaps, takes workforce benchmarks, and adapts an individual plan. The employee creates an assessment process, document learning history, establishes entitlement processes, and develops a custom learning agenda. By taking advantage of these tools employers can maximize their workforce to obtain a competitive edge. The American Bankers Association (ABA) offers the Internet-based 100 training courses for banks' workers.

- Other

One can predict that in the future, the majority of business functions and processes will be automated, informated and put on or integrated through the Web.

E-business, the corporate offspring of the Internet, continues to captivate the attention of business leaders. Fully 97% of 250 IT executives at the *Information Week 500* surveyed in 2000 say e-Business is the No. 1 business

Figure 6-5: The Architecture of e-Business Systems

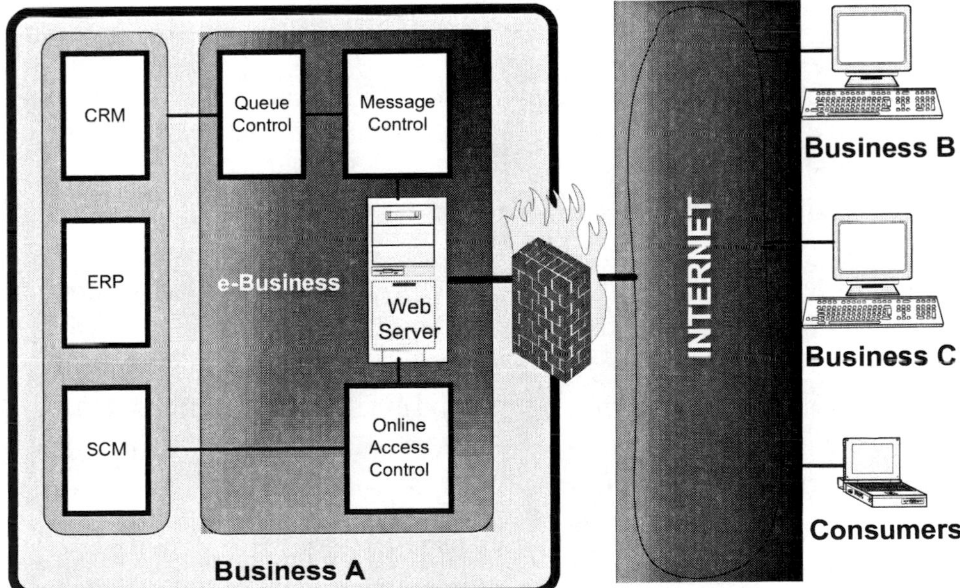

priority of their IT departments which will implement it in the next year. E-commerce applications, intranet and enterprise portals, and B2B electronic networks top the list of key strategic priorities.

Information Week 500 companies, on average, derive 22% of their revenue from e-Business transactions, and 45% of those companies report e-business operations. Up-and-coming *brick 'n click* companies continue to invest heavily in business-to-business operations.

The architecture of e-Business Systems is shown in Figure 6-5.

"DOT-COM" COMPANIES

A dot-com company is an organization that offers its services or products exclusively on the Internet. Although a company that makes only a Web-based software (e.g., Microsoft) might be in the dot-com industry, it is generally not considered a dot-com company. Amazon.com, Yahoo! and eBay are typical dot-companies. "Dot-com" refers to the period (dot) followed by the abbreviation of the commercial domain (.com) at the end of the Internet e-mail or Web address. Since the .dot domain is so widely used, the Internet has become known as the "dot-com" world, and dot-com companies are those that offer their wares on the Web. Since .com addresses are the most popular, Web browsers default to adding the .com to the end of the URL if no other domain, such as .org or .edu is typed.

Dot-com companies are electronic enterprises that differ from old industrial ones, called "*brick 'n mortar*" companies. However, the latter transforms into e-firms and therefore are called "*brick 'n click*" companies. On the other hand, in 2000, when the dot-com companies went through the market correction, they understood that their further success depends on how well they will develop traditional solutions; for example, warehouses. Hence, such transformed companies are being called "*click 'n mortar*" companies.

The Internet is often called the great equalizer of capitalism, a tool that permits almost everyone with an entrepreneurial spirit to start a new business. In 1995-1999 the Internet start-ups created several thousand new companies which within a year have been employing on average 100 people, and that is a very different environment than the entrepreneurial start-ups of five to 10 years ago. The reason that the New Economy start-ups grow more quickly is because the Internet gives them access to broader customer markets than other firms that are limited by geography. In turn, the capacity to increase sales at higher rates helps high-tech firms draw venture-capital from all over, allowing further expansion. After one to two years of their existence, they offer Initial Public Offerings (IPO) and the founders become overnight millionaires or even billionaires.

Dot-com retailers, brandishing fully loaded bags of cash and bravado, staked claim to the e-commerce turf by the end of the 1990's by muscling in on timid *brick 'n mortar* companies, enticing consumers with cheap prices and perks such as free shipping. And while the dot-coms wounded many old-guard companies, what was clear following the 2000 spring's market decline was that the *brick 'n mortar* companies have fought back with highly successful *mortar 'n click* strategies.

Times since 2000 are suddenly tough for dot-coms. A volatile, punishing stock market has cast an unflattering light on some rapidly deflating paper fortunes. Consumer and retail websites are being eulogized and dissected while their little hearts are still pounding and law firms have begun to staff up to handle bankruptcies.

Some experts believe that the vast majority – perhaps 95% to 98% of all dot-com companies – failed in 2000-2002 (Gartner Group, Inc.). According to the same source, the true blending of traditional and Internet business models – and not the pure dot-com model – will be the winning formula. These dot-com companies will get consolidated by the Amazons and Wal-Marts of the world.

So far the cost of building and launching increasingly sophisticated Web-based e-commerce sites requires a funding in a range of $1 million. After the stocks fall in 2000 it is now more difficult to raise funds for new Internet start-ups.

Let's take a look at the most successful dot-com companies such as Yahoo!, Amazon, eBay, and America Online.

Yahoo!.com. It was built by Tim Koogle as a Web portal which in 2000 had 145 registered users and 48.3 million visitors every month. The company has a strategy of partnering with a lot of companies instead of buying them. Rather than trying to own everything from websites to cable-TV systems – not to mention TV studios and print magazines – Yahoo! is a pure Web media play. It offers the masses a friendly gateway to the Webworld. Rather than selling merchandise itself, though, the company partners with retailers. It charges them fees for transactions generated on its websites. The result: its gross margin of 82.7% is more than four times Amazon.com's. It doesn't have to pay for warehouses and labor. As a result of this strategy, Yahoo! could become an e-commerce juggernaut. It added Amazon-style cyberwallets and product reviews. It also teamed with Kmart inc. on free ISP (Internet Service Provider) *bluelight.com*, which has more 1 million users who automatically become Yahoo users.

Amazon.com Inc. It is a superstore which is considered one of the world's great consumer companies. It keeps in inventory about 3 million books and in 1999 achieved $1.6 billion in sales. In 2002 it should reach a level of $6 million and show for the first time profit. This superstore has 25 million customers who are actively spending about $130 per person per year (2000). The e-retailer was developed by Jeff Bezos who was the Time Man of the 1998 year, who has shown others how to organize e-commerce. The company created a huge presence in the Internet Ecosystem and beyond. People who know nothing about e-commerce know about Amazon. It is essentially hoping to follow in the footsteps of AOL and Yahoo! Amazon's theory is that they can scale up first and be profitable later.

eBay.com. It was founded by Meg Whitman, a pioneer of online auctions. The company facilitates trade of flea market items through big-ticket items such as automobiles and real estate, in total about 3 million things. In 2000 the public attention was triggered when somebody advertised for sale human organs. It has local sites in 53 U.S. cities and five countries. In 2000 the company had revenues of about $500 million and about $30 million of a net income.

America Online was founded in the early 1990's by Steve Case, who brought the Internet to 26 million registered and paying fee consumers and 60 million visitors every month in 2000. In the same year, the founder offered the merger with Time Warner Inc. at the $183 billion level. It will be a combination of a quality content and channel provider who can monopolize the market not only in the U.S. but in Europe too. It also will be the electronic solution for how to connect the world in reality.

The key indicators of e-commerce are shown in Tables 6-2, 6-3, 6-4, 6-5.

Table 6-2: The Cost of Acquiring a Customer in 2000

Cost Category	Net Up-starts	Cataloguers On-line	Brick 'n Mortar Store Online
Cost per new customer	$82	$11	$31
Marketing as percentage of revenue	119%	6%	36%

Source: Boston Consulting Group Study of 221 Online Retailers

Table 6-2 shows the reason why the majority of new up-starts (so-called dot.coms) went out of business in 2000-2001 – because they spent too much on marketing – 119% of revenues. Their strategy of neglecting revenues and emphasizing the broad reach of customers did not work. In capitalism, profit is still the most important factor of business.

Table 6-3: Frequency of Using Online Service in 2000

	Net Up-starts	Cataloguers Online	Brick 'n Mortar Store Online
Percentage of visits leading to orders	1.7%	2.1%	1.4%
Percentage of individuals who ordered	3.5%	4.2%	1.8%
Repeat buyers	27%	20%	34%
Abandoned shopping cars	52%	66%	76%

Source: Boston Consulting Group Study of 221 Online Retailers

Table 6-3 shows that every second consumer abandons an online store, perhaps due to a search for a better one, which is a relatively easy operation in the Internet, where through just one "click" one can move from one to another store.

Table 6-4: Customer Satisfaction in 2000

CUSTOMERS SATISFACTION WITH	
Customer service	41%
Easy returns	51%
Better product information	57%
Product selection ability	66%
Price	70%
Ease of use	74%

Source: Boston Consulting Group Study of 221 Online Retailers

Table 6-4 confirms that it is easy to use online shopping which provides better product information and selection.

Table 6-5: Why Customers Buy in 2000

WHY CUSTOMERS BUY?	
Recognize and trust merchant	51%
Purchased from merchant offline	39%
Purchased from merchant online	37%
Can find bargains	36%
Recommendation of others	23%
Merchant offers incentives	17%

Source: Boston Consulting Group Study of 221 Online Retailers

Table 6-5 explains why customers buy online, mostly from recognized and trusted merchants, for example Amazon.com.

B2C e-commerce depends on two types of mainstream consumers:

- Low-income technology optimists – students (16-to-22 year-olds) who are not afraid of technology shop online six times the rate of the overall population. They have $1 trillion (in 2000), (17%) of personal disposable income of $6 trillion. They are interested in what is new, what is cool, are very communicative, and they download music.

- High-income technology pessimists – earliest adopters, clients of Schwab looking for easy shopping and good choices at the bargain prices, they shop online at work and have about 12% of personal disposable income or $2 trillion. They like the style of Banana Republic and J. Crew products.

According to some experts, "being a dot-com in and of itself is not a strategic advantage." There is an advantage in being agile, in being new, in being funded, and having a single purpose to your organization. A lot of traditional companies like Toys "R" US and Wal-Mart are creating e-commerce and are being transformed in *brick 'n click* companies. And vice versa; more and more *click 'n click* companies are being transformed in *click 'n brick* companies.

RETHINKING THE INTERNET

The once-limitless promise of the Internet appears to be fading in at the beginning of the 21st century. The dot-coms that were supposed to topple industry giants have vanished[2] in 2000-2001. No. 1 e-tailer Amazon.com cannot extract a profit from its $2.8 billion in sales. Without advanced technology such as broadband, the Net will take a longer time to fulfill its promises.

Where the Internet may be revolutionary[3]:

- Financial services - most financial services can potentially be handled electronically. But so far, banks cannot even figure out a good way of letting people pay bills online.
- Entertainment – much of entertainment can easily be digitized. But no one knows how to make money yet, and technology is lagging.
- Health care – the benefits of shifting health care transactions to the Web could be enormous. But so far are the institutional barriers.
- Education – e-learning could cut the cost of education, but only at the price of making education more impersonal.
- Government – delivering information to citizens has enormous appeal, but requires massive investments.

Where the Internet's impact may be incremental:

- Retailing – the glitzy websites got all the attention. But dot-com success turned more on who had the best logistics (distribution centers).
- Manufacturing – Web-enable supply chains and intranets are important, but ultimately a manufacturer lives or dies on the quality of its goods.
- Travel – online travel sites are popular, but the ultimate constraint on travel is the physical capacity of the air and road systems.
- Power – online energy exchanges get the publicity, but power generation and transmission capabilities will have bigger economic impact.

With the future of Yahoo! and Amazon.com growing slower, the following business models of B2C can be considered[4]:

- Niches are nice – e-tailers that focus on a niche will fare better. Profitable pet suppliers Waggin' Tails specializes in high-margin products, unlike the defunct Pets.com, which tried to do it all.

- Information brokers – the No.1 thing Netizens do online is look for information. Those that make it pay will win. Job-listing site Monster.com, which charges employers to post positions, makes money.

- The fence-straddlers – business in both the physical and virtual worlds reign. Merck-Medco, the nation's leading provider of prescription drug care, racking up $460 million in online sales in 2000, has clobbered Net up-starts drugstore.com and PlanetRx.

- A la carte models – business models that boast multiple ways of making money have good odds. Real estate listing service Homestore.com, which sells technology and adds, was profitable in 2001 on revenues of $440 million.

What we will pay for[5]:

- Internet access – a few free, plain vanilla dial-up services may persist, but nearly all will charge for a connection and technical support, especially for high-speed broadband access.

- Analysis – highly valued analyses of information, such as stock market prognostications or a city-by-city list of the best doctors, will come with a fee.

- Entertainment – just as we pay for all-movie and music-video cable TV, we will pay for video-on demand and music on the Web, especially now that the courts have outlawed Napster's free file sharing services.

- Specialized services – how about an online personal shopper? Or an advance peek at the Armani line for fall? An upscale e-tailer may offer paying club members such online extras.

What will remain free[6]:

- Commodity data – stuff that is widely available everywhere, such as stock quotes, weather, and news, will be Internet giveaways.

- Shopping information – the Web will remain a great place to comparison-shop and gather information on everything from car models to real estate.

- Search engines – they may cost a bundle to build, but the incremental cost of additional searches is minuscule, so they will stay free and rely on advertising and licensing to companies.

- Purchases – surcharges would make e-shopping lose its competitive advantage over catalog retailers and in-store purchasing.

The e-biz has future. If one looks at how the Net is changing the nature of markets, it is not that it cannot do it, but dot-coms are struggling to find the business models that work. No one has an answer to how to make money. That means it is still a time for experimentation.

FUTURE TRENDS

The early fascination with the Internet potential will slowly transform into more mature and financially sound applications. More emphasis will be put on the issues of security and reliability of Internet operations. The expansion of the Internet applications may be sketched in the main areas as follows:

- The number of consumers using the Internet will grow accordingly to the growth of the number of installed home computers. In the most advanced countries over 60% of households use home computers and only about 20% subscribe to Internet services. In less developed countries the use of home computers is two to 100 times smaller than in the developed countries. This digital divide leads to 1 billion citizens with a computer password and 5 billion without one. It may trigger unpredictable social unrest and political conflict, far beyond the IT professionals' problem solving capability. The most advanced users of the Internet may find that it is a very useful tool for obtaining simple data and information; however, it is not an omnipotent tool for obtaining the most relevant information for free.

- The corporate world will push for the development of e-enterprises that will lead to more innovations and problems which are very difficult to predict today. The new electronic business landscape is very interesting for its creators but less fascinating for its potential victims. It may lead to a fully automated-informated economy that will have electronic robots, and fewer traditional consumers and taxpayers,who will be unable to support this Digital Economy.

It is a question whether humankind will survive peacefully knowledge that has been created in the 21st century.

CONCLUSION

The Internet Economy makes the Traditional Economy more dynamic; however, the failure of dot.com businesses indicates that the "*mortar and click*" or "*click and mortar*" modes of business are so far the best solutions. This only confirms that the Information Wave does not replace the Agricultural and Industrial Waves. The Information Wave just optimizes other Waves' development and operation.

BIBLIOGRAPHY

Sources for survey data come from publications on the Internet and they are mentioned throughout the chapter's text.

ENDNOTES

1 Source: Center for Research in Electronic Commerce, Graduate School of Business, University of Texas at Austin, © 2001

2 This issue (*from dot.com towards dot.con)* is discussed in Chapter 1.

3 "Rethinking the Internet," *Business Week*, March 26, 2001

4 "Rethinking the Internet," *Business Week*, March 26, 2001

5 "Rethinking the Internet," *Business Week*, March 26, 2001

6 "Rethinking the Internet," *Business Week*, March 26, 2001

Part IV

IT Development and Management

Chapter VII

IT Development

INTRODUCTION

In this chapter trends of IT-driven enterprise development are presented. These trends compete among themselves for supremacy. They do not create a well integrated set of techniques; vice-versa, this set is very eclectic and contains techniques very old and still applicable, like the System Development Life Cycle, and new ones, like Web technologies. These trends are extended into issues of an IT vision for the 21st century, IT skills, and computer controversies that may influence IT developers' awareness about how to pursue IT developmental projects.

IT CENTERS

The IT Centers' concept characterizes the main areas of tasks, knowledge and skills that are necessary to develop, operate, and manage EII. Table 7-1 illustrates each center's methodology, examples of projects, and examples of outcomes.

Table 7-1: The Characteristics of IT Centers

IT Center	Methodology	Projects	Outcomes
PLANNING	Information Engineering, System Engineering	Enterprise-wide Systems Configuration Management	Systems Federations Systems Integration Hardware/Network/Soft-ware Configurations
DEVELOPMENT	Information Engineering, Software Engineering	System Analysis and Design Business Process Reengineering Business Process Integration Workflow Integration B2B Integration e-Market Integration	Objects Applets Components Subsystems Systems
MAINTENANCE	Software Engineering	Code Improvements Legacy Systems Integration	Code List, Subroutines, Objects, Components
INFORMATION	Help Desk	Problem Solving	Problem Solved
DATA	Operations Management	Productivity, Security	Data, Information, Knowledge Processing
NETWORK	Topology Planning, Network Administration	Network Services Network Security Network Throughput Mobil Integration	LAN, MAN, WAN, GAN Private or Public

IT DEVELOPMENT CENTER

EII Development Methodologies

To develop an EII one can apply the following methodologies:

- **Information engineering** – to analyze information needs, integrate business and system strategies, and design logic of information systems.

- **System engineering** – to select computer platforms, software packages, and computer/telecommunication networks, and design their configurations.

- **Software engineering** – to buy or design software systems and program their components.

The developmental activities are guided by the System Life Cycle as illustrated in Figure 7-1.

In the EII System Life Cycle, the stage of system construction is replaced by system programming in computer languages or automating editors (CASE-Computer Aided Software Engineering).

Figure 7-1: The EII System Life Cycle

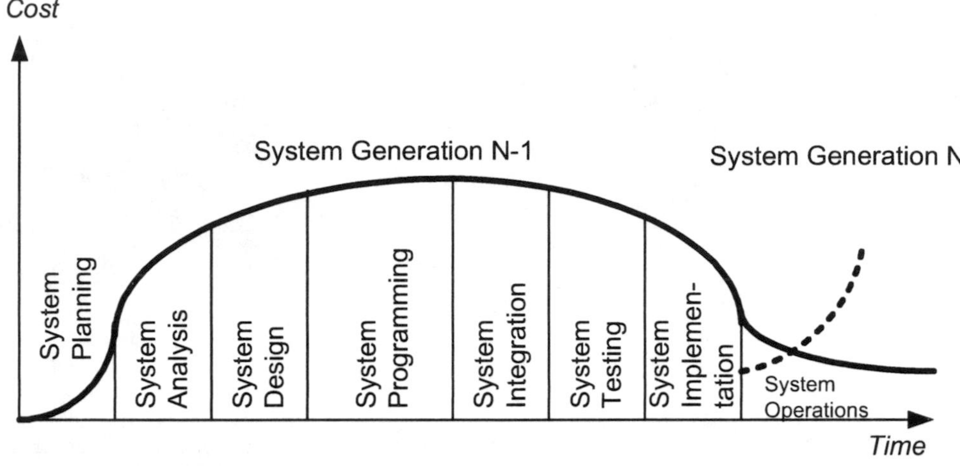

EII Development Strategies

In designing an IS one can apply one of three strategies:

- Bottom-up strategy.
- Top-down strategy.
- Mixed strategy.

The bottom-up strategy used to be the most popular one. It is based on the so-called Application Portfolio Methodology (McFarlan, 1981), which contains only those system projects that are characterized by low risk and useful benefits coming from their implementation. However, this strategy encourages the development of "sure" applications such as "payroll," "inventory control," and "customer orders." This strategy fosters selection of "subsystems" based on the capabilities of individual applications. The application portfolio methodology does not consider holistic issues of Enterprise Information Infrastructure. Therefore this methodology has developed a lot of so-called "legacy systems" that are the subject of reengineering process projects.

The top-down strategy is based on the Federated Systems Methodology (Targowski, 1990), which accepts the premise that the number of information systems/services and their subsystems in the enterprise is, to a certain degree, finite. Each system has its own generic architecture (see Part II of this book), which defines its major components and establishes their relationships formulated by the list of parts, sub-assemblies, and assemblies (called a Bill of System Processor). System federations are enterprise-wide driven, but systems and subsystems are business process-driven.

The mixed strategy is a combination of bottom-up and top-down strategies. The mix strategy is the most realistic strategy. The top-down strategy is the most idealistic strategy which can be applied in the development of a completely new enterprise environment. Such a situation is rare, because in the 1990's practice, we can always find an existing IS. These may be legacy but they are still functioning. In such a case the reengineering process will improve the legacy system according to the idealistic system, expressed under the form of the top-down strategy.

In the 1970's when the maintenance load at Data Processing departments increased from a modest 20% to 80%, many practitioners and theoreticians began looking for the cause behind this reality. Three different causes were discovered:

1. The linear system life-cycle presented a linear way of developing an IS. It was based on the premise that every next step may add new improvements; however, it was not the practice to return to the previous stage and introduce changes into a specification of a given IS. This caused many errors that later were discovered in the operational stage and required additional maintenance activities.

2. The linear system life-cycle was applied on the premise that a system designer can develop a correct IS for a given business process. In fact, this has never happened since this business process is not static, has changed and as a result, has required more maintenance tasks.

3. The linear system life-cycle was applied to the individual application system, without taking into account the complexity of the existing application portfolio, which had to be adapted or vice versa to a new IS. This adaptation required more and more maintenance tasks.

As a result of these false methodological premises, in the 1980's the backlog in system development reached from two to five years at major DP departments. As a response to this backlog, several new methodological activities have been established in the IS developmental practice:

- System quality assurance was developed as a corporate set of policies containing standards for the system's life cycle stages.
- Quality control was introduced at the level of the individual IS developmental process, through the evaluation of every major step's internal solution and its influence upon the adjacent stages of the system's life cycle.
- The system prototyping stage was introduced to discover early errors in the system logic, programming or integration.
- Joint Application Development (JAD) methodology was introduced, which put together system designers and system users.
- Application software packages became more popular than the approach of designing a proprietary IS.

As a result of these new approaches, a "user friendly" software concept (menu-driven) was created and the help function was expanded, including the application of artificial intelligence that can create so-called "wizards" in customizing the user's needs.

STRATEGIC USE OF IT

In the 1960's and 1970's during the early stages of applying information systems, IT was treated as a means of automating clerical routines and reducing employment of clerks. In the 1980's with the emergence of microcomputers and its quiet, creeping revolution, information systems emerged from back offices to front offices and began to affect the competitive positions of businesses.

This type of information system was named strategic information systems (SIS). They differed from the internal organizational IS since they mostly were interfacing a given business with its customers, suppliers, and distributors. In other words, these IS are of an inter-organizational nature.

Parson (1987) identifies (based on Porter's 1980 theory) and this author (A. Targowski) exemplifies the impact of SIS on the business environment at the following levels:

1. The industry level:
    - A product/service can be enhanced by improving its functionality (embedded chips that make a product smart) and as a result, a given firm has a new competitive advantage among its competitors.
    - A product's life-cycle can be shortened by the application of CAD and CAM/CAP (Process) systems and new innovations can be implemented sooner, giving a firm a competitive advantage.
    - The speed of distribution can be accelerated by the system integration of a producer with a distributor through the Extranet, providing a firm with a new competitive advantage (for example, an electronic bookstore *www.amazon.com*).

2. The firm's inter-organizational level:
    - Buyers using SIS can influence a supplier's selection and their prices. An example is a system of searching electronic catalogs on the Internet.
    - Suppliers can reduce prices and increase customer satisfaction by the application of an agile factory, which supports mass customization.
    - New entrants using SIS, particularly in the area of e-commerce, can reduce entry barriers and limit entry deterrence.
    - Substitution of products and services represents opportunities for a firm or a consumer. An Internet service provider substitutes e-mail for snail mail or an e-retailer for a traditional retailer.
    - Rivalry – a firm having access to its own or commercial databases and knowledge bases may establish effective links within the industry and gain a better competitive position among the industry rivalries.

3. The firm's strategy level:
    - SIS can be applied to reduce the overall cost so a firm can gain in cost leadership within an industry. Such is the case of the Japanese auto companies that in the 1980's applied robots, just-in-time inventories, and strong quality controls and were selling cars at very competitive prices.

- SIS can be applied to achieve a firm's product/service differentiation among the industry's producers. For example, the electronic Amazon bookstore provides excellent customer service and traces customers' behavior (knowledge management SIS), so it can offer additional book choices when the customer orders a given book. Due to this service, the customer returns to Amazon to buy more books.

- SIS can be applied to focus on a particular market/product niche. For example, Microsoft gained its very high competitive advantage in the software industry because it specialized in a desktop operating system.

The above mentioned examples of SIS can provide a strategic position for a firm as long as its competitors do not implement similar systems.

In the 1990's the strategic perspective on information systems' role within enterprise operations recognized three trends:

1. The development of a singular SIS as it has been exemplified above.

2. The development of the strategic Enterprise Information Infrastructure architecture.

3. The development of strategic system-driven inter-organizational information systems and services.

The development of the strategic Enterprise Information Infrastructure architecture is based upon choice among media-oriented enterprise

Table 7-2: The Choice of a Mediated Enterprise Type

	Local	***National***	***International***	***Multi-domestic***	***Global***
Off-line	Yes				
On-line	Yes	Yes	Yes	Yes	
Integrated	Yes	Yes	Yes		Yes
Agile	Yes	Yes	Yes		
Informated	Yes	Yes	Yes	Yes	Yes
Communi-cated	Yes	Yes	Yes	Yes	Yes
Mobile	Yes	Yes	Yes	Yes	Yes
Electronic	Yes	Yes	Yes	Yes	Yes
Virtual	Yes	Yes	Yes	Yes	Yes

types. Table 7-2 identifies such choices for a given geography-oriented enterprise.

Once a mediated enterprise type has been chosen, its type characterizes the kind of an enterprise configuration, as it has been presented in Chapter 2.

DEVELOPMENT OF SUBROUTINE, OBJECT AND COMPONENT

Computer programming was first introduced by Ada Lowelace, a collaborator of Charles Babbage, who both developed the first programmable "analytical engine" in 1832. For the last 150 years programming techniques were aimed at the development of convenient instruction sets.

In the 1970's the *structured programming* technique was introduced to minimize the negative effects of "spaghetti" like program codes full of "go to" instructions that call for subroutines.

In the 1990's the *object programming* technique was introduced to make self-dependent code modules=objects more reusable. The term object refers to people, places, things, or transactions about which data is maintained. For example, CUSTOMER, STUDENT, and TAXPAYER are all examples of people objects; similarly, BUILDING, INVOICE, and REGISTRATION are examples of place objects, and transactions objects, respectively. New software solutions are collections of objects that incorporate both data structure and behavior which contains instructions for operating on data (*hire, fire, pay-dividend, open, close, change-job, change-address, close, hide, redisplay,* etc.). This is in contrast to conventional programming in which data structure and behavior are only loosely connected. Most object-oriented software solutions were developed with object-oriented programming languages such as Smalltalk, C++, Object COBOL, Visual Basic, and Java.

In the 2000's now emerges the *component programming* technique which relies on some object-oriented techniques, since a component can be perceived as a set of objects. However, a component is designed to be reused and customized without access or modification of the component's source code, unlike objects, which often come in the form of a class library and which are meant to be customized by subclassing the source code. On the other hand, components have varying granularity and can consist of only one class, a composite of many classes, or an entire application.

Most components cannot process code by themselves, but require a module called a "container," which provides an application context for one or more components and which also secures control services for the components. The container operates as an operating system, which executes the code within the component. The first commercial component system MS COM was created by Microsoft, which incorporated it into its Windows as Object Linking and Embedding (OLE). OLE was designed to make it possible to embed modules from one program into another. For example, when a user of Word clicks on the Excel icon in the menu bar, this icon has the embedded container controlling access to a spreadsheet program. Object applications are the most successful in such cases as is shown in this example. In typical software programming, the reuse of objects is rather rare and in practice, this academic approach did not deliver solutions as was expected. The industrialized object programming led to the emergence of component programming, where objects became less universal and more application-centric.

Components are based on the premise that users can wrap a code module and create an interface (for example in a GUI style) that will respond to their messages (commands). Users are not involved in the manipulations of the internal code of a component. Just the interface intercepts commands directed to the component (in our example to Excel) and then does whatever is necessary to trigger that component's operations. In the object programming, objects must be programmed in the same language (e.g., C++ or Java) in order to interact between themselves. In component programming, two components can be programmed in different languages, since their interaction is secured by the container (interface). However, to ensure a smooth environment for different components' interaction, they should be developed according to standards of CORBA (Common Object Request Broker Architecture) with the Internet Inter ORB Protocol (IIOP) or COM/DNA (Microsoft's Component Object Model - Distributed InterNetwork Application Architecture), or in J2EE (Sun's Java 2 Enterprise Edition architecture, also called Enterprise Java Beans – EJB, where a bean is a kind of self-describing object). Sun's EJB was designed to interact with MS' COM/DNA; on the other hand EJB interacts with CORBA components, thus in such a manner all standardized components can interact among themselves.

MIDDLEWARE-DRIVEN INTERFACING

Middleware systems link a variety of different applications or their components from different computer/software platforms. Middleware keeps track of the locations of the software modules that need to link to each other, and thus manages the actual exchange of information. Because of that, the location of modules is transparent for users. Each linked component must have a standardized interface.

The major types of middleware are as follows:

- **Database middleware (DBM)** – translates SQL requests from applications into the native tongue of the target database;
- **Transaction processing middleware (TPM)** – facilitates updating of multiple databases by a transaction-oriented application;
- **Remote Procedure Call (RPC) middleware** – allows an application executed on one computer platform to call a procedure and/or send data to an application running on another computer platform;
- **Message-oriented middleware (MOM)** – lets applications on different computing platforms (mostly in the client/server configuration) and networks exchange data reliably and securely. Messages are sent and received through an independent layer in the asynchronous mode, which is backed by the buffer capacity;
- **Distributed component middleware (DCM)** – moves messages between components of applications and provides services in security and transaction processing, applying RPC and MOM styles;
- **Distributed object middleware (DOM)** – moves objects of applications between applications and provides services in security and transaction processing, applying RPC and MOM styles;
- **Application server middleware (ASM)** – builds application servers in the n-tier server architecture (client-application-database-directory services-Internet-security) which provides such services as: transactions processing, persistence and data biding (data integrity in multi-user environment), security support, directories, and load balancing as well as the inclusion of all the above middleware types.

Middleware is primarily applied by companies implementing their own application integration. Those companies that buy complete software or outsource their information infrastructure used to ignore middleware applications. Now, with the emergence of object and component-based solutions, almost every computerized organization will sooner or later be using client software which has incorporated object/component solutions that must be linked with other object/components, even with those which are outsourced.

EAI – ENTERPRISE APPLICATIONS INTEGRATION

Integrating information across the enterprise should be at the top of a Chief Information Officer's (CIO) agenda. The information integration goal should be the linkage among business units, applications, data architectures, computer platforms, network topologies, websites, suppliers, customers, etc. An integration strategy can send a company one step forward or two steps backward.

EAI focuses on solving the integration of multiple applications that were independently developed within the enterprise, may use incompatible information technology, and may remain independently managed. For example, SAP applications can be integrated with Peoplesoft applications that are used in different locations, including different countries. EAI aims at the linkage between different application semantics in order to move information seamlessly between systems in short time frames. For instance, within a short transaction, information exchange takes place to support a discrete event, such as the addition of a customer in one application while automatically updating another.

EAI requires layers of data transformation, metadata administration, software adapters and connectors, network connectivity, and integration administration. The EAI integration scenario is about how information is updated between sources and targets within a given organization.

In an average corporation there are about 50 applications developed internally, installed by ERP software or delivered by the third-party, that should be integrated. Major ERP vendors publish application programming interface (API) to enable connectivity with the third-party applications.

The integration between two applications typically occurs at several levels concurrently. Table 7-3 illustrates seven different levels of integration; each level based on services provided by the lower levels.

In the industrial practice of applying EAI one can recognize four levels of possible solutions delivery:

Table 7-3: Layers of EAI

BUSINESS INTEGRATION	**Business Process Development** Business process design/modeling, real-time decision support, state management
APPLICATION INTEGRATION	**Business Event Processing** Automatic event notification, flow control, content routing, transactional integrity
	Application Content Transformation Format translation, data semantics, validation, prebuilt templates
APPLICATION CONNECTIVITY	**Application Bridges and Gateways** For legacy Web, database, and packaged applications
	Application Interaction Style Publish/subscribe, publish/reply, file transfer, request/reply, conversational
	Message Handling Services Queuing, security, message management, administration
	Basic Communications Point-to-point, reliable broadcast, IP multicast, IIOP/ORB, database, Web, 3270 SNA

Source: NASG, 1999

1. The Custom Development Level – involves the implementation of seven layers' requirements by a special project.

2. The Middleware Toolkit Level – is based on the application of a classic packaged middleware, such as RPC's (Remote Procedure Call), message-oriented middleware (MOM), and transaction processing (TP) monitors. These packages support some housekeeping details.

3. EAI Middleware – are built of tools called adapters for custom developed software. For instance, the adapter can integrate a business process of order entry (in software X) with an e-commerce order form (software Y). This approach led to the creation of CORBA (Common Object Request Broker Architecture) specification, supported by Sun Microsystems. Based on CORBA, Active Software, Inc. provides a toolkit to integrate CRM systems with ERP systems.

4. Vendor-Supplied Solutions – the whole set of applications delivered by a given vendor is integrated by the vendor, so the third-party EAI software is not necessary. For example, the Open Application Group Inc. (OAGI) was founded in 1995 by ERP vendors to promote *intra/inter* vendor packages integration solutions.

The Gartner Group, a market research firm based in Stamford, Conn., estimates that 60% to 65% of the money spent on application integration today goes toward maintenance. This is because traditional point-to-point application integration methods cannot keep up with the speed at which information processing requirements change across the enterprise. Acquisitions, mergers, technology updates and changes in management are regular occurrences that must be accommodated by EII. As the number of applications and complexity of internal data routing requirements increase, maintaining multiple point-to-point interfaces becomes harder. Information flow becomes sluggish and unpredictable, and changing or adding anything becomes a major development effort.

WORKFLOW-DRIVEN INTEGRATION

Workflow systems automate business processes from start to finish, managing the pass of information from one participant to another for action, according to a set of rules. The main task of a workflow system is tracking the status of each activity of the process that is triggered by the transferred information as it moves through an organization.

At the end of 2000, workflow systems fell into two categories:

1. **Collaborative workflow system** – takes place in project-oriented processes, where the centralized system allows co-workers from different departments to work on the same e-documents. The leading vendors in this segment are Lotus, JetForm, FileNet, and Action Technologies.

2. **Production workflow systems** – are applied in transaction processing systems, where the control of the whole transaction processing is the key for the successful and fast conclusion. For instance, a fast decision about a loan application (passing or rather "flowing" through many PC's desk computers whose users-officers "approve," "disapprove," or are "uncertain," according to established rules of the system's digital expert subsystem) is a key concern for a bank or the fast processing of a claim is a key apprehension for an insurance company. This system is controlled by a workflow engine (with a GUI interface) which interfaces with a database, recording all the steps taking place in the flow-driven process. FileNet and Staffware are the most important contributors to this type of software.

Workflow systems free co-workers from having to worry about procedures and paperwork. There is no paperwork which is forgotten or may be lost. Therefore many searches, meetings, and disputes can be avoided.

LEGACY SYSTEMS INTEGRATION

Despite the changes triggered by Web technology, large enterprises still process 70% to 80% of their transactions in legacy systems in COBOL-driven software. These systems apply main-frame computers whose shipments continue to increase. However, Internet technology offers completely new possibilities: mobile staff can access relevant information on the road or at home, and project teams can work together across sites and even between companies. In addition, strategic partnerships, performance links and virtual companies can be formed and connected together in internal work. Customers, partners and suppliers can be connected to information relevant to them, and business processes can be "flown" across sites and companies.

These two contradicting situations cannot be tolerated anymore by IT staff. The only noticeable difference between Web-driven transaction processing systems and legacy systems lies in the interface: the former run with a browser, and the browser is thus promoted to a universal client.

The following strategies of integrating legacy systems within the e-enterprise can be recognized:

- Strategy of making a legacy system more user friendly – requires a new user interface, so-called GUI (Graphic User Interface) which is linked with the COBOL code. It improves the use of a legacy system but does not move it into real-time inter-activities by the *front* and *inter-offices*.

- Strategy of extracting key components from legacy systems and incorporating them into EAI's infrastructure, according to rules of CORBA or Enterprise JavaBeans, DCOM, or XML. These standards are designed to allow loosely coupled components to form complete business applications. This strategy allows the integration of legacy systems with ERP, SCM, and CRM systems.

- Strategy of linking Web-driven Java applets and CORBA components with legacy systems. This strategy allows for the use of legacy systems by the *front-office* in real-time.

The integration of legacy systems into the electronic environment should be guided by the following objectives:

1. Minimizing the maintenance cost of systems;

2. Reducing interfaces and redundancies in software which should lead toward higher reliability and manageability of systems;

3. Adding a new value to a business process through better user satisfaction;

4. Improving return on investment in IT system development and operations.

Recognizing these objectives, many IT organizations are now taking an integration-centric approach to deliver "electronized" legacy systems. This means that IT developers are seeking to connect existing systems, building new or reengineering old components to integrate them with new EII.

BPR – BUSINESS PROCESS REENGINEERING

In their book *Reengineering the Corporation* (1993), Michael Hammer and co-author James Champy define a reengineering goal as "achieving dramatic improvements in critical contemporary measures of performance such as cost, quality, service and speed." The basic steps of reengineering are:

1. Define business objectives – reassess your business purpose and reposition for greater market penetration;

2. Analyze existing processes – reconfigurate your work for smoother workflow;

3. Invent new ways to work – reconstruct your jobs to match reality;

4. Implement new processes – for ongoing competitiveness.

Hammer and Champy say that ability to use insight, imagination, and a willingness to challenge all assumptions are key to BPR. In practice, BPR lets people change not only procedures but their rules. In effect, they may change not only rules of a given process but of the entire business.

Reengineering in the 1990's inspired executives and managers in thousands of companies to start rethinking and redesigning such basic business practices as customer service, order fulfillment, product development, etc. For example:

- Ford Motor Company found that it employed 100 times more people in its accounts payable department than smaller Mazda. After reengineering the process, the company cut through the territory of accountants, purchasing department staff, and warehouse receiving clerks, and reordered them. Now, a receiving clerk at Ford checks the database for the order and delivery compatibility and quality and if every thing is right, the computer sends a payment to a supplier, even without its invoice. About 500 workers were moved to other jobs, saving on cost.

- IBM Credit, the organization that finances computers, software, and service sold by IBM, learned that the actual work required to process a new customer could be completed in only 90 minutes, instead of the six days to two weeks it used to take.

The main premise of BPR is based on the reorientation of business procedures from function-driven to process-driven. Whereas the former has roots in the 19th century bureaucracy, when each department had its own internal flow of information, the latter is based on the cross-functional flow of information which supports a given process, for instance order fulfillment. The BPR Model in Figure 7-2 illustrates this change in business practice.

Reengineering approaches defined by Currid (1994) are:

- Streamlining business processes;

- Integrating business processes;

- Transforming business processes.

The seven reengineering business principles defined by Currid (1994) are:

1. Organize work around results, not tasks;

Figure 7-2: Functions versus Processes

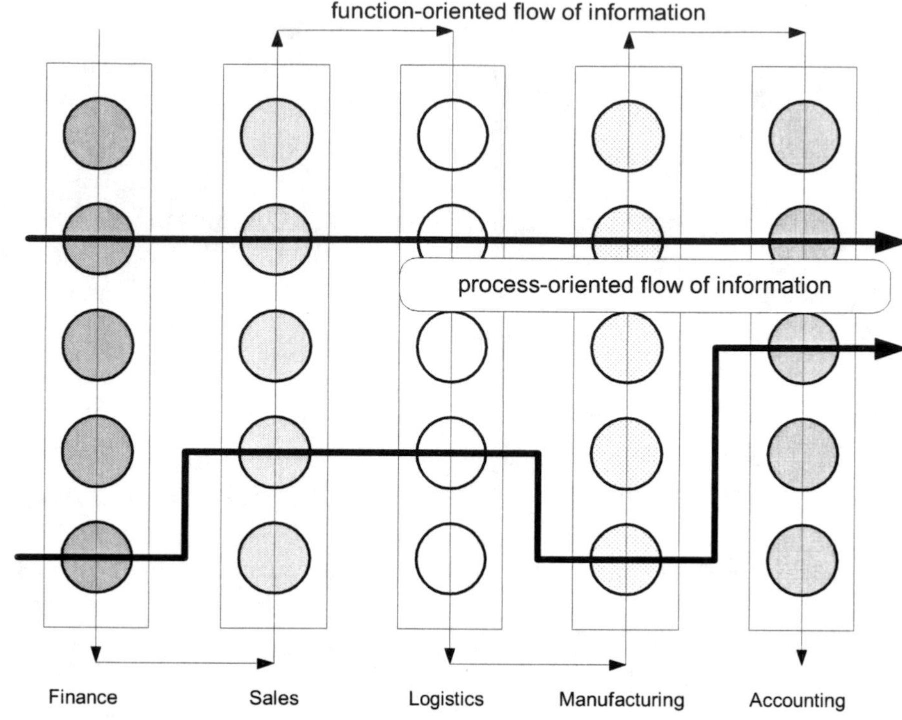

2. Capture data only one time — when it is first created;
3. Allow decision points where work is performed;
4. Incorporate control into information processing;
5. Make people who use a process do the work;
6. Work in parallel instead of sequentially;
7. Treat geographically dispersed resources as one.

The reengineering movement in the 1990's recognized the following issues (Donovan, 1994):

- Global economy changes the business climate and as a result of this many organizations are in crisis. For example, the American airline industry in the first 70 years of their history (1920-1990) generated $3.8 billion in profit. From 1992-94 this industry lost $4.8 billion. In 1994, Sears Roebuck laid off 50,000 employees, closed 100 stores, and sold its insurance and real estate units.

- Business practices turned upside down – in the 1970's major product suppliers (Procter and Gamble, Johnson & Johnson, Unilever) dictated terms to retailers; now Wal-Mart dictates terms to its suppliers.

- Business opportunities are expanding through world-wide privatization, deregulation, globalization, and expansion of internal markets.

- Business and IT are not synchronized and obstacles are caused by mergers, acquisitions, downsizing and layoffs, new consumer-vendor-supplier relationships (mass customization), and low business skills among IT professionals.

- Market expectations are changing – consumers expect better quality products and services, the time-to-market cycle must be shorter, and the profit margin is expected to be higher.

- Dramatic changes in the IT environment have led toward the expanded networking, the client-server architecture, e-commerce (via EDI), tumbling prices and soaring performance, the democratization of IT, adoption of open standards, and so forth.

Despite notable successes at such companies as Bell Atlantic Corp. and Federal Express Corp., many reengineering efforts have fallen short. While countless managers have been persuaded to reengineer, too many have had poor or disastrous results. The main reason that reengineering failed in the 1990's was the fact that operational work cannot be reengineered without changing the way managers do their jobs. Unless the right leadership, teamwork, empowerment, and corporate culture are in place, reengineering cannot succeed.

BPI – BUSINESS PROCESS INTEGRATION

EAI typically involves the exchange of information between two applications without regard for business process. BPI, on the other hand, takes into account the overall work flow and the multiple applications required to complete a business process. EIA ensures software compatibility, while BPI applies business rules to operate integrated applications in order to run a business more efficiently.

Steady business transformations and changes drive business process integration. The result is the frequent integration, de-integration, and re-integration at the business process level, which in consequence influence applications integration.

The architecture of the BPI system is proved in Figure 7-3. Its subsystems are described as follows:

Figure 7-3: The Architecture of the BPI System

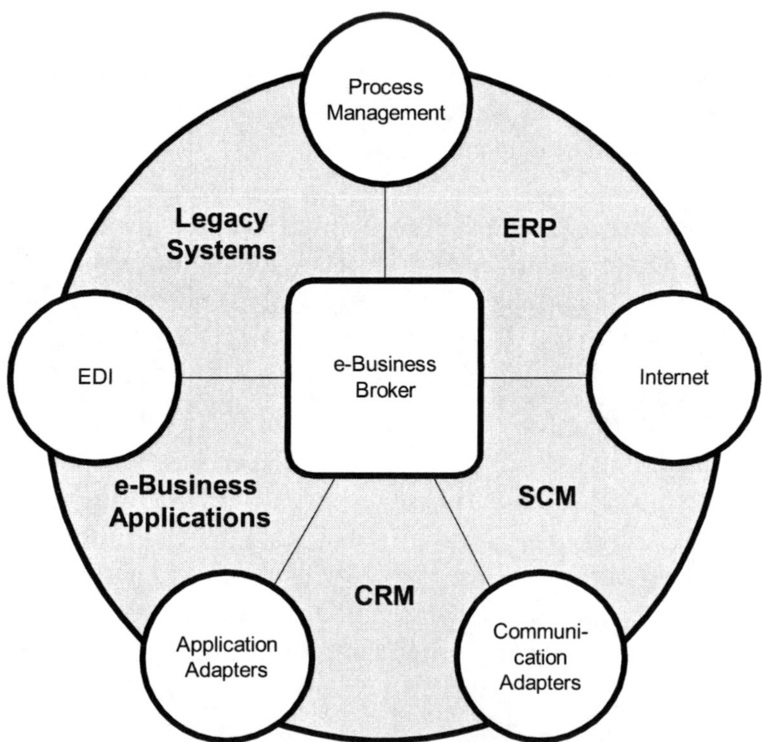

- **E-Business Broker Subsystem** –exchanges business rules, translated data, messages, and files between business operations of a given business process. It audits and tracks information as it moves within and between enterprises. It also performs notification on events and archives all the data processed.

- **Process Management Subsystem** – allows for the modeling, control, and monitoring of the business process' procedures and policies (rules). This subsystem ensures that a business view is included in an IT solution. This subsystem allows the user to develop a graphic model of a business process driven by business rules, without having programming skills. Based on the business model, the e-Business Broker subsystem will receive specific business rules to execute and control the informated business process. Monitoring tools provide a graphical view of business process operations with ad-hoc reporting.

- **Application Adapters Subsystem** – moves data between legacy and packaged applications (ERP, SCM, CRM) and it is a classic interface which translates different codes among applications.

- **Communication Adapters Subsystem** – moves messages and files securely and reliably within and between enterprises (of suppliers, producers, and distributors), no matter how time-sensitive the information is. This subsystem translates different communication protocols between LAN's, MAN's, WAN's, and GAN's at the level of applications.

- **Internet Subsystem** – provides Web technology and transmission services to support BPI operations between enterprises and within an enterprise (Intranet).

- **EDI - Electronic Data Interexchange Subsystem** – supports data transmission through private and public networks that operate outside the Internet environment.

Based on the e-Business Broker Subsystem, BPI replaces static point-to-point integration (EAI) with a flexible infrastructure that can support even the most complicated business process and can accommodate the unpredictable.

B2B INTEGRATION

B2Bi can be implemented in three ways:

- **Cross-enterprise process applications integration** – companies integrate their business processes to optimize existing labor and time utilization. Usually, a limited number of partners are declared in a very static, fixed way and then the processes are optimally adapted (via common infrastructure of e-Business Broker, Business Management Subsystems, and Application Adapters on both ends of the process) to their needs. It reminds one of a hard-wired system once it gets going, driven by a common software/communication solution.

- **Cross-enterprise process data integration** – just data from different application components are translated by a gateway into a common standard such as XML. This reliance on a common data exchange format rather than a common infrastructure makes this solution easier to implement and extend. Instead of requiring all participating firms to utilize the same package, each party needs only to recognize how to process the documents received.

- **Vortal-oriented integration of business partners** – all parties, instead of implementing their own integration solution, apply the vortal as a system to make business deals electronically. In this case, however, only the vortal provides the choice for business partners, who are its members.

Perhaps the biggest source of frustration among firms trying to implement B2B relationships is that their partners are not at the same level of technological advancement. The issue of integrating partners via the same business process can be solved by a number of ways.

Among the first leaders of B2Bi is the Convisint automobile exchange created in 2000 by General Motors, Ford, and DaimlerChrysler. In the same year the GlobalNetXchange was formed by Oracle, Carrfour and Sears Roebuck to connect 50,000 retail buyers and suppliers.

E-MARKET INTEGRATION

E-market integration creates a market for multiple businesses. In this solution there is no common infrastructure like in B2Bi. A new participant can join an e-market within hours. Software like e-Collaboration facilitates business deals in the e-markets. Sabre Holding Corp., a provider of airline ticket reservation services, formed an e-Marketplace for procurement for airlines. Also, eBay, the auction house, was one of the first creators of the e-market for millions of participants. Covisint created e-market for the motor industry.

MOBILE INTEGRATION

So far the integration of *intra/inter* enterprise applications (either through EAI, B2B or e-markets) has taken place at the level of data ad information transfer among servers and users equipped with PC's. However, there is the potential to make enterprise applications – ERP, SCM, and CRM – available for field workers through wireless devices.

In October 1999, the first pilot wireless access was launched by PageMart, renamed WebLink Wireless, teamed with DMR Consulting. Its goal was to develop a system for letting handheld devices tap into a PeopleSoft Vantive CRM application over the WebLink network. The pilot system applied WCTP (Wireless Control Transfer Protocol) protocol which is based on XML-based protocol for transmitting wireless messages over HTTP (Hyper Text Transmission Protocol). To do so, the pilot project used Vitria Technology Inc.'s BusinessWare 3.0 integration software to connect the Vantive applications running at customer sites to WebLink's network.

The system is designed to work like this: when a sales representative (Sales Force Automation) or other mobile employee needs to access information such as a customer's trouble call, a message is sent over a two-way radio frequency to a gateway at WebLink Wireless. That gateway, which is based on Vitria's BusinessWare, uses WCTP to send messages to Vantive applications as well as to wireless devices on the other carrier's networks. That gateway also directs the incoming wireless traffic to the appropriate applications in ERP, SCM, or CRM. Vitria Inc. offers a variety of off-the-shelf connectors ready to integrate Vantive, SAP, Siebel and Oracle applications in a wireless mode.

The mobile integration allows field workers to perform queries of open tickets, update status and close tickets right from the field. Information that would normally have to be written down and logged into a PC can now be transmitted via a wireless messaging device. First among that type of applications would be: an order entry application, a workforce management application, and a time-card system for a construction company. In general, the best candidates for wireless access among applications are those which require a remote real-time data entry and the inclusion of remote workers in a workflow system. For those types of applications, paging networks, like WebLink's, offer a better solution to remote access than the phone network, mainly because an asynchronous messaging system does not require a dedicated, always-on modem-driven connection and, hence, can support more users.

IT DEVELOPMENTAL VISION FOR THE 21ST CENTURY

The IT developmental vision for the 21st century may influence some IT developers about how to develop IT and its applications.

The 20th century introduced the computer and Internet that created the Information Wave. The latter began to intervene in the Agriculture and Industrial Waves. In the 21st century the Information Wave in developed nations (17% of the world population) will transform from intervention into optimization of the other two Waves' development and operations. In developing nations (83% of the world population) the Information Wave should begin to intervene in the other two Waves.

The Information Wave will have the task to optimize the Agricultural and the Industrial Waves in the following scopes:

Agriculture Wave:

- Energy – increase energy efficiency through better control of farming.
- Environment – reduce pollution through better control of recycling.
- Farming – precision farming through better control of irrigation, seeding, fertilizing, and the application of robots.

Industrial Wave:

- Energy – increase energy efficiency through better control of transportation, construction, and manufacturing systems.
- Environment – reduce pollution through better control of recycling and application of "green" technologies.
- Self-assembling materials – through better control of nanosecond processing of composite materials.

- Smart materials – through embedded intelligence applied in homes, offices, and vehicles.
- Production – through better control of eco-industrial parks operating as a closed system to reduce waste pollution.
- Manufacturing – through better control of computer integrated manufacturing leading to mass customization of cars, appliances, and other products.
- Advanced robots – better flexibility through advanced sensors and artificial intelligence and control of mobility.

In order to pursue the task of optimizing these other two Waves, the Information Wave will evolve itself in the following scopes:

Computer Hardware:

- Supercomputers will apply massive parallel and neural processing.
- Computers will apply photons rather than electrons to code and transfer information.
- Biochips should be commercially available.
- Personal computers will be fully integrated with fast telecommunication, television and interactive video.
- Personal digital assistants will be widely applied to manage work and personal affairs.

Computer Software:

- Expert systems will steadily reach a wider scope of users in engineering, management and perhaps even in medicine (the malpractice issue).
- Intelligent software will support net browsers and knowbots to retrieve net-driven information.
- Information systems will be integrated through Enterprise, Local, National and Global Information Infrastructures.
- Information systems will be widely enhanced by knowledge management subsystems based on data mining.
- Software development will enter the stage of manufacturing through the wide application of CASE tools and object/component-oriented programming.

Computer Networks:

- Information super-highway will be organized under the forms of Enter-

prise, Local, National and Global Information Infrastructures (EII, LII, NII, GII) accessed by 80% of citizens of developed nations.
- EII, LII, NII, and GII will be built on ISDN, ATM, and fiber optics that will reach the majority of homes and offices in developed nations.
- Personal communication systems (PCS) for voice and e-mail communication will be popular among the majority of professionals.
- Groupware systems – will be routinely applied for concurrent learning and working at multiple sites of virtual offices and colleges.

Info-Communication Services/Systems:
- E-mail will be the most popular form of communication.
- Videoconferencing – will be the standard for a business meeting.
- Telecommuting – will engage the majority of workers who live in remote places and commute.
- E-commerce – will be the most popular form of closing business transactions.
- Online publishing – will still compete with the traditional form of publishing gazettes and books.
- Distance learning – will enhance lectures and seminars but will not replace them.

Info-tech will be the driving force of the Technology Revolution in the 21st century, which has to eliminate or minimize the threat of the "Death Triangle of Mankind." This Revolution should (but not necessary will) transform modern civilization into sustainable civilization.

BEYOND COBOL – IT SKILLS FOR THE 21ST CENTURY

In May 2000, the Information Resource Management Association (IRMA) conference met in Anchorage and featured representation from 40 countries. It was the author's good fortune to chair a panel on the industry's needs for modern IT tools/skills that are beyond classic COBOL, a very popular language in academic curricula. The author offered a question for discussion: "How to minimize the technological gap between Academia and Industry?"

Panelist Tom Bennett from the U.S. Department of Defense summarized the administration's needs by saying that post-college internships should be the best method to develop IT specialists who would be equipped with current tools. Panelist Mehdi Ghods from Boeing provided a very surprising statistic indicating that industrial software written in COBOL is huge and perhaps for many more years will require COBOL skills.

Virtual panelist Sharm Manwani from Electrolux (UK) stated that legacy systems slow down new IT developments; however, large organizations debate about BRP development via ready-made packages (SAP, JDE, Oracle,) or via in-house Enterprise Application Integration (EAI), particularly in the areas of supply chain management and e-commerce. These integrational tools include middleware tools such as MQ, Tibco, XML, CORBA, COM, EJB, and Java workflow tools. Another area of strong industry interest is the development of data warehouses with SQL/OLAP tools for Decision Support Systems (DSS) including data mining.

Another virtual panelist, Stan Targowski, from Hewitt Associates (USA), characterized the new system landscape of the 2000's as no longer having experts with 20+ years of practice to guide college graduates and in which the user no longer accepts any application. This will be a landscape whose architectures are more flexible and complex and will therefore require a better understanding of not only IT tools, but the whole enterprise organization. A new college graduate can no longer expect a well established career path and his/her career planning must shift from management to employees. To succeed, the new college graduate from an IT curriculum needs to have a mix of skills, crossing many areas of business, from the technical to the communication areas. His/her best approach is to know everything about everything, to be a self-starter and a team player, to be a very quick learner with good organizational and project management skills, to be able to work with minimal supervision, and effectively communicating both orally and in writing. More importantly, he/she should enjoy what he/she is doing. Stan listed specific skills that are needed in the most popular areas of IT:

- Application Development: object oriented analysis and design, experience in designing GUI, event-oriented programming in VBasic, Java, C++, understanding of RDBM (Oracle, DB2, Informix), understanding architecture and tools (HTML, XML, EJB);

- Database Administration: strong RDBM skills, strong Windows NT/2000 and UNIX skills, data modeling and algorithmic skills, Network Management, Netware, Windows NT/2000, UNIX skills, understanding of protocols TCP/IP, IPX, SPX, etc., understanding architecture (bridges, routers, gateways).

Stan also mentioned that advanced skills not necessarily required from a fresh graduate are needed to roll solutions like ERP software (SAP, PeopleSoft, Oracle, Siebel, etc.) with the support from in-house customization, focusing on components and inter-system integration. He argues that globalization and outsourcing may require assigning key in-house leaders to manage IT subcontractors in countries such as India, Ireland, or Poland. He thinks that overall intelligence, ability to learn, and enough proficiency in some specific area will get the IT worker much farther than being an expert in a very narrow area. He is optimistic in saying that if one does not know a specific technology, one will be trained in it.

Panelist Liliane Esnault (France) from Academia stated that some colleges are financially too weak to educate IT graduates in the full range of skills required by the industry today.

As a panelist for Academia, the author stated that some colleges do not train their IT students in current technology but educate them in IT critical thinking and that prepares them for a life-long educational updating. I also noticed that Academia has limited resources but that IT progress is even too fast for the industry and administration which have rich resources. In response to the industry's needs for graduates skilled in communication, the author concluded that Academia cannot "produce" very good communicators, since learning how to communicate is a life-long process, not often completed with success.

I hope that this panel provoked us to a better understanding of industry's and administration's needs for current IT tools/skills. Industry should not blame Academia because we do not train the graduate in the current technologies; we will never do it, since it is not our mission. If industry's IT function must be better managed, particularly within the scope of in-house development of talents and skills, academia must educate more knowledgeable and better motivated graduates to serve their needs.

COMPUTER CONTROVERSIES

The IT developers, who want to be aware of their work, should be familiar with their solutions' social consequences. They should read a book *Computer*

Controversy, edited by Rob King (1996), who opened the debate on such issues as:

- "The seductive equation of technological progress."
  Is it true that in developed countries almost every socio-economic problem can be resolved by technology? Perhaps it is false.

- "The dreams of technological utopianism."
  Technology has its own limits and cannot provide solutions for every issue. Also, too much applied technology may even be too dangerous in cases of employment and customer service.

- "Electronic office: playpen or prison."
  If an e-office limits too much face-to-face communication then it can be a "prison."

- "How information technology can transform organizations."
  IT can transform an organization into a paperless and buildingless organization, very lean and competitive.

- "Great expectations: PCs and productivity."
  A worker with a PC is much more productive than a worker without the information processing capability.

- "Can computer science solve organizational problems?"
  Computer science can solve only limited organizational problems.

- "Mr. Edens profits from watching his workers' every move."
  His "profits" can be shortsighted.

- "Increasing personal connections."
  This is true; e-mail increases personal connections effectively.

- "Finding a happy medium: explaining the negative effects of electronic communication on social life at work."
  E-communication limiting face-to-face communication limits a social tissue that makes humankind an advanced "animal."

- "They call it cyberlove."
  The cyberlove can be a very dangerous play for its participants, particularly for women.

- "The strange case of the electronic lover."
  It is a false promise that electronics can substitute a human touch.

- "I heard it through the Internet."
  The Internet provides a lot of garbage information.

- "On the road again." If information highways are anything like interstate highways – watch out!
  Information highways are new ways of socio-economic operations and it will better if someone will know how to "drive" through them.

- "Privacy and social control."
  Unfortunately, e-communication can be applied to limit privacy and increase social control.

- "Your personal information has gone public."
  In many cases it is true.

- "The government needs computer matching to root out waste and fraud."
  IT may help in discovering waste and fraud.

- "Privacy: How much data do direct marketers really need?"
  They need too much data; to support competitiveness it is better to analyze market as an undeterministic entity.

- "System safety and social vulnerability."
  If social life is too much computerized, it can be unsafe, since technology is technically not perfect.

- "Office automation's threat to health and productivity: a new management concern."
  It is true that work at the computer terminal without breaks can be hazardous.

- "Code of ethics and professional conduct."
  A code of ethics in a digital world should be the same or even stronger than in a physical world.

These controversies add fuel to debates, along with discussion about the development of IT. Will IT challenge and perhaps conquer our culture?

CONCLUSION

- The trends in EII development point strongly towards the profound integration of Enterprise Information Infrastructure, which in effect will become an electronic one with all enterprises interacting with the marketplace through the Internet and private computer networks.

- The development of e-Enterprise today will trigger unpredictable social consequences that should be addressed at the time of an IT project's scope and context definition.

BIBLIOGRAPHY

Chorofas, D. N. (2001). *Enterprise Architecture and new Generation Information Systems*. Boca Raton, FL: Saint Lucie Press.

Cummins, F. A. (2002). *Enterprise Integration*. New York: John Wiley & Sons.

Donovan, J. J. (1994). *Business Re-engineering with Information Technology*. Englwood Cliffs, NJ: PTR Prentice Hall.

Hammer, M. & Champy, J. (1993). *Reengineering the Corporation*. New York: HarperBusiness..

King, R. (1996). *Computerization and Controversy*. San Diego, CA: Academic Press.

McFarlan, W.F. (1981). Portfolio approach to information technology. *Harvard Business Review*. September-October.

Parson, G.L. (1987). Strategic Information Technology. In E. K. Somogyi, & R. D. Galliers (Eds.), *Towards Strategic Information Systems*. Cambridge, MA: Abacus Press.

Robertson, B. & Sribar, V. (2000). *The Adaptive Enterprise: IT Infrastructure Strategies to Manage Change and Enable Growth*. Boston: Addison-Wesley Professional.

Ruh, W.A. et al. (2000). *Enterprise Application Integration*. A Wiley Tech Brief. New York: John Wiley & Sons.

Targowski, A. (1990). *The Architecture and Planning of Enterprise-wide Information Management Systems*. Harrisburg, PA: Idea Group Publishing.

Chapter VIII

IT Management

INTRODUCTION

This chapter presents the main issues of IT management with special emphasis on business, IT strategies integration and on trends that are taking take place in this discipline at the beginning of the 21st century.

IT AS A NEW BUSINESS FUNCTION

In the 21st century the IT function becomes the most visible business function absorbing more new employees than other functions. It is a rather new business function, which is a result of the Information Wave's emergence in the last quarter of that century. In the 1990's IT is recognized as a new business function, complementing such classic functions as marketing, finance, accounting, and management. This function has grown from Data Processing (1960's to 1970's) through an MIS department (1980's) to a Chief Information Officer (1990's) with IRM (Information Resource Management) staff.

Figure 8-1 depicts the IT function's role among other business functions. It is a role of a *back-office's*[1], whose mission is to optimize operations of remaining functions that are composed of *back-offices*, *inter* and *intra-offices*.

Figure 8-1: IT Management Function in the Context of Other Business Functions

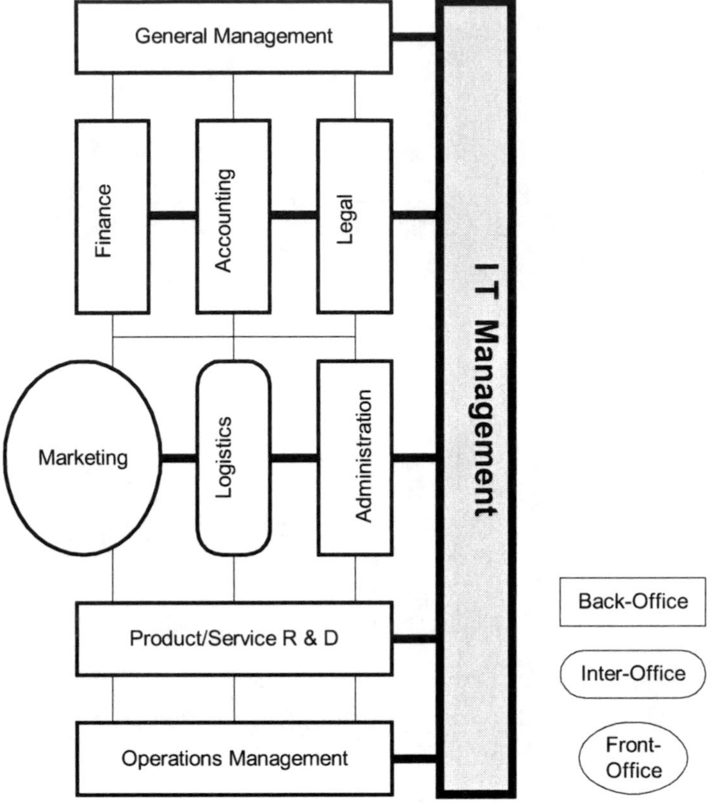

Figure 8-2 illustrates an organization chart of the IT function within a global firm. The chart identifies three major divisions managed by a Chief Information Officer (CIO):

- Global delivery of IT solutions to business units located in different parts of the world through computer and network centers, and user support and help desks;

- Corporate Enterprise Information Infrastructure management, composed of the integration of business and IT strategy, IT solutions quality assurance, mergers integration and IT resources, data and application architecture, EII architecture and new technology and business resumption (by

Figure 8-2: An Organization Chart of the Global Firm's IT Management

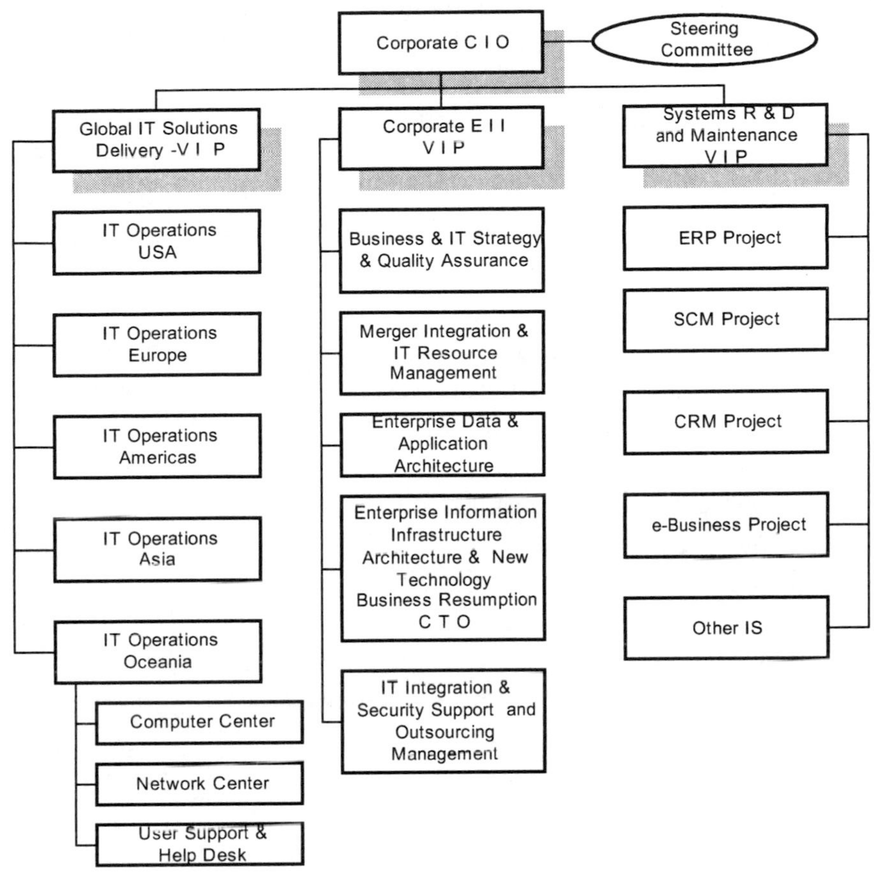

CTO-Chief Technology Officer), integration and security support, and outsourcing;

- IT project research, development, and maintenance.

The management of IT varies greatly from sector to sector and from small to large organizations. However, the presented example emphasizes the complexity and comprehensiveness of the IT function within a business organization.

Nowadays an IT office is costly and must prove that is profitable for the whole company. In the following section an approach towards IT productivity and effectiveness is provided.

IT MANAGEMENT KEY INDICATORS

The measurement of IT performance is provided in the framework of an IT Balanced Scorecard of overall industry average in 2000 in Table 8-1. On average, *InformationWeek* 500 companies in 2000 earmarked 4% projected revenue for IT, about the same level as in previous years. Exceeding the trend are the telecommunications and financial-services, which splurged compared with most other sectors, allotting 17% and 14% of revenue, respectively, for IT spending. The demand for information systems is growing about 30% per year at corporations around the world (Rubin Systems, Inc.'s Report).

According to the same source, top performing companies can support as much as $1,000 in revenue and $50 to $100 in income for every IT dollar invested. Average performers have historically been at $50 in revenue and $1.15 in income supported per IT dollar. Therefore, CEO's and CFO's want their companies to be at the high end of the band, and are demanding answers to questions about IT spending in business terms they understand.

The level of IT investment on a per-employee basis is significant and growing at many companies. IT spending per employee across all industries increased to an average of $12,000 in 2000 from $10,800 in 1998. Companies in the finance sector were the biggest spenders on average, investing about $39,000 per employee, followed by insurance companies at $24,000 and utilities at $19,000 (Rubin Systems, Inc.'s Report).

A MIT professor Erik Brynjolfsson, one of the leading thinkers on the relationship between IT and worker productivity, co-authored with Lorin Hitt of the University of Pennsylvania's Wharton School of Business the study which maintains that productivity goes beyond simply installing a new technology—it's about inventing new ways of working. Accompanied by changing business processes and organization structures, the improvements are dramatic, Brynjolfsson and Hitt state. What is important to realize is that the benefits of technology don't just come from making employees more productive, but the resulting improvements in customer service, product quality and other things that are hard to slap a firm ROI to (Brynjolfsson and Hitt, 1996).

The best of *InformationWeek* 500 companies in 2000 boosted productivity by using the Internet, intranets, and data mining. The latter helps banks gather more, and deeper, information on customers. Net-based computing helps speed information to customers, since fast, accurate customer information is the firm's strongest weapon, particularly in retail.

IT executives at these highly productive companies are making their applications more extroverted:

Table 8-1: IT Balanced Scorecard of Overall Industry Average, 2000

KEY INDICATORS	PERSPECTIVES			
	FINANCIAL	CUSTOMER	INTERNAL BUSINESS	INNOVATION
IT SPENDING IT budget as percentage of projected revenues	4%			
IT SPENDING PER EMPLOYEE	$12,000			
E-BIZ PROFITS Percentage of companies that show profits from e-business operations	45%			
IT REVENUES Portion of companies selling IT services to other firms	32%			
IT SERVICES OUTLAYS Share of IT budget for IT services and outsourcing	15%			
PERSONNEL COSTS Share of IT budget for salaries and benefits	34%			
CUSTOMER SERVICE Inquiries handled electronically, without intervention		21%		
CUSTOMER CONNECTION Percentage of customers included in supply chain		34%		
SUPPLIERS LINKS Suppliers included in e-SCM			28%	
INTERNAL INTERACTION Portion of workweek IT executives meet with line-of-business and departmental managers			36%	
R&D INVESTMENT Share of IT budget for research and development				5%
NEW TECH SPENDING Share of IT budget for new products and technology				19%
KNOWLEDGE WORKERS Portion of knowledge workers using intelligence tools				29%

Source: 2000 CPM Media, Inc.

- Improving communication with customers and suppliers through SCM and CRM systems;
- Improving customer service and because of that, increasing revenues;
- Integrating applications across enterprise boundaries.

IT executives of introverted companies put more emphasis on:

- Improving top management control of IT;
- Accomplishing traditional IT goals;
- Saving on labor and R&D development costs.

Which companies did better? According to Brynjolfsson and Hitt's research, companies with an extroverted strategy had 3% higher productivity when compared with the introverted companies. Their productivity was growing faster, too (*www.informationweek.com*). Interestingly, compared with their competitors, extroverted companies were more likely to report that:

- IT was perceived as being core to their business, which means that CIO's were subordinated to CEO's, not to CFO's or COO's, shortening the distance between the CEO and CIO and creating a two-way dialogue on the interactions of business and technology;
- They were more willing to incur training costs to help their line workers use technology effectively;
- They had a slightly greater tendency to decentralize IT spending.

IT MANAGEMENT LEVELS

Figure 8-3 presents the four-stage model of IT management at the strategic level with the following outcomes:

1. The Strategic Profile Analysis Stage elaborates an IT creed, mission, and goal which will shape the further stages' planning activities;
2. The Preliminary Systems Planning Stage provides a review of available applications, EII technologies, and possible R&D directions;
3. The IT Strategy Planning Stage formulates an IT strategy as a derivative of a business strategy;

Figure 8-3: IT Management at the Strategic Level, Profit and Impact-Oriented

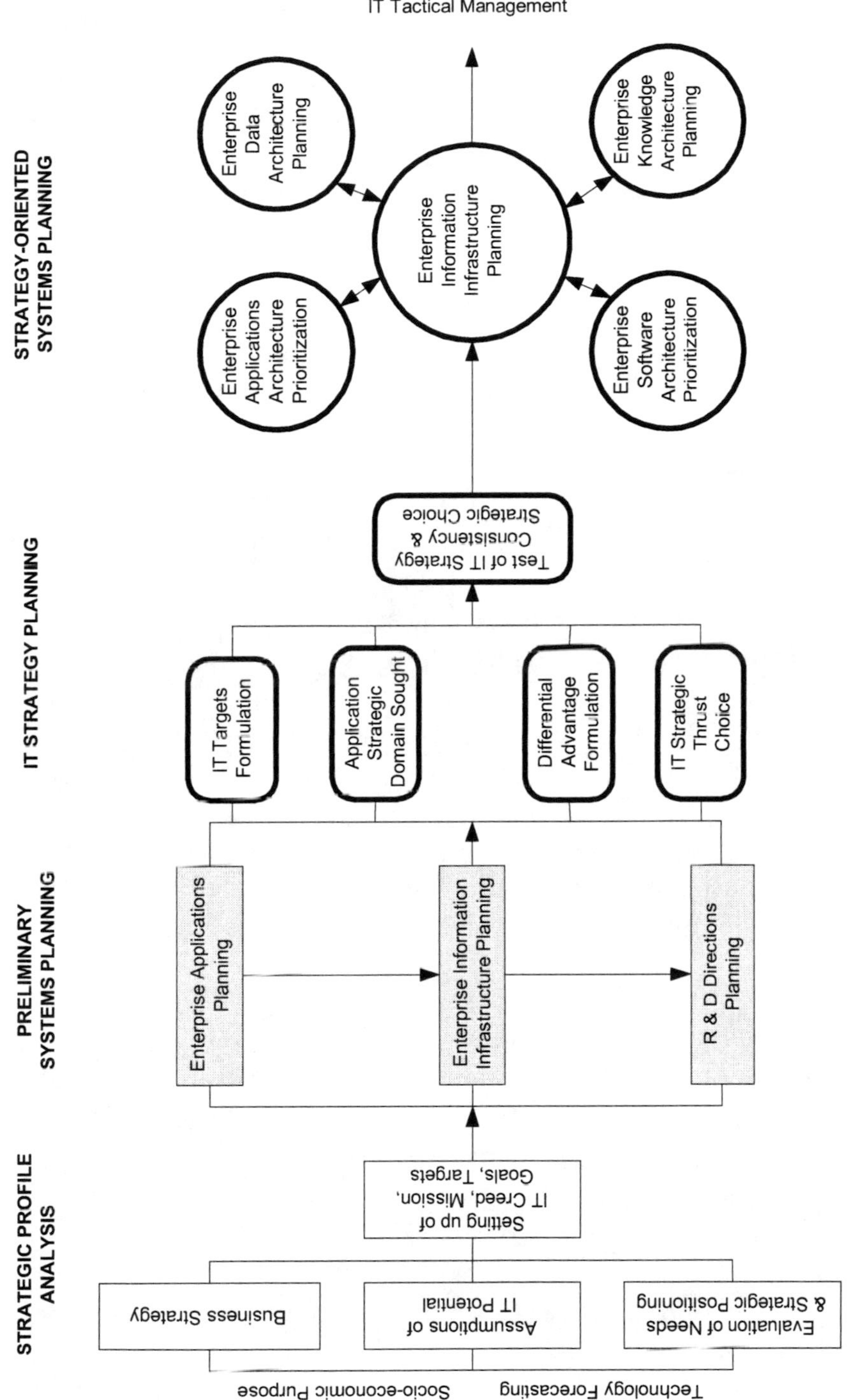

4. The Strategy-oriented Systems Planning Stage re-examines concepts and directions of Preliminary Systems Planning stage. This fourth stage defines all necessary architectures and solutions.

Strategic planning of IT applications in an enterprise is a complex process which requires a systematic effort in defining IT aims (mission, creed, goals, and targets) which support business aims. Based on IT aims one must plan preliminary solutions for enterprise applications, enterprise information infrastructure, and R&D directions. This set of solutions allows the planning of IT strategy composed of IT targets, a strategic application domain, and a concept for how to achieve differential advantage through IT, and choose the IT strategic trust. After testing the IT strategy consistency one can pass to the stage of IT strategy-oriented planning of applications, data, software, knowledge, and EII architectures.

IT management at the tactical level is almost missing in the subject literature and IT professional disputes. It is a matter of fact that IT management at this level is debated as a strategic approach, while the correct strategic one is almost missing in IT management conceptualization.

Figure 8-4 illustrates IT management at the tactical level, which is composed of the three-stage model with the following outcomes:

1. The IT Policy Formulation Stage formulates information objectives and policies;

2. The Implementation of IT-oriented Structures Stage leads towards the setting up of an IT organization, selections of applications and EII technologies, and a service level and capacity, according to available IT budget;

3. The Managing IT Strategy and Policy Stage involves the most critical aspects of IT management because it is based upon art rather than science. It concerns itself with leadership and the spirit of performance, playing the organizational power game, developing expertise and skills among developers and most importantly, setting up an IT strategy supportive culture within the IT developers and users.

Let's review some aspects of IT tactical management:

Information Policy is a general guide to operational action within the scope of IT strategy. It is a set of statements that provide direction for IT specialists and users. One can provide the following example of such policies:

Figure 8-4: IT Management at the Tactical Level, Innovations-Oriented

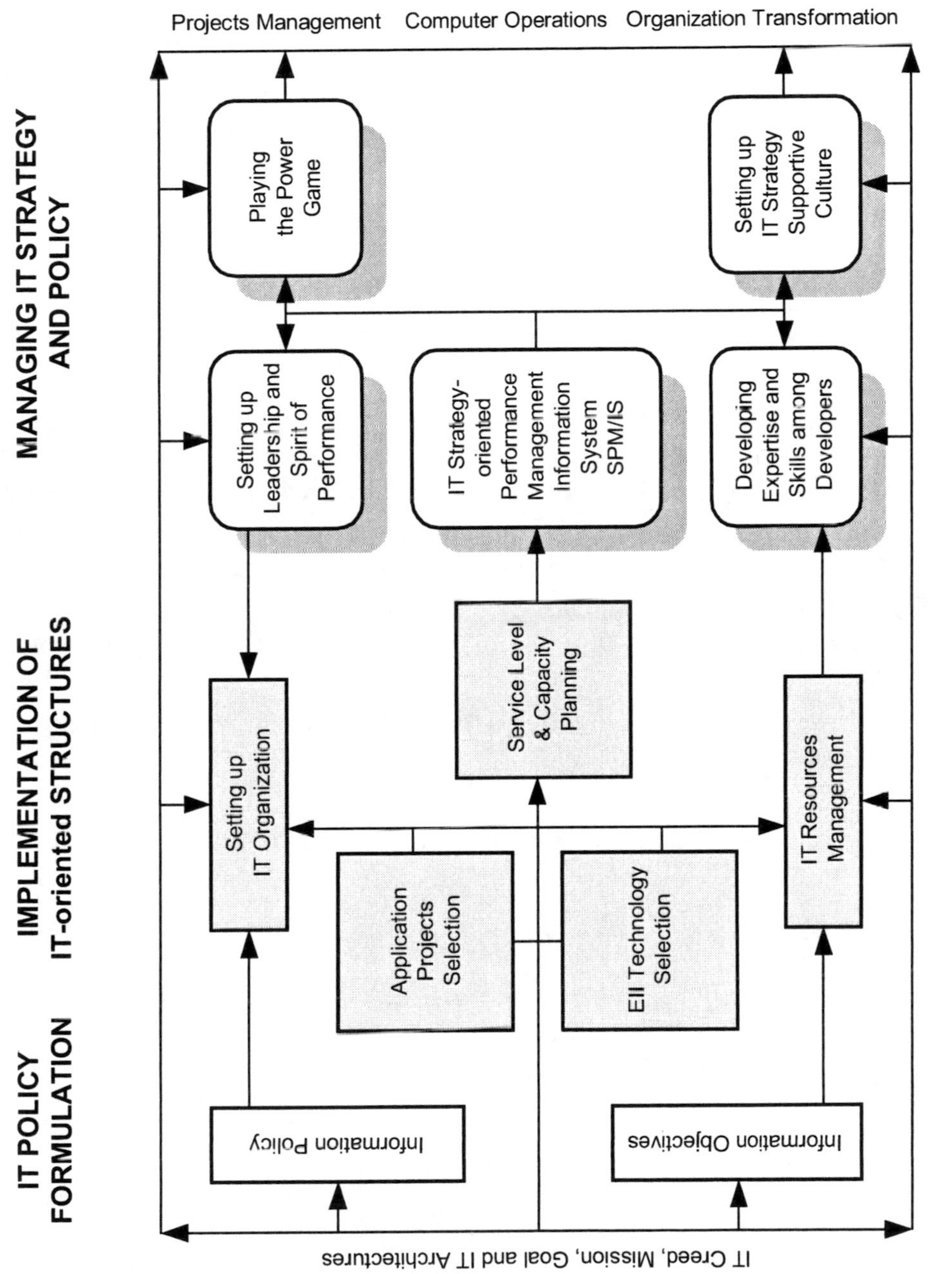

- **IT General Policy** – plan and follow EII architecture for e-enterprise;
- **Line of Applications Policy** – integrate ERP, SCM, and CRM systems through Enterprise Information Portal, and include e-Business systems via a Vortal;
- **Software Policy** – use multi-vendor solutions complying with the open system standards and Web-oriented solutions;
- **Information Tools Delivery Centers** – apply in-house system development;
- **IT Financial Policy** – apply the full chargeout system with the assumption that end-users will make the appropriate trade-offs of computing with other alternatives.

Information Objectives may be planned for the whole IT organization or for major IT projects. Information objectives should be quantitative derivatives of IT goals and strategy. They should guide IT undertakings, set standards for their performance, and control it. For example, if the IT goal is to implement e-enterprise then one of the IT objectives will be to develop the Intranet and Extranet.

Setting up the IT Organization depends on the organization's advancement; for example, one can recognize its following stages:

- *Stage I: IT Initiation* – may lead towards the selection of application champions within users' departments, who will promote IT solutions among peers;
- *Stage II: Application Proliferation* – should create an inter-departmental steering committee, which will promote dissemination of IT applications;
- *Stage III: Enterprise Applications Integration* – requires a strong IT organization, capable of professional supervision which could create an advanced EII;
- *Stage IV: Inter-Enterprise Applications Integration* – leads towards the expansion of the IT organization into a core business function which transforms other functions' ways of doing business.

IT Resources Management is based on the budgeting process. It creates a plan, within certain constraints, covering estimated expenditures involved in pursuing applications development and computer operations. The following items should be included in the IT budget:

- Assets cost (hardware and software, realized cost benefits, previous year's profit);
- Liabilities cost (depreciation reserves, unrealized cost benefits, previous year's net loss);
- Expenses (equipment, personnel, overhead);
- Revenues (outside service, annual realized cost-benefits, applications-attributed revenue increases in business);
- Other.

Investigations deciding whether or not to initiate IT programs should be conducted through feasibility studies. If the cost-benefits analysis cannot be applied, then the impact analysis is recommended.

Service Level and Capacity Planning – involves user service marketing planning, user service level planning, system recovery planning, information security planning, system audit planning, and other planning needs. Decisions that determine the value of service planning focus upon the utilization of IT resources, costs and the workload associated with the service function.

Setting Leadership, and Spirit of Performance – once the strategy-driven EII architecture has been defined, one must bring together capital, people, technology, suppliers, facilities, and communications. The successful IT organization needs dynamic leadership, which guides IT professionals and business users towards the accomplishment of the IT strategy. Greater managerial attention needs to be focused on reward systems and job satisfaction of IT professionals, at least when a firm wishes to maximize organizational commitment and minimize turnover. A CIO should be visible, imaginative and able to foster an IT strategy supportive culture that keeps IT professionals responsive and innovative. One of the techniques used by the best CIO's is to emphasize results and the spirit of high performance ("morale").

Development of Skills and Expertise among Developers and Users – often a new IT strategy requires new expertise and new skills. In the past, when computer skills were based on "COBOL" skills, it was easy to replace an IT professional. Nowadays, the complexity of developing an e-enterprise is so high that IT professionals are a real human resource (capital) to a company. It takes years to develop an IT professional who knows more about a given business than just a programming language. Also, an employer must maintain a reasonable structure of IT personnel in order to attain the IT strategy. A concept of IT Personnel Portfolio (IT/PP) may help in establishing an accurate personnel hiring policy. Figure 8-5 illustrates a concept of the Portfolio, which is based on two criteria: job performance and solutions finesse.

The IT/PP recognizes the following types of IT personnel:

- (C) – Craftsmen
  know the job's routine but, due to the lack of education or motivation, have low job performance and potential. Firms should minimize their employment in jobs that require problem solving skills; however, they can be cost effective at information, data and maintenance centers.

- (P) – Professionals
  have very good skills in a specific domain and are highly motivated. Because of their highly specialized knowledge, their multi-job potential is rather low. They are the best type of employees to carry out mainstream tasks at planning, development, maintenance, data, and network centers. However, they are not good enough to provide strong leadership in company pilot projects.

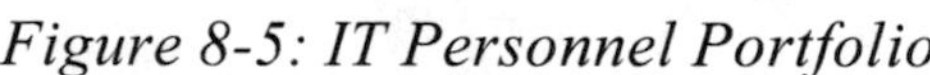
Figure 8-5: IT Personnel Portfolio

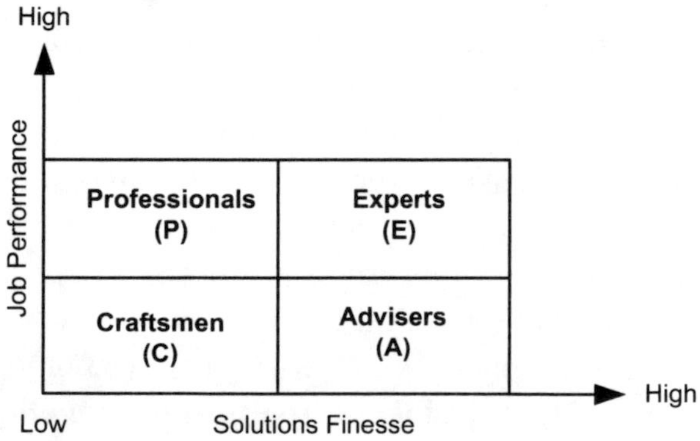

- (E) – Experts
  are well educated, highly motivated, and technically adept. They possess the highest job performance capabilities and have the highest job potential. They are greatly needed at the planning and development centers. They are expensive, but it is better to have one of them than two craftsmen or professionals. Without experts, a firm will pay dearly for expensive external consultants.

- (A) – Advisors
  are, most likely, former experts either in IT or in organizational dynamics; hence, they still can give useful advice (high job potential), but their job performance is limited. They function as developers of IT strategy and culture. To this end, they are important members of the IT organization. At corporations like IBM and Apple, their job-title is "fellow." They mostly are needed in planning centers.

For each center, one can approximate a satisfactory mix for the IT Personnel Portfolio:

- Planning Center – mostly advisors and experts should be employed;

- Development Center – needs some leadership by experts and guidance by advisors but has a majority of employed professionals;

- Maintenance Center – needs both professionals and craftsmen;

- Information Center – can accommodate professionals and craftsmen;

- Data Center – employs mostly professionals and craftsmen;

- Network Center – requires professionals.

IT/PP should be seen as the process of anticipating and making provisions for the movement of IT professionals within and out of the IT organization.

Development Of a Strategy Supportive Culture Among IT Developers And Users – is required for a new IT strategy which brings about new technological or even civilizational solutions. Culture is a value-driven system of people's behavior. Values define cultural man's need for rationality, meaning, emotional experience, richness of imagination, and depth of faith.

Organizational culture creates a communication climate which influences workers to implement aims, such as an IT strategy.

A CIO who develops the healthy culture may include the following plan:

- Developing IT strategy with a strong feedback from the IT personnel;
- Providing a set of awards and recognition for high performance;
- Disseminating success stories;
- Creating meaningful symbols, slogans, jargon, and metaphors;
- Promoting talented professionals to champions;
- Assuring the authority of experts and advisors;
- Securing the development of know-how among workers;
- Other.

A derivative of such an organizational culture should be a set of broad, silently understood rules (policies) which tell an employee how to behave under a variety of circumstances.

Playing The Power Game – must be predicted in the implementation of an IT strategy, which certainly changes structures of somebody's power and/or skills. It should aim at softening resistance to new applications and methods of doing business. One can predict the power game at the following levels:

- Level of workers – focus on educating users about how to develop new knowledge and skills to successfully adapt to new IT tools; however, not all users will be willing to accept the challenge of new knowledge and skills, even with a carefully planned training;
- Level of the formal organization – some departments will have to reconfigurate their ways of operations and they won't be willing to do so, finding rational and irrational obstacles;
- Level of the informal organization – new IT solutions may threaten the established groups (including cliques) by restructuring their influence.

Good tips on successful political tactics may be reccognized as follows (Quinn, 1980):

1. Let weakly supported ideas die through inaction and minimize your political exposure to them;

2. Propose additional tests of solutions that are good but not supported by executives; in other words, do not oppose executives openly;

3. Let more negative decisions come from a group consensus rather than from you;

4. Do a lot of chatting and informal debates to stay abreast of how things are progressing and know when to step in to intervene;

5. Lead an IT strategy but do not dictate it;

6. Reward high performance generously and visibly;

7. Assign pilot tasks to "champions" whose future is linked to their success.

IT solutions can be positive or negative factors in social transformations. Political action should create the social background for controllable applications. Then with proper feedback, computing can create a positive influence for the implementation of organizational and social transformations.

Because IT applications in enterprises do not follow exactly a theoretical framework of strategic-tactical systems planning, one can recognize in practice rather an eclectic set of solutions. Examples of IT management trends which take place in business practice, sometimes in the same enterprise, are presented in the following section.

IT MANAGEMENT TRENDS

Legacy Systems Management (LSM) – still takes place in many companies that do not have the right IT expertise available or begun to implement IT applications long ago and they still work quite effectively. LSM is either in-house or outsourced and its mission is very often to support the core business.

IT Integration Management (ITIM) – is steadily evolving and takes place at different levels of integration, as described in Chapter 7. The first level of integration applies middleware software for different tasks. This leads to more clear applications' integration within one enterprise (EAI). The holistic view of EAI has triggered the appetite for the cross-application integration via workflow systems. In the meantime, a large number of legacy systems have waited for their improvements through their integration via GUI. It is evident that the results of IT integration would be better if the whole business process was re-engineered, and in consequence it would be integrated across business functions. Hence, IT integration is just one step towards B2B integration of the inter-enterprise business process, which eventually may even lead towards the partners' integration within an e-marketplace. However, the ultimate integration is geared to real-time access for field workers via mobile devices. Each of these integration solutions requires very special attention and demands unconventional, innovative management.

e-Transformation Management – embraces the phenomenon of the Internet and its e-business as well as e-enterprise solutions. It requires the radical switch from EAI & ERP architectures to Web technology, which transform brick & mortar firms into brick & click or click & click as well as to click & brick environments. Many IT organizations struggle for the right IT strategy and talent.

IT Outsourcing Management – is caused by cost saving, mergers' problems and management's desire to focus on mainline business issues, and IT low expertise. The most common fully outsourced services are: disaster recovery, application development, user training, software maintenance, and help desk assistance. The other IT services seldom outsourced are data networking and IT planning. If an outsourced service is relatively simple, then usually it meets users' expectations. IT outsourcing takes place when top management perceives IT as a cost center, not a strategic core solution. Outsourcing IT activities abroad is becoming popular as long as the international subcontractors won't complicate (sometimes on purpose) solutions that will be difficult to manage. One can also predict that IT insourcing after outsourcing may take place too, particularly when it will be clear for many businesses that they cannot sustain their competitive advantage through IT, since the outsourcing contractor may pass their competitive solutions to other companies.

ASP – Application Service Provider's Management – a contractual service to their customer for deploying, hosting, managing, and providing access to an application from a centrally managed facility. Among applications wholly delivered by a provider one can recognize the following:

- Enterprise ASP: ERP, SCM, CRM, e-business;
- Collaborative ASP: e-mail, groupware, conferencing;
- Personal ASP: end-user computing and consumer applications.

Among ASP's benefits one can mention rapid deployment and access to state of the art solutions. ASP's essentially host and manage software for companies and provide technical support for that software. Companies may save money with an ASP by avoiding the purchase of copies of software and periodic upgrades for every computer in the office and by reducing the need to train technical staff to maintain the systems. ASP's reduce the total cost of ownership for applications by 30% to 70% (Mark Hall, *www.computerworld.com*).

Among ASP's risks it is possible to perceive flawed execution, ASP's low knowledge about organization issues of a given company, its personnel turnover and even the disappearance of a service provider. According to the Gartner Group's report, 65% of ASP's (out of 480) bankrupted in 2000.

Perhaps the simple applications service providers will win the market's acceptance, and the complex ones may cause many problems on both sides of the service contract. The users cannot be misled that ASP's will solve all their IT problems; for on the contrary, they may even create more problems for them.

After reviewing an IT office's role in an enterprise organization and in increasing its productivity and effectiveness as well as after looking at IT management trends, let's analyze the central issue of how to integrate business and IT strategies, in the following section.

BUSINESS AND IT STRATEGIES INTEGRATION

Business Aims

If a company does not have well-defined business goals and strategy, then the formulation of IT aims may be difficult. Figure 8-6 illustrates a set of business aims for a telecommunication company[2].

Figure 8-6: The Network of Singtel Business Aims

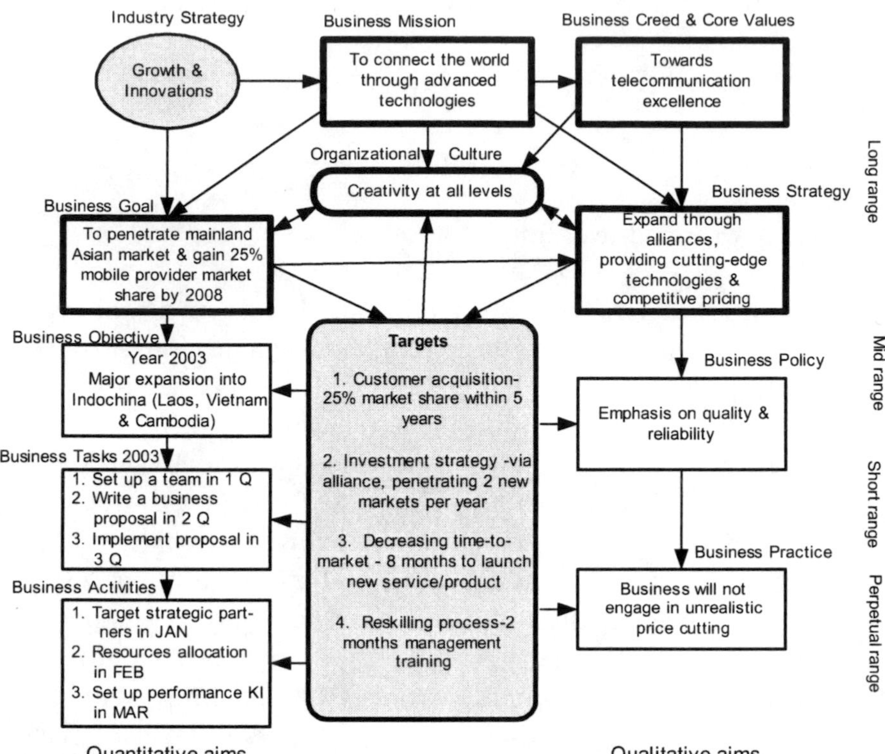

Collins and Popras (1997) state that companies that are built to last have strong core ideology which is composed of **core values and purpose** (mission statement). Core values are organizations' essential and enduring tenets, not to be compromised for financial gain or short-term expediency. For example, core ideologies in the visionary companies are as follows:

- IBM:
    - Give full consideration to the individual employee
    - Spend a lot of time making consumer happy
    - Go the last mile to do things right; seek superiority in all we undertake

- Procter & Gamble:
    - Product excellence
    - Continuous self-improvement

- Honesty and fairness
- Respect and concern for the individual

Very often core values can be expressed under a form of a **company creed**; e.g., Ford's creed is "Quality is job #1."

Among core values one can recognize (after Collins and Popras, 1997) management approaches towards "*building a clock or time telling.*" Most visionary companies are "clock builders" which are *built to last* and tell the time all the time. Among such companies one can perceive: Ford, IBM, Wal-Mart, HP, 3M, Sony, Procter &Gamble, Merck, and others. They are not pursuing one big idea, but step by step they develop and improve their own organization's might.

Core values also reflect management philosophy which is exemplified as a given management style. Visionary companies which have been transforming from good to great ones apply, according to Collins (2002), Level 5 leadership. At this level[3], an executive builds enduring greatness through a paradoxical blend of personal humility and professional will. Such leaders replace their own egos by the larger goal of building a great company. Among such leaders one can mention: Abraham Lincoln, Colman Mockler (Gillette), Darwin E. Smith (Kimberly-Clark), and others.

Another management philosophy of visionary companies moving from good-to-great is first to get the right team of people (Who) and then figure Where to go with business. One "genius" with helpers cannot do it; everything falls when he/she departures.

BUSINESS AIMS

A **mission statement** is the set of reasons for a company being in a given business. 3M's mission is "To solve problems innovatively." Walt Disney's mission is "To make people happy." Merck's mission statement is "To preserve and improve human life."

An **industrial strategy** is a prevailing strategy in a given whole sector of the economy. This type of a strategy influences a given company's business strategy. Figure 8-7 illustrates a classification of industrial strategies.

A **business goal** is a long-term aim looking for an expected company's performance within 2-5 years ahead. A firm should have a clear and compelling measurable goal. For example, General Electric's goal is "Become #1 or #2

Figure 8-7: The Classification of Industrial Strategies

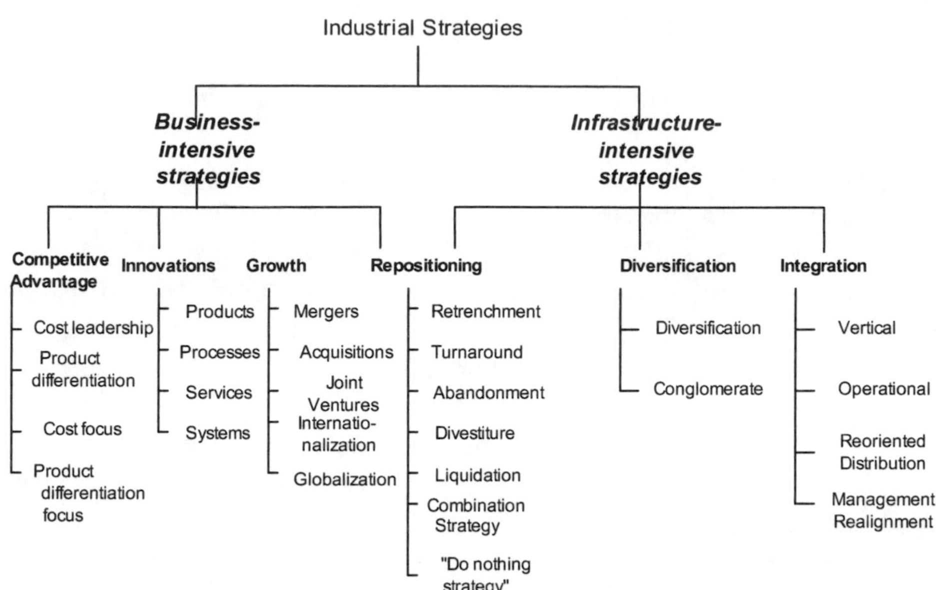

in every market we serve and revolutionize this company to have the speed and agility of a small company."

A business strategy. The concept of business strategy is broad and is the subject of the capstone class in any business curriculum. A business strategy is a plan for how to accomplish a business goal. Napoleon said that "a strategy is a simple act of execution."

Visionary companies based their strategies on *a la* Hedgehog simplicity[4] within three circles: 1) What you are deeply passionate about (Gillette's passion for shaving systems' simplicity), 2) What you can be the best in the world at (Circuit City's 4S model: service, selection, savings, satisfaction), 3) What drives your economic engine (Wells Fargo's stripped-down branches and ATM's) (Collins, 2002).

Organizational culture is a value-driven pattern of employees and management's behavior within a company. For example, Hewlett-Packard's culture is "The HP Way." Walt-Mart's culture is "fanatical dedication to its customers." Marriott's culture is "dedication-to-service atmosphere."

To develop a great strategy, a firm must posses a supportive culture. Visionary companies moving from good-to-great have the ability to *confront the brutal facts*. To know even brutal facts is better than to dream. When

Kroger found that it was losing its market share (1959-1973), it began to confront the brutal facts and started to transform its stores into superstores. Through some experiments, Kroger had found that a classic grocery store (100% of Kroger's stores) was extinct. It was a brutal fact that led to the company's successful transformation into a chain of superstores. A twice bigger competitor, A&P, could not face the brutal facts and lost its market share (Collins, 2002). In 2000, similar crisis began affecting the K-mart company, which cannot face the brutal facts and transform into solutions that could allow it to compete with Wal-Mart.

Visionary companies are famous for developing a culture of discipline. The good-to-great companies built a consistent system with clear constraints, but also gave people freedom and responsibility within the framework of that culture. They hired self-disciplined people who didn't need to manage, and then managed the system, not the people. Examples of such culture are at Circuit City and McDonald's, where people can contribute, but at the same time they have to comply with the system's policy and the Hedgehog concept (Collins, 2003).

A **business policy** is a set of rules for how to go about in certain situations. For example, Nordstrom's policy is "Use your good judgment in all situations. There will be no additional rules."

Business targets are key indicators of a balance scorecard, organized by four perspectives: financial, customer, operations, and innovation. Selected targets should exemplify business aims (including short-term objectives – below one year) and operations of business processes, such as tasks and activities.

A **business task** is a short-term operation of a business process that exemplifies how a business objective can be accomplished. It is a measurable operation carried out within a quarter.

A **business activity** is a short-term operation of a business process that exemplifies how a business task can be accomplished. It is a measurable operation carried out within a period shorter than a quarter.

In planning business aims it is necessary to recognize the long-term ones; however, to go beyond generalization, it can be useful to provide examples of mid-term and short-term aims. Of course such exemplification is limited, but it provides some awareness about current issues and challenges.

Once business aims have been defined, one can pass to the planning of IT aims.

IT Aims

The network of IT aims is depicted in Figure 8-8. The IT aims guide the performance of the IT function and locate it among other business functions. In practice, IT aims are usually reduced to a concept of a strategy or objectives, while the IT aims network indicates that there are 14 types of aims and each one has its own merit.

Until we explain each aim's role, one must notice major aims categories and specific relationships among them. On the left of the network there are quantitative aims and on the opposite side there are qualitative aims. The former's accomplishments can be measured, while the latter's serve as a guide for actions. The IT aims are guided by business aims and this relationship is the most important one, since it justifies the reason for the IT organization's existence.

It is important to observe that an IT strategy is a plan about how to accomplish an IT goal. Without correct goals there is no right strategy. These aims function if the right organizational culture and undertakings are in position, supporting a planned IT paradigm, which will define the whole scope of issues associated with the development of IT solutions, knowledge and skills.

Once long range aims are defined, one can formulate IT targets that are measured key indicators, controlling an organization's performance at all levels of IT management.

Technology as an agent of change is nothing new. The strategic issue is not, what is the role of IT? Rather, the issue is how IT contributes to good-to-great companies that treat IT *differently*. Good-to-great companies apply technology as the change accelerator, not as a creator of momentum (*clock builder*). Circuit City pioneered application of IT to increase denominator for profit per employee. It was not a leader in pharmaceutical R&D – leaving that to Merck, Pfizer, and others that had a different Hedgehog Concept. Walgreen pioneered application of satellite communication to tailor uniqueness of a specific store as a convenient corner drugstore. In such a manner, a company became a giant web of a single corner pharmacy, leading the rest of the industry by at least a decade. Kroger was first in the application of scanners and linked them with the entire cash-flow-cycle, obtaining a competitive advantage in the whole industry at the beginning of the 1980's (Collins, 2003).

Good-to-great companies apply IT in a following manner (Collins, 2003):

- Think differently about technology than their competition,
- Select IT applications carefully,

Figure 8-8: The Network of IT Aims

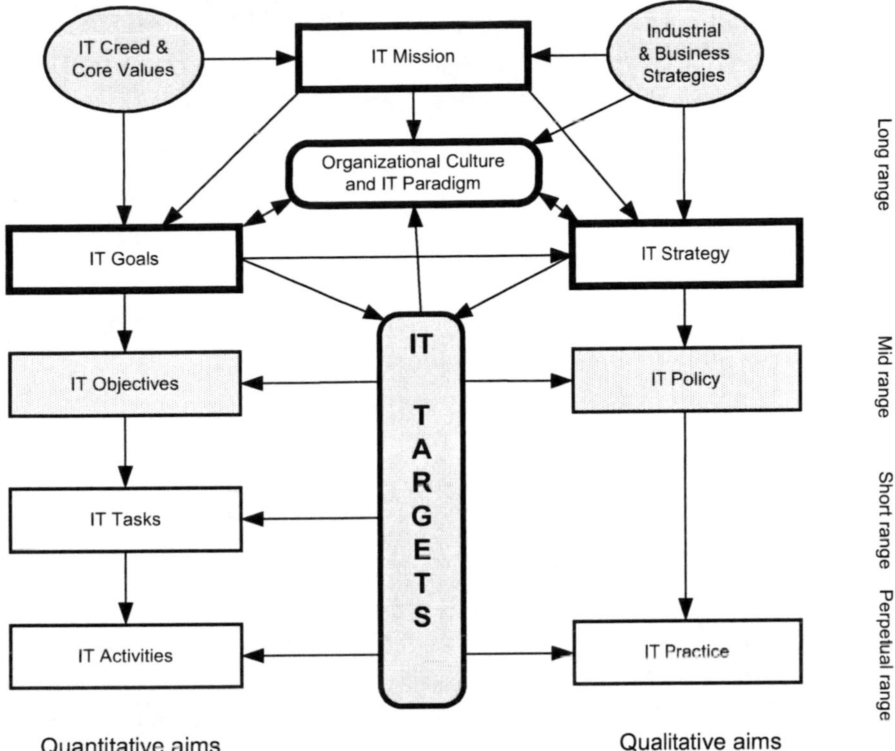

- If the IT solution fits well into the Hedgehog concept, then the IT solution should be at the level of pioneers; otherwise set for parity or ignore it entirely,
- IT should be a change accelerator, not a creator of momentum,
- Respond to IT with thoughtfulness and creativity, driven by a compulsion to turn unrealized potential into results,

Mediocre companies react to IT by fear and they are left behind.

IT Mission

An IT mission should explain the reason for the IT's existence (*raison d'etre*). The IT mission should reflect a given company's business strategy's directions and intentions. It can be structured as follows:

Part I IT's Core Mission, one can recognize three classic missions:

- "IT *supports* core enterprise operations" (e.g., CAD); or
- "IT *fulfills* enterprise operations" (e.g., high volume print of documents such as account statements); or
- "IT is a *strategic* core function of an enterprise" (e.g., customer order application at *www.amazon.com*).

Part II IT's Supportive Mission:

- E.g., "Automate workers' routines and informate executive judgment."

The IT core mission should be short and clear, emphasizing its role in a business' operations. This role can be supportive, or fulfilling, or strategic. The second part of the IT mission can provide directions at the levels below business critical operations. In the provided example IT aims at the issue of what to automate and informate

IT Creed

An IT creed is a philosophy guiding IT operations and workers. It should be a simple, catchy slogan such as "Information is Power," "Information Unlimited," "Friendly Computing," "Beat the System," " Be There," "Quality Data," or "Information Culture." Of course, there should be some relationship between a business creed and an IT creed. For example, if Ford Corporation's creed is "Quality Job no. 1," then its IT organization could apply an IT creed: "Quality Information is Job no. 1."

IT Culture

A human culture is very important for the process of implementing IT aims. We have already discussed issues about how to set up the IT strategy-supportive culture. Very talented professionals usually work in IT organizations and they cannot be managed by a "police" style control of their activities. The right style in IT is management by a culture, which motivates workers to high performance.

IT Paradigms

A paradigm, according to Kuhn (1970), is "a pattern," "model," or "accepted example" of current practice, which includes law, theory, application and instrumentation together. Barker (1985) gives a different definition. He describes a paradigm as a set of rules and regulations that (1) describes boundaries and (2) tells you what to do to be successful within those boundaries. A paradigm shift occurs when the "rules" change and therefore the means of success change also.

In IT development, a shift of paradigm introduces new rules ("era") of development. However, in some case, two or more paradigms can exist coincidentally, since IT grows at a very fast pace. One can recognize the following paradigms in the last 50 years[5]:

- Off line intra-enterprise paradigm (1950's) – punch cards and automated routine processing;
- On-line intra-enterprise paradigm (1960's-1970's) – remote-networked processing;
- Integrated intra-enterprise paradigm (1980's) – ERP with common database processing;
- Agile inter-enterprise paradigm (1992's) – computer-integrated operation processing;
- Communicated inter-enterprise paradigm (1995's) – the Internet-based processing;
- Virtual inter-enterprise paradigm (1996's) – cyberspace office and remote processing;
- Informated inter-enterprise paradigm (1998's) – portal and data mining processing;
- Electronic inter-enterprise paradigm (2000's) – Web-based integration of all processing;
- Mobile inter-enterprise paradigm (2001's) – wireless-based handheld devices access.

The next enterprise level of development includes the previous enterprise level's solutions being either intact, improved, or replaced. Each level of the enterprise development requires new IT professional knowledge and skills. Furthermore, it also requires a new approach to IT strategy. Companies which feel that their IT staff is not up to a new IT paradigm very often seek outsourcing and ASP services.

The relationships between IT paradigms and missions are illustrated in Table 8-2.

Table 8-2: The Relationships Between IT Paradigms and Missions

PARADIGM	SUPPORTIVE MISSION	FULFILLMENT MISSION	STRATEGIC MISSION
Off-line intra-enterprise	X	X	
On-line intra-enterprise	X	X	
Integrated intra-enterprise		X	
Agile inter-enterprise paradigm		X	X
Informated inter-enterprise		X	X
Communicated inter-enterprise	X	X	
Mobile inter-enterprise	X	X	
Electronic inter-enterprise			X
Virtual inter-enterprise			X

Table 8-2 helps to understand how a business strategy's direction is translated into IT's directions. For example, if a business strategy perceives IT as a supportive function only, then a CIO has only three options to pursue: off-line enterprise or on-line enterprise or communicated enterprise. In the 21st century this CIO probably will choose the communicated enterprise option. As such, it shapes the IT solutions and its budget.

The business strategy, which perceives the IT function as a strategic one, provides for the CIO a set of four paradigm options to choose from: agile inter-enterprise, virtual inter-enterprise, informated inter-enterprise, and electronic inter-enterprise. Depending upon the kind of an industrial sector, certain paradigms can be easily eliminated. For example, for the banking sector the agile and virtual enterprise paradigms are not right. Then the choice is between the two remaining paradigms and will depend upon the existing culture and management priorities as well as on the available budget.

IT Goals

Goals are long-term aims in a horizon range of two to five years and they serve as a mechanism to evaluate the organization's performance. A goal is an end towards which managers lead the organization and its business units. "Goals" are very often confused with "objectives," which are mid-range-oriented, in a range below one year. A goal is an aim that differentiates an organization from an undirected crowd of people.

IT goals should be compatible with the chosen IT paradigm; their examples are illustrated in Table 8-3.

Table 8-3: Examples of IT Goals Driven by IT Paradigm

PARADIGM	Examples of IT Goals
Off-line enterprise	Switch from hand design to the CATIA CAD system within 16 months
On-line enterprise	Provide remote monitors for every office worker within 2 years
Integrated enterprise	Implement IBM DB2 database for 8 Peoplesoft ERP applications within 2.5 years
Informated enterprise	Implement IBM Datawarehouse and Data Mining software within 16 months
Agile enterprise	Implement the IBM CIM package for Glenn Plant within 2 years
Communicated enterprise	Implement the Extranet for all of a company's stakeholders within 16 months
Mobile enterprise	Implement Wireless Application Protocol-based server within 2 years
Electronic enterprise	Implement e-enterprise within 3 years
Virtual enterprise	Implement Lotus Notes groupware for all R&D workers within 16 months

IT Strategy

An IT strategy is a plan about how to implement IT goals. Napoleon once said, "Strategy is a simple act of execution." Perhaps for him. To better define the IT strategy components let's take look at its model in Figure 8-9. The IT strategy model is composed of the following choices:

- *Target Results* which translate the strategy into action;
- *Application Strategic Domain* which sets the developmental direction;
- *IT Differential Advantage* which puts a company in the competitive position;
- *Strategic Thrust* which defines the transition steps from the previous to the next stage of IT development.

Let's examine each of the above choices that constitute an IT strategy.

Figure 8-9: A Model of IT Strategy

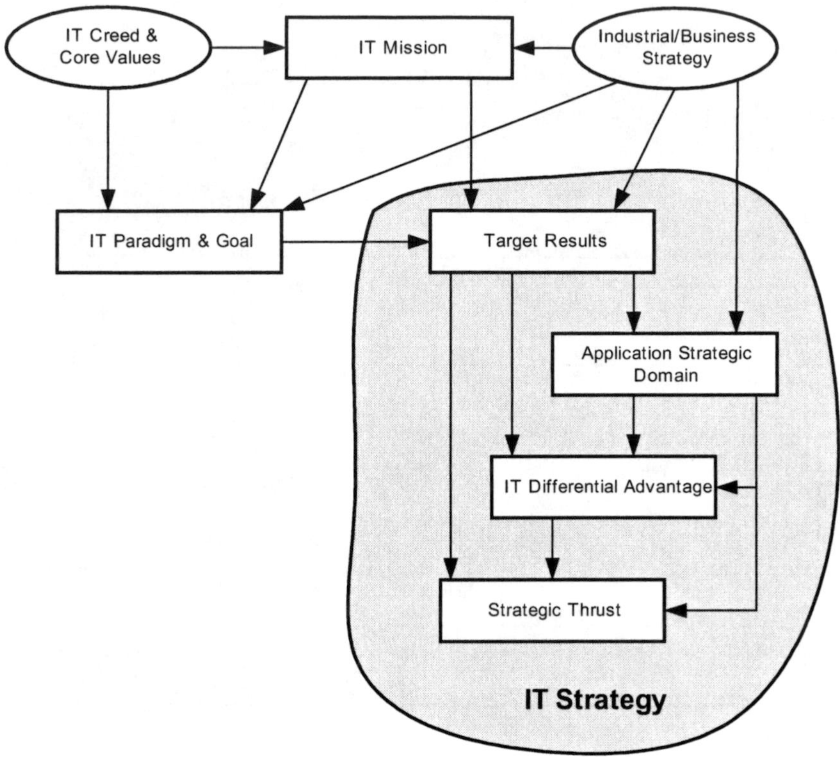

IT Targets

The IT strategy has to be explained in a language of measured key indicators; for example, defined within the framework of the *balanced scorecard* (Kaplan and Norton, 1996). The balanced scorecard translates mission, goals, and strategy into four different perspectives: financial, customer, internal business process, and learning and growth.

Based upon existing industrial practice (Table 8-1) the IT balanced scorecard is presented in Table 8-4.

The selection of IT targets and their values is subjective and depends upon a company's business and IT aims. The balanced scorecard will influence the choices for the remaining components of the IT strategy.

Application Strategic Domain

The selection of application strategic domain should be coordinated with the IT paradigm and goals as well as with the targets. Table 8-5 illustrates a matrix of seven IT paradigms and four main business strategies. Cross-sections of the table list recommended strategic domains of applications[6]. Of course these domains are only some examples of theoretical directions that can be different in every specific case.

Table 8-4: The Example of the IT Balanced Scorecard

KEY INDICATORS	PERSPECTIVES			
	FINANCIAL	CUSTOMER	INTERNAL BUSINESS	INNOVATION, LEARNING & GROWTH
F1. IT budget as percentage of projected revenues	X%			
F2. IT spending per employee	$Y			
F3. Profits from e-business operations	Z%			
F4. Income from IT services to other firms	W%			
F5. Share of IT budget for IT services and outsourcing	A%			
F6. Share of IT budget for salaries and benefits	B%			
C1. Inquiries handled electronically, without intervention		C%		
C2. Percentage of customers included in supply chain		D%		
B1. Suppliers included in e-SCM			E%	
B2. Portion of workweek IT executives meet with line-of-business and departmental managers			F%	
V1. Share of IT budget for research and development				G%
V2. Share of IT budget for new products and technology				H%
V3. Portion of knowledge workers using intelligence tools				L%

Table 8-5: The Selection of Application Strategic Domain

Business Strategies		Off-line Enterprise	On-line Enterprise	Integrated Enterprise	Agile Enterprise	Informated Enterprise	Communicated Enterprise	Mobile Enterprise	Electronic Enterprise	Virtual Enterprise
		IT Paradigms								
Competitive Advantage	Differentiation Focus	**EPM**	**CAM**	**SCM**	**CAD CAM**	**KMS eDOC**	**WFS**	**WAP**	**eBiz**	**EIP**
Innovations		**CAD**	**CAD EUC**	**CAD**	**CAD CAM**	**KMS WFS**	**WFS**	**WAP**	**WFS**	**WFS**
Growth		**TPS**	**TPS**	**ERP**	**CAD CAM**	**KMS**	**eDMS**	**WAP**	**eBiz**	**SCM**
Alliance	Repositioning Diversification Integration			**ERP**	**CAD CAM**	**KMS**	**WFS**	**WAP**	**B2B**	**WFS**

IT Differential Advantage

If the IT organization is to continue to attract a company's business units and their management, it must perform certain functions within industry practice with distinction. Rapid deployment of applications, a sophisticated matrix of applications, a low information processing cost, better user friendly software, and better information quality can all serve to differentiate a particular IT organization from the industrial pack.

IT management may choose the right differential advantage by choosing between in-house and outsourcing of the planning, development, maintenance, information, data and network centers' services. By focusing on all or part of these centers it is possible to implement expected solutions.

Strategic Thrust

This consideration steers a course between strategic moves that are either too aggressive or too passive. Examples of application-intensive and business-intensive strategic thrusts are as follows:

- *Application-intensive thrusts*:
    a. Legacy systems integration
    b. Middleware integration
    c. EAI-Enterprise Applications Integration
    d. Workflow systems
    e. Mobile integration
    f. Other

Figure 8-10: The IT Strategy of Singtel

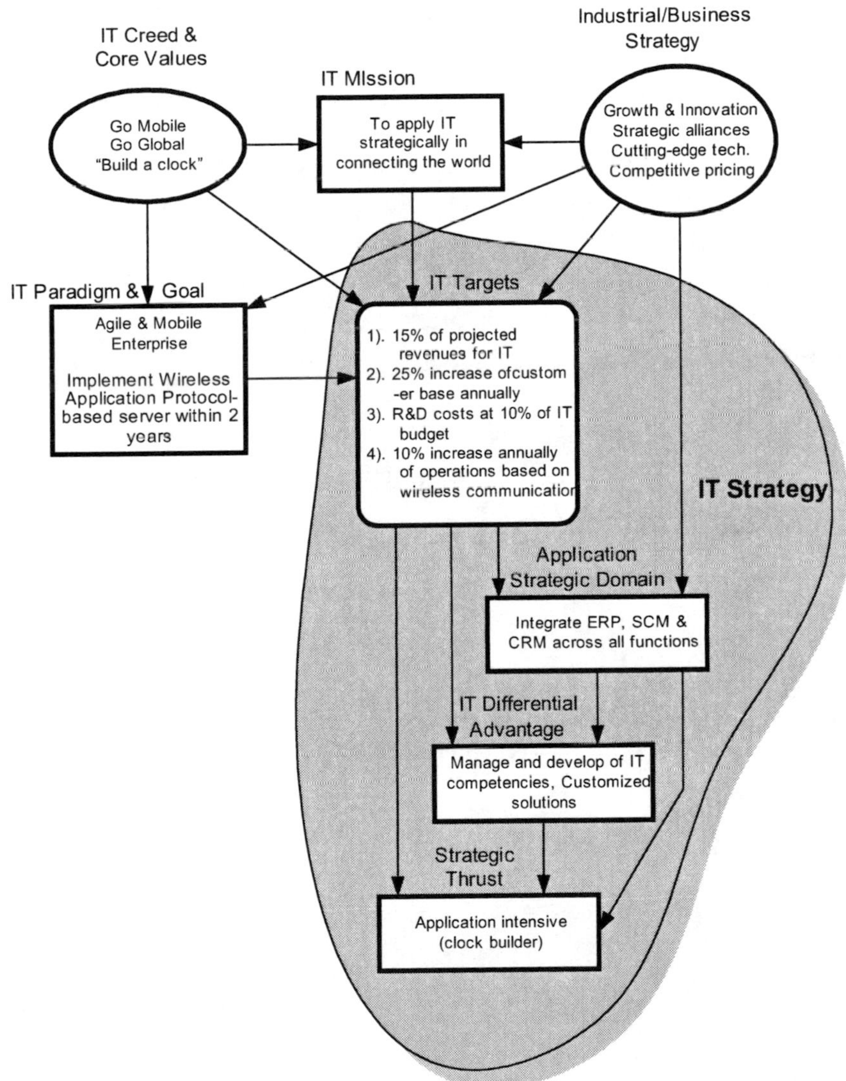

- *Business-intensive thrusts*:
    a. BPR-Business Process Re-engineering
    b. BPI-Business Process Integration
    c. B2B
    d. E-market development
    e. Cost leadership in information tools delivery centers
    f. Other

The strategic thrust selection should concentrate on a critical direction rather than on minor steps. The selected thrust can be seen in a company as offensive or defensive with all related repercussions. The selected trust should be selected in accordance with its IT targets.

Figure 8-10 provides an example of IT aims for a telecommunication company[7].

After defining the IT strategic aims one can pass to the stage of tactical planning and define (Figure 8-4):

- IT Policies,
- Implementation of IT-strategy oriented structures,
- Managing IT strategy and policies.

After the tactical planning stage comes a level of IT operations in the scope of IT developmental projects and information processing and networking.

CONCLUSION

IT management is still an evolving discipline which can hardly follow the accelerated pace of technology development. IT is creating a new Information Civilization, which is about 50 years old but is minute in comparison to 6,000 years of human civilization.

BIBLIOGRAPHY

Barker, J. (1985). *Discovering the Future.* Lake Elmo, MN: Infinity Limited.

Bradley, S. P. & Nolan, R.L. (1998). *Sense & Respond: Capturing Value in the Network Era.* Cambridge, MA: HBS Press.

Brynjolfsson, E. & Hitt, L. (1996). Productivity without Profit?: Three Measures of Information Technology's Value. *Working Paper Series*. MIT Center for Coordination Science.

Collins, J. (2002). *Good to Great*. New York: HarperBusiness.

Collins, J. & Popras, J.I. (1997). *Built to Last*. New York: HarperBusiness.

Cummins, F. A. (2002). *Enterprise Integration*. New York: John Wiley & Sons.

Haeckel, S.H. & Slyvotzky, A.J. (1999). *Adaptive Enterprise: Creating and Leading Sense-And-Respond Organizations*. Cambridge, MA: HBS Press.

Hamel, G. (2000). *Leading the Revolution*. Cambridge, MA: HBS Press.

Kuhn, T.S. (1970). *The Structure Of Scientific Revolution*. Chicago: University of Chicago Press.

Quinn, J. B. (1980). *Strategy for Change: Logical Incrementalism*. Homewood, IL: Richard D. Irwin.

Spewak, S.H. & Hill, S.C. (1993). *Enterprise Architecture Planning: Development a Blueprint for Data, Applications and Technology*. New York: John Wiley & Sons.

Targowski, A. (1990). *The Architecture and Planning of Enterprise-wide Information Management Systems*. Harrisburg, PA: Idea Group Publishing.

ENDNOTES

1 In some organizations IT office can be a front-office.

2 A student project presented by Alison Say, Chau Phan Hong, Dennis Macy, and Karen Hoi, MBA Program of Western Michigan University in Singapore, 2002.

3 Level 1 - highly capable individual, Level 2-contributing team member, Level 3 - competent manager, Level 4 - effective leader, Level 5-executive (Collins 2003).

4 Collins (2003) defines it by analogy that a hedgchog knows one big thing and a fox has a myriad of complex strategies. It comes from Isaiah Berlin's "The Hedgehog and the Fox."

5 More discussion on this issue is provided in Chapter 2.

6 Architectures of these applications are provided in Chapter 4.

[7] A student project presented by Alison Say, Chau Phan Hong, Dennis Macy, and Karen Hoi, MBA Program of Western Michigan University in Singapore, 2002.

List of Acronyms

ABAP/4 – Advance Business Application Programming, a development workbench in SAP R/4
AOL – America Online
API – Application Programming Interface
ARPANET – Advanced Research Project Agency Network
ASM – Application Server Middleware
ASP – Active Server Pages
ASP – Application Services Provider
A2A – Application to Application
ATM – Automatic Teller Machine

BAPI – Business Application Programming Interface
BBS – Bulletin Board System
B-ISDN – Broad-band Integrated Services Digital Network
BIS – Business Information System
BOMP – Bill of Material Processor
BPI – Business Process Integration
BPR – Business Process Reengineering
B2B – Business to Business
B2C – Business to Consumer

CAD – Computer Aided Design
CADD – Computer Aided Drafting and Design
CAE – Computer Aided Engineering
CAM – Computer Aided Manufacturing
CAPP – Computer Aided Process Planning
CASE – Computer Aided Software Engineering
CBD – Component Base Development
CEO – Chief Executive Officer
CFO – Chief Financial Officer
CGI – Common Gateway Interface
CIM – Computer Integrated Manufacturing
CIO – Chief Information Officer
CIS – Computer Information System
CKO – Chief Knowledge Officer
CLR – Common Language Runtime
COBRA – Common Object Broker Request Architecture
COM – Component Object Module
COO – Chief Operations Officer
CRM – Customer Relationship Management
CRP – Capacity Requirements Planning
CTO – Chief Technology Officer
CTS – Common Type System
C2C – Consumer to Consumer

DBM – DataBase Middleware
DBMS – DataBase Management System
DCE – Distributed Computing Environment
DCM – Distributed Component Middleware
DCOM – Distributed Component Object Model
DD – Data Dictionary
DDE – Dynamic Data Exchange
DDI – Dynamic Invocation Interface
DDL – Data Description Language
DES – Data Encryption Standard
DML – Data Manipulation Language
e-DMS – electronic-Document Management System
DNA – Distributed Network Architecture
DOS – Disk Operating System
DRAM – Dynamic Random-Access Memory
DSI – Dynamic Skeleton Interface
DSS – Decision Support System
DWH – Data WareHouse

EAI – Enterprise Applications Integration
EBPP – Electronic Bill Presentation and Payment
EC – Electronic Commerce

EDI – Electronic Data Interexchange
EFT – Electronic Fund Transfer
EFTS – Electronic Fund Transfer System
EII – Enterprise Information Infrastructure
EIP – Enterprise Information Portal
EIS – Enterprise Information System
EJB – Enterprise Java Beans
EPM – Enterprise Performance Management
ERC – Enterprise Computing
ERP – Enterprise Resource Planning
EUC – End User Computing
EXS – Expert System

GAN – Global Area Network
GDSS – Group Decision Support System
GII – Global Information Infrastructure
GIS – Geographic Information System
GNP – Gross National Product
GUI – Graphic User Interface

HBA – Hybrid Applications
HDML – HyperText Device Markup Language
HPC – Handheld Personal Computer
HR – Human Resources
HTML – HyperText Markup Language
cHTML – Cellular Phone HyperText Markup Language
HTTP – HyperText Transfer Protocol

IDL – Interface Definition Language
IIOP – Internet Inter-ORB Protocol
IIS – Internet Information Server
IPO – Initial Public Offering
IR – Interface Repository
IRM – Information Resource Management
IS – Information System
ISDN – Integrated Services Digital Network
ISP – Internet Service Provider
IT – Information Technology
ITIM – Information Technology Integration Management
ITS – Inter-organizational System
IXI – Interexchange Carriers-long distance

JAD – Joint Application Development
JIT – Just-in-Time
J2EE – Java 2 Enterprise Edition
JVM – Java Virtual Machine

KMS – Knowledge Management System

LAN – Local Area Network
LATA – Local Area Telecommunication Access
LDAP – Lightweight Directory Access Protocol
LII – Local Information Infrastructure
LPC – Local Procedure Call
LSM – Legacy Systems Management

MAN – Metropolitan Area Network
MCE – Media Communicated Enterprise
MIS – Management Information System
MNC – Multi National Corporation
MNE – Multi National Enterprise
MOM – Message Oriented Middleware
MRP I – Material Requirements Planning
MRP II – Manufacturing Resources Planning
MSN – Microsoft Network
MVS – Memory Virtual System

NC – Network Computer
NII – National Information Infrastructure
N-ISDN – Narrow-band Integrated Services Digital Network

OA – Object Adapters
OAGI – Open Application Group Inc.
OCA – Oracle Cooperative Applications
OEM – Original Equipment Manufacturer
OIS – Operation Information System
OLAP – Online Analytical Processing
OLE – Object Linking and Embedding
OLTP – Online Transactions Processing
OMG – Object Management Architecture
ORB – Object Request Broker

PBX – Private Branch Exchange
PCS – Pocket-size Telephones
PCS – Personal Communication System
PDA – Personal Digital Assistant
PIM – Personal Information Manager
PIS – Product Information System
POA – Portable Object Adapter
POS – Point of Sale

QR – Quick Response

RAD – Rapid Application Development
RDBMS – Relational DataBase Management System
RIS – Regular-manual Information System

RMI – Remote Method Interaction
ROI – Return on Investment
RPC – Remote Procedure Call

SAP – *Systeme Anwendung Produkte*
SCC – Specialized Common Carrier
SCM – Supply Chain Management
SIG – Special Interest Group
SIS – Strategic Information System
SOAP – Simple Object Access Protocol
SQL – Sequential Query Language

TCP/IP – Transmission Control Protocol/ Internet Protocol
TNC – Trans-National Corporation
TPM – Transaction Processing Middleware
TPS – Transaction Processing System

UDDI – Universal Description and Discovery Integration
UI – User Interface
UML – Universal Modeling Language
U2A – User to Application

VM – Virtual Memory
VMS – Virtual Memory System
VAN – Value Added Network

WAIS – Wide Area Information Services
WAN – Wide Area Network
WAP – Wireless Application Protocol
WFS – Workflow System
WIP – Work in Progress
WML – Wireless Markup Language
WSDL – Web Service Definition Language
WWW – World Wide Web

XML – eXtensible Markup Language

About the Authors

Andrew Targowski is a professor of computer information systems at Western Michigan University, USA, and chairman of the Advisory Council of the Information Resource Management Association. He published one of the first books on enterprise systems architecture — *The Architecture and Planning of Enterprise-wide IM Systems* (1990) and on information infrastructures - *Global Information Infrastructure* (1996) and *Enterprise Information Infrastructure* (1999). He is a pioneer of the information superhighway concept (INFOSTRADA, Poland 1972) and he developed the awarded digital city website (*www.telecity.org*) for Kalamazoo in 1997.

* * * *

Thomas Carey is a professor and chair of the Management Department at Western Michigan University, USA. His teaching and research interests are in leadership, strategic management, and entrepreneurship. He has earned the Western Michigan University Teaching Excellence Award, the State of Michigan Teaching Excellence Award, and the Michigan Association of Governing Boards Faculty Award. For 20 years his undergraduate students have participated in consulting projects for local entrepreneurs, with funding provided by the U.S. Small Business Administration. He has been active in the National Management Association and has received the Gold and Silver Knight of Management as well as their national service.

Index

C

D

E

F

G

N

O

P

Q

R

S

T

U

V

W

X

Y

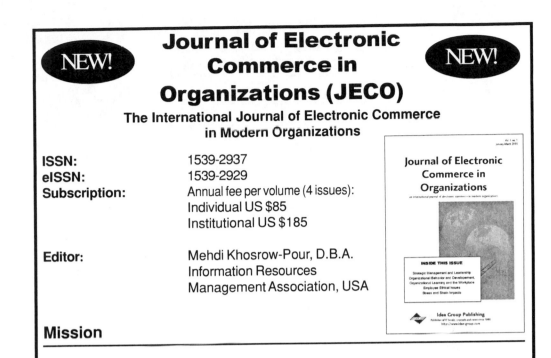

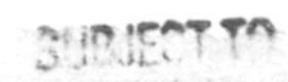

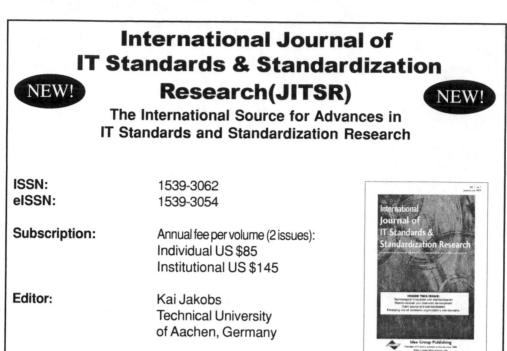